THE CERTIFICATE LIBRARY

* * *

ENGLISH LITERATURE

THE CERTIFICATE LIBRARY

THIS SERIES of books has been designed to cover the various syllabuses of the Ordinary Level Examination for the General Certificate of Education. The books are equally suitable for all students who wish to improve their standards of learning in the subjects of the various volumes, and together they form an invaluable reference library.

The Editor of each book is an experienced Examiner for one or more of the various Examination Boards. The writers are all specialist teachers who have taught in the classroom the subject about which they write; many of them have also had experience as Examiners.

Each volume is comprehensive and self-contained and therefore has far more than an ordinary class textbook: each has a full treatment of the subject; numerous illustrations; questions on the chapters with answers at the end of the book; and a revision summary for each section of the book.

These summaries give the information in a concise and compact way so that examination candidates may easily revise the whole contents of the book—they can soon see how much they readily know, and how much they have forgotten and need to study again. The facts in these summaries serve, therefore, as a series of major pegs upon which the whole fabric of the book hangs.

Advice is given on answering the examination paper and there are questions of examination standard together with suggested answers.

Series Executive Editor
B. E. COPPING, B.A.HONS.

THE CERTIFICATE LIBRARY

* * *

ENGLISH LITERATURE

Edited by

SIDNEY FARRAR, M.A.

Formerly Headmaster, Chippenham Grammar School

Contributors:

ALAN W. RUSSELL, M.A.

Formerly Senior English Master, Wyggeston Boys' School, Leicester

DOROTHY H. ROWE, M.A.

Formerly Senior English Mistress, Talbot Heath School, Bournemouth

THE GROLIER SOCIETY LIMITED

LONDON

First published 1965
Reprinted 1968
Reprinted 1971

ISBN 0 7172 7712 7

Made and printed in Great Britain by
Odhams (Watford) Ltd., Watford, Herts

PREFACE

THIS BOOK, which has been written by experienced teachers of English Literature to help you in your studies, contains a comprehensive background to English Literature. From it you can discover the circumstances in which the special books set for your examination were written; you can read about the lives of the writers, and about the age in which they lived. Such facts will help you to fit each book into its place in the scheme of literary history.

The many illustrations throughout the volume will also help to give you a clear idea of what the authors were like, and of the homes in which they lived. Some of the illustrations show scenes from plays and novels, and you can see the kind of clothes which people of that period wore; others show the development of the theatre, and foreign influences on English Literature. This book, therefore, is a companion to the set books that you are asked to study for the examination.

In addition to all this background knowledge, the book gives much useful information about individual novels, plays and poems, choosing for comment those works which are most likely to appear in the syllabus. The books set for your examination depend on the choice of the examining body, and each examination board changes its syllabus frequently. For this reason, there is a very wide range of books which *may* be set for the examination; but we have selected those which experience has shown to be most frequently chosen by the examiners.

When you have studied all your set books carefully, and learned all you can about the books and their authors, it will be time to turn to the section on Answering the Question, where you will find many pages of helpful advice on how to tackle the different types of question that you are bound to meet in the examination paper. Sample questions have been fully answered in this section; for the best possible results, you should work through the questions and answers in order to learn how to tackle a question paper.

Finally, when you have passed your examination, this book can still be of use and pleasure to you, both as an account of the whole field of literature and as a source of reference in the years to come. We hope that passing an examination will not be an end of your studies, but the beginning of a lifetime's pleasure in the endless wealth of English Literature.

S. FARRAR

CONTENTS

CONTENTS

Coloured Illustrations

Poets' Corner in Westminster Abbey, showing some of the memorials to past masters of English writing: this indicates the nation's high regard for the creators of its literature.

CHAPTER 1

INTRODUCTORY

"Of making many books there is no end." The writer of *Ecclesiastes* hit upon a truth far mightier than he could have imagined when he wrote this statement, and countless generations of students must have heartily endorsed the conclusion of his sentence when he wrote "and much study is a weariness of the flesh." Literature is writing which has cultural and artistic value, and it has developed great scope and variety over the ages. Long before knowledge of written characters made it possible to record in permanent form the thoughts, feelings, memories and hopes of ordinary men, mankind had put their thoughts into words, almost invariably in poetry, in such form as made an appeal to those who heard them. Some survivals of these early compositions, handed down through the generations by word of mouth, remain in our collections of ballads.

The recording of men's compositions by writing, and later the immense increase of the number of copies by printing, brought literature in all its varied forms to an increasingly wide number of people. Today we have a vast production of books, of which only a small proportion will in future years be considered to have permanent literary value; the rest will have their little day and then be forgotten. It is this lasting element with which literature is concerned, and its study is the main concern of this book. The "much study" which might be a "weariness of the flesh" will probably prove, given the necessary interest and application, a pleasant pursuit of great variety and unfailing appeal.

Buying and Borrowing Books

The first necessity is, of course, books, and everybody with any intention of literary studies should build up his own collection of books. This can be a gradual process and the hunting for needed books, on second-hand stalls and elsewhere, has its own fascination. Some books are worth buying and keeping; others of less permanent interest can be borrowed from the public libraries and it is important that the help to be given by those libraries should be known and understood. Not only does each branch library have its own stock of books, but it can call on the resources of its headquarters; and beyond these are larger libraries such as the Central Library and even libraries abroad. It is thus possible through a village branch library to procure almost any book needed for study. Moreover libraries serve not only as providers of books but also as advisers on the choice of books. Through their bibliographies they are in a position to suggest titles of books likely to be of assistance in any field of study. This help will be readily given if asked for, and the independent student especially should avail himself of it.

A growing source of help and interest in the study of literature is to be found in the gramophone records which are being made of poetry and drama. So far the poetry recordings have been read largely by the poets themselves, not always with the happiest results. When we remember that sound is a vital element in poetry, the need for good reading is evident. When we hear a poem well read, we see in it new aspects of beauty and meaning; and this applies equally to plays. If we cannot see plays in the theatre, our enjoyment of them can be greatly increased by hearing them really well spoken in a recording. Poetry would probably come to mean much more to people if their first acquaintance with it came through their ears, rather than their eyes, as they read their books of poetry.

In recent years the scope of books available at relatively low prices has been greatly extended by the publishing of paperbacked books, a venture pioneered by the Penguin series. Many publishers now issue paperbacked editions, and standard works can very often be found in these cheap editions. For private use they are reasonably durable, and over the years it is possible to build up a wide and varied collection. For those who prefer bound volumes there is a wonderful range in the *Everyman* Library; over five hundred authors are represented, including many translations from foreign writers.

Books about Books

It is very helpful in learning to form judgments about literature to read what others have written about their own opinions of literary works. This passing of judgment is known as "criticism," a term which does not denote finding fault, but rather the making of a valuation, high or low, of a work of art. A great critic must be a man of experience, insight and balanced judgment, responding readily to art and having the skill to express clearly his opinions and reactions. Critics do not exist to be agreed with or to be contradicted; their value is in their power to awaken our perception and to reveal qualities which we have failed to see for ourselves. If a critic praises something which makes no appeal to us, it is useless to feel angry with him; he, with equal reason, might feel annoyed at our blindness and lack of insight. The important thing is to try to see how the critic arrives at his judgment; when he has reached his conclusion we may not agree with it, but on the way we shall have caught a glimpse of ideas of which we had been so far unaware.

To read the comments of great critics, such as Coleridge, Hazlitt, Lamb and De Quincey, on a Shakespeare play we already know well is to gain

In the British Museum one can read any book published in Britain.

fresh insight into the play and a realization of beauty and significance previously overlooked.

For literary studies the critic is only a guide; his opinions must not be taken over as our own and reproduced to impress examiners. If we understand the critic's point of view, agree with his opinion and can support it from the text, then that opinion can rightly become our own. Equally, we might find good grounds for forming and supporting an opinion quite contrary to that of the critic; and if we can justify it from the text, we are entitled to hold that opinion. Equally, we must refrain from learning and trotting out second-hand opinions from the notes, introductions and appendices with which many school textbooks are so liberally provided, although we can use them to acquire an understanding and appreciation of the book we are studying.

In all literatures there are certain common elements and some of these will be commented on below.

Narrative Form

Since earliest times the fascination of a story has been present in every nation and age. Its appeal is universal, and arises from many human characteristics. Man loves especially to get outside himself, and to identify himself with heroic figures; he loves to see himself as a champion of the weak and a scourge of the villainous; above all, he has curiosity to know how a situation is finally resolved.

In all primitive literatures, the narrative is the first literary form to appear; the Norse sagas are a mixture of the actions of gods and heroes. Although we have written records of these stories, in their earliest form they were spoken or chanted; that is, they were a form of folk literature.

In ancient civilized countries, the story developed into a highly literary and poetic form. The Greek *Iliad* and *Odyssey* attributed to Homer, stories arising from the war between Greece and Troy, had also elements of description, character-delineation, poetic richness and other qualities which have ensured their preservation for over two thousand years.

This type of magnified and embroidered story, known as an epic, appears again in Roman literature in Virgil's *Aeneid*, in medieval Italian in Dante's *Divine Comedy* and in English seventeenth-century poetry in Milton's *Paradise Lost* and *Paradise Regained*. It is interesting to note the transition from the heroic world of ancient times to the later spiritual and religious world; but the essential struggle which lies at the heart of the epic still remains—the conflict between good and evil.

In English literature our earliest narratives also took poetic form. The ballads which have been gathered during the past two hundred years in such collections as followed Percy's *Reliques* (1765) were poetic narratives on a few general themes such as warfare, magic or heroism. In ballads we have a folk literature in the sense that they were known and passed on by word of mouth from one generation to another. In their earliest form they were songs accompanying dances in the absence of other music. Many of them developed poetic qualities of real and moving effect. Sir Philip Sidney, in his *Apology for Poetry*, belittled the crude popular folk poetry of the sixteenth century, but had to confess that the ballad of *Chevy Chase* stirred his heart "more than . . . a trumpet."

The Importance of the Plot

As literature developed, the story became of increasing importance and interest. Possibly it has reached its highest point of complexity in the modern detective story. This extreme interest in plot came relatively late, in the mystery stories of early nineteenth-century writers such as Mrs. Radcliffe whose work was so delightfully satirized by Jane Austen in *Northanger Abbey*. Opposed to the mystery and horror school, we have the long and involved stories of Scott's Waverley novels, in which interest in events is balanced by an equal interest in people, places, customs and moralizings. It is important to remember that in many of our greatest books the story is not original; Shakespeare rarely relied on his own invention for stories, but often borrowed and adapted some existing and sometimes very slight story. Complexity of plot grew to great lengths and sometimes got out of the author's control, as happened in Dickens' *Little Dorrit*.

There is probably no sterner test of invention and plot management than writing short stories. There are brilliant examples by O. Henry, Somerset Maugham, Kipling, Stevenson and many others. After enjoying their stories, it is a fascinating exercise to trace out the complicated inter-connected events which result in the final outcome of each story.

The Development of Character

One quickly realizes that in almost all types of English literature there is a constant interest in qualities of personality or character, which has called forth a great company of men, women and children born in the imagination of writers. These imaginary people are more vivid and familiar to us than most actual historical characters; Julius Caesar has left an imprint on the records of history, but we feel that we know the Caesar of Shakespeare's play better than the historical character. How many people in real life do we know better and more intimately than H. G. Wells' Mr. Polly, or Bernard Shaw's Eliza Doolittle? This interest in character is a distinguishing mark of English literature.

There has been a marked change over the last fifty years in methods of presenting character in literary work, especially in the novel. In earlier novels, a writer could work either through direct information and comment or by letting us infer qualities through a character's actions, his relationship with other people and what other people say about him. In drama, of course, an author cannot deal with his audience directly, and must rely on the indirect means of description mentioned above. Scott describes Quentin Durward at great length as soon as he appears:

> "The age of the young traveller might be about nineteen or betwixt that and twenty, and his face and person, which were very prepossessing, did not, however, belong to the country in which he was now a sojourner. His short grey cloak and hose were rather of Flemish than of French fashion, while the smart blue bonnet, with a single sprig of holly and an eagle's feather, was already recognized as the Scottish head-gear."

This external description continues for some considerable space:

> "Although his form had not yet attained its full strength, he was tall and active, and the lightness of the step with which he advanced, showed that his pedestrian mode of travelling was pleasure rather than pain to him."

After more physical description we come to some consideration of the hero's personality:

> "His features, without being quite regular, were frank, open and pleasing. A half smile, which seemed to arise from a happy exuberance of animal spirits, showed now and then that his teeth were well set and as pure as ivory; whilst his

bright blue eye, with a corresponding gaiety, had an appropriate glance for every object which it encountered, expressing good humour, lightness of heart and determined resolution."

Here we have a pattern of young manhood, and what he does through the rest of the book will conform to that pattern.

Conrad's Characterization

When we compare this with Conrad's method of characterization, we find a completely different approach. When, in Conrad's novel *The Rover* the ex-pirate Peyrol brings his captured prize-ship into harbour, Conrad writes:

"The course of his life, which in the opinion of any ordinary person might have been regarded as full of marvellous incidents (only he himself had never marvelled at them) had rendered him undemonstrative to such a degree that he did not even let out a sigh of relief at the rumble of the cable. And yet it ended a most anxious six months of knocking about at sea with valuable merchandise in a damaged hull . . . once or twice on the verge of shipwreck and more than once on the verge of capture. But as to that, old Peyrol had made up his mind from the first to blow up his valuable charge—unemotionally, for such was his character, formed under the sun of the Indian seas in lawless contests with his kind for a little loot."

After Peyrol's death and at the close of the book, when Arlette and Réal (whose happiness Peyrol ensured by splendid self-sacrifice) were discussing him, the following dialogue took place:

" 'What sort of man was he really, Eugene? Did you ever ask yourself that question?'

" 'Yes,' said Réal. 'But the only certain thing we can say of him is that he was not a bad Frenchman.'

" 'Everything's in that,' murmured the cripple in the silence that fell upon Réal's words and Arlette's faint sigh of memory."

In Conrad's method of character portrayal we see the hero meeting new people and new sets of circumstances to which he reacts, revealing each time an additional facet of his character. Moreover by Conrad's cinematic use of "flash-back" we become aware of influences which, from early childhood, have moulded Peyrol's character.

Stream of Consciousness

This method of character-presentation, more than any other feature, distinguishes the twentieth-century novel from its predecessors. People have become more important than events; and the study of man's thoughts and feelings, with his response to circumstances in which he is living, is the basis of a modern novel. Sometimes we hear "the stream of consciousness" as a

Falstaff, a great comic figure.

label for the novel of today in its more extreme form. In James Joyce's novel *Ulysses*, a Dublin funeral serves as a peg on which are hung the dreams, fancies, memories and inmost feelings of a motley collection of people who however, at the end of the novel remain as real people in the reader's mind. The novel as a study of character development can be seen in works such as H. G. Wells' *Kipps* and *Mr. Polly*. In these novels the men concerned grow and change as we read about them and see their inmost thoughts and feelings, and we like them better for the greater and more intimate knowledge we gain about them.

The earlier extracts from Scott and Conrad were used to illustrate two different techniques in novel writing, which might be labelled the "representational" and "analytical" methods. This contrast is to be seen also in drama, of which *Waiting for Godot* is a recent and extreme example, and in biography, since Lytton Strachey's innovation in *Eminent Victorians*.

Humour in Literature

English literature is unusually rich in humorous writing, and humour crops up in many unexpected places. Even at the height of tragedy, we come across the drunken porter in Macbeth's castle on the point of the discovery of the body of the murdered Duncan; and the clownish grave-diggers in *Hamlet* chatter unconcernedly as they dig the grave and await the arrival of Ophelia's body for burial.

Hamlet talking to the grave-digger.

This mixture of comedy and tragedy is characteristic of Shakespeare's tragedies, and a source of shock and bewilderment to foreign readers. Voltaire concluded that Shakespeare must have been drunk when he wrote these and similar passages!

What makes us laugh? The answers are many and various. Horace Walpole distinguished between comedy and tragedy in his saying, "This world is a comedy to those that think, a tragedy to those that feel." If we can stand aside and disinterestedly watch life going by, it must seem to be made up of amusing figures, with occasional flashes of human worth. If we feel sympathy with our fellow-beings, their sorrows will make life appear sad and pathetic.

True Humour and Wit

Of course, we never see life neatly divided in this way, and the same event can evoke both laughter and pity. Walpole's saying, however, does give us a clue to the distinction between humour and wit; true humour will arise only if our sympathies are engaged, but wit must appeal primarily to our intellect and is dependent on our understanding of words.

It would appear that the unexpected plays an essential part in humour, and this unexpectedness appears in its crudest form in the play upon words known as a pun. Such unexpectedness or surprise can be invoked not only by actions; a peculiar voice or intonation, grotesque appearance or unusual gait, "wickedness" which is so obvious that it can deceive nobody, and many other elements, singly or in combination, are the substance of humour.

Falstaff, a Great Comic Character

Possibly the greatest comic figure in our literature is Shakespeare's Falstaff, a man of gross fatness, a liar, thief, drunkard and coward who is also greedy and selfish, and yet we can neither hate nor despise him. His appeal to us is largely compounded of two elements; firstly, his vices are so open and obvious that they cannot be taken seriously, and secondly, we all have within us elements of deceit, greed and selfishness, and are only too happy to load our particular burden of sin upon the monstrous scapegoat in the person of Falstaff. Though a rascal, he is an engaging rascal; he has a glib tongue, he can find excuses in the blink of an eyelid and assume an air of complete innocence when he is found out. In spite of his abundant flesh, he has a youthful zest and eagerness, and in his more solemn moments he glimpses the degradation into which he has sunk, and is immensely sorry for himself because of the hard way in which the world has used him. Whatever faults the man may have, we have sympathy and not censure for Falstaff; we accept his faults and discount them, and warm to the human characteristics of this delightful rogue. It is this element of sympathy which is essential to true humour, and which differentiates it from wit and satire.

A scene from Oscar Wilde's comedy, The Importance of Being Earnest.

Wit, or Impersonal Humour

We have seen that humour lies in the perception of incongruities in human character, where censure is neutralized by sympathy or liking, and we are left to enjoy the comedy created by the unusual or unexpected. There can be similar unexpectedness and absurdity in ideas and mental impressions where sympathy has no part, and we are concerned purely with an activity of the intellect. This type of humour is known as wit, and is rare in English literature because the average Englishman can seldom keep his feelings separate from his understanding. Wit can be savage or mild, but it is at the same time impersonal and detached; and this is why we have in English relatively few writers of true wit, although we have had so many humorous writers. Sometimes if we separate feeling from comedy we may find cruelty, and then it becomes satire. In Restoration comedy we get an intellectual, and therefore witty, attitude to the characters. If we judged these characters by normal standards we should say that they were shallow, selfish and immoral. Actually they are impersonal, having neither vice nor virtue, because their feelings are never engaged in the action of the play. Of the relatively rare comedy of intellect or ideas we have had examples in Goldsmith, Sheridan, Wilde and Shaw: *She Stoops to Conquer*, *The Rivals*, *The Importance of Being Earnest* and *Pygmalion* are admirable examples of this type of comedy.

Satire, or Reforming Humour

In dealing with humour it has been pointed out that this stems from a combination of comic attributes and sympathy. Wit arises from ideas, comic in themselves or by contrast or comparison, but is free from the influence of emotion. Satire has to do with the comic allied with a deliberate purpose to amend or moderate folly, vice or other human failings by means of ridicule. The satire may be savage and ferocious, as with Swift who despised his fellow-men, or mild and even kindly, as in Jane Austen's penetrating sketches of foolish people.

In almost all literatures, satire appears early and plays a prominent part. Aristophanes in Greece and Juvenal in Rome held up to ridicule the vices and follies of their times. Before 1400 in our own literature, in the *Vision*

Mrs. Bennet and her husband, from Jane Austen's Pride and Prejudice.

Concerning Piers Plowman, Langland attacks many abuses of his time. To our day, satire has remained a vigorous and prominent element in literature.

Satire in Verse Form

Probably the most effective and penetrating satire has been written in verse, where economy of words and directness of expression give added power. Dryden, Pope, Byron and Browning attacked men's follies, or men they disliked and to whom they attributed follies or vices. In *Absalom and Achitophel* Dryden deals with the attempt by Lord Shaftesbury and his followers to secure succession to the throne, after Charles II, for the Duke of Monmouth, Achitophel representing Shaftesbury, and Absalom the Duke of Monmouth. Of Achitophel Dryden writes:

"Pleas'd with the danger, when the waves went high,
He sought the storms; but, for a calm unfit,
Would steer too near the sands to boast his wit.
Great wits are sure to madness near allied,
And thin partitions do their bounds divide;
Else, why should he, with wealth and honour blest
Refuse his age the needful hours of rest?
Punish a body which he could not please,
Bankrupt of life, yet prodigal of ease?
And all to leave what with his toil he won
To that unfeathered two-legged thing, a son."

Pope had his particular enemies against whom he directed his satire, but much of his scorn was lavished on all humanity; in his *Essay on Man* he shows man's folly, baseness, treachery and many other faults without any relenting mercy or sympathy. He sums up the futility of man's struggles in a few lines and makes life seem tawdry and empty:

"See! some strange comfort every stage attend,
And pride bestowed on all, a common friend;
See! some fit passion every age supply,
Hope travels through, nor quits us when we die.
Behold the child, by Nature's kindly law,
Pleased with a rattle, tickled with a straw:
Some livelier plaything gives his youth delight
A little louder, but as empty quite.
Scarfs, garters, gold amuse his riper stage,
And beads and prayer-books are the toys of age;
Pleased with this bauble still as that before;
Till tired he sleeps and Life's poor play is o'er."

So Pope dismisses man's life in four meaningless stages. Shakespeare allotted man his seven ages ending with the emptiness of death, but we are led to believe, with Shakespeare, that there was something warm and pleasant in those ages, brief as they were.

Satire in Prose Form

Prose satire in English has been equally effective and, at times, possibly more virulent. Usually satire is expressed in a figurative form, often in the framework of an imaginary era or country. No fiercer or more bitter satire on humanity has been written than Swift's *Gulliver's Travels.* Taken purely on surface value, the first two voyages to Lilliput and to Brobdingnag have become a firm favourite as a children's book of attractive fantasy. The picture of man first as a giant and then as a pigmy gives a fairy-like quality to the story, which sharpens the point of Swift's satire when he holds up man's follies to our view. The other two books have no fairy-tale appeal; one is a fierce attack on theorists who are complete fools in practical affairs, the other is an attack on humanity in general.

Another effective satirist who wrote in the framework of an imaginary country was Samuel Butler, who died in 1902. In his invented country *Erewhon* he attacked the self-satisfaction of his fellow-men and their placid acceptance of ideas and institutions which, in his opinion, had become outworn and obsolete. His attacks are effective through their element of surprise and the calmness of their presentation. He felt keenly about the prison system and its debasing effects, and urged the need for a wrongdoer to be treated with understanding and sympathy. In *Erewhon*, a man caught burgling a house was sent to hospital; his friends brought fruit and flowers, and made kind inquiries about his moral progress. If, however, a man caught a cold, he would be committed to prison and shunned by others. Butler wanted to make the point that a man is a criminal through influences often beyond his control, but illnesses are things that can usually be avoided by any man who will take reasonable precautions.

It is interesting to note that satire has flourished in periods of calm and general prosperity. Soon this country will have been living under the effects of wars and their aftermath for half a century, and prospects of settled peace are still remote. However, in George Orwell, by whose early death literature recently suffered a great loss, we had a satirist of real power and appeal. His two books *Animal Farm* and *1984* portrayed and exposed some of the major follies which still threaten the future of humanity.

Pathos, the Art of Arousing Pity

Before we leave this consideration of various basic types of writing, we should give some consideration to pathos as a mood of expression which can be used with great effect. *Pathos* means *pity*, and whilst we shall see later in the discussion of tragedy that pathetic or pity-arousing writing is an

Children spy on adults in the grim world of George Orwell's 1984.

essential element in some plays, we find pathos also in the writing of poetry, novels and history. In these instances pathos is usually most effective when unexpected, but it can be worked up with equal effect. In concluding his account of *The Rise of the Dutch Republic* Motley pays a moving tribute to William the Silent who had led the Dutch people through a long and bitter struggle for their independence:

> "The people were grateful and affectionate, for they trusted the character of their Father William, and not all the clouds which calumny could collect ever dimmed to their eyes the radiance of that lofty mind to which they were accustomed, in their darkest calamities, to look for light. As long as he lived, he was the guiding star of a brave nation, and when he died the little children cried in the streets."

Expression and Communication

Men communicate with each other in various ways, sometimes by signs, gestures, smiles or scowls, but most commonly by words. These words, particular sounds which we recognize, grow in our minds as we grow in our bodies, until they come to have a definite significance. Words, however, have not only sound and meaning; they have associations and evoke memories and emotions. In a well-known poem, Edward Thomas says of words:

"I know you;
You are light as dreams,
Tough as oak,
Precious as gold,
As poppies and corn
Or an old cloak
. . . familiar
To the eye
As the dearest faces
That a man knows
And as lost homes are:
Let me sometimes dance
With you,
Or climb
Or stand perchance
In ecstasy
Fixed and free
In a rhyme
As poets do."

We have, then, two characteristics in words: (*a*) denotation, i.e. meaning; and (*b*) connotation, i.e. qualities or associated ideas. Writers use this double nature of words with deliberate art, and can produce widely varying effects; but the primary necessity is that meaning shall be conveyed. Efforts have been made, and no doubt will continue to be made, to convey feeling and associations without meaning, as in James Joyce's *Ulysses:*

> "That it was not a heaventree, not a heavenbeast, not a heavenman. That it was a Utopia, there being no known method from the known to the unknown; an infinity, renderably equally finite by the suppositious probable apposition of one or more bodies equally of the same and of different magnitudes."

Compare this with the following, from Landor's *Imaginary Conversations:*

> "Laodameia died; Helen died; Leda, the beloved of Jupiter, went before. It is better to repose in the earth betimes than to sit up late; better, than to cling pertinaciously to what we feel crumbling under us, and to protract an inevitable fall. We may enjoy the present while we are insensible of infirmity and decay; but the present, like a note in music, is nothing but as it appertains to what is past and what is to come. There are no fields of amaranth on this side of the grave; there are no voices, O Rhodope, that are not soon mute, however tuneful; there is no name, with whatever emphasis of passionate love repeated, of which the echo is not faint at last."

Here the meaning is clear; it could be said to imply that death is to be welcomed as a refuge from the decrepitude of age; today can mean nothing when detached from yesterday and tomorrow; all things lovely, however much loved, must finally perish. But there is in Landor's prose much more than literal meaning. By its sounds, thoughts and images and by its stately rhythm, it emphasizes for us the sadness of mortality.

Rhythm and its Effects

So far we have been dealing with words from the points of view of meaning and association, and of the effect words have on us. The writer has at his command still another powerful means of emphasizing his meaning and heightening the emotional effect of what he writes, through *rhythm*. In a later chapter we shall consider more fully this topic of the nature and development of rhythm, and its effects in writing, but it is important from the outset to realize and look for those effects. Here it must suffice to give one instance of rhythm in a poem conveying a mood and ideas similar to those expressed in the passage from Landor. This passage is from Shirley's *Death the Leveller*:

"The glories of our blood and state
Are shadows, not substantial things;
There is no armour against fate;
Death lays his icy hand on kings.
Sceptre and Crown
Must tumble down,
And in the dust be equal made
With the poor crooked scythe and spade."

Stephen D. *is based on incidents from the works of James Joyce.*

Here the solemn, balanced rhythm of the verse gives an added intensity to the awe and menace of death.

Literature and the Time-Spirit

Most literature is written to be read by somebody other than the author, and to be sold to the public for the writer's benefit. It follows that a writer, to achieve material success, must appeal to the prevailing tastes and interests of his day.

It now seems difficult to realize that the detective story was established by Conan Doyle barely eighty years ago. H. G. Wells's *First Men in the Moon* is but seventy years old, though he was preceded by some forty years by the Frenchman Jules Verne in the field of what we now call Science Fiction. The Elizabethan period and the early eighteenth century were fascinated by travel and exploration; in the late seventeenth century men were deeply interested in religion and philosophy. Each age and era has its special interests which are largely conditioned by forces existing at the time.

It has often been said that literature is a reflection of life and that the poet holds the mirror up to Nature. In his *Apology for Poetry* Sir Philip Sidney wrote, "Among the Romans the poet was called 'Vates' which is as much as a Diviner, Fore-seer or Prophet"; and this prophetic quality (which Wordsworth called, "Seeing into the heart of things") is seen from time to time in poets, who, by their greater imagination and insight, seem to penetrate the curtain between us and the future. A remarkable instance of foresight is to be found in Tennyson's *Locksley Hall* where he wrote in 1832:

> "For I dipt into the future, far as human eye could see,
> Saw the vision of the world, and all the wonder that would be;
> Saw the heavens fill with commerce, argosies of magic sails,
> Pilots of the purple twilight dropping down with costly bales;
> Heard the heavens fill with shouting, and there rained a ghastly dew
> From the nations' airy navies grappling in the central blue;
> Far along the world-wide whisper of the south wind rustling warm,
> With the standards of the peoples plunging thro' the thunderstorm;
> Till the war-drum throbbed no longer, and the battle flags were furled
> In the Parliament of man, the Federation of the world."

These lines, written seventy years before the first aeroplane flew and over eighty years before poison gas was first used in war and the League of Nations founded, show a remarkable insight. We can only hope that the vision of the last two lines quoted will one day be realized in its turn.

Social Background of Literature

We have seen that most literature has been conditioned by the feelings and aspirations of the generation in which it was written. If, therefore, we wish to enter fully into a writer's thoughts and feelings, we must make some effort to find out for ourselves the characteristics of the times in which he wrote. Firstly we must know about the conditions and people of that time. Pope said, "The proper study of mankind is man," and as literature is largely a reflection of man's condition and feelings, the more we know of these in different ages, the better we shall understand what is written. Much of what Samuel Johnson wrote would be less significant for us now had he not had probably the greatest of biographers in James Boswell, who, by his record of Johnson's words, actions and even his thoughts, revealed the man's inmost nature.

We must, if we wish to understand the literature of varying periods, have at least a background knowledge of history—not lists of kings and battles, but the varying conditions of life through the ages. We must know something, too, of the inter-action of events and ideas of one country with those of another. The impact of the French Revolution on thought, politics and society in England was profound and lasting; the Jacobite rebellions in Scotland inspired some of our best novel-writing; factory conditions and the effects of industry in general on the lives of the people laid the foundations of much mid-nineteenth-century writing. In more recent years campaigns such as the Spanish Civil War have inspired stories and poems. Unless we know something of the events and causes which affected their writers, we cannot hope to realize fully the plan and purpose of literary works.

One of the most useful and enjoyable background books for a student of literature is G. M. Trevelyan's *English Social History* which traces the conditions under which men have lived since Chaucer's day. We can read what men thought, how they were fed, housed and clothed, how they were governed, what prompted their revolts, the mistakes they made and the triumphs they achieved. For the student of literature this knowledge is essential, and Professor Trevelyan's book is the more valuable since much of its material is drawn from the literature of the period under consideration.

Writers' Diaries

Diaries are another fruitful source of background knowledge. Dorothy Wordsworth's journals give us an insight into her brother's feelings, his methods of composition and the sources of his inspiration. To read her account of the events leading to the writing of the best known of Wordsworth's poems, *Daffodils*, is to gain a new insight into the poem itself. Anybody twenty years hence wanting to read and understand much of what is being written today will have to know something of political forces since 1945, especially Communism and Fascism, together with the views and outlook of young people in the affluent age in which we are now living. A period of depression, stagnation and unemployment would probably, in a space of two or three years, either change the views now finding expression in current literature or give them new and extreme forms.

One period in English literature and history which clearly shows change and development in progress is the latter half of the fourteenth century. The Black Death had broken down the system of serfdom which had survived the feudal system and against which discontent found an outlet in the Peasants' Revolt. The first rumblings could be heard of the Reformation which was to have its full effect in England a century and a half later; the weaknesses in the medieval church were giving rise to protest and satire such as we see in the writings of Langland and Chaucer. Petrarch, who died in 1374, marked the first stirrings in Italy of the Renaissance which was to reach England nearly a century later, and to flower into the richest period of our literature under Queen Elizabeth I. The exciting period 1350-1400 presents us with our first truly English poet, Chaucer, writing against a background of political, social and religious change. With such a book as G. G. Coulton's *Chaucer and his England* to guide us, Chaucer's poetry comes alive; and the period in which he lived is illuminated by his writings. Similarly a book such as J. Dover Wilson's *Life in Shakespeare's England* adds immensely to our understanding and enjoyment of Shakespeare's plays.

Enjoyment of Literature

This has been said to be "the crowning fruit of long experience," and this is equally true of the enjoyment of any art. It is an enjoyment which can never become stale and can never be exhausted. The pleasures to be gained from literature grow richer with the widening of one's experience and knowledge. It touches life and humanity at countless points; we become more acutely aware of our fellow-men through the penetrating studies of humanity which we find in literature, and our own surroundings become novel and surprising when we read the poets' reactions to their own environments and to things we had seen each day of our lives without having really noticed them. If the atomic catastrophe occurred, and television, wireless, record-players, tape-recorders and cinemas could no longer function in an age deprived of electric current, a survivor of the catastrophe who had a hundred good books would have rich and satisfying entertainment for as many years of life as were left to him.

CHAPTER 2

THE MAKING OF ENGLISH

THE language that the Anglo-Saxons brought to this country in A.D. 449 belonged to the Teutonic group of languages and thus was closely related to the German, Dutch and Scandinavian tongues. It was a highly inflected language with as wide a variety of endings in its declensions and conjugations as there are in classical Latin. The spelling is archaic and many of the words became obsolete through later Norman influence. Thus the language impresses the general reader as a foreign tongue, and study of Anglo-Saxon literature has remained a preserve of scholars. Nevertheless this Anglo-Saxon tradition exercised a persisting influence upon the development of Middle English: the student will find annotated editions which will assist his reading, or modern paraphrases which, although losing some of the direct impact of alliterative verse, convey the atmosphere and outlook of this early age.

In spite of divisions by dialect, this language was known from the first as *Englisc*. The influence of Celtic missionaries who came from Ireland by way of Scotland made Northumbria the first centre of scholarship. Here our first poet, Caedmon, wrote his versions of parts of the Bible. All prose literature

This Caedmon manuscript shows how the English language has changed.

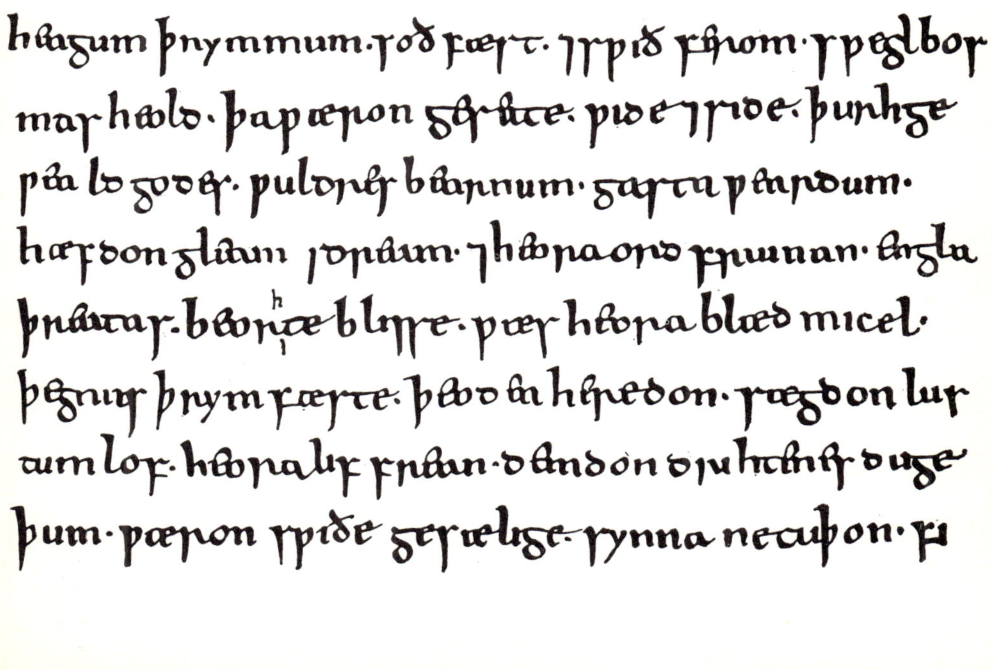

was the work of clerical scribes in monasteries, and was written in Latin. Their work prepared a way for the development of English prose under King Alfred, and their use of Latin idiom gave to English a standard of clear and simple statement. The Venerable Bede was the most eminent of these scribes: his *Ecclesiastical History of the English Race* not only gives us valuable historical information, but in its literary quality reveals the sensitive and gentle personality of its author. By King Alfred's time (*c.* 848-*c.* 900), Danish invasions had checked advance in Northumbria and the centre of culture had moved to Wessex. Alfred's influence in inviting scholars from the Continent to raise the standard of learning was more important than his own authorship. The introduction of *The Anglo-Saxon Chronicle* was his outstanding achievement: it was the first continuous history of a people in Europe, and one form of it, compiled at Peterborough, persisted for over a hundred years after the Norman Conquest.

The First English Poem

Beowulf, a poem on a grand and heroic scale, is the only pre-Conquest and pre-Christian Saxon poem to reach us, and even that only in versions written by clerical scribes who have reconciled it with Christian ethical ideas. A little history mingles with a lot of legend. Beowulf, besides winning victories for the Geats and becoming their king, is a slayer of monsters, a kind of Teutonic Hercules. The supernatural enters into his exploits, for example, when he slays the monster Grendel and the monster's mother. The poem conveys a primitive love of fighting that characterizes the Scandinavian sagas, but some episodes have been given a quality of vague allegory. The mood, as in most Anglo-Saxon poems, is melancholy: nature is grim and grey, inflicting hardship on man; there is no Mediterranean buoyancy. The note of humanism, that even defeat and tragedy can be accepted because of the heroism and intensity of experience that have been displayed, does not appear until the Normans bring us under the French influence of the *Chanson de Roland*, a famous French poem about Roland and Charlemagne.

Anglo-Saxon Poetry*

This is written in alliterative verse. The lines each divide into two parts and vary in length, but there are a uniform two stresses in each part of the line,

* Poems that can be recommended to the general reader are *The Dream of the Rood* and *Judith* (a fragment of the biblical story); both of these can be obtained in paperbacks in Methuen's Old English Library. *Saint Helen*, by Cynewulf, tells the story of a search by the mother of the Emperor Constantine for the True Cross. *The Seafarer* is interesting as a more lyrical poem conveying the mood of a sailor who, while he hates and fears the sea, at the same time is fascinated by it and loves it. The grim hardships of the sea and gentler pleasures of the land are vividly contrasted. The poem, in a modern rendering by Stopford Brooke, should be available in public libraries. Finally, *The Battle of Maldon*, an historical poem describing the last stand of Byrhtnoth and his men before the Danish invaders, has the tragic quality of the *Song of Roland.*

and use of alliteration (words beginning with the same sound) reinforces these stresses in giving pattern to the verse. The tone of the verse is heavy because words are dominated by consonants rather than by vowels. There is little variation to convey changes of mood; joy is expressed in much the same tone as sorrow. Instead of forming words by the use of prefixes and suffixes (as in Latin), Anglo-Saxon tends to form compound words: thus *to crucify* is *rod-faestnen* (to fasten to the cross). Everything is visualized: the Biblical "And the earth was without form and void" is rendered "The earth as yet was not green with grass." This process passes readily into copious use of imaginative but often over-indulged metaphor, producing a roundabout style: eyes become "the jewels of the head," and the sea "the path of the whale."

The Norman Conquest

Unlike the Danes, the Normans were felt as an alien race. They became the ruling class; Norman French became the language of Court and Law Court, and it was also taught in schools. Englishness became a mark of inferiority, and it was something of a miracle that English survived. Norman influence was strongest in the South, but the Midland dialect continued to develop as a spoken language. A "come-back" of English was started by John's loss of Normandy (1200-1250). The Normans who elected to stay here and give up their Norman lands became more English. Gradually, assisted by the growth of trade, the Mercian or East Midland dialect gained ascendancy and became standard English. It was significant that this area included London, Oxford and Cambridge. The English that emerged had adopted many Norman-French words in its vocabulary.

The Norman Conquest, linking England with France, had a great influence on verse form. Regular metrical lines were introduced, together with rhyme and variety of stanza form. Gradually the English acquired the French spirit: poetry lost its monotonous Anglo-Saxon rhythm and became more responsive to mood. Chivalry and courtly love became themes of the new literature. The effect was to give clearness and colour to English verse.

Such changes developed only gradually. At first secular writers turned to Latin, which was the only language common to the races.

Geoffrey of Monmouth has been called the first of our writers of fiction, and he certainly used legends freely. In *Historia Regum Britanniae* he introduces Arthurian legends.

Both Normans and Saxons claimed Arthur as a national hero; the historical Arthur, a very vague figure, seems to have been a leader of the British against the Saxons, Picts and Scots in the period after the Romans left the country, but now he rapidly became romanticized into the heroic leader of the Knights of the Round Table. This was invaluable material for the new verse romances in the French manner. Magic enters with Merlin, and early fairy-lore (later

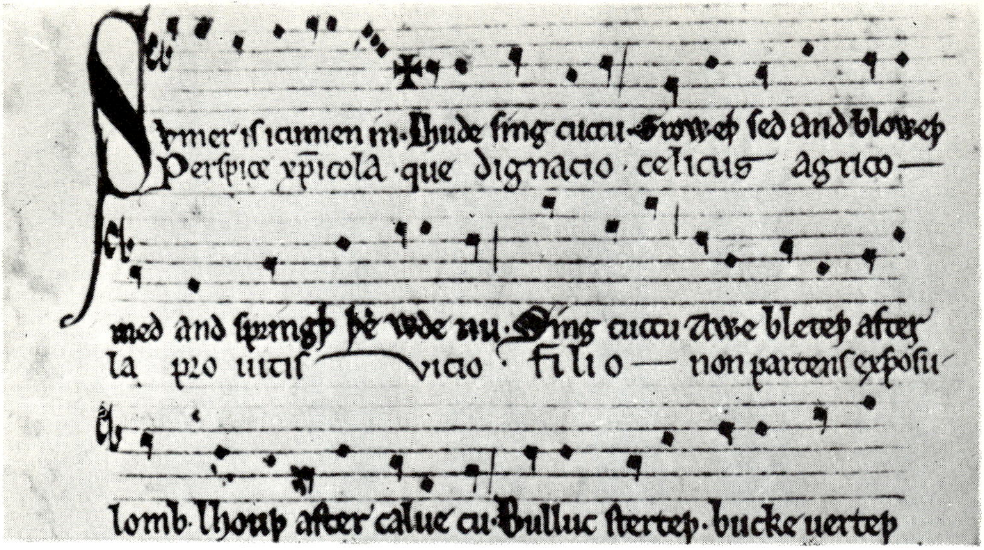

An eleventh-century manuscript of the famous song, Sumer is i-cumen in.

used by Shakespeare) mingles in the stories. Gradually the stories of Tristram, Lancelot and the Holy Grail gather from many sources round Arthur.

Sir Gawain and the Green Knight

This poem is written in the dialect of the North-West. Challenged in Arthur's Hall to strike off the head of the Green Knight, Gawain does so and is told by the knight (who has gathered his head under his arm) that in a year's time he must journey to a certain chapel where the Green Knight will deliver a similar blow upon him. After a year, Sir Gawain goes on his quest and comes to a castle where he is entertained by a hospitable lord and two ladies. Each day the lord goes hunting, and meanwhile Gawain stays sleeping to prepare for his ordeal with the Green Knight. To him comes the beautiful lady to tempt him, but Gawain withstands the temptations without sacrificing his courtesy to the lady. Thus the theme of courtly love and the conventions of chivalry appear. However, Gawain makes a concession to the lady, accepting her green girdle which, she says, will protect him against a mortal wound. When at last he faces the Green Knight, who proves to be his host at the castle, the blow merely grazes the skin of his neck.

In the language of the poem there are many Northern and Scandinavian words, but there is an irregular French stanza division with a brief rhyming lyric concluding each stanza.

Piers Plowman

This is a very different type of poem, in West Midland dialect, and a social document of the time. William Langland was a humble clerk in religious orders, who spent a life-time observing the human scene with shrewd insight.

The poem's power emerges not so much from its poetry as from the earnest sincerity of the poet in pursuing his moral and religious purpose. The poet lies down to sleep among the Malvern Hills, and in his dream sees a plain crowded with people who are all so immersed in their various occupations that they are indifferent to the purpose of God in human life. To these people comes Piers Plowman, a simple countryman who offers to lead them on a pilgrimage to find Truth. Piers has great dignity, which reminds us of the Apostles and anticipates something of the dignity that Wordsworth gave his humble characters. In the visions that follow, showing different levels of Christian living, Piers is identified first with the Good Samaritan, and ultimately with Christ himself; this is the poet's way of showing that the human side of Incarnation gives man a part in the life of God, and links him to God's eternal purpose. The triumph of Antichrist at the end of the poem is not an anti-climax; it restores the situation to where the poet began, reminding us that evil is a constant presence in the world.

Most of the devices in *Piers Plowman* are medieval. There is a framework of allegory in the poem (i.e. it has a second moral meaning), and allegorical figures like Lady Holy Church and Conscience appear. Its loose unity and seeming digressions are medieval. The parade of the Seven Deadly Sins was constantly being presented in verse and in morality plays, and the episodes of the Crucifixion and the Harrowing of Hell resemble Mystery plays in their presentation. One might conclude that here is concentrated the essence of the Middle Ages, before the curtain falls upon them and Chaucer introduces a modern approach. But Langland in some ways anticipates Chaucer. By describing what he actually sees, he brings individual characters vividly to life; the Seven Deadly Sins are not mere Morality figures, but almost Chaucerian in their individual and personal quality.

Alliterative Verse

Both these poems are written in the alliterative verse of the Anglo-Saxons. In reading them, a student will sense the poetic qualities of alliterative verse more readily than in the Anglo-Saxon poems from which they derive. Chaucer and his East Midland fellow poets were using French verse patterns with a regular number of syllables to a line; but English poetry has always been impatient of poetic forms that limit the number of unstressed syllables, as the verse of Shakespeare and Milton shows. This may have sprung from the influence of Saxon verse, and indeed an alliterative pattern can often be seen in the two halves of Chaucer's line.

The Age of Chaucer, edited by Boris Ford (Pelican Books), is a useful companion for the study of the later Middle Ages. Besides giving the text of *Sir Gawain and the Green Knight* in full and that of *Piers Plowman* in part, it contains critical essays on both poems. The two poems are also published by Penguin Books; *Piers Plowman* in a prose translation by J. F. Goodridge is eminently readable and conveys something of the quality of Langland's language.

CHAPTER 3

CHAUCER

GEOFFREY CHAUCER was born about 1340 and died in 1400. Thus he saw the decline of Edward III's fortunes in the French wars, and the economic and political troubles of the reign of Richard II. The slow process was beginning that was to transform the Middle Ages into the modern world. At first this bred doubt and uncertainty in men's minds and some of the old social, political and religious forms were declining, but there was an air of expectancy, and men's minds were receptive to new ideas; literature was beginning to feel the first influence of the Renaissance from the Continent, and Chaucer responded joyously to the challenge and promise of his time.

He was the son of a London wine-merchant, and perhaps it was the growing financial dependence of king and Court upon the wealth of the merchant class that enabled Chaucer to obtain a place as page in the household of the Duchess of Ulster, later the wife of the Duke of Clarence, third son of Edward III. Soon Chaucer was promoted to the king's service, and is described as a "valet" in the Court. Like his Squire in *The Canterbury Tales*, he took part in a military expedition into France, "In Flaundres, in Artoys and Picardye." He was taken prisoner at Rheims, and ransomed a year later, the king paying part of his ransom. Back at Court, he was appointed by the king to go abroad as an ambassador on trade missions; upon such employment he went to Italy in 1372 and again in 1378. In the meantime he was appointed Comptroller of Customs at the Port of London. Chaucer owed most of his appointments to the patronage of John of Gaunt. In later life he became Justice of the Peace for Kent, and in 1386 represented that shire in Parliament. He was also Clerk of the King's Works in repairs to the riverside between Woolwich and Greenwich, and later in repairs to St. George's Chapel at Windsor. He died in 1400, and was buried in the Chapel of St. Benedict in Westminster Abbey, thus being the first poet to be buried in what is now known as Poets' Corner.

Chaucer's Wide Experience of Life

Chaucer's interests brought him into direct contact with every class of the community. By birth, and therefore probably by inclination, he belonged to the middle-class merchants; by training he acquired the manners and courtesy of Court life. In the wide experience of his business life he was studying his fellow men with shrewd insight; and when he came home in the evening he acquired, by extensive reading of books and manuscripts, the learning and literary ability displayed in his works. All great writers have had models on which to build their own genius: Chaucer had virtually no models in English literature to go by, and the only literature available to him was in Latin, French and Italian. In all of these languages he read widely. In his time the Court spoke French, and Chaucer's education at Court and direct experience of living in France enabled him to absorb all the conventions and devices of French writers.

Chaucer's Early Poems

One of Chaucer's earliest works was a translation of the French *Roman de la Rose,* a poem of immense length begun by Guillaume de Lorris and vastly extended by Jean de Meung. This poem employed all the French conventions of the period, both in its metre and rhymes and in the manner of presenting its themes: the framework of a dream device, the double meaning of allegory, the idea of courtly love, and (in the part written by Jean de Meung) a sly laugh at all these things. Chaucer's achievement in this translation was that for the first time a poet of genius had shown that the East Midland dialect of English contained literary resources capable of conveying all the grace, refinement and delicacy of French.

There followed poems in the French manner, imitations lit by touches of original genius. *The Book of the Duchess,* a poem of allegory and classical story, was written outwardly as a tribute to John of Gaunt's wife Anne, who had died of plague at the age of twenty-two. *The Parliament of Fowls* is built upon an allegory of birds, a form popular in the Middle Ages to convey human outlook and values. In *The House of Fame,* with delightful originality, Chaucer embarks on space-travel, carried to the House of Fame by an eagle; he talks to his escort on the way about stars and the nature of sound waves. Each of these poems covers thousands of lines, but each is left unfinished. It seems as if Chaucer felt that he had not yet found his true form of self-expression.

Chaucer and the Renaissance

Then Chaucer went to Italy, where the Renaissance was in full swing. The Renaissance (meaning "re-birth") will be discussed more fully later: suffice it here to say that it was started by the re-discovery of Greek learning and literature, which placed at the disposal of Western writers the models of Greek poetry and their manner of presenting a subject. Its influence was to take away the artificiality of allegory and the obvious moral purpose, and to substitute a true picture of life. Chaucer drew upon the Renaissance in Italy 150 years before it reached England, and he had a mind great enough to absorb its influences. He visited Genoa, Milan and Florence, the city of the great Italian poet Dante. Dante had been dead for fifty years, but his work and influence remained. Chaucer may have met Boccaccio and Petrarch, two other famous poets of the day; but it was the manuscripts which Chaucer brought back from Italy, rather than personal contacts, that stamped the Italian influence upon his mind.

Chaucer is in a very real sense our first novelist. He combines the descriptive power of a poet with a dramatic interest in what people do and why they do it —in other words, in action and character; and he has the further dramatic gift of writing dialogue in which characters reveal themselves by their talk. The immediate works that Chaucer wrote under Italian influence were *Troilus and Creseyde* and a poem which later became *The Knight's Tale* in his *Canterbury Tales*. Both of these are dramatic in their basic construction. Chaucer presents us with real and convincing men and women, whom we should recognize if we met them in the street. He has now found reality, and this is what places Chaucer among modern writers, and links him with Shakespeare. The poet does not begin with his own ideas and attach them to the figures he creates: he lets ideas emerge from the way his characters behave, and from how they talk and think. Moral purpose is no longer stated but it is there by implication: moral law determines issues of good and evil in all that men do, so there must be a moral issue in all dramatic representations of men and women acting and reacting in the human scene.

Troilus and Creseyde

Chaucer took the love story of *Troilus and Creseyde* from Boccaccio's *Il Filostrato*. He is faithful to the original story in his portrayal of the sentiment and high passion of the lovers; but his originality is seen in his development of the character of Pandarus, a go-between who brings the lovers together. Chaucer's mind did not naturally run on the high level of tragedy: he was not sympathetic to the extremes of character that produce it. His true gift was for comedy, and Pandarus takes his place beside Falstaff and other great comic characters of literature. In *Il Filostrato*, Pandarus is a young cousin of Creseyde, but Chaucer makes him a talkative middle-aged uncle, a busy-body who is full of worldly wisdom which he utters with a sprinkling of pithy sayings and proverbs. It is the conversation of Pandarus that makes the character. Chaucer must have been very fond of conversation: he wrote his poems primarily to be spoken, as is shown by a contemporary picture of him reading to the Court from a pulpit. When his characters are not talking, he frequently addresses his audience, taking them into his confidence, which gives the reader a very intimate feeling of Chaucer's personality.

Chaucer's presentation of Troilus reaches high tragedy, but he retains our sympathy for Creseyde as well. Besides her beauty he gives her intelligence and sensitiveness of mind: her sin is weakness, not wickedness. "To understand everything is to forgive everything," is a very common result of artistic presentation. Chaucer extends to her the charity that derives from his impartial contemplation of the human scene.

The medieval conception of courtly love is the basis of the love story, and must be understood if an understanding of the poem is to be reached. The modern mind is inclined to be impatient at the inactive melancholy of Troilus before Creseyde yields to him. The over-riding condition of secrecy, even when Creseyde is to be delivered to the Greeks, is part of the convention: there was no solution through marriage to their problem. Courtly love was a reaction in romance and literature against marriages of convenience in the real world, at a time when marriage determined the holding of land, and when holding of land determined political and military loyalties. Even middle-class marriages were often very unromantic.

In this poem Chaucer abandons the eight-syllable line for a longer line of ten syllables, which is more variable. This ten-syllable line is one of his outstanding gifts to English poetry.

The Prologue to *The Canterbury Tales*

In *The Canterbury Tales* Chaucer becomes original and entirely English in his presentation of the English scene and of a cross-section of English

Chaucer's pilgrims going to Canterbury, from an old manuscript drawing.

society. The device of linking a series of stories to a central idea was an old one; *The Arabian Nights* is an early example. Boccaccio, in his book *The Decameron* (which Chaucer probably did not know) presents in a garden of a villa on the River Arno a group of noblemen who have fled from the plague in Florence, and who tell stories to pass the time. Boccaccio thus loses the wide social range that Chaucer obtains by writing about a mixed group of pilgrims of all classes who are making a pilgrimage to Canterbury. Gower, a poet contemporary with Chaucer, had told a series of love stories in *Confessio Amantis*, but he is himself the narrator of all the stories. Chaucer devised the idea of allowing each pilgrim to tell, in the original plan, four stories. He thus interposes the mind of the narrator between himself and his readers, and the stories become revelations of their narrator's character. *The Canterbury Tales* was the first work in English to become known throughout Europe.

Medieval Background

A pilgrimage, originating earlier in the Middle Ages as an occasion for pious devotion, was now as often as not merely an occasion for a holiday; life was uneventful and dull. The state of roads made travel difficult, and the law was not a great safeguard, so that pilgrims were obliged to travel in a company. Probably Spring was the best time of year for a pilgrimage; Chaucer's *Prologue* begins with a lively description of Spring. Bad roads, poor food, primitive dwellings and the menace of illness made people of Chaucer's time hail the return of Spring with a relief that is difficult for us to realize. The pilgrimage to Canterbury was considered spiritually the most effective that English shrines offered, but a pilgrimage to the Holy Sepulchre or to other famous shrines in Christendom was popular with English patrons. Pilgrimages were selected according to income: the Wife of Bath, a weaver's widow, had been to most of them, which shows how wealthy the weavers were. Inns for accommodation were few; the main hospitality was provided by monasteries.

A pilgrimage broke down normal social barriers, and so Chaucer is able to gather together a wide range of social types. There is, however, a definite upward limit to this range: none of the higher clergy is present, and none of the nobility. Chaucer's picture of the medieval world divides itself into four divisions: Military, Church, Country-life, and Industry and Commerce.

The Knight, Squire and Yeoman represent the army. A Squire would one day become a Knight; and the Yeoman was a non-commissioned rank whose long-bow had been the decisive weapon in Edward III's victories in France. Standards of chivalry pursued by the Knight—"Trouthe and honour, fredóm and curtesye"—reflected in a very real sense the ideals of the Middle Ages, and all the pilgrims show him the utmost respect.

The medieval Church was the largest single organization in the Middle Ages and its influence was felt in every department of life. Since the only educated men were churchmen, much of the administrative business of the country was performed by churchmen of low rank. The Church took part in personal life in ways unknown today: Summoners took men and women into the Archdeacon's court for moral offences (for example swearing, gambling or immorality) which would be left to a person's conscience nowadays. The process of forgiveness of sins provided well-paid occupations for men like the Friar and the Pardoner, whose lack of any real feeling for religion made them parasites of the medieval community. The religious vocation had declined with the increase of wealth. Monasteries, originally founded in lonely and remote parts of the country, had grown rich by their own honest labour in the fields, particularly in sheep-farming, for the wool trade with Flanders was now the most prosperous industry. Moreover, rich men left bequests to the Church for the good of their souls, and more priests were required to sing masses for the dead. Thus parish priests were tempted to London to earn a second income, leaving their parishes in the hands of ignorant priests who would take a mere pittance for the job. However, there were many parish priests performing their duties as conscientiously as did Chaucer's poor Parson. Here Chaucer's account agrees with that of his contemporary Wycliffe, as indeed does his whole picture of the Church.

Town and Country in Chaucer's Day

Towns were growing with the development of trade, but the great majority of people still lived in the country. The Franklin was a prosperous middle-class farmer, indulging his sense of the good things of life in wholesome farmer's fare. He was a freeholder, paying a money rent for his land, and becoming valuable to the king as a local magistrate in the Shire Court, an early Justice of the Peace. There is considerable detail in *The Prologue* relating to the manorial organization of agriculture in the villages. The Reeve was an official of the manor in charge of the complicated organization: villeins' labour services on the land and co-ordination of fencing, sowing and reaping of strips in the large open fields were under his direction. There would be abundant opportunity for dishonesty, especially as many payments were made in farm produce or in service. The Miller was a very important member of a village community: the mill, usually driven by water, was an example of the partnership between man and nature, and gives a good illustration of the influence of religion. The stream's speed was regarded as an act of God, and therefore a miller living by a sluggish stream was allowed a higher fraction of grain as his payment than was allowed to a miller living by a fast stream. It is easy to see why millers acquired a reputation for dishonesty.

Trading interests of Chaucer's day are represented by the Merchant,

Gildsmen, Manciple and Shipman. Trade was beginning to free itself from its medieval fetters and to assume modern characteristics. The Church had condemned lending money and charging interest on it as immoral, but this attitude was weakening, as the Merchant's contracts for loans show. Trade was expanding on a basis of credit. The Merchant's insistence on command of the sea, and his speculations with foreign currencies, have a modern ring. The Gildsmen represent the manufacturing interest, still in the craft stage but bringing rapid wealth to master-men and breeding that snobbery of wealth which trade usually fosters; their wives were especially pleased with their social position. The Manciple illustrates the growing practice of bulk-buying, the ebb and flow of prices, and the need for business sense and shrewdness. The Shipman is half pirate and half trader: the king's ships could command the narrow seas "betwixe Middelburgh and Orewelle," but in more open parts of the Channel there was still plenty of opportunity for smuggling and piracy.

The Literary Qualities of *The Prologue*

In presenting his characters, Chaucer gives us the types of his day, but he gives his pilgrims personal and individual qualities which bring them vividly to life. These two elements are mingled in varying proportions: sometimes a character is almost completely a type and fails to arouse much interest. The Doctor, Lawyer and Manciple are almost exclusively professional men, and such characters are merely described; but others are presented by the dramatic method. We see the Miller in action, smashing a door by running against it with his head, and we watch with amusement the fastidious table manners of the Lady Prioress, as Chaucer saw her across the dining-table at the Tabard Inn. Chaucer does not give much direct conversation in *The Prologue*, but we virtually hear the Monk expressing his impatience at the strictness of monastic rule; and we hear Chaucer agreeing with him that "his opinioun was good":

> "What! sholde he studie and make him-selven wood,
> Upon a book in cloistre alwey to poure,
> Or swinken with his handes, and laboure
> As Austin bit? how shal the world be served?
> Lat Austin have his swink to him reserved."

This is the language of medieval conversation: we hear it again when the Friar hypocritically justifies taking money for absolving the sins of hard-hearted rogues, or when the Parson says, "If gold ruste, what shal iren do?"

Chaucer uses physical appearance, dress and ornament to convey character. The pimples on the Summoner's face and the gangrenous sore on the Cook's shin seem to imply their loose habits. In actual life, what is accidental may dominate, and all kinds of people may have warts on their noses or black gaping nostrils; but artistically everything has significance, and these symptoms seem to convey the coarse toughness and carelessness of the Miller.

Chaucer's Female Characters

Chaucer uses all these devices in his description of the Lady Prioress, whose personal beauty is indicated by her eyes, which were "greye as glas," her long and well-shaped nose, and her forehead, which was a span broad and boldly displayed when it ought to have been concealed beneath a nun's veil. Her cloak was very neat and her head-dress carefully pleated; her rosary had ornaments of worldly vanity when it should have been a symbol of religious vocation. The two women in *The Prologue* are directly contrasted —the affected refinement of the Lady Prioress and the coarse bold features, extravagant head-dresses and red stockings of the Wife of Bath, the vulgarian of the company, whose wealth had outrun her taste; but her love of loud gossip and her hearty relish of life give her a vitality that places her among Chaucer's masterpieces.

These women characters best illustrate the subtle vein of irony that runs through *The Prologue*. Irony conveys by implication the opposite to what is said. It is an art of the novelist, and Chaucer here anticipates Jane Austen and Thackeray, the nineteenth-century novelists. Satire is too strong a word for it: the ridicule that is implied is too affectionate, too good-humoured, like much of the humour of Shakespeare. In Chaucer's description of the Lady Prioress, the irony lies in what is *not* said of her: religion is only mentioned once, and then only to show her pride in her tuneful voice. All her charity was expended on lap-dogs, who consumed enough wholesome meat to feed several beggars. The spurs that the Wife of Bath wore seem to imply that she was as hard on her pony as she had been on her several husbands.

Chaucer's Moral Attitude

What then was Chaucer's moral attitude? Wycliffe's picture of the period is in close agreement with Chaucer's, especially on the subject of the Church; but where Wycliffe is angry and anxious to reform his fellow men, Chaucer is lenient and humorous. He presents a picture and leaves us to judge it for ourselves: the implication of his moral judgment lies in his selection of significant detail. His rogues are more interesting than his virtuous men, but this is always true both in literature and in life. This does not imply that Chaucer approved of vice. He obviously has a deep admiration for his poor Parson, but cannot make him as interesting as the Friar or the Miller. When he said the Monk's "opinioun was good," he was probably reproducing the politeness that one shows to a chance acquaintance on a holiday. Chaucer is an unobtrusive observer of his fellow men, with an imagination that relishes the rich variety in human nature. He leaves it to moralizers and reformers to reprimand sinners.

The central character on the journey to Canterbury is Harry Bailey, host of the Tabard Inn, briefly described at the end of *The Prologue*, when he proposes his plan for the journey and becomes compère of the tales. Imposing in stature, he must be, like all good inn-keepers, "all things to all men": he is deferentially polite to the Knight, and shows his appreciation of the delicate feelings of the Lady Prioress; he gently bullies the modest Clerk, and with characters of coarser grain he can become, as with the Pardoner, almost blasphemous. He is a commanding influence holding the company together.

The Canterbury Tales

The stories themselves are drawn from every branch of medieval tradition: there are tales of chivalry and courtly love, like the Knight's tale; and tales of magic and fairy-lore like the Squire's tale and the Franklin's tale. The Lady Prioress tells a miracle story about a little boy who was murdered by Jews as he passed through a ghetto, a story well adapted to her tender "conscience." Stories at the other extreme derive from popular *fabliaux*, which Chaucer had probably heard recited, for example the Miller's and Reeve's tales. Always Chaucer's art shapes a story to fit its narrator, not only in the kind of tale but in the manner of its telling. A few tales he leaves almost as he found them in his sources: for example, the Clerk's tale of a patient wife, Griselda, is virtually a translation of the poem by Petrarch from which he takes it.

In the course of the journey to Canterbury, we catch our one glimpse of Chaucer himself. The Host invites him to tell a story and adds this comment:

> "Thou lokest as thou woldest finde an hare,
> For ever upon the ground I see thee stare."

And then he adds to the company:

> "He in the waist is shape as wel as I;
> This were a popet in an arm t'embrace
> For any woman, smal and fair of face.
> He semeth elvish by his contenaunce,
> For unto no wight doth he daliaunce."

Chaucer's *Tale of Sir Thopas* is broken off because it is so dull. He embarks on a fresh story, *The Tale of Melibeus*, in long tedious prose, but his audience, accustomed to these scholarly discourses, listens politely. Thus Chaucer, with sly and disarming modesty, labels himself as a bore.

The Knight's Tale

Chaucer took his *Knight's Tale* from Boccaccio's *Teseide*. It is the most spectacular of the stories, embodying all the colourful and romantic pageantry

The Greek writer Sophocles (495-406 B.C.), one of the world's first dramatists, wrote many fine plays, including the *Antigone*. This scene shows the heroine, who has just thrown dust over her dead brother.

Euripides (480-405 B.C.), also a Greek dramatist, wrote many plays, including the *Electra*. In this scene, Electra is threatened by her wicked mother Clytemnestra, who has murdered Electra's father.

The great Italian poet Dante Alighieri (1265-1321) is remembered for his long poem *The Divine Comedy*. In this scene from *Purgatory*, Dante kneels before Cato, watched by his guide, Virgil.

The Spanish writer Miguel de Cervantes Saavedra (1547-1616) wrote the first great novel, *Don Quixote*, about an eccentric Spanish gentleman who sets forth with his squire to find adventure.

Comedies by the French playwright Molière (1622-1673) are still enjoyed today. Here is a scene from *The Gay Invalid*, in which Argan, who enjoys thinking that he is ill, discusses the state of his health.

Johann Wolfgang von Goethe (1749-1832) wrote the great poem *Faust*, using an old tale of a man who sold his soul to the devil to gain his heart's desire. Here Faust is with villagers near the town gate.

Victor Hugo (1802-1885), the French novelist, dramatist and poet, wrote *Notre-Dame of Paris*, the story of the ugly hunchback, Quasimodo, who fell in love with the pretty gipsy dancer, Esmeralda.

Gustave Flaubert (1821-1880), a French novelist, wrote *Madame Bovary*. This scene shows the wedding feast of Emma and Dr. Charles Bovary, celebrated in true country style at her father's farm.

of chivalry. The ornate splendour of the three temples in the lists that Theseus builds for the knights' combat, and the sumptuous array of knights who come to support the rival lovers, are lavish in their detail of myth, fable and legend. The natures of the two knights are nicely contrasted; Emily herself is a passive cause of all the strife but conforms dutifully to the code of courtly love, which here ends in marriage. In his instinct to relieve a tragic theme, Chaucer has reduced the stature of Theseus from the heroic to that of a kindly middle-aged gentleman with a sense of humour.

The Nun's Priest's Tale

In this tale, we get a very direct reflection of Chaucer's mind. The Monk has just been depressing the company with a tale of "tragedies," and the Nun's Priest is bidden to cheer up the pilgrims with a lively tale. Tragedy, to a medieval mind, was the fall of great men through pride from great prosperity to utter ruin: *The Nun's Priest's Tale* is the story of a cock who suffers a fall through pride. Thus the story of Chanticleer is a burlesque on the Monk's tale. The ridiculous—a mere cock, hen and fox—is raised to the level of the sublime. Not only is Chanticleer given the dignity and regality of heroes of old, but he is also an authority upon the literature and learning of the

Woodcut of the Knight, from a 1490 copy of the Canterbury Tales.

The Nun's Priest, from a manuscript of Chaucer's Canterbury Tales.

Middle Ages. The story thus becomes a good-humoured burlesque upon medieval learning, and Chaucer is laughing at himself and the whole company of learned men for the entertainment of his readers. The story itself occupies barely a fifth of the poem, and all the rest is digression prompted by incidents in the story. The source of the story lies buried in the wealth of fable that goes back to Aesop and has been expanded and varied by centuries of recitation. The story would be well known to Chaucer's hearers, so its attraction would lie solely in Chaucer's treatment of it.

The setting of the story is the humble cottage of a poor widow, which houses the widow, her daughters and the farm creatures. The poverty of her life is described simply but vividly, and is set in deliberate contrast with the lordly splendour of Chanticleer. All the details of Chaucer's description of him imply aristocracy, from the burnished gold of his plumage to the serrated "castel wal" of his comb; and his favourite wife, Pertelote, has all the qualities of a medieval lady. Chaucer's cock and hen are both animal and human. Chanticleer, like any husband, complains of bad dreams; so Pertelote, like any wife, gives him a lecture on the folly of believing that dreams have any significance: his blood is out of order, and he must take some laxatives. So we are off on the first digression, Pertelote's review of medical theory. Piqued by his wife's reproaches, Chanticleer supports his belief in dreams by telling in considerable detail three stories that prove his point. Two are taken from Latin authors (Cicero and Valerius Maximus) and the third comes from

English legend. Chaucer deals freely with his sources, giving interesting glimpses of medieval towns and inns; and the discovery of a dead body and the arrest of a criminal in the first story are vividly presented. Chanticleer follows up his stories with brief examples from the Bible or classical literature, only ultimately to be soothed into the false security that is the fore-runner of tragedy by the beauty of Pertelote and the thought of their wedded bliss.

So the story proceeds again, but only for some sixty lines to introduce the fox, lying concealed among the cabbages in the yard. This tempts the Nun's Priest into further digression upon biblical and classical arch-traitors, to whom in horror he compares the fox:

> "O newe Scariot! newe Genilon!
> False dissimilour, O Greek Sinon
> That broghtest Troye al outrely to sorwe!"

He then proceeds to discuss the views of medieval theologians and philosophers upon whether man has free will, or whether he is bound by God's fore-knowledge of what is going to happen. At last Chanticleer is undone; the fox appeals to his family pride, another of his aristocratic qualities. With precise detail, Chaucer pictures a cock crowing, and Chanticleer is betrayed. The Nun's Priest denounces princes for listening to flatterers, and accuses fate, in the manner of classical tragedy, of being responsible for Chanticleer's downfall. The cries of Pertelote are likened to the lamentations of Queen Hecuba when Troy was burnt by the Greeks.

But the story has now reached its climax, and Chaucer is too good a story-teller to halt his story when he should let it run. There are no further digressions: the hue and cry is up; the whole village takes part in a chase after the fox. This is the most vivid and lively passage in the poem: even the geese and ducks join in. This ending to the story, told in under one hundred lines, illustrates Chaucer's economy and power of condensed narrative, which we shall see again in *The Pardoner's Tale.* The fox is duped in his turn by a similar trick of flattery, a shaping of the story that is typical of fables and moralities, and which is echoed in the statement, brief and to the point, of the tale's moral when both victims confess in turn to their weakness. So, with the conventional prayer for God's blessing, the story ends, and we have seen something of the range of Chaucer's reading and learning, his high spirits, his elvish sense of humour, and the keen relish with which he observes details of the life of his time.

The Pardoner's Prologue and Tale

Both *The Wife of Bath's Tale* and *The Pardoner's Tale* have prologues in which the characters reveal themselves by self-confession, in both cases unashamed and frank—in the Pardoner's case an impudent revelation of his technique "in wynning silver." Some critics are unconvinced that such a cunning rogue as the Pardoner would have been so frank when he intended, after his sermon, to exhibit his relics and claim offerings from the faithful; but Chaucer uses the confession very much as Shakespeare uses a soliloquy, to put the audience wise. The Pardoner had been drinking, and in such a situation it would please his vanity to boast of his cleverness. In any case he gets nothing but insults when he approaches the Host for a contribution, and he does not seem to have imposed on any of his audience.

Chaucer has already given a lengthy description of the Pardoner in *The Prologue*: he now dramatizes the character by showing him in action in his pulpit:

"Than peyne I me to strecche forth the nekke,
And Est and West upon the peple I bekke,
As doth a dowve sitting on a berne."

Chaucer's dramatic instinct combines with his poetry to bring the Pardoner vividly before our eyes. He is a "spiv" of the Middle Ages, a confidence-trickster whose primary instinct is to avoid work.

Pardoners were important among the different types of churchmen who dispensed forgiveness for sin, because they were armed with Papal Bulls (licences from the Pope that gave them the direct authority of the Pope). These licences to sell Indulgences were easily forged, and fake relics were easy to obtain, so the countryside swarmed with false pardoners. Chaucer's Pardoner exhibits a sheep's bone that gives healing qualities to drinking-water or cures jealousy; he also has a mitten that multiplies the crops of any man who pays a handsome sum for the privilege of slipping his hand into it. The Pardoner's cunning is seen in his warning to the audience that his relics have no efficacy for people who have secret sins on their conscience. He speaks bitterly against those who do not fall for his tricks, and trades upon the credulity or fear of his victims. *The Pardoner's Tale* consists of a sermon and a story that illustrates it, a common form of medieval sermon.

The Pardoner's Sermon

The Pardoner commences by setting a scene in a tavern, which he describes with a relish that he cannot disguise. He then digresses to denounce the sins of blasphemy (swearing), gluttony, drunkenness and gaming. These are presented vividly to his audience by the Pardoner's eloquence. He has the formal style of a sermon at his fingertips, addressing inanimate things or abstractions; and he is not squeamish in his choice of words. He echoes the Epistles of St. Paul, and he makes copious allusion to classical stories and to history. In these ways the argument is kept concrete and visual: the drunken man is presented in the manner of the Deadly Sins in a Morality play.

Some features of contemporary life can be deduced from the detail of the sermon: Chaucer is indulging in irony in his description of the way in which cooks disguise their concoctions until a man hardly knows what he is eating. This has a very modern ring, and Chaucer has given to the Pardoner some of his own humour. Chaucer is also speaking of his own experience in the wine trade when he enlarges with ironical humour upon the vintners' habit of diluting choice wines with cheaper products.

The Pardoner's Tale

Three cardinal sins are all illustrated by the story which follows. Three "riotours" in an inn are recovering from a night of drunken revelry: they have been gambling, their language is full of oaths, and they are drunk. Death is a constant presence in the background of the story: sudden death dealt by violence and anger, or by a stroke of plague, which was looked upon as a punishment for sin. Again this would be a well-known story, but

The Pardoner, from a manuscript of Chaucer's Canterbury Tales.

Chaucer gives it an individual character. The old man whom the rioters meet in their search for Death seems to hover between natural and supernatural, like the Wandering Jew or the Ancient Mariner. At first he opposes mildness to their rudeness, and in words of simple pathos expresses a wish to die. We feel the strange burden of humanity. To him death is not to be feared, as the robbers fear it: his feeling for Mother Earth is almost religious. As the incident proceeds, the old man seems to be undergoing a transformation. Who is he? Is he Death himself? No, he is not, but he directs the robbers where to find Death.

From this point the story moves swiftly to its close. Each rioter plots to destroy the others, and they all succeed and all fail by their plotting and counter-plotting. The condensed narrative aids the patterning of incident which is so essential to a moral story. But Chaucer has allowed himself one indulgence, in a thumb-nail sketch of a medieval apothecary plying his trade in poisons, and of his neighbour who had a pole-cat that was destroying his chickens, an obliging customer who will give him a testimonial.

So the Pardoner has justified his text, "Love of money is the root of evil," but before he reverts to his impudent hypocrisy, Chaucer allows us to glimpse one redeeming feature in his mind: from behind all his roguery there emerges an inner conviction of the truth of the doctrine that he exploits and perverts:

> "And Jesu Crist, that is our soules leche,
> So graunte you his pardon to receyve,
> For that is best, I wol yow nat deceyve."

Chaucer's Versification

The Prologue and most of the tales written expressly for the Canterbury series are written in the heroic couplet, or ten-syllable lines rhymed in pairs. Chaucer, unlike Pope and the eighteenth-century poets, does not make the sense-unit coincide with the couplet, but frequently carries the sentence beyond the couplet; and the caesura (or sense-pause) may fall anywhere within a line, giving variety to the rhythm. Prevalence of the ending *-e* (usually sounded like the *a* in *China* except before a vowel or *h*), sounded plurals of nouns in *-es* and verb endings (*-es*, *-est*, *-eth*) give a liquid smoothness to the verse, and lines often end with feminine (two-syllable) rhymes. This adds an eleventh weak syllable to the line:

> "Whan that Aprillë with his shourës sootë
> The droghte of March hath percëd to the rootë."

Sometimes Chaucer omits a weak syllable at the beginning of a line, thus reducing the line to nine syllables:

> "Twènty bookës, clàd in blàk or rèed." (Clerk)

The metre is *Iambic* (unstressed syllable followed by stressed), but Chaucer will frequently introduce a *Trochee* (stressed syllable followed by unstressed) anywhere within the line, usually at the beginning:

> "She wolde wepe, if that she saugh a mous
> *Caught in a trappe*, if it were deed or bledde." (Prioress)

These are common variations in later English poetry, but Chaucer was the first to adopt this freedom, and the only writer of his own day to use them.

Chaucer's English

With the aid of an annotated edition and a glossary, we can soon get on terms with Chaucer's English without going into a great many details of syntax. Sometimes two words are contracted into one, e.g. *noot* (= do not know), *everich* (= every one), *ywis* (= certainly, I know), and *nis* and *nas* (= is not, was not). There are frequent double negatives, and the relative pronoun is often omitted. The prefix *y-* is the Anglo-Saxon prefix *ge-* for the past participle. Some constructions look strange, e.g. impersonal use of the verb with the dative case:

> "For *hym was lever* have at his beddes head
> Twenty bokes, clad in blak or reed." (Clerk)

and such constructions as:

> "He never yet no vileinye ne sayde
> In al his life unto *no maner wight*."

where the genitive case has been attracted to the case of the noun it defines. These are a few brief examples of what we must look for in the notes. We must also check carefully the meaning of words in the glossary. Words are living things, and in six hundred years meaning has often travelled a long distance. The word *vileynye* from the above quotation, for instance, meant "rude" (the opposite of *curteisye*), or an expression that one might expect from a villein or peasant. The Clerk speaks words of *hy sentence*, i.e. wisdom or opinion; the word comes from Latin *sententia* (= opinion).

Norman French Words

Many of Chaucer's words come from Norman-French, and often the French spelling is still evident: "a *povre* widwe" (French *pauvre*) is one example, and the Prioress "*peyned* hir to countrefete chere of court," where nearly every word is Norman-French. Sometimes he gives us both English and French equivalents where, perhaps, the English word was dying out:

> "Or *swinken* with his handes, and *laboure*
> As Austin bit." (Monk)

We recognize many words of today in a different garb, as in *dette*, *faute* and *vitaille*, which came into Norman-French from the Low Latin that the Romans left behind in Gaul. The Renaissance, a hundred years after Chaucer, was shocked by the spelling, and brought these words into line with the classical

The village of Charing, on the Pilgrims' Way to Canterbury.

Latin of Cicero; and so today we spell them *debt*, *fault* and *victuals*. In two cases the old pronunciation has persisted; but in *fault* we sound the letter that has been added. These are brief indications of the interest that lies in Chaucer's words for those who trace their development.

Chaucer's language is generally direct and literal, but he is very fond of a brief simile taken from things of ordinary experience and springing from his lively imagination to make his descriptions immediately recognizable. Here is his description of the Miller in *The Prologue:*

> "Up-on the copright of his nose he hade
> A werte, and thereon stood a tuft of heres,
> Reed as the bristles of a sowes eres . . .
> His mouth as greet was as a greet forneys."

Chaucer's language is very close to the spoken language of his day, as a poet's language should be. It is not only the final *e*s and the old-fashioned words that impress our minds with the poetry's simplicity and quaintness; behind the simplicity there is considerable art. Chaucer had few predecessors when he wrote at the beginning of English literature, unhindered by tradition: if he says that grass is green, he makes an original statement and runs no risk of being charged with imitation. So to our modern minds his language is spontaneous and refreshing in its impact.

The Poet Chaucer by Coghill (Home University Library) is a profitable Life and Commentary at moderate length.

Most leading publishers produce annotated editions of *The Prologue* and of individual tales.

Medieval background can be obtained from *Chaucer and His England* by Coulton, and from *A Commentary upon the General Prologue to the Canterbury Tales* by Muriel Bowden (Macmillan). *The Age of Chaucer*, published in Pelican Books, is useful for background and criticism.

QUESTIONS

1. From Chaucer's *Prologue*, either describe in detail two pilgrims who pointedly contrast with one another, or, selecting at least four pilgrims to illustrate your answer, show how and to what extent Chaucer reveals his own admiration or dislike of them.

2. In *The Prologue*, Chaucer sometimes conveys the character of a pilgrim by describing his or her dress or physical appearance; but sometimes he gives us virtually no description of the man himself but only of what he does. Select *two* pilgrims, one of each type, who illustrate this varied treatment, and describe your impression of their characters from the material Chaucer has given.

3. What impression of country *or* of town life in Chaucer's time have you gathered from your reading of his *Prologue*?

4. Illustrate Chaucer's delight in detailed treatment of his theme by writing about *two* of the following episodes from *The Nun's Priest's Tale:*

(*a*) His description of the widow, her cottage, and her life in it.

(*b*) The story of the murdered pilgrim.

(*c*) The chase after the fox.

5. From your reading of *The Nun's Priest's Tale*, show with close illustration how Chaucer gives to his birds and animals both animal and human qualities.

6. What picture of medieval life do we gather from the Pardoner's sermon?

CHAPTER 4

FROM THE DEATH OF CHAUCER TO 1660

IN the days when few people could read, stories in lilting verse, called ballads, were passed from one generation to the next as a popular form of entertainment.

It is difficult to assign a definite date to these ballads, because they were not collected in the form in which they now exist until the seventeenth and eighteenth centuries. However, they are generally ascribed to the later fourteenth and fifteenth centuries. The genuine ballad is medieval, and belongs to the countryside in the days before the coming of the printing-press. It was handed down through the generations, and naturally became modified in the process. Local in origin, ballads often spread rapidly, and varying forms of the same story are found in different districts, and even in different countries.

The word *ballad* derives from Low Latin *ballare* (= to dance), and ballads developed out of dance songs and carols (or ring dances) of earlier times; the refrain, particularly in early ballads, indicates this link with choral singing and dancing; and perhaps the dialogue so frequently introduced into ballads has a link with part-song such as we still find in some children's games. But the theory that a village community shared in composing ballads is not generally held today. Authors of ballads are anonymous; but, impersonal and artless as ballads usually are, they tell a story with such condensed dramatic shaping that it is hard to avoid the conclusion that they bear the stamp of an individual mind. Probably the community affected a ballad most in the long process of modification that it underwent during its existence. However, authors of ballads, whoever they may have been, were so completely identified with the ingenuous and natural simplicity of the people they wrote for, that the ballad becomes, of all forms of poetry, the most difficult to imitate in more sophisticated days.

Popular taste in earlier times was much like it is today. Love and war, violent death and murder, are the most prominent themes. Magic and the supernatural are often introduced; a few ballads are religious, a few humorous, and many are based on historical incidents. The ballad usually conveys a strong feeling of locality, arising out of some local incident that has made a deep impression upon people's minds. Some areas are more favourable than others to the growth of a ballad tradition. In Britain the Scottish Border country, with its constant warfare, produced the richest crop. Again, in the

Robin Hood meets the minstrel Allan-a-Dale, who sang ballads about him.

English ballads of Robin Hood, it is the people's point of view that we see; Robin is their champion against a greedy landlord or a tax-collector, or an incompetent local-government officer such as the Sheriff of Nottingham.

The Metre of the Ballads

The common stanza-form of the ballad has four lines, in which two longer lines of four feet (eight syllables) alternate with two shorter lines of three feet (six syllables). These shorter lines rhyme, but the longer ones commonly do not. Composers of ballads allowed themselves considerable metrical freedom: half-stresses and extra syllables abound, and approximate rhyme is often thought sufficient. The one principle insisted on, essential for dance purposes, was that a line should have well-defined musical rhythm, a condition that it admirably achieved. Language is simple and literal: virtually no figures of speech are employed, and vocabulary consists of stock images and adjectives which become conventional in their use. Thus *bonnie* and *sweet* are applied freely to both men and women, and *gold* is used as a symbol to indicate high rank or what is highly desirable in the people's eyes.

Repetition is a popular device and gives to the ballad a patterning that is linked with its origins in singing and dancing. Conventional phrasing gives repetition of rhythm:

> "They hadna sailed a league, a league,
> A league but barely three. . . ." (*Sir Patrick Spens*)

Another form of repetition, probably sung in chorus, was the refrain, which usually occurs in the two shorter lines, alternating with two longer lines of narrative:

> "There were twa sisters sat in a bower;
> Binnorie, O Binnorie!
> There cam a knight to be their wooer,
> By the bonnie milldams of Binnorie." (*Binnorie*)

Proper names were frequently used in these refrains, and there is relevance to the story in "the milldams." The refrain eases the tension of a starkly tragic story; it occurs in all kinds of ballads, and sometimes suggests a vague natural background which has distinct poetic beauty:

> "The broom blooms bonnie and sae it is fair." (*Leesome Brand*)

The ballad derives its dramatic power from the condensed brevity with which it tells its story. Normally we are given only the barest indication of how the situation has come about; we plunge into the story on the verge of a climax. A few "stage directions" are given as the story proceeds, but essential incidents are directly dramatized by introduction of dialogue spoken by the characters involved.

Sir Patrick Spens

This tale illustrates most features of the ballad as noted above. The stanza is traditional, repetition is frequently used in varying forms, and assonance (approximate rhyme) is sometimes employed as a substitute for rhyme (*morn—storm* in ninth stanza; *deep—feet* in the last; and *twine—in* in the extract below). Brief details of the storm are given, but the real quality of the desperate situation is conveyed by the Master's frantic calls:

> "O where will I get a gude sailor,
> To tak' my helm in hand,
> Till I get up to the tall topmast,
> To see if I can spy land?
>
> Gae, fetch a web o' the silken claith,
> Another o' the twine,
> And wap them into our ship's side,
> And let nae the sea come in."

The ship's foundering is not described, but there is sufficient material for our imagination to work upon. The ballad never comments or reflects: it is purely objective, telling its story vividly and leaving it to imply its own significance.

The Twa Brothers

This poem, in which one brother has accidentally killed the other, is even more marked in its economy in telling a story. Here the ballad employs climax, first in the effort to staunch the blood, and then, when the brother goes home, in the succession of questions from the father that ultimately forces the confession that he has killed his brother.

Binnorie, O Binnorie

This poem weaves both love and magic into the tragedy. The ugly elder sister has drowned the younger through jealousy, and a minstrel makes a harp of the lady's hair and breast-bone, which he takes to her father's hall, where the harp denounces the murderess. There is both beauty and pathos in this ballad. There are short bursts of climax in the dialogue; and when the miller's son finds the body in the mill-dam, there is no realistic repulsiveness of death by drowning, but all the colour and glitter of a fairy tale in the lady's golden girdle, the golden fringes of her dress, the pearls in her hair and the diamond rings on her fingers.

The Wife of Usher's Well

This is one of the most powerful ballads introducing the supernatural. The wife's three sons have gone to sea and been drowned. In her grief, their mother contrives to will them back from the dead, but they come with birch sprigs in their hats plucked at the gates of Paradise. In her joy the mother lays a supper and makes a bed, and sits beside them. But

> "The cock doth craw, the day doth daw,
> The channerin' worm doth chide,"

the ghosts fade at daybreak and the mother is left thrice forlorn. No poem better illustrates a ballad's power to convey intense emotion simply by the imagery employed: there is no direct mention of feeling or grief.

A strong sense of the inevitable also occurs in other ballads which reproach undue mourning for the dead, notably *The Unquiet Grave*.

The Ballad of Chevy Chase

Historical ballads are the nearest approach ballad poetry makes to the more literary epic.

Chevy Chase is the best-known of the historical ballads. Primitive in style and bare of ornament, it is one of the few ballads that exist in fifteenth-century manuscript, although a later version from the early seventeenth century is usually printed nowadays. Addison's comment on this version in his *Spectator* essays well repays reading; Sir Philip Sidney wrote, "I never heard the old song of Percy and Douglas, that I found not my heart moved more than with a trumpet." *Chevy Chase* reflects the outlook and values of chivalry at the time of the incident, and swift transitions of mood between violence and courtesy. Percy embarks on his hunting in Chevy Chase deliberately, to

Sir Philip Sidney, the poet whom one of his contemporaries called "the miracle of our age," was born at Penshurst in Kent, in 1554.

provoke Douglas to a fight. The zeal of their followers prevents the issue from being decided by single combat; there are vivid descriptions of sword-play and of the tactics of bowmen. Percy and Douglas fight like Achilles and Hector; and, like Homer, the poet is impartial. *The Battle of Otterburn* is a similar ballad, perhaps a variant of the same.*

Elizabethan Poetry

The Renaissance represents a general movement of human intellect much wider than a mere literary movement. Religious bonds of the Middle Ages were loosened by the Reformation; Copernicus and Galileo re-interpreted the universe; in Britain Bacon established the experimental method which made scientific progress possible, and Harvey revolutionized medicine by discovering the circulation of the blood. In the meantime, explorers were widening men's horizons by their discovery of new continents. This concentration upon the nature of the world, its beauty and the variety of man's experience in it is called Humanism. The Greeks and Romans were Humanists; and so, in its widest sense, the spirit of the Renaissance represents a classical revival.

In this atmosphere of general expectancy and wonder, men of letters were making their own discoveries, exploring their own minds and fashioning a new instrument of language by which to express their experience. There was

* All the ballads referred to here will be found in *English Verse*, Volume II (No. 308 World's Classics, Oxford) or in *A Book of Narrative Verse* (No. 350 World's Classics, Oxford). Comment on Ballads will be found in *The Age of Chaucer* in Pelican Books, or *British Popular Ballads* by Housman (Harrap).

a new awareness of the power of language and expression: words were not only capable of expressing an intellectual meaning, but could arouse men's feelings and convey those feelings by their sound-values and by the associations they raised in men's minds. Poets were discovering new verse forms, new patterns of thought and word-music, which they took from Greek and Latin sources, either directly or from the models of Italy and France, where the Renaissance developed earlier; but they were by no means mere imitators. There were no fixed standards in English; the syntax of the language was still fluid, and, unhampered by endings, parts of speech could be interchanged with a freedom unknown in other languages. Moreover, words derived from Latin were transforming the English vocabulary. Classical diction was meeting native Anglo-Saxon and medieval Norman-French. Renaissance poets used classical and Italian verse-forms to give English poetry the models it sorely needed, but within those models they preserved a freedom that gave English poetry a character of its own which rivalled, and may even have surpassed, the literary sources from which it developed.

Wyatt and Surrey

These two men, courtiers at the Court of Henry VIII, were early poets who experimented in verse-forms. Both were preoccupied with the theme of love, which became the dominant theme of courtly poetry. Wyatt produced a variety of lyrical forms; in the examples in Palgrave's *Golden Treasury* (Numbers 21 and 33), he combines a rhyming triplet with a refrain to emphasize the main point of his theme. Short, simple words convey the sincerity of his feelings. Surrey was a pioneer in adopting blank verse for his translation of Virgil, which enabled him to reproduce the unrhyming verse of his original. He also used the same deca-syllabic (ten syllable) line in the rhyming pattern of the sonnet.

Sidney, the Elizabethan Gentleman

Like Sir Walter Raleigh after him, Sir Philip Sidney (1554-1586) was a typical gentleman of the Elizabethan Court, at once soldier, scholar and poet. His sonnets, gathered under the title of *Astrophel and Stella*, establish the Elizabethan sonnet-sequence devoted to the theme of love, in which can be traced the progress of the poet's suit to his lady. These poems are often conventional addresses to reigning beauties at Court, and they become a means by which the poet pursues platonic conceptions of beauty, truth and goodness. But Sidney's feeling was genuine; like Astrophel he worshipped from afar his Stella, a lady to whom he might have been betrothed as a child, but who was now married to another. His style is often artificial, inspired by Lyly's *Euphues* (*p.* 71) but the strained use of words to associate or contrast ideas in puns, paradoxes and antitheses was introducing pattern and form as well as elegance into both poetry and prose. Later writers, especially Shakespeare, learned how to moderate these "conceits" or extravagances of language. The sonnet* "With how sad steps, O Moon, thou climb'st the skies" is genuinely poetic in its opening. This line imposes a laboured effort with its gathering of stresses on "how sad steps," the long vowel-sound of the word "moon," and the cumbrous consonant-grouping of "climb'st." Sidney then becomes more artificial and euphuistic in exploiting this image of the moon to convey his arduous persistence and scanty reward. The song "My true love hath my heart and I have his" (*Golden Treasury*, No. 24) similarly strains genuine feeling to the point of artifice.

Spenser, the Poets' Poet

Edmund Spenser (1552-1599), one of the major poets of English literature, was of humbler origin than Sidney, and so dependent on Court patronage, which did not treat him generously. He was given a government post in Ireland, which exiled him for most of his life, but gave him the landscape of *The Faerie Queene*. In Spenser's verse, English flows melodiously. He went back to Chaucer for the smoothness of his rhythms and word-music, and so his spelling and pronunciation are sometimes old-fashioned. In his *Shepherd's Calendar* Spenser was the first English poet to adapt pastoral poetry to a variety of themes—love, elegies and theological controversy. (For treatment of the Pastoral Convention, see Chapter 7, page 139.) He wrote a pastoral eclogue for each month of the year, and also composed sonnets, *Il Amoretti*, which trace his courtship of his future wife. *Prothalamion* (a poem written before a marriage, see *Golden Treasury*, No. 36) illustrates most of the qualities of Spenser's work, the smooth contemplative flow of verse, and the elaborate stanza with occasional variation of line-length and intricate rhyming-pattern. The pastoral and romantic setting on the banks of the Thames, with its symbolic imagery of nymphs and swans, brings the poem to the verge of allegory; but it retains its link with reality by glimpses of London and the houses of the nobility that fringed the Thames between Whitehall and the City. The poem is formal and complimentary in tone, and illustrates the attentions a poet had to pay to his patron.

The Faerie Queene

Spenser's high conception of his vocation as a poet is seen in the bold design of *The Faerie Queene*, which was planned to comprise twelve books, although Spenser lived to complete only six. Each book presented one of the virtues of chivalry. It was the first work in English literature to rival the epics of old or works of the Italian Renaissance such as Ariosto's *Orlando Furioso*. Spenser's adoption of allegory sprang partly from his medieval taste but

* *English Verse*, Vol. I (No. 308 World's Classics, Oxford), or *Oxford Book of Verse*, No. 93.

mainly from his Puritan cast of mind. Like Milton, he associated the beauty he sought as a poet with virtue, and believed that it was the function of a poet to instruct. The allegory is very complex and sometimes obscure. In Book I, devoted to holiness, a Red Cross Knight is riding on a quest with a damsel, Una, to deliver her father's castle from siege by a dragon. On their journey many adventures befall them: they shelter from a storm in the wood of Ignorance, but the Knight slays the monster Error; by the contrivance of a magician, who represents Fraud, he is parted from Una, who represents Truth; Duessa, in the guise of Una, but a false lady, is foisted upon him. In Duessa's company he defeats pagan enemies but in consequence is defeated by the Giant Pride, and rescued only by King Arthur, who exposes Duessa and restores Una to him. As a result of his pride he comes to the Cave of Despair, where he is prevented from taking his own life only by Una's strength of mind. Finally, in the House of Holiness, he gains strength to kill the dragon, and is betrothed to Una as a reward.

Clearly the primary purpose of this allegory is to represent symbolically the living of a Christian life with all its attendant hazards and temptations, the need for moral discipline and the ultimate triumph. But in a secondary vein of allegory, the Faerie Queene is Queen Elizabeth, Una represents the Church of England, Duessa the Roman Church, and the Magician the Pope.

Edmund Spenser wrote The Faerie Queene *in honour of Queen Elizabeth.*

The story is over-burdened with allegory and becomes tedious, but it is read nowadays for its poetry, the rich colourful imagery and the enchanted landscape which was inspired in Spenser's mind by the elfin quality of the mountains and wide desolate tracts of open country which he saw in Ireland.

The great merit of the poem is its series of word-pictures, each presented in the paragraph unity of the stanza which Spenser invented for his purpose. This is a nine-line stanza, eight lines of which have ten syllables, the ninth an alexandrine of twelve syllables. The rhyme-scheme is intricate: ABAB, BCBC, C. Thus the two quatrains and the final alexandrine are interlocked by the rhyme-scheme; the rhythm is unbroken until the final alexandrine draws the stanza to a gradual lingering close. In rhythm one stanza is very much like all the others, which produces a soothing effect on a reader, and could act as a sedative drug, were it not for the variety of Spenser's imagery.

"Next him was *Feare*, all arm'd from top to toe,
Yet thought himselfe not safe enough thereby,
But feard each shadow moving to and fro,
And his owne armes when glittering he did spy,
Or clashing heard, he fast away did fly,
As ashes pale of hew, and wingyheeld;
And evermore on daunger fixt his eye,
Gainst whom he alwaies bent a brasen shield,
Which his right hand unarmed fearefully did wield." (III xii 12)

This picture of Fear gives an emblematic figure of Spenser's allegory, and if, in spite of Spenser's imagery, the conception remains rather abstract, here is another impression where the image is the delicate art of the painter to present convincing men and women:

"Withall she laughed, and she blusht withall,
That blushing to her laughter gave more grace,
And laughter to her blushing, as did fall." (II xii 68)

So human beings mingle with allegorical figures. This passage illustrates the repetition which Spenser is fond of weaving into the pattern of his verse. Other devices are unforced use of alliteration and coining of compound words.

Palgrave's Golden Treasury, First Book

This anthology has been chosen to show the range and variety of Elizabethan lyrics, and to give the student some guidance in stating the theme of a lyric, summarizing its substance, and making critical comment upon its images and form.

The first two poems are written on the same theme, the coming of Spring; but they adopt directly-opposed methods of presenting this theme. The first is simple and literal, relying for inspiration on native English tradition. The second poem, not a very good one of its kind, adopts an indirect classical method and shows the mythological and figurative approach. Greek myths are here used as metaphors to give personification to the countryside in Spring. It is a matter of taste which of the two poems is preferred.

Poems 3 and 4 introduce the Elizabethan sonnet, and many of the examples are taken from the works of Shakespeare. The Elizabethan sonnet is composed of fourteen iambic pentameters (lines of ten syllables with five stresses). The lines divide into three quatrains (groups of four lines) with alternate rhyming and a concluding rhyming couplet, ABAB, CDCD, EFEF, GG. The poet develops his thought in the three quatrains and then in the final couplet states an emphatic conclusion.

A sonnet is a very personal poem, and conveys a strong personal emotion. Shakespeare obeys the Elizabethan convention by writing a series of sonnets, sometimes to a male patron, sometimes to a woman the poet loves; but he avoids the artificiality of so many sonnets of his time by generalizing or universalizing a personal thought. Thus the theme of Poems 3 and 4 is the ruthless passage of time, which threatens the beauty and youthfulness of his lady; but the imagery escapes to a wider conception of this universal and inevitable process. The conclusion he draws in the second sonnet is that art is independent of time in its power to immortalize an experience. This vein of melancholy is persistent in the humanist's mind because time and death threaten his sense of the world's beauty and his experience of it. It is as dominant in the poetry of Walter de la Mare and Rupert Brooke as it is in Elizabethan poetry.

Poem 12, probably addressed to Shakespeare's patron, shows some of the metrical variations that were conventional in the sonnet: in the first foot of lines 1, 5, 6, 9, 10 and 11 the emphasis is on the first syllable of the two-syllable foot, making the foot a trochee (′◡) instead of an iambus (◡′), thus varying the rhythm by bringing two short syllables together (′◡◡′); and an extra weak syllable is added to lines 9 and 11 to give a double or feminine rhyme. Shakespeare's sonnets contain some of his finest images and metaphors. Poem 23, whose theme is that true love is not mere physical attraction but a sympathy of mind with mind which can therefore defy time, has a very imaginative metaphor which again links the personal to a wider range of experience, a mariner steering by the stars. In the lines

> "Love's not Time's fool, though rosy lips and cheeks
> Within his bending sickle's compass come,"

imagery and word-music reach a perfection that defies analysis. Notice that the first four words each take a stress; perhaps again this is strictly a trochee (′◡) followed by an iambus (◡′), but in English scansion technically unstressed syllables may acquire at least a secondary stress. This is an example of the freedom an English poet can indulge within the sonnet form.

Drayton's sonnet (Poem 37) shows in its first two quatrains how ordinary conversational speech will fall naturally into verse form. The personification in the third quatrain is natural and unforced, abstractions merging into an image of friends gathered round a death-bed. Compare this with Daniel's sonnet (Poem 35) where personification is more artificial.

Elizabethan Lyrics

Poetry and music still went hand in hand, and lyrics were accompanied on the spinet, virginals or guitar. In this anthology only major poets are represented, but there were many anonymous poets writing lyrics which were printed in broadsheets and sold up and down the country by pedlars like Autolycus in Shakespeare's *The Winter's Tale.* England at this time was "a nest of singing-birds."

The lyrics are characterized by great variety of verse-forms. On the theme of love, Marlowe's poem *The Passionate Shepherd to His Love* (Poem 5), with its delightful music, was inspired by the Italian Pastoral, with an idealized natural background and rich, artificial imagery. Shakespeare, in a similar treatment of the theme in Poem 8, avoids the artificial, and is more English. Most of Shakespeare's lyrics come from his plays and are designed to convey the mood and atmosphere of scenes where they occur. They vary over a very wide range, from the fragile delicacy of Poem 50 conveying the air of fancy in a lover's mind as Bassanio makes his choice of casket, to the heavy stresses and satirical intention of *Blow, blow, thou Winter wind* (Poem 42), where the poet compares the harsher moods of nature favourably with the cruelties of man to man.

Poems About Death

There is variety of attitude and mood in the poems on death. In Ariel's song on the supposed death of Alonso by drowning (Poem 46), the word-music and imagery turn what is realistically repulsive into beauty, and the poem seems to enlarge into a wider significance showing how an experience, passing through the imaginative mind of a poet, suffers "a sea-change into something rich and strange." Webster's Dirge (Poem 47) strikes a quiet note of beauty in the grimmest of his plays, *The White Devil.* The rhythm changes to convey the contrast of the last two lines. The sounds of the letters *r, v, f* and *m* are weaving a subtle pattern of music in this poem.

Shakespeare's beautiful dirge *Fidele* (Poem 45) is taken from *Cymbeline,* occurring in a very poignant incident in the play when the two brothers who have been driven into the mountains by the intrigue and false values of Court life come upon the body of Imogen and believe her to be dead. Death is inevitable, but death in youth is especially tragic. The poet gathers into the

Autolycus selling broadsheets.

John Donne.

word "golden" all the humanist delight in youth—its beauty, energy and high spirits, and then perhaps, in the last line of the stanza, its capacity to smile even at death.

Finally, Lord Bacon's *Life* (Poem 57) is based primarily on thought rather than on feeling or emotion. The substance of the poem belongs to prose, but metre and rhyme give a patterning to the thought that increases its effect on the reader's mind.

Donne, the Seventeenth-Century Metaphysical Poet

The poetry of John Donne (1573-1631) marks a break with tradition and introduces and inspires the Metaphysical school of poets. Donne belonged to a Catholic family when the Catholic faith was under persecution in England: he was a scholar whose introspective mind habitually meditated on his own experience and the deeper issues of life. Eventually he adopted Anglicanism, was ordained a priest and became Dean of St. Paul's, in which capacity his prose sermons enriched the tradition of English prose. In early life he wrote secular satires and love poetry, but later turned to religious verse; but the same passionate, scholarly and mystical qualities underlie all his works. As a young man, he realized and indulged the sensuous qualities of love, but even here he was preoccupied, like Hamlet, with an effort to reconcile body and soul, the physical and the spiritual. His poems make difficult reading: his metres are irregular and the lines often cumbrous,

He did not pour his thought into a ready-made mould like the Elizabethans; his thought is so urgent that it determines the form of his expression. He is fond of paradox, sudden strange images, and metaphors that appear strained because the reader's mind cannot always jump with his across the gulf of his implied meaning, or follow the violent transitions of his mind passing from one image or metaphor to another. He derives these images both from his medieval scholarship and from his interest in the new scientific processes of thought that were developing.

A Valediction, Forbidding Mourning

This poem illustrates most features of Donne's poetry. The lovers are threatened with parting, and the central idea pervading the poem is that, since their love is of the soul, transcending physical limitations, they can part without suffering a sense of separation. The poem progresses through a succession of images, each connected with the one that follows. As a strong-minded man would wish to die without claiming undue grief from friends, so lovers should not display self-pity at parting. To describe their love, he uses a material image that trembles on the verge of the immaterial—the fine thinness of gold leaf beaten out by goldsmiths. Though the lovers are parted, they will still be united like the two arms of a pair of compasses, she the fixed centre, he describing a circle controlled by that centre. This poem illustrates what is meant by metaphysical wit, a close interplay of passionate feeling with a precise intellectual process. Shakespeare's image (G.T. No. 28),* "Bare, ruin'd choirs, where late the sweet birds sang," adopts the trees in winter as a metaphor for his advancing years. Here is a metaphor within a metaphor: the trees in winter for the poet's age, and then a metaphor for the trees, "bare ruin'd choirs." The conception strikes our senses with its beauty; but in Donne's poem metaphors of planets and compasses are used primarily to illuminate an obscure intellectual argument. This distinction between poetic and explanatory effects can often be found in metaphors.

Donne's two sonnets on death in his later religious verse (E.V. II, *pp.* 40-41) are more regular, and in their deep harmonies resemble the prose of his sermons. *Death, be not proud* is the more personal of the two, expressing his own Christian hope in the Resurrection. Again the method is by the deduction and logic of precise argument, comparing death with drugs in its power to confer sleep and rest.

Other Religious Poets of the Seventeenth Century

There is a strong vein of religious poetry in the seventeenth century, most of it Anglican, but devotional rather than institutional.

* Most poems referred to in this section are taken from *English Verse*, Vol. II (World's Classics, Oxford); references are given as E.V.II. Reference to *The Golden Treasury* is shown as G.T.

George Herbert (1593-1633) wrote lyrics which are always carefully patterned. He conveys his thought through imagery that tends to become symbolic. In *The Collar* (E.V. II, *p.* 170) he pulls against the discipline of spiritual life; and in *Virtue* (E.V. II, *p.* 182) the theme is again the lure of the world. Both conclude with a concise climax in which the spiritual claim is accepted. In *The Elixir*, well known today as a hymn, there is mysticism and depth behind its apparent simplicity:

"A man that looks on glass,
On it may stay his eye;
Or, if he pleaseth, through it pass,
And then the heaven espy."

The outward world around us may hold our eyes, or we may penetrate through it to the spiritual reality that informs it. This Christian insight imparts a unique quality (or elixir) to living. The metaphor is metaphysical and allies Herbert with Donne.

Richard Crashaw (*c.* 1612-1649) was a convert to Roman Catholicism. He was less intellectual than Herbert, whom he admired, but his poetry is richer in imagery and music. His paradoxes and conceits in *The Ecstasy* (E.V. II, *p.* 352) and *The Weeper* (E.V. II, *p.* 346) link him with Donne and the Metaphysical poets. His *Hymn to Saint Teresa* (E.V. II, *p.* 348) and *The Flaming Heart* (E.V. II, *p.* 345) reach magnificence of language.

Henry Vaughan (1622-1695), who lived in Wales, is a delightful if uneven poet, whose anthology pieces should certainly be read. Another disciple of Herbert, he is a poet of the open air who uses natural imagery to convey his religious thought and his mystical contact with other worlds than ours. His feeling for nature will appeal strongly, even if his religious thought is not acceptable. He is a poet of childhood, and *The Retreat* (E.V. II, *p.* 409; G.T. No. 75) anticipates Wordsworth's *Immortality Ode* in its conception of childhood as a time of natural joy derived from a previous, more perfect existence.

Cavalier Poets

Secular poets of the seventeenth century, composing light but elegant love lyrics, owe more to Jonson than to Donne. Jonson's work breaks with the Spenser tradition: he is classical but not French or Italian. The Pastoral spirit remains, but its imagery becomes less artificial and more English. Virtually all these poets are Cavaliers.

John Suckling (1609-1642), careless and natural, sometimes gallant and sometimes cynical (G.T. No. 101), produced in his *Ballad upon a Wedding* (E.V. II, *p.* 321) a mock epithalamion (a hymn sung after a wedding ceremony) which is a lively picture of English peasant life.

Richard Lovelace (1618-1658) was very unequal in his work, but two of his lyrics (G.T. Nos. 83 and 99) embody the ideal Cavalier, with courtly wit and honour as well as gallantry. Both Suckling and Lovelace suffered for their king in the Civil War; Suckling died abroad and Lovelace in poverty during the Commonwealth period.

Among these poets, Robert Herrick (1591-1674) is outstanding for the lyrical quality of his light poems, in which he shows himself a master of the short line:

> "Whenas in silks my Julia goes,
> Then, then (methinks) how sweetly flows
> That liquefaction of her clothes." (G.T. No. 93)

Herrick died a bachelor. His verse has a spontaneous and sophisticated quality. A Londoner, he sought the company of poets and wits; but eventually he entered the Church to gain a livelihood, and coming to his parish of Dean Prior in Devonshire, he brings the imagery of the English countryside into his poems, and at times seems to convey something of Wordsworth's feeling that a flower "enjoys the air it breathes."

In *Corinna's Going a-Maying* (E.V. II, *p.* 137), written in five stanzas with sonnet form, the approach and method are classical, but it is actual English life and English countryside that are so delightfully presented.

Marvell, the Garden Poet

Apart from Milton, Andrew Marvell (1621-1678) is the poet of this period of highest stature after Donne. He served the Puritan government under Cromwell, and after the Restoration carried on a battle for religious and political liberty. But Marvell has a balanced mind: he does not allow his virtue to dull his relish for the life of the senses. He is a Christian humanist, metaphysical wit, patriot, humorist and lover of nature. He shows his patriotism in his *Horatian Ode* to Cromwell (E.V. II, *p.* 390; G.T. No. 65), in which he pictures Cromwell as a modest country-gentleman rising to the challenge of his times, and not afraid to:

> ". . . cast the kingdom old
> Into another mold."

But Marvell shows his balanced mind by paying tribute to Charles I as well:

> "He nothing common did or mean
> Upon that memorable scene:
> But with his keener eye
> The axe's edge did try."

To His Coy Mistress, perhaps his masterpiece, is written in the buoyant and rapid tetrameter couplet, a form that he favours. The first part shows the humour and inventiveness of his fancy: the Ganges, where she is, is colourful;

Robert Herrick spent thirty years as vicar of Dean Prior in Devonshire.

the Humber, where he is, is grey. Then imagination takes over from fancy in the finely-conceived metaphor conveying the ruthless passage of time:

"But at my back I always hear
Time's wingèd chariot hurrying near:
And yonder all before us lie
Deserts of vast eternity."

Chariots rode men down in battle, and "deserts" is full of implied meaning. When he brings the lady's beauty to dust, he is as ruthless as Donne; and the last part of this poem illustrates the humanist zest for experience.

His poems on Gardens (G.T. No. 111; E.V. II, *p.* 138) show an England which, despite civil war, was cultivating the arts of peace. The pattern of flowerbeds, green lawns and shady trees shows the civilizing influence of prosperity and leisure:

"Annihilating all that's made
To a green thought in a green shade."

These metaphysical lines convey a meaning to the feelings rather than to the mind. He had a feeling for wild country too, as he shows in his *Song of the Emigrants in Bermuda* (G.T. No. 114; E.V. II, *p.* 395). The Puritan emigrants see in the colourful landscape of their new home the temple of their new-found freedom of worship. Andrew Marvell, of all these seventeenth-century poets, is the most representative of the England of his day.

English Prose after 1500

In 1500 there were few models of English prose, for scholars such as Sir Thomas More and Bacon still wrote their more serious works in Latin. The coming of the printing-press (about 1494) gave a great stimulus to the development of what might be called popular literary prose. Malory's *Morte d'Arthur* was one of the first books to be printed. English prose was in search of a standard even more than poetry was, and this was given to it by a meeting of native and classical traditions. In the native tradition literary prose began its evolution by diverging from poetry, and kept many of its poetic qualities, its use of imagery, cadences and rhythms, over nearly two centuries. Not until Addison wrote his *Spectator* essays (about 1700) was modern prose really established as a vehicle of expression with laws of its own, though it must always be remembered that poetry and prose never completely separate.* They are complementary to one another; all expression is conditioned by a combination of thinking and feeling, but in poetry the feeling is primary, while in the more literal prose the thinking faculty is uppermost.

The Translation of the Bible

This was one of the strongest influences in giving style and standards to English prose. The translation was a decisive result of the Reformation in England, and sprang from the desire of the people to read the Bible for themselves and to understand church services. The Authorized Version of the Bible did not appear until 1611, but it embodied much of the work of earlier translators such as Coverdale and Tyndale in the time of Henry VIII. Many books of the Hebrew original are poetic, for instance the Book of Job is a poetic drama, and the Psalms are Hebrew poetry.

The Book of Common Prayer, where the Latin Collects are adapted to English prose style, reinforced the influence of the Bible. This liturgical English is the work of scholars, and is more indebted to Latin in its vocabulary than is the English of the Bible. The long Latin words enrich the deep harmonies of the English of the Collects. Another characteristic that conditions the rhythms of this liturgical English developed from a habit, which grew up in the Middle English period, of setting an Anglo-Saxon word alongside a Norman-French synonym so that one or other would be understood. This developed into a settled idiom of the language—today we have the alliterative phrases "safe and sound," "hale and hearty"—and it is

* See Sir Arthur Quiller Couch's *The Art of Reading* and *The Art of Writing*, which will be found stimulating, especially on *The English of the Bible* and *The Capital Difficulty of Verse*.

frequently used in the Collects of the Prayer Book, as in the following extract:

> "O Lord, raise up (we pray thee) thy power, and come among us, and with great might succour us; that whereas, through our *sins and wickedness*, we are sore *let and hindered* in running the race that is set before us, thy bountiful *grace and mercy* may speedily *help and deliver* us."

Though modern prose is no longer superficially biblical or liturgical, upon examination all these features will be discernible; but the feature which determines the genius of English prose is prevalence of the *loose* sentence built up of co-ordinate main clauses, rather than the *periodic* classical sentence built up with a complicated architecture of subordinate clauses. Thus, Sir Thomas North, translating Plutarch's *Lives of the Noble Grecians and Romans*, describes Coriolanus' arrival in the city of Aufidius:

> "When he came thither, he got him up straight to the chimney hearth, and sat him down, and spake not a word to any man, his face all muffled over. They of the house, spying him, wondered what he should be, and yet they durst not bid him rise."

Classical Influence

Numerous translations of classical works, of which Sir Thomas North's was one, brought classical stories to the Elizabethan reader and spread classical influence. Lyly's *Euphues* and Sidney's *Arcadia* can be considered as the earliest novels, but they are so rich and Italianate in their ornament and imagery that they belong to poetry rather than to prose. *Euphues* has already been referred to for its effect on the style of poetry and drama. Its balance of contrasted statements by antithesis, often with alliteration superadded, becomes self-conscious and artificial, but it did serve a purpose in its day by giving style and elevation to expression:

> "Among a number of ladies he fixed his eye upon one, whose countenance seemed to promise mercy and threaten mischief, intermeddling a desire of liking with a disdain of love; showing herself in courtesy to be familiar with all, and with a certain comely pride to accept none, whose wit would commonly taunt with despite but not without disport."

Sidney's *Apology for Poetry*

The *Apology for Poetry* is the first substantial work of English criticism. In it, Sidney reflects on the function of the poet in society and, like Aristotle, analyses the art of fiction. He calls the poet a prophet, and places him above the historian, who deals with facts, and the philosopher, who deals with abstractions. Speaking of painters, he condemns those "who counterfet onely such faces as are sette before them," i.e. mere realists, but commends the artist who, wishing to paint "the constant though lamenting look of Lucrezia . . . painteth not Lucrezia, *whom he never sawe*, but painteth the outward beauty of such a virtue." So Sidney realizes the penetration of an artist, whether painter, poet or novelist, through the actual to the universal. Thus Leonardo da Vinci paints the enigmatic smile of the Mona Lisa and Shakespeare creates a Hamlet or a Macbeth.

Bacon's Essays

Francis Bacon was a man of great intellect, both philosopher and scientist, and in both roles he was a seeker after truth. His scientific experiments supplied data from which he deduced general laws of the material world, and in his moral essays he is equally impartial in deducing general laws of human behaviour from observation of his fellow-men. His advice is for men of a high social level, statesmen, diplomats and courtiers; he is very much a man of the world, purveying the wisdom of self-interest and expediency rather than of disinterested virtue. He is a more scrupulous Machiavelli, the Italian writer who advocated a selfish cunning to gain one's ends; and in his essay *Of Cunning*, he gives a list of the tricks and manoeuvres that will assist a diplomat abroad or a master of Court intrigue at home. Many of his essays, however, reflect on general human behaviour.

In his prose style Bacon is quite apart from all his contemporaries: his style has a modern ring, concise, epigrammatic and clear as crystal. Every sentence is an aphorism with a parade of wisdom in it, and many sentences have become proverbial. He derives this conciseness from his mastery of Latin, in which he wrote several of his major works. In *Novum Organum*, he points to tendencies in the human mind which distort a man's thinking, and calls them "idols of the mind." He hated inaccuracy, whether of thought or expression, and every word in his essays is precisely used. He uses imagery sparingly, with brief but illuminating similes or metaphors, e.g.

> "Men fear death as children fear to go in the dark; and as that natural fear in children is increased with tales, so is the other." (*Of Death*)

The balance of these sentences is perfect. He is fond of antithesis, and it is interesting to compare his use of it with Lyly's. Lyly's prose is descriptive, but Bacon's prose is expository, developing an argument: the contrast of antithesis clarifies ideas, and aids Bacon's impartial way of giving both sides of the case.

The openings of Bacon's essays are notable: he dives straight to the heart of his subject, and at once a reader grasps the topic-theme of the essay and its writer's attitude to it:

> "Revenge is a kind of wild justice." (*Of Revenge*)
> "God Almighty first planted a garden." (*Of Gardens*)

Bacon's essays are so condensed that it is difficult to summarize them, but they are logical in development and very clear in exposition. Many regard Bacon's *Essays* as the first English prose classic. He died in 1626.

Seventeenth-Century Prose

Works of this period that continue the development of prose towards the more modern style of Dryden and Addison are Izaak Walton's *Compleat Angler*, Sir Thomas Browne's *Urn Burial* and *Religio Medici*, and Jeremy Taylor's *Holy Living* and *Holy Dying*. Walton is intimate, gentle and serene, a lover of the countryside. Browne is a writer whose discursive interests,

Bacon, essayist and politician.

Thomas Browne, a Norwich doctor.

ranging from the local to the cosmic, reveal the mind of an eccentric who never fails to be interesting. Taylor's devotional books were written at a time when Anglicanism was suffering persecution, and Taylor pleads for toleration and integrity.

One of the few books written by authors on the Puritan side is Lucy Hutchinson's biography of her husband, *The Life of Colonel Hutchinson*, which though not a skilled work, nevertheless gives a direct impression of Commonwealth times by an author who is one of the first women to emerge from domestic seclusion into English literature.

QUESTIONS

1. Give brief accounts of *two or three* ballads that tell a story from history or legend, commenting on and illustrating their appeal both for earlier audiences and for modern readers.
2. Making reference to at least *four* characters, show the variety of men and women that Spenser introduces into *The Faerie Queene*.
3. Write a critical appreciation of the poetry of Herrick *or* Marvell, illustrating your points by reference to at least *four* poems.
4. Choose *two* of the following themes, and show how they are introduced into the poetry of the sixteenth and seventeenth centuries:
   Satire, Humour, Fantasy, Peasant Life, Court Life.
5. (*a*) Outline Bacon's argument in *two* of his essays that have interested you, and (*b*) use extracts from these essays to illustrate his style.
6. Read the following passage from Donne's *Devotions*, then:
   (*a*) Re-write the passage in your own words; and
   (*b*) Show what devices of style Donne has used in developing his argument.

"Perchance he for whom this Bell tolls, may be so ill, as that he knowes not it tolls for him; and perchance I may thinke my selfe so much better than I am, as that they who are about mee, and see my state, may have caused it to toll for mee, and I know not that. The Church is Catholike, universall, so are all her Actions; all that she does belongs to all. When she baptizes a child, that action concerns mee; for that child is thereby connected to that Head which is my Head too, and engraffed into that body, whereof I am a member. And when she buries a man, that action concerns me: . . . As therefore the Bell that rings to a Sermon, calls not upon the Preacher onely, but upon the Congregation to come; so this Bell calls us all: but how much more mee, who am brought so neere the doore by this sicknesse. . . . The Bell doth toll for him that thinks it doth; and though it intermit againe, yet from that minute, that that occasion wrought upon him, he is united to God. Who casts not up his eye to the Sunne when it rises? but who takes off his eye from a Comet when that breakes out? Who bends not his ear to any Bell, which upon any occasion rings? but who can remove it from that Bell, which is passing a peece of himselfe out of this world? No man is an Iland, intire of itselfe; every man is a peece of the Continent, a part of the maine; if a Clod be washed away by the Sea, Europe is the lesse, as well as if a Promontorie were, as well as if a Mannor of thy friends or of thine owne were; any man's death diminishes me, because I am involved in Mankinde; and therefore never send to know for whom the Bell tolls; it tolls for *thee*."

CHAPTER 5

ELIZABETHAN AND JACOBEAN DRAMA

DRAMA, wherever it has developed in the course of history, has always had a religious origin. In England in the early Middle Ages, drama began to emerge from the ritual of the early Church which, with its responses and processions, was essentially dramatic in its appeal. On Good Friday the Cross was taken down from the High Altar and laid in the Easter Sepulchre, a recess in the chancel wall. Then, on Easter morning, a priest would stand by the Easter Sepulchre to represent the angel at the tomb, while a party would advance across the chancel, representing the women coming to the sepulchre. The angel would sing: "*Quem quaeritis?*" (Whom do you seek?) and the women would respond: "*Ihesum Nazarenum Crucifixum*" (Jesus of Nazareth, the Crucified). And so the part-song would continue in Latin following the Gospel text: "He is not here, He is risen, and has gone before you into Galilee." All would then turn and face the High Altar where the Cross was again elevated, to sing a *Te Deum* in praise of the risen Lord. Here we have the germ of drama. Priests encouraged it because it directly represented, to people who could not understand the Latin of the service-books, incidents of the Easter story. The Nativity was similarly represented, and perhaps the Ascension. Drama, of all forms of literature, has always made the most direct appeal to the mass of the people. The people demanded more plays, and more scriptural stories were added; soon the church was not big enough to hold them, and plays moved out into the churchyard, or to a square of the town. Native English was introduced instead of Latin, and lay actors took the place of priests. We cannot date all these developments, but in 1294 Pope Urban IV established the festival of Corpus Christi in the week following Trinity Sunday, which developed into a summer festival of several days' duration in which the *Miracles*, as these plays were called, were performed by members of the town's Craft Guilds.

Miracle or Mystery Plays

Cycles (or series) of plays now extended over the whole of the Bible stories, showing the development of God's purpose for Man and reaching their climax in the plays of the Crucifixion, the Harrowing of Hell, and the Resurrection. Each guild acted one of the plays, usually being allotted a theme related to its occupation. Thus the shipwrights might build the

Ark, and the goldsmiths might undertake the visit of the Magi with their gifts. The pageants, as the stage-settings were called, were usually on wheels, and the plays moved to different "stations" in the town, so that an audience gathered at any one station saw a number of plays in the course of a day.

These plays were written in verse: a wide variety of rhyming and lyrical verse forms was used, but the poetry was halting and imperfect in workmanship. The authors, all anonymous, were bound by their biblical material, but developed considerable freedom in their treatment of the stories. Just as paintings of the Gospel story by medieval Italian masters are given an Italian setting, so English playwrights were intensely English in their presentation of workmen putting up the Cross, or soldiers on guard at the Sepulchre.

Some Miracle plays reach a high standard of dramatic power. Abraham, about to sacrifice Isaac, displays a conflict of mind between his sense of duty to God and his love for his son; and Isaac shows a human fear of death that stirs pity in an audience and shows some quality of tragic power. Comedy and farce were freely introduced into the plays: in the story of the Flood, Noah is afflicted with a scolding wife, who declares that she will not go into the Ark, but will stay with her friends; in the end Noah has to instruct his sons to carry their mother aboard, and she gives Noah a slap on his face as they carry her past him. This is a beginning of domestic comedy.

The Wakefield Nativity Play

This is a most daring mixture of comedy with a scriptural story. The shepherds, again very English, have lost one of their sheep, and suspect that Mak, a local rogue, has stolen it. They go to Mak's cottage in the middle of the night, to investigate. Mak pops his head out of a window to inform them that his wife has just given birth to a baby. One of the shepherds hits on the idea of asking Mak to let them come in and see the babe, and present gifts to him:

"*Shepherd:* Mak, with your leave, let me give your bairn but sixpence.
Mak: Nay, go 'way. He sleeps.
Shepherd: Methinks he peeps.
Mak: If he wakes, he weeps.
I pray you go hence.
Shepherd: Give me leave him to kiss, and lift up the clout*.
What the devil is this? He has a long snout."

They find that the baby in the crib is their stolen sheep, and toss Mak in a blanket for his sins. As they are returning to their flocks, an Angel appears above, and sings, "*Gloria in Excelsis*," announcing to them the birth of

* covering.

This scene from the York Mystery Plays *shows typically simple scenery.*

Christ at Bethlehem. Thither they go, again to bend over a crib and delight in a new-born child:

> "*Shepherd:* Lo, he laughs, my sweeting,
> A welcome meeting!
> Here's my proper greeting—
> Have a bob of cherries?"

And so this divine event comes right into the experience of simple English peasant folk. This mingling of the farcical with the holy is done so ingenuously that all offence is taken out of it. Religion played such an all-embracing part in the Middle Ages that men did not distinguish between the religious and the secular as we do today. All drama was religious, but they enjoyed comedy as much as we do, so they introduced comedy into their religion. It was this same instinct for the comic and grotesque that made them carve imps and devils in their churches. The Devil frequently appears in Miracle plays, and is always, along with Herod and Pilate, comic and grotesque. These plays were still performed in Shakespeare's age, and it was from such models that Elizabethan dramatists learned to mingle comic relief with their tragedies.

Morality Plays and *Everyman*

The Morality play, which probably dates back to the mid-fourteenth century, was the next development of drama. Men were beginning to think upon moral problems of conduct, so Morality plays were more intellectual than the Miracles, which merely provided spectacle and told a story. Morality plays dramatize the conflict between Good and Evil. Abstractions are made visible by personifying such qualities as Pleasure and Covetousness, which are seen as characters disputing for the soul of man; so the Morality is a form of allegory, so popular in the Middle Ages. There is a more perceptive presentation of character in the Moralities; to present the Seven Deadly Sins, an author must have observed men and women in whom these sins are displayed. The Morality also frequently introduces conflict in a character's mind. These developments are preparing the way for the secular drama of Shakespeare's century.

Everyman, a play that can still hold a modern audience by its simple sincerity and the seriousness of its theme, was the most notable Morality play. The play embodies the Christian teaching on death: Death summons Everyman to die and appear before God, but Everyman, dismayed, pleads for a brief respite to gather friends to go with him and support him before the Judgment-throne. Fellowship, Kindred and Goods (riches) all refuse to go with him; Good-Deeds alone is willing to accompany him, but she lies wounded on the ground. Knowledge, with the aid of Discretion, Strength, Five-Wits and Beauty, brings Everyman to Repentance and Confession. He receives the Last Sacrament, and Good-Deeds is revived. When Everyman comes to the grave, all desert him except Good-Deeds, and together they pass into the presence of God.*

Drama in the Sixteenth Century

From 1500 onwards, drama separated itself from religion, in accordance with the Renaissance spirit. Moralities persisted, but they began to be applied to politics, as in Sir David Lindsay's *Satire of the Three Estates*. The Morality form readily lent itself to religious controversies of the Reformation. At this time drama became enormously popular, and it was through the theatre that the Renaissance made its direct impact on the mass of the people. Medieval drama had been largely amateur, but now professional actors took over. Strolling players performed in barns and inn-yards throughout the country, and in 1576 the first permanent theatre was established in London, built outside the City, in Shoreditch, to avoid the ban of the civic authorities, who feared riot and the spread of plague. Strolling players were classed as vagabonds and escaped a precarious existence only by obtaining the patronage of the nobility. They frequently gave performances in noble houses; and in London, performances at Court furnished a substantial part of their income. Aristocratic culture influenced the character

* There is a very readable selection of Miracle and Morality plays, including *The Wakefield Shepherds' Play* and *Everyman*, in the Everyman Edition published by Dent.

Satire of the Three Estates.

of the plays, but one theatre catered for all tastes, which accounts for the mixed features of plays in which crude comedy mingles with romantic drama, tragedy and courtly wit.

Amateur effort persisted among students of the Inns of Court, at the Universities and in the schools. These sources produced two early farces, *Ralph Roister Doister* (1533) and *Gammer Gurton's Needle* (1575). University men wrote plays for the popular theatre, and were known as the University Wits. *Gorboduc* (1562), by Thomas Sackville and Thomas Norton, is notable for its adoption of blank verse to give dignity and force to tragedy; it also illustrates the influence exerted on the Elizabethans by the Roman plays of Seneca, with their blood-curdling crimes and violence.

Thomas Kyd (1558-1594), not a university man, follows the Senecan influence in *The Spanish Tragedy* (1586) by piling up crimes and horrors, but brings action directly on to the stage; it is a revenge tragedy of crime, poisoning and madness, and started a fashion. *Hamlet* is in a direct line with it. Marlowe was soon to reserve tragedy only for the great men of the world.

While these plays were introducing blank verse as the language of tragedy and melodrama, John Lyly (1554-1606) was establishing prose as the language of comedy. He wrote for the cultured taste of Court and nobility, but he influenced popular dramatists, and Shakespeare imitates his mannered style in the early comedies. His most notable play is *Campaspe*, a play of quieter emotions which looks forward to some of Shakespeare's delicate pictures of womanhood. In Lyly's plays, character and events begin to exercise an influence upon one another.

The Elizabethan Theatre

Shakespeare spent his working-days at the theatre in Moorfields, and later at the Globe Theatre in Southwark on the south bank of the Thames. The structure of an Elizabethan theatre determined and controlled the construction of plays to be performed in it. This applies to the theatre of any period: the form of a modern play is determined by the proscenium stage, footlights and scenery. All these features were absent from Shakespeare's theatre. The general plan of early theatres may have been inspired by the inn-yards in which strolling players gave their performances. A balcony extending round the yard to give access to the upper rooms was a ready-made gallery; a platform to serve as a stage was readily built. The wooden walls of the Globe Theatre were circular in shape, with balconies built on for the more wealthy members of the audience; in *King Henry V*, Shakespeare calls the theatre "This wooden O." On the floor of the theatre the "groundlings" thronged on *three* sides of the stage, which was a platform projecting into the circle of the theatre. At the back of the stage were two entrances from the dressing-rooms, on top of which was a higher stage forming a balcony and described as "above" in stage directions. There the Governor of Harfleur would stand to parley with Henry V, who would be on the lower stage; and there Juliet would emerge to talk with Romeo. This balcony overhung the lower stage, and the portion beneath it was curtained off to form a recess; the curtains might be completely drawn while properties were assembled behind them for a scene like the banquet in *Macbeth*, or they might be partly opened as Prospero's cave or the tomb where Juliet lay.

Setting the Scene

Here, apart from lavish costumes and properties, realism ended; there was no scenery. This is a significant feature, calling for an effort of imagination by the audience such as a modern play does not stimulate. The dramatist had to describe the scenery for his play, and it is to this that we owe most of Shakespeare's descriptive poetry—the description of Macbeth's castle, for instance, when Duncan enters it:

> "This guest of summer,
> The temple-haunting martlet, does approve
> By his lov'd mansionry that the heaven's breath
> Smells wooingly here: no jutty, frieze,
> Buttress, nor coign of vantage, but this bird
> Hath made her pendent bed and procreant cradle." (I vi 3)

Time of day or night had also to be indicated in dialogue. The theatre was open to the sky; and in the absence of effective lighting, performances took place in daylight. Brutus, therefore, in his orchard at night reading Cassius' letter, must continually refer to the night around him:

> "The exhalations whizzing in the air
> Give so much light that I may read by them." (II i 44)

A large part of *Macbeth* takes place in the dark, and an audience must realize this darkness if they are to catch the atmosphere of the play: hence one reason for the many images of night dispersed throughout the text:

"Light thickens, and the crow
Makes wing to the rooky wood." (III ii 50)

The soliloquy, in which a Shakespearean actor speaks his thoughts aloud to "put the audience wise," would seem unnatural in a modern realistic play; but the Elizabethan audience was close to the stage on three sides of it, creating an intimacy between actor and audience, so that he was speaking directly to them.

In the absence of a drop-curtain in the Elizabethan theatre, a scene could not end on a dramatic climax. Actors must leave the stage in an organized way. If there were dead bodies on the stage at the end of the play, as in *Hamlet*, arrangements must be made for their proper removal: and so the audience relaxed and returned to normality before again making contact with the real world outside the theatre.

Shakespeare's Contemporaries

There was a strange mixture of barbarism and culture in Elizabethan and Jacobean England, and its drama is a faithful reflection of the age. We must not look in Elizabethan drama for the kind of realism that we find in modern plays. Popular taste demanded exaggerated incident and violent passion, both of which features required the heightened language of blank verse to support them. Sometimes verse is declamatory, sometimes rhetorical, often pure poetry; but always it is the crowning glory of Elizabethan drama.

Discounting exaggeration, the characters of Elizabethan drama are true to life, but are drawn on broad, simple, sometimes crude, lines. In their drama, the Elizabethans used broad splashes of colour rather than intricate patterning.

The First Great English Dramatist

Christopher Marlowe (1564-1593) establishes the tragedy of consuming passion. The exuberance of his plays seems to reflect the national spirit of his time. The plays were immensely popular, and reflect his own short and violent life. He was born in the same year as Shakespeare, and died mysteriously in a tavern brawl. In most of his plays a single character dominates the stage. In the two parts of *Tamburlaine the Great* the hero is motivated by lust for power and conquest which he indulges without any scruple of moral restraint. The play is melodramatic in its horrors, luxurious and exotic in its splendours (as when Tamburlaine weds the divine Zenocrate), and tragic in the ultimate nemesis that falls upon a man who has come to believe that he is above the Gods. In *Doctor Faustus* the hero has a similar ambition, but his thirst is for power through unlimited knowledge, which takes him beyond lawful knowledge into magic, and ultimately he faces damnation when his bargain with Mephistopheles expires. This play is near Marlowe's own mind, for he dabbled in atheistic opinions, and, like Faustus, was uneasy in his defiance of God and the Church.

Doctor Faustus is a strangely uneven play: many comedy scenes are crude and trivial, for example, when the clowns exploit their master's magic. Marlowe disapproved of clowning, but bowed to popular taste. Good and Evil Angels appear to argue with Faustus for his soul, and there is a procession of the Seven Deadly Sins. Some transitions of the play are abrupt and disconcerting; a passage describing Rome as seen from the air by Faustus and Mephistopheles in their aerial tour of Europe exhibits the glory of poetry that is henceforth to fill the bare and empty stage of the Elizabethan theatre; but only a few lines later, Faustus is entering the Pope's apartment in a cloak of invisibility, slapping the Pope in the face and snatching away his food. *Doctor Faustus* is generally considered Marlowe's best work, not for its sense of theatre (which is slight), but for the peaks which Marlowe attains in his use of blank verse, particularly in the soliloquies.

Marlowe has a sense of rhythm that enables him to re-group stresses and weak syllables in varying combinations. Here is Faustus expressing his

Tamburlaine's chariot is dragged along by the kings he has captured.

rapture at a vision of beautiful Helen for whose sake Troy was burned down:

'Was this the face that launch'd a thousand ships?
And burnt the topless towers of Ilium?
Sweet Helen, make me immortal with a kiss.
Her lips suck forth my soul: see where it flies!
Come, Helen, come, give me my soul again. . . .
O, thou art fairer than the evening air
Clad in the beauty of a thousand stars;
Brighter art thou than flaming Jupiter
When he appear'd to hapless Semele."

In the third line, three stresses are gathered within the first four syllables; and in the fifth line there are four stresses within the first five syllables, and the stresses in the line are increased to six.

Mephistopheles tempts Faustus.

Faustus' final monologue of despair as he faces his damnation has been held to bear comparison with Shakespeare's tragic endings. In the line, "See, see, where Christ's blood streams in the firmament," the stresses are increased to seven,* and grouped to give a harsher rhythm to the line, which seems to reflect Faustus' distraught mind. In all passages quoted, the quality of hyperbole (exaggeration) will be noted.

These qualities of verse were innovations by Marlowe, but became conventional in the work of his successors. Shakespeare was to indulge in even greater freedom, but it was Marlowe who had shown the way.

Marlowe's *Edward II*

A later play by Marlowe is *Edward II* (1592), a strangely subdued piece after *Tamburlaine* and *Doctor Faustus.* Edward shows a confident bravado while Gaveston is about, and Gaveston himself is the most animated character in the play; but when he disappears the play droops, and the Spencers are a poor substitute for him. In the duel between king and barons, victory and

* Or perhaps six: Marlowe has a way of letting his line fall away to a weak or feminine ending. Compare this line with the last line of the Helen passage.

defeat seem to come quite arbitrarily, like prizes in a lottery. In his final despair and murder, Edward wins little sympathy, because there is nothing in his character to compensate for his weakness and to give him distinction in his ruin. There is no glow of patriotism in the play to relieve the depression of the political situation. The play inevitably takes our minds on to Shakespeare's *Richard II*, and suffers by comparison. The verse is on the whole declamatory rather than poetic, but nevertheless the play shows more sense of theatre than do his other plays; dialogue and action are taut and rapid, and dialogue achieves effective interplay between characters. There is economy in craftsmanship too; the affair between Mortimer and the Queen develops convincingly with a few effective strokes. The play's significance lies in its preparation of the stage for Shakespeare's historical plays.

O Rare Ben Jonson

Ben Jonson (1572-1637) was a classical scholar who in critical writings condemned the loose constructions of his rivals; but he was not always true to his theory as a practical playwright. Ben Jonson was a satirist who lashed with his wit the vices of the age. Hence he posed as a moralist and corrector of manners. His early satirical comedies are based on the Elizabethan conception of "humours"; his characters are eccentrics or oddities of London life, men with one predominating mood or disposition. Thus, in *Every Man in his Humour* (1598) there is a jealous husband, two self-confident but foolish fops known as Town Gull and Country Gull, and Bobadill, who is a more complex creation, a boaster who can lie with complete self-possession. These plays tend to become tedious in their insistence on humours, and we long for some normal character to appear.

Bartholomew Fair is an entertaining play. What plot there is satirizes the Puritans, but the Fair gives Jonson an opportunity to present a rogues' gallery of sharpers and impostors with characteristic extravagance, with an animated and swarming picture of London life in the Fair. *Sejanus* and *Catiline* are two Roman tragedies, perhaps inspired by the success of Shakespeare's Roman plays. They make some approach to classical form, but become cumbrous in dialogue through Jonson's anxiety to parade his knowledge of Latin authors.

The Alchemist and *Volpone the Fox*

These are Jonson's two best plays. In both he is bitingly satirical: characters divide into two categories, one displaying a roguery that almost passes belief, the other displaying an equally incredible capacity for being duped by the rogues. In *The Alchemist*, a group of servants take advantage of their master's absence to turn his house into an alchemist's den, and various gullible and greedy types fall ready victims to their imposture and charlatanry.

Volpone and Mosca in a scene from Ben Jonson's play Volpone.

Volpone draws its inspiration from Italian Renaissance drama, which it resembles in its gusto and in the total absence of moral sense in most of the characters. Volpone has amassed fabulous wealth, not by working for it, but by practising on the greed of his dupes, who make costly gifts to him in hope of inheriting his wealth when he dies. But Volpone is no conventional miser living on a crust of bread so that he can gloat over his hoard; his appetite for sumptuous and luxurious living is equally monstrous when he leaps from his sick-bed after the departure of his fawning visitors. He is served by something between a hanger-on and a servant, Mosca by name, who ultimately trips himself up by the fantastic ingenuity and inventiveness that he displays in gulling would-be inheritors of Volpone's wealth. The whole play is fantastic, but the son of one suitor and the wife of another intervene effectively to reassure us that there is still honesty and virtue in the world, and they upset Volpone's apple-cart.

The virtue of Jonson's verse is its clarity: his style is clearer than Shakespeare's, because Jonson is less burdened with thought. His language is usually literal, with only a light play of metaphor and simile; and there is a rapid succession of images giving the verse a visual quality and buoyancy that appeal to eye and ear. Here is Mosca congratulating himself on his superiority to mere flatterers and hangers-on; they, he says,

"... can fawn and fleer,
Make their revenue* out of legs and faces,†
Echo my lord, and lick away a moth."

But Mosca, with his quick inventive mind, is a master of intrigue out of which he carves his fortune; he is

"... your fine elegant rascal, that can rise
And stoop, almost together, like an arrow;

* income. † bowing and flattering.

Shoot through the air as nimbly as a star;
Turn short as doth a swallow; and be here,
And there, and here, and yonder, all at once;
Present to any humour, all occasion;
And change a visor swifter than a thought." (III i)

It was verse such as this that gave vitality to Elizabethan drama.

The Duchess of Malfi

Sensational or melodramatic tragedy finds its highest achievement in *The Duchess of Malfi* by John Webster (*c.* 1580-*c.* 1625), a revenge drama deriving its story from Italy, where violent feuds of families such as the Medicis and the Borgias gave rise to a Renaissance drama of blood-curdling crimes and horror. Duke Ferdinand and his Cardinal brother have forbidden their sister, the dowager Duchess of Malfi, to marry again. She ignores their warning and marries beneath her rank a virtuous officer of her household, Antonio, by whom she has three children. Antonio and the Duchess conceal their marriage, but are betrayed to the brothers by Bosola, who has been introduced into the Duchess' household as a spy. The brothers pursue revenge by subjecting their sister to a long ordeal of suffering. She first becomes aware of their vengeance when Ferdinand creeps behind her into her bedroom as she sits combing her hair, while she thinks that she is talking to her husband, who has withdrawn from the room unknown to her. Ferdinand, behind her, offers a hand which she takes, only to find that it is the severed hand of a dead man. She adopts flight, separating from her husband and eldest child for their safety, but she is captured and submitted to tortures. She sees waxen effigies of her husband and child and believes them murdered; and she is condemned to live amidst madmen, who dance grotesquely and sing lunatic ditties. In the end, she and her children are strangled, in full view on the stage. The brothers and Bosola are overcome with remorse, and in the course of the final act, in a succession of misunderstandings and accidents, they contrive to kill first Antonio and then each other, so that at the conclusion the stage is strewn with corpses.

A Comparison of Webster and Shakespeare

Webster was a conscious imitator of Shakespeare, and comparison with Shakespeare is instructive. Shakespeare adopted all the devices and fashions of the theatre of his day, and introduced witches and ghosts, crimes and bloodshed; but he always strictly subordinated these to his artistic purpose. For instance, events that bring about four violent deaths at the end of *Hamlet* have emerged from a taut process of cause and effect and so assume the quality of the inevitable. In Webster's play the horrors appear as if introduced to satisfy the grim appetite of the audience. Moreover, time lapses

Her two brothers warn the Duchess of Malfi against re-marrying.

in the course of the action for no apparent reason: why did the brothers wait for three children to be born before proceeding to their revenge? Webster is also careless in ascribing motives to his characters; the brothers do not mention a motive until overcome with remorse, and then it is hardly valid, for the Duchess has a son by her former marriage who will inherit her wealth. Bosola is a faint shadow of Iago in *Othello*, but he is very dull-witted to fail to realize who the father of the children is until three have been born; and he has an academic conscience which never seems to affect his actions. Nevertheless *The Duchess of Malfi* can hold a modern audience, partly through the quality of Webster's verse, and partly because Webster has so strong a sense of theatre that he disarms the critical faculty by the convincing reality he gives to his array of horrors; he can raise emotions of pity and fear that involve an audience with what is happening on stage. Moreover, the atmosphere of gloom is relieved by the virtuous character of the Duchess: and the scenes of her courtship and marriage are happy and full of charm, though both lovers have premonitions of woes to come. When her ordeal of suffering comes, the Duchess displays great strength of mind:

> "The Heaven o'er my head seems made of molten brass,
> The earth of flaming sulphur, yet I am not mad.
> I am acquainted with sad misery
> As the tanned galley-slave is with his oar." (IV ii)

Webster had learned from Shakespeare to endow his characters with tragic greatness.

The Shoemaker's Holiday

Two comedies of London life very popular in the theatre were Dekker's *Shoemaker's Holiday* and Beaumont and Fletcher's *The Knight of the Burning Pestle*; both blend romance and realism. Thomas Dekker (*c.* 1572-*c.* 1632) was a Londoner of little education, but so shrewd an observer of the London scene that he presents it with lifelike and animated reality. In his play *The Shoemaker's Holiday*, the London craftsmen who formed a large part of the theatre audience saw themselves portrayed without any touch of satire or burlesque. They are gloriously alive, expressing themselves with all the vigour of colloquial speech. They are proud of their skill as craftsmen; they quarrel without bitterness, and enjoy their ale and occasional holidays with tremendous relish. Supremely contented with their lot, they accept the social order as they find it, regarding themselves as the equals of lords and ladies, even of the king, in esteem if not in rank. Simon Eyre, Master Shoemaker in the reign of Henry VI, is the central figure: diverse elements in the play are held together by the story of his rise from a mere apprentice to become the Lord Mayor of London who built Leadenhall Market and instituted an annual feast for apprentices. He is invariably good-humoured, even when abusing his wife and employees, which he can do without offending them and with a marvellous vocabulary of oaths and terms of abuse that has to be heard to be believed.

Romance appears in the love of Rowland Lacy, nephew of the Earl of Lincoln, for Rose, daughter of the Lord Mayor who precedes Simon Eyre in his office. Both Earl and Lord Mayor are too jealous of their respective ranks to countenance the match, and Lacy becomes a shoemaker's apprentice to win his Rose. Parallel to this runs the love story of humble Jane for her shoemaker Ralph, parted from her by the wars. But virtue is triumphant and both pairs of lovers are united by the contrivance of the shoemaker fraternity and by intervention of the king at the Feast of Apprentices that celebrates Simon's elevation to the Mayoralty.

The Knight of the Burning Pestle

This is one of many plays written in partnership by Beaumont and Fletcher. It is a good-natured burlesque of the literary fashions of artless citizens, reflecting the appeal of stories of chivalrous romance to their imaginations. They were familiar with all the jargon of out-moded chivalry, and projected themselves into the adventures of the knights errant of the stories. In spirit the play is akin to the Spanish *Don Quixote*, which the authors may have known, although there was no English translation.

The realistic element in the comedy is supplied by the Citizen and his Wife, who interrupt the opening Prologue from their place among the audience to protest against plays that satirize and belittle merchants, demanding a play "in honour of the commons of London." The Wife suggests that Ralph, their apprentice, should take part in the play to show the actors how to do it. The actors consent to this intrusion, and Ralph's adventures as a knight errant are superimposed on the play. The Citizen and his Wife go up and occupy seats on the stage and keep up a running commentary as the play proceeds. The Wife's observations are particularly artless, but always pungent: she takes sides violently and is completely absorbed by the dramatic illusion. Ralph's adventures range from a visit to an Eastern Court where he resists the proposal of a princess in order to be faithful to his plain Jane at home, to neat satirical reflections on London life. A giant that he encounters is a London barber, and the victims that Ralph frees have gone to the barber to have teeth extracted or minor operations performed. Running along with this, and virtually independent of it, is the story of the love of the apprentice Jasper for his master's daughter, also presented as burlesque: when Jasper is thrown out of the house by the angry father, he has his death announced and gains access to the house again by being carried in in a coffin, whence he arises to terrify his master as a ghost while his beloved escapes from the house in the coffin. The apprentice's father, Master Merrythought, is a parody of Jonson's humours. The play is thus a medley, but the authors keep firm control over their material. The dialogue is skilfully varied from the colloquial London speech of the Citizen and his Wife to burlesqued rhyming verse, lyrical songs, and quite estimable blank verse.

Three of the plays commented on in detail in this section can be obtained in *Six Plays by Contemporaries of Shakespeare* (No. 199, World's Classics, Oxford); and *Volpone* is one of *Four English Comedies* (Penguin). For critical essays, the reader may refer to *The Age of Shakespeare* (Pelican Books).

QUESTIONS

1. "The English Mystery Plays mingle simple piety with broad comedy." Using close reference to the play, show how these contrasted features are blended in either the *Wakefield Nativity Play* or *Noah* in the Towneley cycle of plays.
2. Explain what is meant by allegory. State the theme of the Morality play *Everyman*, and show clearly how the author uses allegory in the development of his theme.
3. Using close reference and some quotation, show how Dr. Faustus reveals his character and his emotional conflict in the soliloquies he speaks.
4. Do you consider that the appeal of Ben Jonson's plays derives from their plots rather than from the characters that appear in them? Use varied illustration from either *Volpone* or *The Alchemist* to support your answer.
5. Illustrate from *The Duchess of Malfi* (*a*) the happy womanliness of the Duchess in the first part of the play, and (*b*) her tragic greatness in facing suffering.
6. Both Beaumont and Fletcher in *The Knight of the Burning Pestle* and Dekker in *The Shoemaker's Holiday* give us a picture of London life, its merchants, craftsmen, apprentices and courtiers. Give your own impression of London life as you have gathered it from your reading of either one of these plays.

CHAPTER 6

SHAKESPEARE

LITTLE is known of Shakespeare's life: information from many sources is like pieces of a jig-saw puzzle, and the missing pieces have led to much guess-work, picturesque rather than profitable. Nevertheless the main lines of his life are known. To judge by a Baptismal Register at Stratford-upon-Avon, he was born on 23 April, 1564, St. George's Day. Before Shakespeare's birth, his father prospered as a businessman in Stratford, and had been mayor of the town; but by the time that his son William was born, he had fallen upon harder times, and was living in comparative poverty. Shakespeare went to the local Grammar School, but left at an early age because it was necessary that he should earn his living; but his short stay at Grammar School is important because he learned some Latin and French, which he could study in later days to gain access to French and Italian literature, which provided virtually the only literary models of that time. He unwisely married at the age of eighteen, and in 1586 he left Stratford.

The period 1586-92 is a gap in our knowledge of him. He may have seen something of the world in these years, in the company of Gentlemen Adventurers; but however that may be, by 1592 he was working in the theatre, discovering his craft as a playwright by patching up old plays for revivals. Soon he wrote entire plays of his own, inviting the opposition and scorn of the University Wits, who were disturbed that a mere actor of little education could successfully rival them in the theatre. As an actor frequently performing at Court, he would have easy access to courtiers and nobility. He published poems (*Venus and Adonis*, *The Rape of Lucrece*) under the patronage of the Earl of Southampton; and by the turn of the century (1600) he was becoming a rich man, for besides being actor and playwright, he had become a shareholder in the theatre. About 1605 he returned to Stratford, bought a gentleman's house, and obtained a coat-of-arms. In 1611 he wrote his last play, *The Tempest*, and in 1616 he died. He was buried in the chancel of Stratford Church, not because he was a great poet and dramatist, but because he owned lands that paid tithes to the Church.

The Early Comedies

From 1592 to 1601, Shakespeare concentrated on writing comedies and historical plays. The general feature of his comedies is their infinite variety, both in their internal composition and in the individual quality of each play. In *A Midsummer Night's Dream*, an early comedy, Shakespeare's invention weaves five stories into the plot, all related ultimately to the marriage of Theseus with Hippolyta. The love in the play is that of a young man's fancy; and the attitude to it is summed up in Puck's words, "Lord, what fools these mortals be." Fairies, unstable in their affections, are the agents of this midsummer madness. Puck, the mischievous and loutish hobgoblin of English folk-lore, is here entirely at home with the delicate fairies of Italian romance. Nick Bottom is also in strange company, both in Fairyland and at the Court of Theseus, but nothing can shake Bottom's self-confidence: he is the man of resource in the company of rude mechanicals. Like Dogberry in *Much Ado About Nothing* and Justice Shallow in *King Henry IV, Part II*, he is incompetence masquerading as authority. Such figures have their roots deeply set in English character and manners. But Shakespeare is fond of what he laughs at, and there is no malice in his ridicule.

The Merchant of Venice

In *The Merchant of Venice*, Shakespeare attempts to blend romantic comedy with melodrama which verges on tragedy, but is not altogether successful. The story of Shylock may have been suggested to Shakespeare by the success of Marlowe's play *The Jew of Malta*; but if Shakespeare began with an intention of making the Jew a conventional moneylender, greedy, cunning and cruel, Shylock so took possession of his imagination that he created a man rather than a monster. The persecution of Jews by Christians is not disguised:

> "Fair sir, you spit on me on Wednesday last;
> You spurn'd me such a day; another time
> You call'd me dog; and for these courtesies
> I'll lend you thus much moneys." (Act I, Sc. iii, line 121)

Shylock has genuine pride in his race, and exhibits characteristic Jewish puritanism in his contempt for the frivolity and extravagance of Bassanio and his fellow nobles. Moreover he is genuinely fond of Jessica, although admittedly his affection for her is sorely tried when she takes his ducats with her. Shakespeare's workmanship is seen at its most skilful in the scene between Shylock and Tubal, where comedy, pathos and character are blended together in the skilful dialogue. Shakespeare gives Shylock a case, which Shylock himself states:

> "Hath not a Jew eyes? hath not a Jew hands, organs, dimensions, senses, affections, passions? . . . If you prick us, do we not bleed?" (III i 60)

The speech is a good example of Shakespeare's balanced prose with its parallel rhetorical questions and its pattern of climax.

In the trial scene Shakespeare has diminished our sympathy for Shylock; despite Portia's plea for mercy, Shylock relies on the literal and legal strength of his bond. He is defeated by a verbal quibble, but, apart from the law, the moral issue was in favour of Antonio. Shylock, however, is great enough to refuse to submit to the ignominious terms imposed upon him, and even to suffer death; but that would have made the play a tragedy, and Shakespeare has still to conclude the Belmont story, so he must keep the play in a vein of comedy; therefore we have a fifth act without Shylock, which is rather like *Hamlet* without the Prince of Denmark.

The Casket Scene

Portia is the presiding genius at Belmont, so redolent in its splendours of the Italian Renaissance. She is designed to come face to face with Shylock in the climax of the play, and may be considered as Shakespeare's intellectual heroine. Nevertheless she has the high spirits and fondness for practical jokes of a Rosalind or a Viola. We see all these qualities in her early scene with Nerissa, when she makes critical and biting comments upon her foreign

In The Merchant of Venice, *Bassanio debates which casket to choose.*

suitors. She is deeply in love, and when Bassanio is successful in his choice of casket, she becomes modest and submissive, afraid of the excess of her joy:

> "O love! be moderate; allay thy ecstasy;
> In measure rain thy joy; scant this excess." (III ii 111)

The Casket Scene is in the fairy-tale manner, and Shakespeare lavishes rich imagery upon it. Only in a fairy-tale would logic work so perfectly to produce a genuine lover. The suitors' addresses before the caskets reveal their characters: the self-centred egoism of Morocco, and Arragon's disdainful rejection of the barbarous multitude without himself having any quality of mind to give him distinction, unless it be the stupidity which makes him a forerunner of Sir Andrew Aguecheek. It would be a mistake to criticize Bassanio's character realistically: he may be extravagant and pleasure-seeking, but these qualities are within the expected make-up of a romantic lover. Shakespeare intends us to take the humility of his choice of casket seriously: there is no cunning in it. His speech over the caskets is a succession of developed similes and comparisons upon the theme:

> "So may the outward shows be least themselves:
> The world is still deceiv'd with ornament." (III ii 73)

The Garden Scene

In this scene of Act V, the poetry of the play rises to a summit:

> "How sweet the moonlight sleeps upon this bank!
> Here will we sit, and let the sounds of music
> Creep in our ears: soft stillness and the night
> Become the touches of sweet harmony." (V i 54)

Here is a philosophy of beauty; heaven and earth seem to be linked by the blending of moonlight with the beauty of the garden. As in a Greek myth the Moon stooped to kiss Endymion, so in the garden Lorenzo kisses Jessica. The music of the minstrels playing to Lorenzo and Jessica becomes the music of the spheres as the lovers gaze at the stars. This harmony of sight and sound exercises a refining influence by purging the mind of violence and anger:

> "The man that hath no music in himself . . .
> Is fit for treasons, stratagems, and spoils." (V i 83)

There is something of the idealism of Plato in this glimpse of divine patterns in heaven of what is imperfect and fleeting in the realistic world of experience.

As You Like It, a Pastoral Play

As in *The Merchant of Venice* Shakespeare sets the realistic and the romantic side by side, the one as a corrective to the other, so in *As You Like It* he gathers into his miniature world of the Forest of Arden the literary attitudes or conventions that amused and diverted the Elizabethan mind.

Shakespeare took the story from Lodge's *Rosalynde*, a pastoral novel of artificial country life written in the manner of Lyly's *Euphues*. Through this pastoral convention the Elizabethans saw themselves projected into the life of Arcady; it was their "escape" literature in which they were free to see their lives enhanced by romance. In *As You Like It*, the Court is a realistic world of low motives, sordid intrigue and greed. The Duke in his exile can indulge idealistic values; he can find

> "Tongues in trees, books in the running brooks,
> Sermons in stones, and good in everything;" (II i 16)

but, for all his exalting of nature, he is leading an artificial life and indulging sentimental values. Nature is not his appropriate background, and he is ready enough to return to Court when an opportunity arises. Another sentimentalist is Jaques, the melancholy philosopher and self-appointed critic of society. Silvius and Phebe, the languishing lover and his scornful lady, are Arcadian shepherd and shepherdess derived from the classical poetry of Theocritus and Virgil. The only genuine country-folk in the forest are the shepherd Corin and the down-to-earth lovers Audrey and William.

On all these extravagances the wit of Touchstone plays: he laughs at Jaques' affected melancholy (though Jaques does not realize it), reconciles Court and country with the forced parallels of his chop-logic arguments, and finally proposes a union of the two in his own proposal of marriage to Audrey. Only Corin's honest common-sense is proof against his wit: all the others are sitting targets. But the real touchstone that gives a true measure of all these extravagances is the love of Orlando and Rosalind, which is so woven into the texture of the play that it gives a unity to the diversity. Rosalind's love is both real and romantic; it falls upon her with the suddenness of discovery, but, though it transfigures the world she lives in, she can detach herself from it, criticize it, and even make a jest of it.

The songs of *As You Like It* sustain the play's atmosphere which, apart from the early Court scenes and the melancholy musings of Jaques, is lyrical throughout. Even the prose of Rosalind and Orlando has a buoyancy on which their high spirits ride. The most dramatic episode in the play is the wrestling-match; in the Elizabethan theatre this would be conducted with professional skill, and the audience would show their keen appreciation of the technical points displayed.

Twelfth Night, or *What you will*

Twelfth Night is regarded as embodying the perfection of Shakespeare's comic art. Written about 1600 on the eve of his tragic period, it may very well have been designed for performance at Court on the twelfth night of Christmas festivities, an occasion for the abandonment of normal restraints, a healthy outlet for high spirits when all normal authorities were flouted and even ridiculed.

Illyria is a country of Shakespeare's imagination, not very far away from Charing Cross and the houses of the nobility that were situated between the City of London and the City of Westminster where the Court resided. The success of *Twelfth Night* lies in its all-round excellence: there is no dominating character, unless it be Malvolio. Most of the characters are touched with a light ironic ridicule, but there is no malice behind it. Thus Olivia, declaring theatrically that she will mourn for her brother for seven years, falls in love with the first handsome youth who comes to her gate—and "he" happens to be a woman. Orsino is more in love with love than with any particular person, and can easily shift his choice from Olivia to Viola when the situation at the end of the play demands it. He can languish in the sweetness of his emotion without seeking the presence of his lady:

> "If music be the food of love, play on:
> Give me excess of it, that, surfeiting,
> The appetite may sicken and so die." (I i 1)

And so he can send Viola (in disguise as a page, under the name of Cesario) to do his wooing for him. Always protesting his own constancy, his mind is (as Feste tells him) "a very opal," changing colour and direction with every impulse of his whimsical nature. It is Viola who knows the nature of true love; and being herself in love with the Duke, she can speak its true language. Already feeling Viola's spell, Olivia asks her, "Why, what would you?" meaning, "How would you woo?" And Viola replies:

> "Make me a willow cabin at your gate,
> And call upon my soul within the house." (I v 252)

This is how Olivia would like to be wooed. Orsino recognizes the same quality in Viola's speech when, asked her opinion of the music, she replies:

> "It gives a very echo to the seat
> Where Love is thron'd." (II iv 21)

Much of the poetry of the play is given to Viola. There is nothing sentimental in her love: it grows and deepens by virtue of the restraint she puts upon it.

Viola's Character

Viola is the strongest character in the play, perhaps the only one not touched with irony. When she fears her brother is drowned, she is like "Patience on a monument," she smiles at grief; she never forgets her brother and constantly refers to him throughout the play, but she does not shirk the task of living. In her disguise as a page, she shows a fund of resource and adaptability that steers her safely through all the complications that her disguise sets in motion; she can talk love to Orsino, swagger before Olivia, or exchange wit with the clown; she is only at a loss when challenged to prove her manhood with a sword, but here she is lucky, for the timely arrival of Antonio enables her to save face.

Olivia's Character

Olivia is in direct contrast to Viola. Olivia's grief for her brother is as sentimental an emotional indulgence as the Duke's love. Feste can see through her pretence when he proves her a fool. Once Cesario's appearance has charmed her, she loses all self-control; she cunningly sends a ring after him to ensure his return, and when he comes back she throws modesty and pride to the four winds:

> "Cesario, by the roses of the Spring,
> By maidhood, honour, truth, and every thing,
> I love thee so that, maugre all thy pride,
> Nor wit nor reason can my passion hide." (III i 146)

Yet Shakespeare enables her to keep her dignity as a lady presiding over a great household; Sebastian comments upon her "stable bearing," and Toby and the servants seem to have a healthy respect for her authority.

The play is far from exhausted by its main theme. The rest of the play is the "trappings" of the love story. Yet what trappings! They threaten to eclipse the romantic comedy. Sir Toby Belch is presiding genius below stairs in Olivia's household. "I hate . . . an unfilled can," he says, and, "I am sure care's an enemy of life." These two utterances sum him up: he belongs to the "cakes and ale" school of life. In his self-indulgence and flouting of authority, he is an embodiment of the spirit of Twelfth Night. Sir Andrew Aguecheek is the stooge of Sir Toby, an admirer of his wit and of the dash he cuts; he is also unconsciously the butt of his humour. Sir Toby is exploiting Sir Andrew's three thousand ducats a year, but Sir Andrew is blissfully unaware of his own stupidity; reputed to know "three or four languages . . . without book," he asks the meaning of "Pourquoi"; and his appearance, dancing and wooing are all ridiculous. Sometimes we could almost credit him with wit, as when he is commenting on Sir Toby's fooling: "He does it with a better grace, but I do it more natural." The mock duel with Cesario in which Sir Andrew becomes involved is Sir Toby's most ingenious device, and his conduct of the challenge and the duel, so that ultimately Viola and Sir Andrew "will kill one another by the look like cockatrices," is the most humorous episode in the play.

This is the point at which various threads of the plot begin to weave together. Viola is drawn into the duel, and Antonio's intervention, her denial of the purse, and his charging of Viola with ingratitude and cowardice, tempt

Sir Andrew to renew the duel. Mistaken identity persists: Sir Andrew strikes Sebastian, Olivia intervenes to prevent the fight, and this paves the way for the *dénouement*, or laying bare of the facts of the situation.

Malvolio, from Twelfth Night.

Malvolio, the Pompous Steward

One thread of the plot persists in isolation, the gulling of Malvolio. Olivia has a high opinion of Malvolio as a steward in a large household. "Where is Malvolio?" she says, "he is sad and civil, and suits well for a servant with my fortunes" (III iv 5). On several occasions she summons him to deal with a situation in the household. But Olivia also recognizes his faults: "O, you are sick of self-love, Malvolio," she says, "and taste with a distempered appetite." Malvolio has no sense of humour, which is really a sense of proportion. He is the direct opposite of Sir Toby: if Sir Toby stands for the "cakes and ale" of life, Malvolio represents repression and discipline. To Sir Toby he has all the vices of a Puritan, but Maria knows him better: "The devil a Puritan that he is," says Maria, "or anything constantly but a time-pleaser." In Malvolio the virtues of a genuine Puritan are used to feed his own egoism and conceit, and righteousness becomes self-righteousness; he is a character often pilloried in literature, the moral humbug. His delusion that Olivia loves him is fantastic. Maria is the brains of the plot against him, and Sir Toby calls her a "most excellent devil of wit"; she is a shrewd observer of character and knows how to play upon him where he is most vulnerable, in his conceit:

> "an affectioned ass, that cons state without book, and utters it by great swarths: the best persuaded of himself; so crammed, as he thinks, with excellencies, that it is his grounds of faith that all that look on him love him." (II iii 139)

As the plot proceeds, we become sympathetic towards Malvolio, especially when he is put in a dark room and treated as a madman. It is the only part of the plot of *Twelfth Night* that is not satisfactorily concluded at the end of the play. To fit with the rest of the play, Malvolio should have seen the joke; but there has been malice behind the ridicule, and it has eaten deep. Like

Shylock, Malvolio has the makings of a tragic character, and does not fit readily into comedy.

Feste the Jester

Feste alone remains, as he does at the end of the play to sing the Epilogue. The Fool was a privileged person in an Elizabethan court, a professional wit paid to be funny; he was given licence to make his betters the butt of his jokes, but must use this freedom with discretion. Feste is carefully estimating the length to which he can go when he proves Olivia a fool for mourning for her brother, and tells Orsino that he is a creature of wayward and whimsical moods:

> "Now the melancholy god protect thee, and the tailor make thy doublet of changeable taffeta, for thy mind is a very opal." (II iv 72)

Viola sums up the Elizabethan jester after her encounter with Feste at the gate of Olivia's house:

> "This fellow is wise enough to play the fool;
> And to do that well craves a kind of wit." (III i 57)

A Fool's stock-in-trade consisted of puns, paradoxes, and all the tricks of word-juggling that were so fashionable in the sixteenth century. Feste can make nonsense sound like sense:

> "I did impeticos thy gratillity, for Malvolio's nose is no whipstock. My lady has a white hand, and the Myrmidons are no bottle-ale houses." (II iii 25)

Yet to Shakespeare Feste is a man, not a mere word-machine. The Fool was usually an oddity and often appeared crazy, but Feste has the cleverest mind in the play. He moves spectator-like among all groups of characters, and implicit in his fooling is a vein of melancholy. He feeds the Duke's love-sick mood with a song of a deserted lover, and even when Sir Toby and Sir Andrew ask for a song, he sings of the fading of beauty and youthful love with the inevitable passing of time. Feste surveyed and assessed the human scene, and everywhere he saw folly. One could suppose that, like Hamlet, he saw too deeply into human nature to be really happy. His final song is a pessimistic review of the human lot. Shakespeare often reminds us that laughter is very near to tears, and when he wrote *Twelfth Night* he was on the verge of his Tragedy period.

The Historical Plays

From 1597-8 Shakespeare wrote in quick succession *King Richard II*, the two parts of *King Henry IV*, and *King Henry V*. He had already told the story of the reigns of Henry VI and Edward IV in the three parts of *King Henry VI*, plays that he had revised at the beginning of his career; later he had written

King Richard III, a Marlowesque play with a colossal central figure. And so, with the completion of *King Henry V*, Shakespeare had presented on an epic scale an entire period of English history, the Wars of the Roses, a century of disruption and civil strife that preceded the Tudor monarchy. Shakespeare was writing at the close of the Tudor monarchy, when the Queen could not live many more years; it may be that one of Shakespeare's purposes was to emphasize the importance of national unity.

But the History plays have a far deeper significance than this. The Elizabethan conception of the religious, social and political order of the human community was that it was divinely appointed by God. God was at the apex of the pyramid, and below Him were national kings, the Vicars of God; then, on levels broadening down to the base, were the nobility and the various ranks of commoners. Every man had his appointed place in the divine order, and rebellion was the arch-sin.

But kings are men and therefore mortal, and subject to human frailty. Each play focuses upon a king, and each king is a failure with the exception of one in the middle of the sequence, Henry V, who alone is fully integrated in his personal and political qualities to his function as a ruler. Each of the others offends the moral order in one way or another. Richard II puts his own personal gratification before the needs of his subjects, and when faced with rebellion he has not the practical ability to cope with it, so he is rightly deposed. But the man who deposes him, Henry Bolingbroke, sins by his act of rebellion, and so must meet retribution as well.

King Richard II

King Richard II is a tragedy. Richard undergoes a change of character in the course of the play. At first he is seen in success, a youthful king taxing his people heavily for the costly maintenance of upstart favourites. Opposed to him is Bolingbroke, calculating son of John of Gaunt and a claimant to the throne; and Bolingbroke's challenge to Mowbray is indirectly a challenge to the King. Richard, politically incompetent, wavers; he orders a duel, then cancels it, and banishes Mowbray for life but Bolingbroke for only ten years. His confiscation of the Lancastrian revenues and his departure for Ireland are acts of political folly: the one gives Bolingbroke a motive for return that enlists the unanimous support of the barons, who feel their own security of succession threatened; and the other leaves a way open for Bolingbroke's return to an undefended land.

Richard's Changing Character

So far all is straightforward, but when at last Richard returns from Ireland and meets his small band of followers on the coast of Wales, he is a changed man: he makes no effort to resist, and becomes an object of self-pity dramatizing his own despair; but he shows the imagination of a poet, and acquires tragic greatness in his fall. In this long scene, Shakespeare displays with sharp dramatic contrast the swaying of the King's mood as each successive messenger brings further news of Bolingbroke's easy progress. From an arrogant confidence in his own divine right—

"God for his Richard hath in heavenly pay
A glorious angel," (III ii 60)

—Richard develops a penetrating insight that sees kings, like all mortal men, as subject to Fate:

". . . for within the hollow crown
That rounds the mortal temples of a king
Keeps Death his court, and there the antic sits,
Scoffing his state and grinning at his pomp." (III ii 160)

Richard sees all the conditions of his situation when, at Flint Castle, he comes down from the upper stage to surrender to Bolingbroke in the base court:

"Down, down I come, like glistering Phaethon,
Wanting the manage of unruly jades." (III iii 178)

The brief comparison with Phaethon's ambition to drive the chariot of the

In Richard II, *the Queen and her ladies hear the gardeners talking.*

Sun-god across the sky is appropriate in all details to Richard's position. It implies the presumption of his early years when he was drunk with the sun-like glory of kingship, and the disaster that follows from his failure to curb the turbulent barons. Imagery and word-music blend to produce the magic of Shakespeare's poetry.

The same swaying of Richard's mood between despair and consciousness of his kingly office can be traced in the deposition scene. Shakespeare sees the soul of a nation in its king; when that soul is diseased, the whole body-politic is affected. Yet in spite of Richard's incapacity in his high office, Shakespeare gives him many moments of grandeur:

> "Though some of you with Pilate wash your hands,
> Showing an outward pity—yet you Pilates
> Have here delivered me to my sour cross,
> And water cannot wash away your sin." (IV i 239)

This passage shows the direct relationship of the king to God. In his prison dungeon, suffering has purged Richard's mind of all its weaknesses. He makes a little world of his prison and peoples it with his thoughts. When he hears music played outside by some well-wisher, he compares its broken time to the broken harmonies of his life. When the murderers arrive, he shows a spirit and decisiveness that we could wish he had displayed earlier, and kills two before he is himself struck down by Exton.

Variety of Characters

The play is rich in variety of character. The dramatic contrast of character lies between Richard and Bolingbroke, who is practical because he is unimaginative; his efficiency is uninspiring against Richard's more perceptive mind. In the words of the Queen, "triumph is become an alehouse guest." The calculating quality of Bolingbroke's mind is seen in his courtship of the people:

> "Off goes his bonnet to an oyster-wench;
> A brace of draymen bid God speed him well
> And had the tribute of his supple knee,
> With 'Thanks, my countrymen, my loving friends'." (I iv 31)

John of Gaunt is a patriot and admonishes Richard for his early sins. Gaunt speaks Shakespeare's well-known lines on England and the quiet beauty of English life and landscape. There is an undertone of patriotism running through the whole play, not only a love of its people but also of its soil, its flowers, its "high wild hills and rough uneven ways." On landing from Ireland, Richard says: "Dear earth, I do salute thee with my hand" (III ii 6). The gardeners compare England with a garden, and the Bishop of Carlisle talks of the defilement of the soil by the blood of Englishmen shed in civil war.

The Duke of York, another of the king's uncles, is weak because he can see right on both sides, and wishes to find a compromise. He reproaches Richard for confiscating the Lancaster estates, and reprimands Bolingbroke for coming back in rebellion. In the end he bows to the necessity of events and joins Bolingbroke; and having once yielded, he takes his stand on rigid principle, and condemns his son Aumerle.

Medieval Content

There is much that is formal and medieval in the style and structure of many scenes in *King Richard II.* The Middle Ages were fond of ceremonial and ritual; the trial-by-combat scene in the lists at Coventry, with its ceremonial of heralds, reflects the formalism of chivalry and the tournament. The speeches of Richard, both in the surrender scene at Flint Castle and in the deposition scene in Westminster Hall, display the repetitive quality of the language of church services:

> "I give this heavy weight from off my head,
> And this unwieldy sceptre from my hand,
> The pride of kingly sway from out my heart;
> With mine own tears I wash away my balm,
> With mine own hands I give away my crown." (IV i 204)

The brief scene in the Duke of York's garden is unique in the Histories. In its comparison of the State of England with a garden, it has the character of a medieval allegory. The gardeners, like the Chorus of a Greek play, are detached spectators of political events; their insistence on harmony and proportion, in a garden or in a kingdom, emphasizes the underlying theme of the History plays. It is worth noting that Shakespeare puts this political wisdom into the mouth of a common man. The Queen, in this scene and elsewhere, is a pathetic figure; and the gardener's thought for her is the kindest in the play:

> "Here did she fall a tear; here, in this place,
> I'll set a bank of rue, sour herb of grace.
> Rue, even for ruth, here shortly shall be seen,
> In the remembrance of a weeping queen." (III iv 104)

King Henry V, the Ideal of Kingship

Shakespeare may have regarded the deposition of Richard II as the last act of the Middle Ages, and has given it a medieval style. In the plays that follow we enter the modern world: Shakespeare gives the stories of Henry IV and Henry V an Elizabethan background. History is no longer merely an affair of kings and nobles; the common people enter and comedy runs side by side with history. *King Henry V* is a national pageant, a cross-section of national life as Shakespeare saw it. Whatever our views on modern war may be, we must remember that in the past war was the instrument whereby a nation proved its greatness. The spirit of aggressive conquest that won the Battle of Agincourt was akin to the Elizabethan defeat of the Spanish Armada, a vindication of England's place in the world.

At the outset, the play poses a problem for Shakespeare. He is proposing a theme that extends over a period of years, yet he must compress it within the limits of a three-hour performance, in the course of which the scene will shift from England to France. Down-at-heel actors must assume the majesty of kings and princes; and rusty old swords and battered helmets must represent the martial array which met in battle at Agincourt. How can he hope adequately to realize his theme on the bare platform of his theatre? So Shakespeare devises a Chorus to fill the void of the theatre with poetry. The Chorus appeals to the imagination of the audience to join in partnership with the actors, to realize the full glories of the theme from the bare essentials:

> "Piece out our imperfections with your thoughts:
> Into a thousand parts divide one man,
> And make imaginary puissance.
> Think when we talk of horses that you see them
> Printing their proud hoofs i' the receiving earth;
> For 'tis your thoughts that now must deck our kings." (Prol. I 23)

Setting the Scene

In the Prologue to Act III we see all the splendour and colour of Elizabethan galleons as the king's fleet sets sail for Harfleur; and the Chorus to Act IV contains perhaps the finest word-picture of the play, presenting the scene on the battlefield as the two armies face each other on the night before Agincourt:

> "Fire answers fire, and through their paly flames
> Each battle sees the other's umber'd face:
> Steed threatens steed, in high and boastful neighs
> Piercing the night's dull ear; and from the tents
> The armourers, accomplishing the knights,
> With busy hammers closing rivets up,
> Give dreadful note of preparation." (Prol. IV 8)

Notice how both eye and ear are appealed to, in this conjuring up of the scene. So far the Chorus has shifted the scene: but now it has a different function. The Chorus to Act V spans a period of time, the winter that follows Agincourt, when the troops are in winter-quarters at Calais and the king comes to England before returning to France for the Peace Conference that ends the play. So Shakespeare, with his Choruses, justifies the "loose" construction of his plays, which was coming under fire from Ben Jonson and academic critics who favoured the more restricted unities of time and place that characterized classical drama.

Henry's Character

The personality of the king is naturally the centre-piece of the play. First his random youth is glanced at by the two bishops; Shakespeare's audience was familiar with this from the two parts of *King Henry IV* which had preceded this play. There the prince escapes from Court formality to the Boar's Head Tavern in Eastcheap, where Sir John Falstaff is presiding genius. Prince Henry shares Falstaff's escapades and learns a great deal about the subjects he will one day have to rule; but he never forgets his royalty, which indeed he proves by slaying Hotspur in personal combat at the Battle of Shrewsbury. When, at the end of *King Henry IV*, *Part II*, the prince ascends the throne, he rejects Falstaff; he cannot take Falstaff into history with him. It is interesting to note that, in an early scene of *King Henry V*, Shakespeare enacts the death of Falstaff. Falstaff had emerged from fiction into life, and could only be finally disposed of by the proper enacting of his death. Although the description of his death is in the broadly comic vein of Mistress Quickly, it is one of the most moving passages in the play.

To the two bishops, the king's reformation seems a miracle, for the king has emerged a soldier, a statesman and a theologian. It is clear to them that in his youth he was "covering discretion with a coat of folly." We first meet the king in his presence-chamber, awaiting the arrival of French ambassadors. He is deeply conscious of his duty to God and his responsibility for his subjects, and seeks assurance from Canterbury that his cause is a righteous one. Next, he explores the necessity of home defence while the army is campaigning abroad. Canterbury's detailed comparison of a human community with a hive of bees emphasizes that the diverse activities of different orders in the community are all co-ordinated into a harmony of effort by the directing authority of the king.

Under the insult of the tennis-balls the king is angry but controlled, and his determination sets as hard as flint. When he encounters conspiracy against his life he is merciless, not on personal grounds, but out of concern for the safety of his kingdom. He shows compassion for victims of war in his plea to the Governor of Harfleur, and it is this same concern that makes him hang Bardolph for looting.

Before the Battle of Agincourt

As battle approaches, the finer qualities of his leadership emerge in his efforts to sustain the morale of his troops. He identifies himself with them by sharing their hardships, and by emphasizing his common humanity with them rather than his kingship:

Henry V sits alone before Agincourt, musing on his responsibilities.

> "I think the king is but a man, as I am: the violet smells to him as it doth to me; the element shows to him as it doth to me; all his senses have but human conditions." (IV i 104)

The king's talk with Court, Williams and Bates shows that it is no narrow view of the glories of war that Shakespeare is taking: he is probing deeply into the suffering, endurance and anxieties of common soldiers. This is the most significant episode on the night before battle. In his soliloquy following the interview, the king reflects on how the ceremony and distinction that surround his person and make his subjects bow before him, ironically take away from him the power to know truth from flattery; and in his luxurious bed the king, sleepless under the burden of rule, envies the sound sleep of the peasant on his hard boards.

Back among his nobles, in the second long scene of the night, Henry, in reply to the doubts that he has overheard Westmoreland expressing, delivers his famous speech on honour:

> "If it be a sin to covet honour,
> I am the most offending soul alive." (IV iii 28)

The speech is a characteristic piece of rhetoric, in contrast to the more contemplative verse of *Richard II.* The address by Henry to his troops before the breach at Harfleur is another example. The purpose of rhetoric is to persuade by communicating *feeling* from a speaker to his audience; today we call it propaganda. The sentiment of this speech on honour proclaims itself genuine when we reflect upon how truly it echoes the feelings of veterans of either of the world wars of this century; they all have their St. Crispin's Day, when they renew old comradeships of war. Henry goes on to use the phrase "a band of brothers," which was also the theme of his address before Harfleur when he paid tribute to the mettle of English yeomen.

Left to meditate alone, the king prays before the battle, "O God of battles, steel my soldiers' hearts." He is conscious of past events and his father's sins controlling the present, and attempts to free himself from the vicious circle by offering repentance to God.

The Battle of Agincourt

But how is Shakespeare to stage a battle? As if aware of his limitations, he makes the first battle scene a comic one: Pistol, of all people, has encountered a greater coward than himself and taken a French prisoner! A succession of short scenes follows, suggesting simultaneous battle-action in many parts of the field. An heroic note is sounded with an account of the death of the Dukes of York and Suffolk. In victory Henry is modest, giving all praise to God and refusing any credit for it himself.

Immediately after the battle, Henry lends himself with relish to a practical joke on Williams, which began in an encounter of the previous night. This king has a sense of humour; and we are reminded of his early days with Falstaff. The human side of Henry's character is sustained in his wooing of Katherine in the last act of the play, but the only valuable passage in Act V is Burgundy's description of the desolation of the French countryside, the ultimate curse of war.

The French Scenes

Shakespeare's presentation of the French is a travesty of history, but a good dramatic contrast. The French king shows discretion, but the Dauphin represents most of the others. From the outset, when he sends tennis-balls, he under-estimates both the power of the English and the king's character. England is a "nook-shotten isle" where men drink beer instead of the spirited wines of France. He concedes that the English have animal courage but believes that, like a flea on the lip of a lion, they have not sufficient brains to realize the danger they are in. The spirit of a "band of brothers" is sadly absent from the French host: the nobles despise the peasantry and wish they could fight their battles without them. However, the Dauphin fails to relieve Harfleur, and when he arrives at Agincourt he is vying with the other nobles in boasting of horse and armour and playing at dice for "the low-rated English." Against this arrogant display, Grandpré's description of the

English drawn up for battle is perhaps the finest descriptive contrast in the play:

> "The horsemen sit like fixed candlesticks,
> With torch-staves in their hand." (IV ii 45)

The Minor Characters

The other characters of the English scene may be briefly dealt with. The gang in Eastcheap are hangers-on of the army. Pistol, the only one to be given much development, is an eccentric, belonging to the type that the Elizabethans called "humours." Pistol in his extravagant speech reveals the smattering of culture that ignorant men picked up in the Renaissance, full of quotations (usually faulty) from plays that he has seen.

Fluellen is Pistol's antagonist in his conscientious pursuit of duty. He is the Englishman's good-humoured laugh at the excitable Welshman. As a soldier he is a strict disciplinarian and very proud of his knowledge of the military art, although it dates back to the Romans! He has no sense of humour, and labours the obvious. Monmouth and Macedon are much the same sort of place because each has a river, "and there is salmons in both." His Welsh excitability makes him pile word upon word in his effort to speak English, and he confuses all the parts of speech. Henry approves of Fluellen:

> "Though it appear a little out of fashion,
> There is much care and valour in this Welshman." (IV i 84)

The Period of Tragedies, 1601-1609

From 1601 to 1609 Shakespeare was almost exclusively engaged in writing tragedies: his mind was preoccupied with the mystery of evil, which does not appear in his tragedies merely as the negative of good, but rather as a positive force in the world. This probing into evil is so deep that it seems to have come from some very personal feeling in Shakespeare's mind.

The hero of a Shakespearean tragedy is a great man, a king, a prince, or at least a man wielding great power. The fall of such men, carrying with it political disruption, is much more charged with dramatic power than any private disaster:

> "When beggars die, there are no comets seen:
> The heavens themselves blaze forth the death of princes."
> (*Julius Caesar*, II ii 30)

This tragic hero commits an act that creates circumstances which carry him by an inevitable process to his death. In his struggle against these hostile circumstances, he is like a man who has caught part of his clothing in a machine and becomes, in spite of all efforts, inexorably drawn into the mechanism. But not only is his own death involved: as the tragic action proceeds, he becomes an agent of death; for example, Cinna and Portia die in *Julius Caesar* as innocent victims of circumstance. The action in a tragedy develops by a taut process of cause and effect: there is little scope given to accident or coincidence in tragedy.

Character and Fate

Thus Shakespearean tragedy emerges from an interaction of character and fate. In *Shakespearean Tragedy* (Macmillan), A. C. Bradley maintains that character *is* fate, and, following the lead of Coleridge,* sees the plays as psychological dramas. All serious students of Shakespeare will find Bradley's book a fascinating study. But fate as well as character is strongly felt in a Shakespearean tragedy; it lies outside the hero himself, beyond his direct control. It may be the world of circumstance, or it may seem to acquire the dimensions of a spirit world, satanic in nature and directly influencing, or even possessing, the human mind. The witches in *Macbeth* give this impression.

The hero of Shakespearean tragedy is noble-minded and a man of strong passions; his nobility is essential to gain the sympathy of the audience in his fall. But there is a tragic flaw in his make-up, which defeats his finer nature and sets the tragic action in motion. He is not a balanced character, but is built too strongly to submit to the hostile circumstances he has raised. He is too great to submit, and in his struggle he generates such resistance that he wins our admiration and sympathy. We have seen a human nature greater than we thought. Comedy fastens on human weaknesses, but tragedy concentrates on its strength; and so the hero's death is not merely depressing, but also inspiring. This reaction is aesthetic, not necessarily moral, as the case of Macbeth shows.

Julius Caesar, a Roman Tragedy

Julius Caesar was an early Shakespeare tragedy (1599) and does not contain the complexities of later plays. Shakespeare took his story from history because the story of Brutus and his murder of Caesar coincides with the tragic formula. The play is named *Julius Caesar* because of Caesar's historic eminence; he disappears from the play comparatively early, although his spirit lives on and influences the ending. But Brutus is the real tragic hero, and it is from his viewpoint that the tragedy develops.

Rome in 44 B.C. had been ruled in recent years by victorious generals. Julius Caesar was sole survivor of the second Triumvirate, having defeated his partners, and was now virtual dictator of Rome. This offended a group of patrician Romans whose political ideals were still republican and democratic. Brutus was the most conspicuous and high-minded of these, a political idealist; but he had two serious faults. He did not realize that Roman

* *Shakespearean Criticism* by Coleridge (162 and 183, Everyman Library, Dent).

Cassius and Brutus discuss the dangers of Caesar's growing power.

character had declined through conquest and riches; the people of Rome no longer possessed the moral fibre that alone was capable of making democracy work. His second fault was that he stooped to political murder, or in other words tried to combine idealism and murder. These tragic flaws were caused by his failure to understand his fellow-men; he assumed that everybody was as high-minded as himself, and thus he became the tool of men of meaner motive.

Shakespeare usually opens his tragedies with a brief, dramatic scene to introduce the underlying influence that is to bring about the tragedy. Here it is the Roman mob, and we see their demoralization: they are idle in their dependence on doles of corn from conquered Africa distributed by the dictator, and they are fickle in their desertion of Pompey, their previous idol. Clearly they are politically inept.

The second scene lays the foundations of the tragedy. Brutus is beset by Cassius, a man who follows political intrigue for his own purposes; his practical instinct is in dramatic contrast to Brutus' idealism. He has noted Brutus' discontent, and needs Brutus as figurehead of a conspiracy against Caesar, to give it an air of respectability and patriotism. His shrewd insight into character enables him to use arguments that will most influence Brutus. Cassius' weakness is passion, and he cannot at first suppress his own personal jealousy of Caesar: the story of how he saved Caesar's life in the Tiber shows this. He is on stronger ground with Brutus when he describes the personal slavery into which they are sinking, and sees the remedy in the self-help of independently-minded Romans:

> "The fault, dear Brutus, is not in our stars,
> But in ourselves, that we are underlings." (I ii 139)

In the distance, the crowd's shouts dramatically confirm Cassius' fears.

In this play the drama emerges from close interplay of character, and the opinions that major characters hold of one another is very significant; Caesar, returning from the Lupercal, shrewdly sums up Cassius as a lean, hungry man who always has a grievance; as the scene closes, Cassius sums up Brutus as noble but easily led.

The Storm Scene

This scene is one of atmosphere. Each character reacts to the storm according to his temperament: Cicero looks for a rational explanation; Casca is superstitious; Cassius welcomes the storm, which echoes the storm in his own mind—it is a fitting night to set on foot a conspiracy. When Cassius sees Casca's superstition, he plays on it to draw him into the plot. In his tragedies, Shakespeare uses imagery with cumulative effect. The strange supernatural omens that accompany the storm, here and later in Caesar's house, introduce images of fire and blood and the strange behaviour of animals, and they seem to suggest some external power of evil luring men to their doom.

In his orchard in the early hours of the morning, Brutus is complaining that he is unable to sleep. Broken sleep is another image recurring through the play: Calphurnia recounts her nightmare; Cinna dreams that he feasted with Caesar; and at Sardis, Brutus envies the sleep of the boy Lucius.

Conflict in *Julius Caesar*

Drama is based upon conflict. Here the pattern of conflict is extremely complex: there is the external conflict of parties—Caesar and the conspirators—but outside that conflict, a more subtle one is soon to develop between Cassius and Brutus; and, perhaps most dramatic of all, there is a conflict in Brutus' mind. It is this last conflict that Brutus is trying to resolve at the beginning of the orchard scene. The conflicting elements in Brutus' mind are his love for Caesar (a personal friend) and his earnest desire for the freedom of Rome. His soliloquy:

> "It must be by his death, and for my part,
> I know no personal cause to spurn at him,
> But for the general . . ." (II i 10)

conveys his state of mind. At present he acknowledges Caesar's moderation and restraint, and resolves to kill him, not for what he is, but for what he may become. The nightmare imagery returns:

> "Between the acting of a dreadful thing
> And the first motion, all the interim is
> Like a phantasma, or a hideous dream." (II i 63)

But when the conspirators come and he consents to assume leadership, he is on his idealist level again. He makes three mistakes: he will not allow an oath to be taken because that implies mutual mistrust; he will not include Cicero because he is a manoeuvring politician; and he will not allow Antony to be slain. This last was the fatal mistake, as Cassius sees. There is dramatic irony in Cassius' position; his own device recoils against him. He brought Brutus into the conspiracy to make it a success, and Brutus ruined it. Cassius has the necessary lack of scruple that makes conspirators, and he sees beneath Antony's mask of levity the "shrewd contriver" who may undo them all. Brutus has the weakness of most idealists; it never occurs to him that he may be making a mistake.

The Female Characters

After the conspirators leave, two concluding incidents of the scene, the intervention of Portia and the visit of Caius Ligarius, emphasize the high-mindedness of Brutus. The two women of the play, Portia and Calphurnia, are directly contrasted. Both are the wives of great men: but Calphurnia wishes to persuade her husband to forsake his greatness and descend to the level of her fears, while Portia seeks to be worthy to share her husband's greatness. To Portia it is the complete sympathy of mind with mind that makes a perfect marriage. It is the Stoic philosophy of Brutus that Portia wishes to emulate; the Stoics advocated fortitude and patient endurance of evil. Ultimately Portia finds that she has not the strength of mind to endure her husband's absence and the uncertainty of his fortunes, but she chooses a courageous way of taking her life.

Caesar is not the world conqueror of history: Shakespeare has debased him in order to enhance our sympathy with Brutus. He is appalled by storms and omens; he consults augurers, yields to his wife's fears after making a show of despising them, and then changes his mind again under the flattery of Decius Brutus. In the scene in the Capitol, when on the verge of being murdered, he is arrogant and bombastic. Refusing to repeal the banishment of Cimber's brother, he likens himself to the Northern Star for constancy and steadiness of purpose. In almost his last words he is comparing himself with the Gods:

> "Hence! Wilt thou lift up Olympus!" (III i 74)

This is the *hubris* of Greek tragedy, the arrogance that makes the Gods jealous of human greatness.

The Murder of Caesar

This event is the central crisis which turns events against the tragic hero. But in *Julius Caesar*, as later in *Macbeth*, the central climax has two peaks, the death of Caesar and the speech of Antony. Not until Antony has spoken does the ultimate failure of Brutus become apparent. With the death of Caesar, Antony enters the play as an effective character. He genuinely loves Caesar, but he knows that his life hangs on a mere thread, and that if he shows too much love for Caesar, he will be killed as dangerous; if, however, he shows too little, the hypocrisy will be transparent. So he delicately walks the tight-rope between these two extremes, and is given permission to speak in the funeral. Cassius protests, but Brutus, with characteristic lack of insight, thinks Antony's motives are as honest as his own, and declares that they too loved Caesar when they struck him. It is Brutus' words that Antony throws at Cassius when Cassius challenges his too outspoken grief.

> "Pardon me, Caius Cassius,
> The enemies of Caesar shall say this;
> Then, in a friend, it is cold modesty." (III i 211)

This is masterly interplay of character, and Cassius can only bite his lip in impotent rage. Antony is an even more shrewd politician than Cassius; he has a more generous mind, at any rate until the death of Caesar embitters him.

In the Forum, where the people are assembled, Brutus speaks in prose, Antony in verse. Verse is more capable of conveying deep feeling, and it is to the emotions of the crowd that Antony addresses himself. Brutus makes an intellectual appeal in precise prose. His argument proceeds by rhetorical questions and contrasted ideas of antithesis:

> "Had you rather Caesar were living and die all slaves, than that Caesar were dead, to live all free men?" (III ii 24)

and by climax:

> "As Caesar loved me, I weep for him; as he was fortunate, I rejoice at it; as he was valiant, I honour him; but, as he was ambitious, I slew him." (III ii 28)

The crowd are impressed by both his style and his obvious sincerity, but they completely fail to understand him. One of them shouts: "Let him be Caesar!", dramatic irony in four words. Brutus, who has killed Caesar to destroy Caesarism, finds that the spirit of Caesar lives on.

Antony shows courage and resource in facing a hostile mob. He begins quietly, briefly and swiftly undermining Brutus' argument with convincing

Shakespeare's birthplace at Stratford is visited by many tourists.

facts, but always assuring the crowd that Brutus is an honourable man, a concession that he is soon able to turn into biting sarcasm. Then comes the first appeal to passion, grief for a dead friend, an emotion that goes to the heart of everyone. He appeals to their self-interest by mentioning the will, making them more eager by refusing to read it. Brutus had spoken in the abstract, but Antony is visualizing and dramatizing all the time: he refers to Caesar's past victories for Rome, re-enacts the murder by pointing to dagger-slashes in the robe that wraps the body of Caesar. He has all the tricks of a demagogue at his finger-tips. Modestly (and ironically) he disclaims his powers of oratory; he is only an ordinary man like themselves. Finally he shows them the body of Caesar and works them up to such a pitch of frenzy that they are ready to set out on their work of destruction, and he has to remind them of the will he promised to read. The brief scene that follows, the murder of Cinna the Poet, registers the full effect of Antony's triumph. The touches of grim, ironical humour are Shakespeare's way of conveying the irrational behaviour of a mob.

Scenes Leading to the Death of Brutus

The crisis past, Act IV introduces events that are to lead to Brutus' death. The brief scene that introduces us to the new Triumvirate of Antony, Octavius and Lepidus in Rome shows a marked fall in the moral level of political atmosphere in Rome; Antony is cheating the people of the legacies in Caesar's will, and planning to discard Lepidus as soon as he has ceased to be useful; and there is a veiled hostility between Octavius and Antony.

Meanwhile, in Sardis, Brutus and Cassius are still uneasy yoke-fellows. In the need to raise money and an army, Cassius has not been scrupulous in his methods. Brutus is still applying his ideal principles of government, and will not compromise with the imperfect world he lives in, even when disaster threatens. The quarrel that ensues forebodes their final defeat, but Cassius' nature is changing: long contact with Brutus has given him some of Brutus' nobility of mind. He is about to die with Brutus and so he must share the sympathy that the audience gives to Brutus. In their long comradeship, Cassius has learned to love Brutus, and it is a grief to him that they are quarrelling, so he lets Brutus have his way. This is the prelude to defeat. Brutus sees the ghost of Caesar in his tent that night, a reminder that Caesar's spirit is still potent in the Roman world.

In these final acts of the play, Brutus does not meet impending disaster with frenzied action, as Macbeth does. Brutus' resistance to his fate lies in his own mind. Stoic fortitude does not desert him, even when he hears of Portia's death; and he still attempts to detach himself from pressing circumstances around him by reading a book before retiring to rest. He shows gentle sympathy towards his slave-boy Lucius, and the ghost of Caesar does not terrify him. Cassius, in contrast, shows the impatience of a practical man. He is an Epicurean who believes that the Gods are indifferent to human fate, and that a man has only himself to rely on; his only armour against disaster is suicide. It is characteristic of Cassius that he dies on a mistaken impulse. In the end Brutus compromises with his Stoic principles when he chooses the Roman way of suicide rather than the ignominy of returning to Rome as a prisoner. Both he and Cassius in their ruin are able to inspire heroic devotion in their followers. There is something of the nature of martyrdom in their deaths.

Macbeth, a Scottish Tragedy

As in *Julius Caesar*, the evil in *Macbeth* is murder; but the force of evil in this play is much more insistent. As represented by the Weird Sisters, it seems supernatural and Satanic, like a bird of prey extending its talons to clutch the soul of Macbeth and possess him. The play is more poetic than *Julius Caesar*, and oblique and indirect in its words and images, which are used with great atmospheric effect.

Images of blood and violence dominate the play. In the initial battle against the rebels, Macdonwald is "unseam'd from the nave to the chaps," the battlefield is "another Golgotha," and the sergeant who describes the battle is bleeding from his wounds. Macbeth and Lady Macbeth are preoccupied with blood in the scene following the murder of Duncan; Banquo's ghost has "gory locks," and the apparition in the cavern is a bloody child. "Here's the smell of the blood still," says Lady Macbeth in her sleep-walking; and finally the severed head of Macbeth is presented to victorious Malcolm by Macduff.

Sleep, or broken sleep, is another image persisting through the play. Sleep is a symbol of security, one of man's most precious boons, and it is thus that Macbeth sees it in the poetic line, "Sleep that knits up the ravell'd sleeve of care" (II ii 38). Duncan sleeps trustfully; Banquo cannot sleep for disturbing temptations of evil; Macbeth sees himself as a destroyer of sleep, and later speaks of the terrible dreams that haunt him nightly. Lady Macbeth's ultimate breakdown is brought about by "thick-coming fancies that keep her from her rest."

Much of the play takes place in darkness; the old conception peopled night with evil spirits, witchcraft and "pale Hecate's offerings," mortal and material dangers, and a belated traveller hurried to reach his inn. Often the darkness of a scene is the more felt by the presence of a light that comes to break it, such as Fleance's torch on two occasions, and Lady Macbeth's candle in the sleep-walking scene. The old man speaks of an uncanny darkness covering the land on the morning after Duncan's murder.

Moreover, here and there throughout the action of the play, short daylight scenes offer promise of relief from the tension of evil with their sunlight and happiness, but there is always some grim evil lurking behind the deceptive appearance. Such scenes are Duncan's arrival at Macbeth's castle, and when young Macduff precociously and charmingly chaffs his mother when they are both on the verge of being murdered.

Shakespeare's Use of Dramatic Irony

These two scenes furnish examples of dramatic irony, which Shakespeare uses throughout the play with tragic effect. Events work out to results that are directly opposite to what the characters expect. The audience realize the deception, and this heightens their feeling of the workings of fate. Macbeth says to Banquo, "Fail not our feast," and Banquo replies, "My Lord, I will not"; and sure enough he comes—as a ghost.

There are many questions in the text of *Macbeth*: all the characters ask them. It seems that they are all groping in a mysterious world of evil that baffles their understanding. The scene in which Macbeth and Banquo meet the witches is one long sequence of questioning. At the opening a witch asks, "Where hast thou been, sister?" and when Banquo enters, he asks, "How far is't call'd to Forres?" There follows the questioning of the witches by both men, and the questioning of Ross and Angus. Finally Macbeth, in his soliloquy, questions himself. Later, at a tense moment in the play, Macbeth and Lady Macbeth answer one another's questions with further questions:

People come from all parts of the world for Shakespeare's birthday.

This portrait of Shakespeare is probably the best likeness.

"*Macbeth:* I have done the deed. Didst thou not hear a noise?
Lady Macbeth: I heard the owl scream and the crickets cry.
Did not you speak?
Macbeth: When?
Lady Macbeth: Now.
Macbeth: As I descended?
Lady Macbeth: Ay.
Macbeth: Hark!
Who lies i' the second chamber?" (II ii 16)

All these short questions make us feel tense and involved, as we too await the answers.

Macbeth's Character

Macbeth is a much more complex character than Brutus. We give him our sympathy, not on moral grounds, but because we are given such an intimate insight into the workings of his mind. We see how it all comes about; we see the ordeal of an imaginative mind. Early scenes in Duncan's camp reveal Macbeth as a great warrior and loyal subject, held in high honour by both his king and his fellow thanes. This reputation he throws away, partly to satisfy ambition and partly because he is fascinated by the evil powers that address him in the person of the Weird Sisters. His character seems to undergo a revulsion, a sudden unaccountable swing-over to opposite characteristics. (Some critics think that Shakespeare was interested in this device as good theatre, rather than in close psychological analysis of character. It makes human behaviour mysterious, and is certainly a convenient way of accounting for the behaviour of Hamlet, Macbeth, Othello and perhaps Brutus.) When he is first accosted by the witches, Macbeth's mind leaps to the thought of foul play. Banquo says:

> "Good sir, why do you start, and seem to fear
> Things that do sound so fair?" (I iii 51)

Perhaps Macbeth had had the thought before: his first words when he enters this scene, "So fair and foul a day I have not seen," seem to echo the witches' incantation and suggest that he is sympathetic to them. In his soliloquy at the end of this scene, his imagination conjures up an image of Duncan murdered, and though he shrinks from it, he is fascinated by it. Here is a very subtle internal conflict. Duncan's naming of Malcolm as heir to his throne strengthens Macbeth's prompting to use foul play, and fate sends Duncan to his castle. But when Macbeth meets his wife, he is still full of doubt and uncertainty. His soliloquy when he comes from the banqueting hall (I vii 1-28) reveals his state of mind. Then, as subject and host of the king, his sense of loyalty protests, and the finer side of his nature realizes the saintliness of Duncan: Macbeth will feel, like Cain, the curse of his fellow-men upon him.

The Murder of Duncan

At this point he might have recoiled from his purpose, but Lady Macbeth's single-minded determination sways him again. In failing to withstand her taunt of cowardice (which he knows is untrue), he proves himself a moral coward; and he seizes upon Lady Macbeth's ready-made plan of action as an easy way out of the conflict in his mind. After this his resolution does not waver, but his sensitive imagination makes murder an ordeal. He sees a vision of the dagger, and the bell that his wife rings is a final stimulus. The torment of his mind during and following the murder is the protest of his better self: he has cut himself off from God's blessing, and has murdered sleep. The vision of blood on his hands will always persist. He sees these things figuratively and obliquely, as a poet sees truth, and his language is very exaggerated; but he communicates his tense emotion to his audience and so the statements appear natural. Already he wishes the deed undone, "Wake Duncan with thy knocking! I would thou could'st!" (II ii 75).

However, he is cool enough to play his part when Macduff discovers the murder, though there is a subtle double meaning in his words:

> "Had I but died an hour before this chance,
> I had liv'd a blessed time; for, from this instant,
> There's nothing serious in mortality." (II iii 89)

Macbeth as King

He becomes king, but is compelled to murder Banquo who threatens his security. He is now no longer a free agent, but a victim of circumstances he has created. He feels stronger for a second murder, but employs hired murderers in hope of avoiding imaginative horrors. "Thou canst not say I did it!" he says to Banquo's ghost in the banquet scene. Here it is not his finer nature protesting, but his fear for security. After the encounter with Banquo's ghost, he is stronger for further crimes: experience is blunting his imagination, and soon after the thanes have left the banquet he is plotting fresh murders. There can be no turning back:

> "I am in blood
> Stepp'd in so far, that, should I wade no more,
> Returning were as tedious as go o'er." (III iv 136)

He is now identifying himself with the evil forces that beckon him, but the feeling is beginning to grow that they are cheating him, and that security is always running before him. Therefore he will visit the witches again and extract from them a pledge of security.

The violence of Macbeth's language to the witches when he visits them in their cavern exhibits the egoistic self-centred mania of a complete tyrant: if he is to fall, he will bring the world down with him. He even demands that the seeds of life shall be destroyed, if necessary, for his satisfaction:

> ". . . though the treasure
> Of Nature's germens tumble all together,
> Even till destruction sicken; answer me
> To what I ask you." (IV i 58)

He hugs the security the witches offer him through apparitions, yet the vision of Banquo's seed as kings is a gap in his security that leaves a background of despair in his mind. "But no more sights!" he says: he feels strong enough now to go on alone, and orders the murder of Lady Macduff and her children, a completely irrational crime serving no purpose but blind revenge.

Scenes Leading to the Death of Macbeth

In Act V, when he waits in Dunsinane for his enemies, Macbeth no longer has a divided mind, and perhaps this is why daylight returns to the scenes.

He has completely integrated his mind to the evil forces that have for so long fascinated him:

> "I have almost forgot the taste of fears.
> The time has been my senses would have cool'd
> To hear a night-shriek, and my fell of hair
> Would at a dismal treatise rouse and stir
> As life were in't. I have supp'd full with horrors;
> Direness, familiar to my slaughterous thoughts,
> Cannot once start me." (V v 9)

Shakespeare, however, still gives us a fleeting glimpse of the man beneath the monster, conscious of the good things of life that he has thrown away:

> "My way of life
> Is fall'n into the sear, the yellow leaf;
> And that which should accompany old age,
> As honour, love, obedience, troops of friends,
> I must not look to have." (V iii 22)

However, he soon casts off these softer moods. When he hears of his wife's death, he dismisses it with a casual, "She should have died hereafter." When he hears that Birnam Wood is coming and realizes the equivocation or double meaning of the promises of the Apparitions, he realizes the destructive character of the evil forces whose instrument he has become:

> "(Life) is a tale
> Told by an idiot, full of sound and fury,
> Signifying nothing." (V v 26)

His courage is now the one thing that he believes in, and he dies displaying it.

Macbeth and Lady Macbeth

Macbeth is a dynamic character: we see his nature changing as it is moulded by his experience in the play. Lady Macbeth is likewise dynamic, but whereas Macbeth commences in weakness, disabled by his imagination, but becomes progressively stronger in purpose, Lady Macbeth is strong in her single-minded determination at the opening of the play, but breaks up and is overwhelmed by horrors she has passed through. So husband and wife cross one another in their development during the play: she ends where he began. Where Macbeth is imaginative, Lady Macbeth is literal-minded, and does not realize horror until she sees it. Her prayer to the spirits of evil to unsex her (I v 40), and the forced image of dashing out her baby's brains, seem to imply at least a subconsciousness of the womanly tenderness she is outraging. Nevertheless she is the driving-force that holds Macbeth to his purpose: she lashes him with her tongue, and breaks down his resistance by her taunt of cowardice, by challenging his love for her, and by producing the plan. She herself drugs the grooms, and it is then that she realizes her weakness:

> "Had he not resembled
> My father as he slept, I had done't." (II ii 12)

But she steels herself for her husband's sake, and it must have been a terrible ordeal to take back the daggers and smear the grooms with blood. This scene (II ii) is a conspicuous example of Shakespeare's workmanship; the dialogue admirably contrasts Macbeth's imaginative and his wife's literal mind. He hears a voice in his imagination, and she asks who spoke. He knows he can never cleanse his hands of blood, but she says, "A little water clears us of this deed." He develops strength as he meets Macduff, but she faints. When next we see her, after Macbeth is crowned king (III ii), she is disillusioned:

> "Nought's had, all's spent,
> Where our desire is got without content." (III ii 4)

Joining her, he expresses the same thought:

> "We have scotch'd the snake, not kill'd it."

Husband and wife are at the same point here, crossing one another's path. He goes on without her to fresh crimes, realizing she cannot help him.

The three Weird Sisters, from Shakespeare's Macbeth.

However, when the ghost of Banquo appears, she makes another supreme effort to save him; but when the ordeal is over, she is exhausted, and no longer lashes him with her tongue; she merely says,

"You lack the season of all natures, sleep." (III iv 141)

When next we see Lady Macbeth, she is sleep-walking. There are three obsessions in her mind: she is trying to cleanse her hands of blood; she is living over the past again; and she is revealing her horror at what has happened:

"The Thane of Fife had a wife: where is she now?" (V i 40)

The dramatic irony in this scene is intense: the woman who prayed for darkness now has light by her continually; her earlier remedy, "A little water clears us of this deed," has now become, "Not all the perfumes of Arabia will sweeten this little hand"; and when she says, "What need we fear who knows it, when none can call our power to account?" here she is, in her sleep-walking, called to account by her womanly nature, or by fate, or God, or what you will.

It remains to consider further features of the play and characters worthy of notice. The brief dramatic opening scene introduces the underlying influence in the play, and the witches' incantation denotes the subversal of moral values that is to be the theme. Duncan is a gracious king, saintly in his people's eyes, but far too trustful to those who immediately serve him.

The Minor Characters

The scene when Macbeth and Banquo first encounter the witches (I iii) should be studied for its dramatic development. Shakespeare takes the detail of witchcraft at the opening from contemporary superstition. Banquo, in his reaction to the witches, is a dramatic foil or contrast to Macbeth, interested but sceptical; when he sees the deep impression they have made on Macbeth, he gives him sane advice:

"And oftentimes, to win us to our harm,
The instruments of darkness tell us truths,
Win us with honest trifles, to betray's
In deepest consequence." (I iii 123)

The fact that we already know that Ross and Angus are going to announce fulfilment of the second prophecy gives suspense and dramatic power as we watch Macbeth's reaction. Macbeth's concluding soliloquy in this scene gives a first real clue to his mind.

Banquo, like Macbeth, cannot forget the witches; their prophecy slowly germinates in his mind. When he meets Macbeth in his castle just before the murder, he reveals that he is troubled with evil thoughts that keep him from rest. To Macbeth he is non-committal, but when the murder is discovered, he keeps silent and so in effect has sold himself to evil.

Macduff, on the other hand, is the most honest character in the play. He suspects Macbeth when he kills the grooms, and never disguises his suspicions. He refuses to go to the feast and puts his forthright patriotism before safety of wife and children. He is the primary agent of Macbeth's downfall.

In the scene at the English Court in Act IV, Malcolm never really takes hold of our imagination as a living character: rather he is a symbol of sovereignty, and the true royalty that must ultimately triumph. In Malcolm's real virtues and pretended vices, Shakespeare is pursuing his favourite theme of true and false kingship, connecting it vitally with a sound or diseased commonwealth. The interlude with the English doctor in this scene sets up the healing powers of King Edward as positive sovereignty in contrast to the negative, self-destructive sovereignty of Macbeth.

The scene (II iii) in which the Porter imagines himself the porter of Hell-gate is perhaps Shakespeare's most daring introduction of comic relief. It relieves the tense emotion of the previous scene, but there is a grim relevance in it: if he did but know it, the porter *is* porter of Hell-gate. The allusions in the porter's speech are topical.

The Tempest, Shakespeare's Final Play

In 1609 Shakespeare emerges from his tragic period to write four plays that are known as tragi-comedies. These plays commence with every appearance of developing into tragedies, but at a certain point in the action, good prevails over evil and they turn to a happy ending. *The Tempest* (1611) is the last of these plays and the concluding play of Shakespeare's career if we exclude *King Henry VIII* (1614), which was written in collaboration with John Fletcher.

Owing to the moral quality of its theme, some have looked upon *The Tempest* as a parable. Setting on the magic island, fairy characters, and features of music, singing, and dancing, give it a romantic and spectacular quality that resembles the character of the Masques, which had reached their most elaborate development in performances at the Court of James I. There is an unusual emphasis on setting in this play, and it may have been performed before scenery in the roofed Blackfriars Theatre, which had recently come into the possession of Shakespeare's company.

In the story a great wrong is committed, years follow, and then the former enemies come together again; but the feud is healed through forgiveness and reconciliation. The tempest that brings Prospero's former enemies within his power is the incident that links past and present. It occurs in the opening scene of the play, since the past is not dramatized but merely narrated in a long second scene. This has the effect of giving the play a classical construction: all events shown in the play take place in one place, within a period of three consecutive hours.

Narration of the Past

The narration in the second scene is made dramatic by Miranda's reaction to it: at first she is inattentive, distracted by distress for the people on the wrecked ship, but gradually she becomes more attentive as she realizes its significance for her. The language is difficult: in Shakespeare's latest style his mind seems to work too fast for his pen, and so the thoughts are condensed and packed into lines with the aid of ellipses (gaps in the sentences). The second part of the introduction, revealing what the island was like when Prospero arrived there, is made dramatic by Ariel's rebellion and by Caliban's grumbling.

Antonio's persuasion of Sebastian to kill Alonso, which might at first sight appear an irrelevance to the theme, also dramatizes the past because it enables us to feel the villainy in Antonio's character; so far we have taken it on hearsay from Prospero. These are technical points involved in adoption of the classical structure of the play. Features of the island can be gathered into a composite picture from indications dispersed through the play: caves by the sea-shore, the bay where the ship is hid, an "odd angle" of the isle where Ferdinand lands, a barren interior where Trinculo cannot find shelter, and pine woods where wolves howl.

Prospero the Magician

Prospero, as a magician, is lifted above his fellow-men. Such a man might be tempted to use his magic to wreak revenge on his enemies. Some conflict of mind is at times evident in Prospero, but there is not much impression of internal struggle conveyed. Almost like a god, he is lifted above mortal weakness by his moral purpose; but forgiveness cannot be granted gratuitously, and must be earned. Therefore, Alonso, the arch-enemy with whom Prospero desires reconciliation, undergoes suffering—the shipwreck, apparent loss of his son by drowning, and a feast spread by spirits and then snatched away. Alonso at once connects these sufferings with his past sin: unlike Antonio and Sebastian, he has a conscience and so can come to repentance and reconciliation with Prospero. Prospero states his moral purpose to Ariel:

> "Though with their high wrongs I am struck to the quick,
> Yet with my nobler reason 'gainst my fury
> Do I take part: the rarer action is
> In virtue than in vengeance: they being penitent,
> The sole drift of my purpose doth extend
> Not a frown further." (V i 25)

This is the main theme of the play: Gonzalo states in symbolic terms the philosophic conception that out of the conflict of good and evil has emerged a higher good:

> "Was Milan thrust from Milan, that his issue
> Should become kings of Naples?" (V i 205)

The plot against Alonso's life by Antonio and Sebastian doubles the theme of murder, and then the conspiracy of Caliban and Stephano triplicates it. This has the effect of generalizing murder as a common ingredient of evil in human nature. It is prevalence of this evil that temporarily depresses the optimistic mind of Prospero in a speech that, in its imagery and word-music, is one of the peaks of poetry in the play, but which in its conclusion despairs of a divine pattern in human affairs:

> ' We are such stuff
> As dreams are made on, and our little life
> Is rounded with a sleep." (IV 1 156)

Prospero will recover from this mood: he goes on to apologize to Ferdinand for it as a weakness.

Ferdinand and Miranda

Reconciliation is assisted by the betrothal of Ferdinand and Miranda, whose love heals the feuds of their elders. Miranda is a high-born girl brought up in completely natural surroundings: in her, Shakespeare is indirectly emphasizing the artificiality of civilization as he was in Perdita in his previous play, *The Winter's Tale*. Perdita, daughter of a king, was brought up among simple shepherds. Miranda is entirely free from the conventions and hypocrisies of Court life: she expresses her love naturally, and even proposes marriage to Ferdinand without any loss of modesty (III i). Ferdinand finds the experience refreshing after the blandishments of Court ladies in Naples.

Ariel and Caliban

Ariel, servant of Prospero's magic, is a spirit of the air, and therefore akin to moral good in the elemental theory of spirits. He is a good servant but inclined to rebel owing to his instinct for freedom. Like Puck, Ariel is mischievous and likes a practical joke, but he goes beyond Puck in acquiring human feeling, affection for his master, and sympathy for human suffering.

In so far as Caliban is a spirit (his father was a demon), he is the opposite to Ariel, a creature of the earth element and therefore evil. He is ungrateful, lazy and gross, though he has a case in claiming the island. Caliban is a natural savage where Stephano is a civilized savage; Stephano is a degenerate who has absorbed the vices of civilization, but Caliban's emotional and intellectual powers are unimpaired and capable of rich development, and he

Early Mystery plays were acted on rough wooden platforms like the one shown above; these platforms, or "pageants," were wheeled from one spot to another. The curtained-off area beneath the platform was used as a dressing-room. The earliest theatres (see the cut-away model below) were only partly roofed, so performances could take place only in the summer and during daylight hours.

Later, theatres were built with a roof, so that plays could be acted during bad weather. Theatres were closed by the Puritans, but reopened after the Restoration in 1660. The Duke's Theatre (above), built in London in 1671, introduced the elaborate proscenium arch framing the stage on three sides. The Georgian Theatre Royal in Bristol (below) was built a century later, in 1766.

Drury Lane Theatre, London (above), rebuilt in 1812, was lit by candles, but gas lighting was installed five years later. The Victorian Haymarket Theatre (below), built in London in 1880, was the first to have a proscenium arch surrounding the stage on all four sides, like a picture frame. "Stalls" now replaced the "pit", and a dress circle ousted most, though not all, of the boxes.

Since 1945 several new theatres have been built in England. The Belgrade Theatre at Coventry (above) follows the traditional type of stage; but the Chichester Theatre (below) seats the audience on three sides of the projecting stage, which in some ways resembles the Elizabethan theatre stage—this arrangement gives the actors greater freedom of movement and puts them in closer touch with the audience.

is far superior to Stephano in intelligence. He becomes the brains of a conspiracy against Prospero and is not deceived by the rich robes that Prospero hangs out to distract the plotters. In the end he sees through Stephano:

"What a thrice-double ass
Was I, to take this drunkard for a god." (V i 295)

Although at present he has virtually no moral sense, Caliban has the future on his side. Apart from the deformity of his figure, which Shakespeare uses dramatically to suggest his primitive mind, he has the psychological qualities of a savage, particularly a feeling for nature and music which redeems him:

"Be not afeard: the isle is full of noises,
Sounds and sweet airs, that give delight, and hurt not.
Sometimes a thousand twangling instruments
Will hum about mine ears; and sometime voices,
That, if I then had wak'd after long sleep,
Will make me sleep again: and then, in dreaming,
The clouds methought would open and show riches
Ready to drop upon me; that, when I wak'd,
I cried to dream again." (III ii 130)

Here, in The Tempest, *Prospero uses his magic powers for the last time.*

Shakespeare's understanding and sympathy were never greater. He probably gathered material for Caliban from accounts that Gentlemen-Adventurers brought of native inhabitants in newly-discovered lands. The atmosphere of oversea adventure runs through the play: Ariel's "still-vex'd Bermoothes" are the Bermuda islands recently discovered by Sir Thomas Gates in his voyages to Virginia. Strange noises at night had made sailors associate the islands with magic. Looked at in this light, one can feel that Shakespeare was aware, in his treatment of Caliban, of problems inherent in the white man's first contacts with coloured races. The first influence on the native was white man's liquor, and in Virginia colonists had been very dependent on natives, who pointed out natural resources of the land:

> "I'll show thee the best springs; I'll pluck thee berries;
> I'll fish for thee, and get thee wood enough." (II ii 150)

CONTEXT QUESTIONS

(A) "It must be by his death: and, for my part,
I know no personal cause to spurn at him,
But for the general. He would be crown'd:
How that might change his nature, there's the question:
It is the bright day that brings forth the adder;
And that craves wary walking. Crown him?—that!
And then, I grant, we put a sting in him
That at his will he may do danger with.
The abuse of greatness is when it disjoins
Remorse from power." (*Jul. Caes.* II i 10)

(i) Who is the speaker? When and where is he speaking?
(ii) Explain the appropriateness of the metaphor of the adder.
(iii) Re-write in your own words the last two lines.
(iv) Give the meaning in this passage of *the general* and *would be.*
(v) What light does this passage throw upon the character of the speaker?

(B) *Antonio:* "But O! how vile an idol proves this god.
Thou hast, Sebastian, done good feature shame.
In nature there's no blemish but the mind;
None can be call'd deform'd but the unkind:
Virtue is beauty, but the beauteous evil
Are empty trunks o'erflourish'd by the devil."
(*Twelfth N*, III iv 349)

(i) Briefly describe the situation when Antonio speaks these words.
(ii) Why does Antonio describe Sebastian as a god, and why does he say that this god has now proved to be an idol?

(iii) What does Viola deduce from Antonio's words?

(iv) What other *major* characters are present, and what is the effect of Antonio's words upon them, with, briefly, what further results?

(v) Paraphrase the second and third lines of the passage.

(C) *Henry:* "Alas, your too much love and care of me
Are heavy orisons 'gainst this poor wretch!
If little faults proceeding on distemper
Shall not be wink'd at, how shall we stretch our eye
When capital crimes, chew'd, swallow'd, and digested,
Appear before us?" (*King Henry V*, II ii 52)

(i) Re-write the passage in your own words.

(ii) Who is "the poor wretch," and what was Henry going to do to him?

(iii) To whom is Henry speaking, and why are his words sarcastic?

(iv) What trick does he go on to play on these men, and with what effect?

(v) What light does this passage throw on the character of the King?

(The student should select further passages and devise his own questions.)

ESSAY QUESTIONS

The Merchant of Venice

1. Describe *either* the scene in which Antonio negotiates his loan with Shylock, *or* Shylock's duel with Portia in the trial scene. How far do you sympathize with Shylock in the scene you have selected?

2. Show how the three suitors who take their choice of the caskets indicate their characters by the choice each makes.

Twelfth Night

1. Contrast the behaviour of Orsino, Olivia, Viola and Sebastian as lovers.

2. Give a clear and concise account of *one* of the following scenes and show briefly how it affects the development of the play:

(*a*) the scene in which Malvolio interrupts the revelry of Sir Toby, Sir Andrew and the Fool;

(*b*) the garden scene in which Malvolio finds the letter;

(*c*) the scene of the duel between Sir Andrew and Cesario.

Richard II

1. Describe *one* incident from the play in which Richard appears in an unsympathetic light, and *one* in which you sympathize with him. Account for the difference in your reaction to these two incidents.

2. Select *three* of the following characters, describe the part played by each of them, and show their dramatic importance in the play: Aumerle, the Bishop of Carlisle, Northumberland, the First Gardener.

King Henry V

1. Show how Shakespeare, in his picture of war in *King Henry V*, has contrasted the heroic and the unheroic.

2. Give an account of *two* scenes in the French camp before Agincourt. What dramatic purpose is served by these scenes?

Julius Caesar

1. Contrast the characters of Brutus and Cassius. Do you notice any change in Cassius' character in the last two acts of the play?

2. By close reference to the first part of the play, describe the development of the plot to murder Caesar. What warnings of his danger are left unheeded by Caesar?

Macbeth

1. Describe the second meeting of Macbeth with the Weird Sisters, and the effect of this on Macbeth's thoughts and actions during the remaining scenes of the play.

2. Describe *two* of the following scenes and estimate their importance in the development of the play:

(*a*) Macbeth's preparations for the murder of Banquo;

(*b*) the scene at Macduff's castle in which his wife and children are murdered;

(*c*) the scene between Macduff, Ross and the old man, following the discovery of the murder of Duncan.

The Tempest

1. By describing and commenting on their first appearances in Act I and their conversations with Prospero, contrast the characters of Ariel and Caliban.

2. With close and varied reference to the text, write a character sketch of *either* Miranda *or* Alonso.

CHAPTER 7

MILTON

MILTON is perhaps the most isolated of our poets: his work has little relationship to that of poets writing in his time. He owes something to Spenser and to Shakespeare and, above all, to his knowledge of Greek and Latin verse: but these sources of his style develop into a product that is peculiarly his own; he rises, a solitary but majestic figure, in the middle of the seventeenth century.

Milton's poems are closely related to his personal life and to public events of his time. He lived through the Puritan Revolution, of which he was, in some ways, the poet. The Puritans have not produced many poets. The musicians, painters and poets were among the Royalists, and we shall see particularly in his early work to what extent Milton's heart, if not his mind, was with them. A poet rises to his highest theme through an effort to resolve some conflict in his own mind; and in Milton's case we shall see how the poet within him, sensitive to the pagan and mythological inspiration of Greek and Roman poetry, to music and the beauty of nature, meets in his

Milton spent six years at Horton, Bucks, where his mother is buried.

poetry the disciplined and exacting thought and ideals of the Puritan, and is merged and reconciled with them to form one harmonious and very exalted view of life.

Milton's personal life was not eventful. Born in London in 1608, he went to St. Paul's School and later to Christ's College, Cambridge. Here he was nicknamed "The Lady of Christ's" owing to the delicate and feminine cast of his features. Before he left Cambridge he had written two significant pieces: *At a Solemn Music* and *Ode on the Morning of Christ's Nativity.*

Milton's father was a solicitor in easy circumstances, and he was in very close sympathy with his son's literary ambitions. This harmony between father and son was very significant in Milton's development: as a result of it, he was not pressed to adopt a career. When Milton left Cambridge University in 1629, his father had retired to the Buckinghamshire village of Horton in beautifully-wooded Chiltern country. Here Milton lived until 1637, the only time in his life when he was living under the direct influence of nature. Here he found the opportunity for strenuous leisure that his mind required.

Milton's Early Poems

In these years he wrote *L'Allegro*, *Il Penseroso*, *Comus* and *Lycidas.* If the Nativity ode is linked with these, we have a formal ode, two lyrics, a dramatic piece and an elegy. Milton is clearly experimenting in various forms of poetry to develop his poetic art. He had no thought of publishing them (they were eventually published in 1645); his mind was already directed by a feeling that he was destined to write a great poem which would (in the later language of *Paradise Lost*) "justify the ways of God to men," and he devoted himself to preparation for this destiny with all a Calvinist's exacting discipline. A poem *On His Being Arrived to the Age of Twenty-Three* should be read in connexion with this phase of his life: he has no definite results of his training to show to the world; his contemporaries may have entered professions and he is feeling their implied criticism of his "idleness"; but in the last six lines that form the sestet, his feeling that he is destined for great things reassures him.

In 1638 Milton left England to go on a Grand Tour of Europe: he spent sixteen months in Italy, meeting scholars and absorbing all the influences of Renaissance art.

Milton's Political Career

In 1640 the approaching outbreak of civil war in England hastened his return: he linked himself ardently to the Puritan cause, and for some fifteen years politics kept him from poetry. During this period his only poetic writing was a number of sonnets reflecting closely upon his own life, a kind of poetic diary. After the execution of King Charles in 1649, Oliver Cromwell appointed Milton to be Latin Secretary to the newly-formed Council of State, which made Milton virtually Cromwell's Foreign Secretary. He also wrote numerous pamphlets for the Republican government in the war of words that followed the death of the king. In 1652, under stress of all these activities, Milton went blind. Under the shock of this, he composed his most moving sonnet, *On His Blindness.* He still believed that God had designed his life to find its fulfilment in writing a great poem to make God's purposes clear to men. Why then had God allowed him to go blind? However, before the Restoration of the monarchy in 1660, with the help of his daughters and personal secretaries, he had made a beginning upon *Paradise Lost.* Perhaps, with his eyes blind to earthly reality around him, he was better able to conceive in his imagination the unearthly and fantastic scenery of his Heaven and Hell.

At the Restoration Milton was imprisoned, and his life may have been in danger; but after a short time he was released and lived an obscure life in London for the remainder of his days. The causes he had fought for were in ruin and his enemies triumphant around him; yet in those years he was doing his greatest work. He wrote the major part of *Paradise Lost*, and followed it with *Paradise Regained*, a natural sequel to it and yet ineffective in comparison. Milton's last poem, *Samson Agonistes*, which he wrote in the form of a Greek play, is full of reflection on Milton's own life in these later years: as Samson sits "eyeless in Gaza," captive among his enemies, he shakes off his despair as a feeling takes hold of him that God's purposes are still working through his life; Milton was not the man to doubt his views or his cause because they had come to disaster in the world of men. Milton died in 1674.

Ode on the Morning of Christ's Nativity

This poem is a regular ode written in the form of a hymn and introduced by a brief Proem, or Preface, which states the paradox, or seeming contradiction, that shapes the poem and much of the contrasted imagery: this humble babe lying in a lowly stable is God Himself, Creator of Nature and the vast forces of the Universe, Creator of Man and therefore Ruler of Princes, and the Bringer of Peace.

The complex pattern of the eight-line stanza of the hymn shows the influence of the Elizabethan poet Spenser. The rhyme-scheme is AAB,CCB,DD. Thus rapidly-recurring rhymes mingle with more distant rhymes, an effect which is heightened by varying length of line. The longer alexandrine of the last line (extending to twelve syllables) brings the verse-paragraph to a gradual stately close.

The cadence or rhythm of the poem is almost uniformly smooth, with an occasional gathering together of accented syllables to give spondaic, or hammering, effect where this suits imagery or theme. (You will recall that a spondee is a foot with two equally-stressed beats.)

> "He saw a greater Sun appear
> Than his bright thròne or bùrning àxle-trèe could beàr."

There is complete orchestration of sound in the poem: gentler violins, the thunder of brass, and woodwind leading the deeper harmonies. All these effects are a matter of choice of words, variety of vowel sounds and consonant-grouping:

> "Peor and Baalim
> Forsake their temples dim."

Rhythm and music are linked very intimately with the theme, and must be felt if the full meaning of the poem is to be realized.

Milton is thinking in images in this poem, conveying his thought and feeling to us in a succession of word-pictures. The imagery is very varied: snow covering the earth, shepherds on the lawn, and the Virgin and Babe in a stable require homely and simple imagery. Some imagery is used symbolically: "the hookèd chariot" and the trumpet suggest the ferocity and terror of war. So the imagery in the poem ranges from the simple and quietly beautiful to the majestic and sublime in such a passage as the second stanza of the Proem.

Milton's Use of Music and Nature in the *Nativity* Ode

In the middle section of the poem, Milton links music very intimately with his theme. The song of the angels is conceived as the music of the spheres, the music that the stars were believed to make as they revolved in their nine concentric spheres round the earth.

Now, at the birth of Christ, the music of the spheres rings out again to create, not physical laws of matter, but moral law in the heart of man, to promote harmony and love among men, which was the ultimate purpose of creation. So, when Christ was born, human life seemed suddenly to leap forward to perfection, but this was only a glimpse of the ultimate redemption that lay open to men now that Satan's power was chained.

In the *Nativity* ode, Nature is in sympathy with the birth of Christ. The snow is earth's garment of repentance; sun and stars pay homage. Nature as well as man is at peace, and "the birds of calm," kingfishers, show their sympathy with the theme of birth by "brooding on the calmèd wave." When the music of the angels sounded,

> "(Nature) was almost won
> To think her part was done."

Nature is here the principle which informs all matter and all forms of life, and is conceived as herself moving slowly and laboriously towards ultimate

In Ludlow Castle, now a picturesque ruin, Comus *was first performed.*

perfection. When, in the last part of the poem, Milton banishes the pagan gods before the power of Christ, these are the gods who, to the early mind, presided over the processes of nature. Milton's mind responds to the beauty of the myths that inspired Greek poetry and peopled the earth with greater gods like Apollo of the Delphic Oracle, and also with lesser deities, nymphs of the streams and dryads of the woods.

L'Allegro and *Il Penseroso*

These poems are the first-fruits of Milton's life at Horton. They are a pair of lyrics, written with deliberately contrasted imagery to present in their picture of the light-hearted man and the melancholy man, not two different personalities, but rather the same person, Milton himself, in two contrasted moods. Thus they constitute two poetic essays in autobiography. The metre is the iambic line of four feet (i.e. each foot has an unstressed beat followed by a stressed beat), rhyming in couplets, and sometimes varied by the trochaic measure (a stressed beat followed by an unstressed beat). It is a metre rapid in movement and buoyant in spirit.

Personification

The two poems are parallel in structure: thus a brief introduction opens each poem banishing the opposite quality; then, in a brief mythological passage, the mood of the poem is personified and its descent traced from Greek gods. The care-free country life described in *L'Allegro* is very aptly derived from the warm West Wind wooing the Goddess of Dawn, but the student's mood in *Il Penseroso* is traced to Vesta, Goddess of Wisdom. Then the personification becomes more modern: Mirth is "laughter holding both his sides," and we see the complete figure in a single line; the corresponding figure in *Il Penseroso* is the pensive nun, "sober, steadfast, and demure . . . with even step and musing gait."

In *L'Allegro* Milton is a man of scholarly and cultured tastes relaxing in the countryside: in *Il Penseroso* the melancholy mood is that of a studious and meditative mind (a meaning that the word retained through the eighteenth century).

Royalist v. Puritan

In this pair of poems Milton might be balancing Humanism (delight in the beauty and wonder of the things of this world), which was the Royalist way of life, against the more Puritan ideals, and settling his choice on the Puritan. Nevertheless, *Il Penseroso* is just as much a poem of the feelings and senses as *L'Allegro*: the poet responds to the beauty of nature, music and philosophy with a deeper, richer poetry than *L'Allegro* produces. There is more atmosphere in the imagery of *Il Penseroso*.

So the poems are developed through a series of directly-contrasted features. *L'Allegro* is a poem of day-time, sunshine and the lark; in *Il Penseroso* the poet prefers night-time, moonlight and the nightingale. In *L'Allegro* the poet seeks company: the hunt is out; he watches peasants at their work in the fields; and on the holy day he is a detached spectator of their simple and care-free sports and dancing. When evening comes, he follows them to their cottages to listen with a scholar's interest to their simple tales of English folk-lore which embody country superstitions. In *Il Penseroso* the poet avoids company and sunlight: either he withdraws into the solitude of his own study, or, if the sun is flaring, he seeks some shady grove.

The Poet at Night

The poet in both poems comes to a city at night-time. In *L'Allegro* he delights in the masques, tournaments and pageantry that lingered on in the tradition of medieval chivalry at Court in Milton's younger days. He visits a theatre to see Ben Jonson's intellectual comedies of wit, or Shakespeare's comedies of the English country scene.

By contrast, in *Il Penseroso*, the poet burns the midnight oil in the solitude of "some high lonely tower" where he studies the stars and philosophy, communing across the ages with Plato's mind by reading his treatise on immortality. He now exchanges the comedies of *L'Allegro* for the tragedies of Greek dramatists, or perhaps Shakespeare's tragedies ("the buskined stage") which rival Greek drama in their treatment of character and fate. He regrets the unfinished work of Chaucer in his Squire's Tale, where romantic middle-eastern names give the verse a rich and haunting quality;

and he refers briefly to the moral allegory of Spenser's *Faerie Queene.* These are some of the literary pleasures of a studious mind.

The Poet and Music

Both poems close on the theme of music. In *L'Allegro* the music is "soft Lydian airs," i.e. light, tuneful music: in a long passage of many lines, sense flows over the rhymes without a pause, representing in its sustained rhythm the very music that Milton is describing:

"In notes, with many a winding bout
Of linkèd sweetness long drawn out."

In *Il Penseroso* the poet comes again to music as an expression of his mood; this time he listens to the deep solemn music of the organ blending with the beauty of Gothic architecture and the colour of stained-glass windows.

The classical allusion to Orpheus descending into the Underworld to win back his wife Eurydice from the dead by the power of his music is used with much the same force in the two poems, perhaps serving to remind us that the two moods are not so far removed from each other after all.

Lycidas and the Pastoral Convention

In 1637 Milton experimented in the form of the Elegy: he was stimulated to compose *Lycidas* by the death of Edward King who was drowned off Anglesey. King had been a contemporary of Milton at Cambridge; he was a fellow poet, and a man with Puritan leanings who was designed for the priesthood. *Lycidas* is a difficult poem: different readers will appreciate it at different levels. It is possible to enjoy it merely as a lament for Edward King, and also for the poetry of its natural descriptions. Many will appreciate its reflection of the personal problems of Milton; but only a few will pick up all the echoes of Greek and Latin poets, of Theocritus, Virgil and Horace, that Milton introduces into the poem.

The Pastoral Convention

The poem is written in the Pastoral Convention. A Greek poet, Theocritus, had written poems which were a direct, if idealized, portrayal of Sicilian shepherd life. These shepherds lived in Arcady, an ideal world: in the leisure of watching their flocks, they composed love idylls to their shepherdesses, and sang lyrics to the accompaniment of a flute made from an oaten straw cut in the fields. They also composed elegies on suitable occasions. Virgil followed Theocritus in writing this kind of verse, "eclogues" of country life as he saw it round his home on the River Mincius; and this form of writing became a convention, an agreed device of Renaissance poets to represent the characters in their poems as shepherds and shepherdesses, to give them the names of the shepherds of Theocritus (which Milton had already done in *L'Allegro*), and to place them in a pastoral setting. We have seen Elizabethan poets adopting this device, Sidney to some extent in his *Arcadia* and Spenser in his *Shepherd's Calendar*.

To some tastes the Pastoral Convention will appear very artificial, but by using it Milton gains both a colourful natural setting for his theme and an opportunity to introduce imagery that enhances the poetry and blends naturally with the copious classical mythology he wishes to employ. By adopting this method in preference to a more realistic approach, Milton gives his theme a universal quality: it ceases to be merely a story of the incidental death of a man named Edward King, and becomes a lament upon the theme of the waste and tragedy of death in youth. If the student compares this oblique and figurative approach of poetry with the literal and more personal approach of, say, the novel, he will have realized one essential difference between the methods of prose and those of poetry.

Analysis of *Lycidas*

At the opening of the poem, the poet comes to pluck laurels as his emblem of mourning, and invokes the Muses ("Sisters of the Sacred Well") to inspire him in his lament. He then goes on to describe in pastoral terms his life with Edward King at Cambridge, when together they wrote their poems, and their tutor ("old Damoetas") criticized and encouraged their youthful efforts. In the passage that follows, Nature is portrayed as being in sympathy with human events, and three brief similes from nature emphasize the theme of death in youth:

> "As killing as the canker to the rose,
> Or taint-worm to the weanling herds that graze,
> Or frost to flowers, that their gay wardrobe wear
> When first the white-thorn blows:
> Such, Lycidas, thy loss to shepherd's ear."

Milton transfers the nymphs quite naturally from Greece to Snowdon and Anglesey, and the introduction of a mother's grief in the allusion to Calliope mourning for Orpheus has the universalizing effect already mentioned.

In the procession of figures that come to pronounce upon the death of Lycidas, Milton mingles Greek gods with a figure of his own (Father Camus, representing the University) and with St. Peter, whose presence seems quite natural in this strange company. The poet associates these Greek and Christian conceptions because in his mind they are equivalents: he ignores time and place, and fastens on the universal. St. Peter comes to denounce the English clergy of the time and thus introduces a theme of religious controversy. This lends itself to the Pastoral Convention because Christ, in the Gospel of St. John (Chapter 10), likens himself to the Good Shepherd.

To avoid the Great Plague of 1665, Milton and his wife and three daughters fled from London to this cottage at Chalfont St. Giles.

Again, by an abrupt transition, Milton reverts to Nature: in a passage of sustained beauty the flowers come in procession to mourn for Lycidas:

> "Bid Amaranthus all his beauty shed,
> And Daffadillies fill their cups with tears,
> To strow the laureate hearse where Lycid lies."

In order to gain respite from his grief, Milton indulges a fancy that Lycidas is exploring the ocean with all a poet's wonder at this new and strange beauty. Finally a firmer consolation is reached in the Christian hope of resurrection. In this concluding passage, allusion to the New Jerusalem and the Saints in Heaven as presented in the Book of Revelation (Chapter 7) mingles with the Greek conception of the Elysian Fields as the Abode of the Blest, another fusion of Greek and Christian themes.

Milton's Personal Problems

In the above analysis of *Lycidas*, one important passage has been omitted:

> "Alas! what boots it with incessant care
> To tend the homely slighted shepherd's trade,
> And strictly meditate the thankless Muse?"

This was perhaps the primary problem of Milton's earlier life, and we have already seen it reflected in the sonnet he wrote *On His Being Arrived to the Age of Twenty-Three*. The death of Edward King had emphasized in Milton's mind the chance and accident of life that rides rough-shod over ambition, desire for fame, and the long-term purposes that a man envisages in his mind. The passage is thus linked intimately to the central theme of the poem, waste of youthful powers by accidental death. Milton asks himself whether he is wise to plan his life for fulfilment of some ultimate lofty purpose that he may never live to achieve. Would it not be better to set his sights lower and write poems of lesser scope which might win immediate success, like the love-lyrics of Court poets of his time:

> "To sport with Amaryllis in the shade,
> Or with the tangles of Neaera's hair?"

As in the sonnet, he is reassured by his religious faith. Apollo God of Poetry, Jove and Jehovah are here all assimilated into one: God assures Milton that a man's achievement does not lie in worldly success or the verdict of public opinion ("broad rumour"); to seek such fame is the "last infirmity of noble mind." Rather a man's reward is the assessment that God puts on his work in the light of eternity. The passage is written in pastoral terms and is very oblique in conveying the thought.

The passage denouncing the English clergy of the time is also intimately linked with Milton's religious views. The worldliness and ignorance of many of the clergy offended Milton: there was a lack of spiritual power, and their sermons failed to teach true doctrine, so the people fell a ready prey to Jesuit priests who were working in secret throughout the land to win converts to Rome ("the grim wolf with privy paw"). The passage is bitter and full of argument. Puritans were still within the Established Church, and Milton feels that the spiritual force of a man like Edward King would have been a valuable quality in the decadent church of his time.

The basis of the verse is the heroic deca-syllabic (ten-syllable) line, but Milton uses it with considerable freedom, varying the length of line at will by introducing shorter lines which have the effect of unexpectedly hastening the rhyme. He uses rhymes with the same freedom: some occur in alternating lines, some in couplets; and occasionally a rhyme will produce a distant effect by echoing back across a number of lines. Milton is so much a master of rhythm that he can adopt this freedom without any intrusion of false cadences.

The Sonnets of Milton

Milton enlarged the scope of the sonnet by breaking away from the love interest for which the Elizabethans had reserved it. He also abandoned the Elizabethan form of sonnet, adopting the Italian or Petrarchan model in which the fourteen iambic pentameters (lines of five feet, each an unstressed beat followed by a stressed one) are divided into octet (eight lines) and sestet (six lines). The octet consists of two closed quatrains (groups of four lines), the rhyming sounds being identical in the two quatrains—ABBA, ABBA. The sestet divides into two tercets (groups of three lines) introducing three rhyming sounds (sometimes only two)—CDE, CDE or DCE, etc. The octet generally states a topic or situation, and the sestet moves to a concluding thought upon it; but frequently the content of a sonnet moves independently of the technical framework, developing from opening to close in a single sweep of language. The sonnet thus becomes a most disciplined form of poetic utterance, a reflective and intellectual type of poem.

Milton's Occasional Sonnets

The occasional pieces (i.e. inspired by a special occasion) written by Milton during the Civil War (between king and Parliament) and Commonwealth that followed, refer to political events and pay tribute to public figures of the time; but they always concentrate upon some personal conviction of Milton's, political or religious (the terms meant virtually the same in Milton's time). In his sonnet dedicated to Cromwell, after paying tribute to his victories, Milton pleads with him to save the nation from the tyrannies that had arisen in the war of Puritan sects that followed the execution of the king. Each sect strove to set up its own views as an infallible authority:

> "Help us to save free conscience from the paw
> Of hireling wolves whose gospel is their maw."

In thus pleading for toleration and freedom of mind, Milton is far ahead of his time: he hated all forms of persecution, and his most notable sonnet on topical events is that on the massacre of the Waldensians by the Piedmontese in Savoy, which is a trumpet-note of denunciation.

Milton's verse in this sonnet is "the organ-voice of England": the variety of the deep open vowel sounds gives a rich and solemn music to the words, which are simple as befitting such an occasion, and yet rise to the grand style. The language is biblical, appropriate to the metaphor of the sheep and the echo of the Parable of the Sower. The sonnet illustrates Milton's masterly use of overflow, with the caesura (or sense-pause) falling at different places in different lines. The division between Octet and Sestet is ignored, and the rhymes ring solemnly in the ear as the long-sustained sentences pass over them.

Sonnets About Himself

The most interesting sonnets are autobiographical pieces reflecting various facets of Milton's mind in his day-to-day personal life. The early sonnet *To the Nightingale* is a youthful piece, interesting as giving a hint of the strength of passion that is normally concealed by Milton's severe self-control. *When the Assault was Intended to the City* reads rather like an exercise: it was expected that the king's army would attack London, and the poet pleads with a soldier to spare his life and house, giving classical examples of how soldiers have recognized that there is a natural alliance between soldier and poet, since the poet immortalizes the deeds of the soldier. The sonnets *To Cyriac Skinner* and *To Mr. Lawrence* show Milton in a mood of relaxation: he urges Cyriac, whom he is coaching, to put away his books and take a half-holiday; Lawrence shares Milton's cultural and artistic tastes, and the friends are relaxing in a long winter evening with a meal of delicate food and wine which is followed by classical chamber music. These are two of the lightest pieces Milton wrote, and warn us against regarding Milton as invariably severe in his way of life. The style cannot be called colloquial but they are the nearest approach to informality that Milton's rather formal mind allowed him to make.

In striking contrast are two sonnets, poignant in their pathos. *On His Blindness* is written with biblical simplicity, and contains biblical allusion: his poetic talent under the handicap of blindness is compared with the talent entrusted to the unprofitable servant of the parable in the Gospels; it is likely to be buried in the ground profitless. The sestet of this sonnet contains one of the humblest passages that Milton wrote: no man is indispensable to the purposes of God, who has His angels to perform His commands; God accepts the service of those who, though unable to aspire to tangible achievement, wait upon the will of God, whatever it may contain for them. The quiet pathos of *On His Deceased Wife* is heightened as we reflect that Milton is seeing in an inward vision a woman whom he never saw in actual reality. The final elusiveness of the vision conveys the acute sense of isolation that blindness brought to Milton:

> "But O as to embrace me she inclined,
> I wak'd, she fled, and day brought back my night."

Paradise Lost (Books 1 and 2)

Milton's models for *Paradise Lost* were Homer's *Iliad* and *Odyssey*, Virgil's *Aeneid*, and Dante's *Divine Comedy*. An epic poem was originally a long narrative poem dealing with the legendary beginnings of a nation, in which characters assume heroic proportions and gods mingle with men in the story. Milton had toyed with the idea of an epic poem on King Arthur, the natural epic hero of England. But ultimately he adopted the story of the Archangel Lucifer's rebellion against God in Heaven, his fall into Hell as Satan with the archangels who had joined him in rebellion, the creation of Earth by God to compensate Himself for the loss of the angels, and the plot of Satan to win Man to Hell and thus to rob God of His new creation. Thus the theme of *Paradise Lost* is the Fall of Man, and instead of the beginnings of a nation, Milton gives us the beginning of a world. The characteristic which unites all epic poems is that in them we have the embodiment of an age: its life, character and thought. Milton's *Paradise Lost* in its theme and thought is the voice of Puritan England resting upon the ultimate authority of the Bible for its interpretation of God and His purposes for Man.

In *Paradise Lost* Milton abandons rhyme and employs blank verse, solemn and sonorous, and sustaining a high poetic level. His style, as in all his later poems, tends to become latinized in syntax and idiom, notably in his use of the relative pronoun and the participle:

"They heard, and were abash'd, and up they sprung
Upon the wing; as when men wont to watch
On duty sleeping, found by whom they dread,
Rouse and bestir themselves ere well awake."

This gives a condensed and very concise style. Quite frequently, however, a romantic note appears, as in the passage in which Milton is comparing the legions of Satan to the colourful array of armed knights in medieval chivalry:

"And all who since, baptized or infidel,
Jousted in Aspramont, or Montalban,
Damasco, or Marocco, or Trebisond,
Or whom Biserta sent from Afric shore
When Charlemain and all his peerage fell
By Fontarabia."

This is another fine instance of that long sustained rhythm flowing from line to line, of which Milton is a master. But Milton can use simplicity when a

In Milton's Samson Agonistes, *Dalila seeks to win back Samson's love.*

theme requires it, as when Satan leaps into the Garden of Eden and only mono-syllabic Anglo-Saxon words can convey the dramatic climax of such a moment:

"So clòmb this fìrst grànd thìef into Gòd's fòld." (Bk. iv)

Milton's Idea of Hell

Like Homer and Virgil, Milton opens his poem in the middle of the story, reverting to the beginning when the Archangel Raphael visits Adam in the Garden to warn him of the approach of Satan, when he relates to Adam the story of the revolt in Heaven. In Book I the story opens in Hell. Unlike Dante, whose Hell is within the earth and more earthly and precise in its various levels and departments, Milton fills Hell with a vastness of suggestion rather than with clearly-defined scenery, which would have been too earthly:

"A dungeon horrible, on all sides round,
As one great furnace flamed; yet from those flames
No light; but rather darkness visible
Served only to discover sights of woe,
Regions of sorrow, doleful shades, where peace
And rest can never dwell, hope never comes
That comes to all, but torture without end
Still urges, and a fiery deluge, fed
With ever-burning sulphur unconsumed."

The two continents separated by the River Lethe, one burning and the other frozen, belong to this class of imagery. Pandemonium is an earthly palace carried into the realm of fantasy by Milton's imagination; and the vast concave dome of Hell with its gates guarded by Sin and Death, in their colossal dimensions, mingles definite imagery with vast suggestion. Here fantasy conveys allegorical meaning like Spenser's dragons and monsters in *The Faerie Queene*; but Milton invests his demons and monsters with a terrifying reality. Sin and Death are revealed as offspring of Satan's sin of pride and rebellion. To describe the vortex of Chaos, perhaps the biggest challenge to his imagination, Milton dramatizes what was then abstract scientific theory:

"For Hot, Cold, Moist and Dry, four champions fierce
Strive here for mastery, and to battle bring
Their embryon atoms; they around the flag
Of each his faction, in their several clans,
Light-arm'd or heavy, sharp, smooth, swift or slow,
Swarm populous."

This description of Chaos again has the double meaning of allegory: as there is no physical law relating the different forms of matter in Chaos, so there is no moral law; this is an inversion of what is always implied in Milton's themes, that moral laws of the universe are as rigorous in their working as physical laws that hold the stars in their courses. The journey across Chaos can only be described in human terms, and Milton, in his imaginative conception of it, seems to have anticipated (in the air-pockets and the clouds "instinct with fire and nitre") the hazards faced by airmen pioneers of our own century.

Similes in *Paradise Lost*

The scenes of *Paradise Lost* are set in Heaven or Hell or the Garden of Eden: thus the story, both in its location and in its characters, is remote from human experience. Milton is under the necessity of constantly relating the unreality of his Hell to the reality that his readers know. One of his devices to achieve this is the use of simile. Thus, to convey the colossal dimensions of his fiends, Milton compares them with some of the vaster conceptions of earthly reality: Satan is compared with the whale ("Leviathan"). This is the first simile in the Homeric manner, a simile which is developed for its own sake and becomes a miniature poem within the poem. In the building of Pandemonium, Milton compares the flowing of metal into the pattern of the mould in the ground to air that carries sound through the pipes of an organ, appropriate because the walls rose to "dulcet symphonies and voices sweet." (Note that music is again performing the act of creation.) In order to enter Pandemonium, all but Satan and his archangel peers are compelled to shrink in size, and they swarm at the doors of their palace like bees before their hive, or like elves of English folk-lore seen by a peasant as they hold their midnight revels:

> "While overhead the moon
> Sits arbitress, and nearer to the earth
> Wheels her pale course."

These two similes relieve the mind from the tension of the story by their touches of gentle beauty; they are an ornament to the poem, not vital to it.

Another way in which Milton enlarges the scope of his story and anchors it to reality is by copious allusion to the history of the world that lay ahead of events that he is recording. Thus, as the Fallen Angels arouse at Satan's call and fly in to join him on land, Milton describes their future on earth, where they are destined to become the heathen gods that tempt Man into idolatry; and so we have a review of Old Testament history.

Satan's Character

Satan is not only colossal in stature; his qualities of character and his passions are built on an heroic scale: he holds a worthy place among epic heroes. His character is implicit in all his actions, but Milton has given some

The living-room of Milton's home at Chalfont St. Giles is now a museum, containing many relics of the famous poet.

analysis of it when the Fallen Angels have gathered on shore to hear the rallying-call of their leader. In form he towers above them all "proudly eminent." He has not lost all his celestial glory but his face is intrenched with care. Courage is his foremost quality; he has dared the Almighty, and only he of all the spirits dares to undertake the journey to earth. Pride is linked with his courage; and presumption was his original sin. He is cunning, and his eye is cruel; but as he beholds his followers, their glory shorn, remorse and grief qualify his pride in their loyalty. These qualities can all be illustrated from events in the story, but the quality that gives Satan his uniqueness is his indomitable spirit that refuses to submit, even to the Almighty. Satan is the villain of Milton's story; but Milton too is a rebel, against king and bishops, and he has, perhaps only subconsciously, a sympathy with Satan that invests the arch-fiend with tragic greatness:

> "To reign is worth ambition, though in Hell:
> Better to reign in Hell than serve in Heaven."

We have heard this sentiment already, when Satan aroused his followers from their trance on the burning lake: "Awake, arise, or be for ever fallen!" It is the language of Satan's leadership.

The Debate in Pandemonium

The debate that is held between Satan and his peers in Pandemonium in order to determine a policy for the continuance of their rebellion against

God is a very human episode. The language here is the political rhetoric of the Long Parliament, Pyms, Hampdens and Cromwells, when parliamentary art reached one of its peaks of distinction. Each speaker in the debate represents a distinct type of statesman. Moloch is the crude advocate of brute force and direct counter-attack upon the battlements of Heaven: "My sentence is for open war!" Belial is a more subtle statesman: he has "persuasive accent" and "his tongue dropped manna." Cunningly he puts the case for the appeasement of God and counsels "ignoble ease." He is followed in the debate by Mammon, a calculating and mercenary mind, who recommends the exploiting of Hell to develop its rich mineral resources, above all, gold, the "precious bane" of Hell. Finally Beelzebub arises, the mouthpiece of Satan to urge the compromise policy of the invasion of earth to rob God of his new creation. He is represented as a statesman of experience and responsibility; he might be a Gladstone or a Winston Churchill:

> ". . . with grave
> Aspect he rose, and in his rising seemed
> A pillar of state; deep on his front engraven
> Deliberation sat and public care;
> And princely counsel in his face yet shone,
> Majestic though in ruin."

This debate shows Milton's political sense and his shrewd estimate of political motive.

QUESTIONS

1. Show how, in *Lycidas*, Milton reveals his own personal problems, and how he relates these problems to the death of Edward King.
2. Show how Milton uses the Pastoral Convention in *Lycidas.* What does he gain by introducing this device into the poem?
3. Use varied illustration to show some of the contrasts of imagery that Milton introduces into his *Ode on the Morning of Christ's Nativity.*
4. Describe the Debate in Pandemonium—the appearance of the chief speakers and the arguments they put forward.
5. Using varied illustration from Books I and II of *Paradise Lost*, compose a character-sketch of Satan.
6. *L'Allegro* is a poem of the open air, *Il Penseroso* of indoors. Use varied illustration from the two poems to show these contrasted preferences of the poet.

CHAPTER 8

FROM THE RESTORATION TO 1714

At the Restoration of the Monarchy in 1660, the feeling of romantic wonder excited by the Renaissance had largely passed away, and had given place to a more critical mood in which men examined and criticized the gains of the Renaissance. It was an Age of Reason which stimulated a big development of prose; in poetry the romantic attitude was succeeded by the classical, in which exuberance of feeling was disciplined to conform to fixed patterns of expression. This change of attitude was determined partly by historical events. Men were tired of the excesses of religious feeling that had produced the strife of the preceding fifty years. The Restoration was a triumph of reason and common-sense over fanaticism. The middle-classes, with their large Puritan element, wished to develop and enjoy their growing commercial prosperity; and men of letters, largely recruited from the Royalist ranks, still gathered round the Court in their dependence on patronage. Literature still did not provide an independent living. At Court, the king and many of the aristocracy had spent years of exile in France, where classical influences of the Age of Reason were concentrated in the splendours that were to culminate in the Court of Louis XIV at Versailles. The Court of Queen Anne, in its patronage of literature and the Arts, was to become a miniature Versailles in England. Since attitudes and outlook were very similar to those of the early Roman Empire, where such poets and satirists as Virgil, Horace and Juvenal were gathered at the Court of Augustus, the time of Queen Anne has come to be known as the Augustan Age. It was an age of sophistication and wit when the culture of the aristocracy determined fashions of literary taste.

Dryden, a Satirical Poet

John Dryden (1631-1700), in both poetry and prose, set the mould for future developments, particularly in his use, as a satirist, of the heroic couplet. He was a versatile writer, at once poet, critic and dramatist. In the theatre he contributed to an attempt to revive heroic tragedy, and his adaptation of Shakespeare's *Antony and Cleopatra* in his play *All for Love* deserves to be judged in its own right. But heroic tragedy was an outworn convention: the tendency in the theatre was towards the wit and satire of social comedy, and so Dryden's plays achieved no conspicuous success.

A duel, from Dryden's play Marriage à la Mode.

Their chief value for us lies in the critical prefaces and prologues which Dryden attached to them, and in his two essays on *Dramatic Poesy*, which contain much valuable dramatic criticism.

In an early poem he pays tribute to Oliver Cromwell (1658), and two years later, in *Astraea Redux*, he is welcoming the returning Charles II. In a time when loyalties were changing rapidly, Dryden is revealed in both poems as a patriot rather than the turn-coat that he has sometimes been represented as being. In 1667 comes a more ambitious poem, *Annus Mirabilis*, celebrating in picturesque verse the naval exploits of the king's brother, the Duke of York, against the Dutch, and concluding with a dramatic description of the Fire of London. The poem is written in quatrains (groups of four lines, each of ten syllables) which rhyme alternately, the metre of the later Gray's *Elegy*. The verse has a solemn and rather formal dignity. Other eighteenth-century qualities are the use of personification, and of abstract for concrete:

> "The diligence of trades and noiseful gain,
> And luxury, more late, asleep were laid."

Sustained metaphors and similes are developed with clear and precise detail, as when flames, personified as marauding bands on a battlefield, leap over the gap blasted by gunpowder in a frantic attempt to stem their progress.

Some conceptions resemble the Elizabethan conceit and there is a good deal of roundabout expression, as in the description of Father Thames:

> "Deep in his ooze he sought his sedgy bed,
> And shrunk his waters back into his urn."

In other words, the tide went out. The poem is most moving when, in utterly simple style, the pathos of human suffering is conveyed:

> "Those who have homes, when home they do repair,
> To a last lodging call their wandering friends:
> Their short uneasy sleeps are broke with care,
> To look how near their own destruction tends."

Absalom and Achitophel

This satirical poem is Dryden's finest work. The art of satire, or ridicule, flourishes in an age of reason. Satire is in essence the art of criticism, an intellectual art which is given special flavour by the wit with which it is presented. The object of satire is to expose frauds, shams and abuses: it flourishes at Courts because such society is always highly conventional, governed by unwritten laws of social behaviour, behind which insincerity, intrigue and hypocrisy flourish. Hence personal and social satire finds its opportunity. Moreover, personal and political rivalries tend to become very acute and bitter in the atmosphere of courts, and it is as a political satire that Dryden presents *Absalom and Achitophel* (1680).

Dryden uses the biblical story of Absalom's revolt against David, his father, to expose the political manoeuvres of the party group which in the reign of Charles II sought to pass through Parliament the Exclusion Bill. By this Bill the King's brother, James, Duke of York, would be excluded from the throne in favour of the Duke of Monmouth, a natural son of Charles II. James adhered to the Roman faith, and political agitation sprang from the distrust of Roman Catholicism so deeply embedded in English minds since the Reformation. Absalom in the poem is the Duke of Monmouth; and Achitophel, the cunning counsellor, is the Earl of Shaftesbury, a man of shrewd ability and daring who had a long record of political intrigue. He determined to exploit the handsome and attractive personality of the Duke of Monmouth. The agitators resorted to all manner of unscrupulous devices: Titus Oates, an impostor and charlatan of low origin (Corah in the poem), was induced to declare upon oath before a London magistrate the lurid details of a bogus popish plot, and next day the magistrate was found murdered. King David in the poem is of course Charles II; Jerusalem is London; and the stiff-necked Israelites are the rebellious Londoners. The Jebusites, earlier inhabitants of Jerusalem, are the Roman Catholics of the pre-Reformation faith. All personalities on both sides of the political struggle are presented with lively portraiture, loyalists with lavish praise and those wishing to exclude Monmouth with pointed and pungent satire. Dryden is never merely abusive in his satire: rather is he precise and detached in his analysis of character. Although it is at once obvious whom he is attacking, his satire extends beyond the merely personal to create types of character that every political crisis throws up. This is an essential quality of genuine satire: as Swift puts it, speaking of himself,

> "Yet malice never was his aim;
> He lash'd the vice, but spared the name;
> No individual could resent,
> Where thousands equally were meant." (*On the Death of Dr. Swift*)

The most developed character in Dryden's poem is the Earl of Shaftesbury:

> "For close designs and crooked counsels fit;
> Sagacious, bold, and turbulent of wit;
> Restless, unfix'd in principles and place;
> In power unpleased, impatient of disgrace:
> A fiery soul, which, working out its way,
> Fretted the pigmy body to decay,
> And o'er-inform'd the tenement of clay.*
> A daring pilot in extremity;
> Pleased with the danger, when the waves went high,
> He sought the storms; but, for a calm unfit,
> Would steer too near the sands to boast his wit.
> Great wits are sure to madness near allied,
> And thin partitions do their bounds divide."

The Heroic Couplet

The effectiveness of this character-sketch in verse derives from Dryden's use of the heroic couplet, a verse-form soon to be perfected by Pope and to prevail for most of the eighteenth century. The deca-syllabic (ten-syllable) lines, rhyming in pairs, had already been used by English poets; Chaucer introduced them in his *Prologue* and in many of his *Canterbury Tales*; but Dryden and Pope use them in a way so different that it appears to be a verse-form quite distinct from that employed by earlier poets. Chaucer allows the sense to flow on independently of the couplet, but eighteenth-century poets make the sense conclude, or at least pause, at the end of each couplet. The rhyme therefore seems to punctuate the sense, and the couplets stand out as so many verses (which indeed they are). The line itself tends to divide, usually at the fourth syllable (second foot), which enables the two parts to be pointedly balanced by the contrasted ideas of antithesis. This is illustrated

* Physical body.

by lines 4 and 10 in the paragraph quoted above. A single line is often given the condensed force of an epigram, as in the imaginative metaphor of line 8 and the brief contradictory terms of paradox in line 12. We shall see Pope perfecting these devices; Dryden is feeling his way towards them, but is not so rigid in his technique.*

Dryden's Later Poems

Two later poems by Dryden, *Song for Saint Cecilia's Day* (*Golden Treasury* No. 63) and *Alexander's Feast, or the Power of Music* (G.T. No. 116), look forward to the eighteenth-century odes of Collins and Gray. The Ode, following the pattern of the Greek poet Pindar, is a poem written for a formal occasion, and therefore adopts a formal and elevated language and a complex stanza construction. Both Dryden's odes are written in honour of Saint Cecilia, who was believed to be the inventress of the organ. Dryden, ranging over various musical instruments, makes the rhythm and sound of words represent the music of the instrument he is describing. In *Alexander's Feast* the world-conqueror is celebrating his victory over Darius, seated at a banquet with "lovely Thais" by his side. Timotheus the minstrel sways Alexander's moods by the power of his music.

Pope, a Classical Poet

The work of Alexander Pope (1688-1744) marks the perfection of the classical period of poetry. Until dethroned by Wordsworth (1800), he was so generally regarded as an infallible authority in poetry that Dr. Johnson, in the middle of the eighteenth century, virtually lays it down that if a poet does not write in the manner of Pope, he cannot lay any serious claim to be a poet. Born in London of middle-class parents, he was a sickly child and puny in build. Moreover, he had a Roman Catholic upbringing at a time when Catholics in England were still subject to disabilities, and Pope was thus debarred from going to university. These handicaps, in a self-conscious and sensitive mind, probably account for his aggressiveness and venom in the many personal quarrels in which he became involved and which figure so strongly in his satirical works. He read widely in the classics, and before reaching adult years had written *The Pastorals* in imitation of Virgil, showing a precocious and spontaneous instinct for poetry.

Windsor Forest followed, showing a feeling for nature in descriptions of scenes amidst which he lived, and yet carrying a foretaste of the intellectual and comparatively abstract subjects, such as History and Moral Philosophy, that were to characterize his later works. However, before these weightier

* This poem may be read in *The Poems of Dryden*, Penguin Poets, where there are brief footnotes as a guide to allusions; but the student without a knowledge of historical background should use an annotated edition—there is one published by the Oxford Press.

subjects really preoccupied his mind, Pope composed a poem of sparkling vivacity and airy grace as a first essay in satire.

The Rape of the Lock

This poem is a good-humoured satire, ridiculing with delicate and ironic gallantry the vanities and affectations of ladies in the social life revolving about the Court of Queen Anne at Hampton Court Palace. In the circle of Roman Catholic families in which Pope moved was a Miss Arabella Fermor, a celebrated beauty of the Court. Lord Petre was an ardent admirer of the lady, who attached him to her circle of admirers without accepting or rejecting his advances. Ultimately, exasperated by these tactics, Petre cut off one of the lady's locks of hair and bore it away as a trophy. A social scandal ensued, and it was suggested to Pope (probably by Caryll, a friend of his) that he should write a burlesque of the incident which by its good humour might dissolve social hostilities into laughter. Apparently it did, for we are told by a niece of Miss Fermor that "Mr. Pope's praise made her aunt very troublesome and conceited."

Homeric Parallels

The poem was first written in a shorter form, and later expanded by addition of the supernatural element of sylphs and gnomes. So it ultimately

Hampton Court Palace, "a structure of majestic frame," was the scene for Pope's amusing poem, The Rape of the Lock.

took the form of a mock-heroic poem written in five cantos. The mock-heroic raises the trivial and ridiculous to sublime heights. This is achieved in *The Rape of the Lock* by a burlesque imitation of the epic form of Homer's *Iliad* and *Odyssey*; characters are raised to heroic dimensions, and the Gods (in this case sylphs and gnomes) take part in the human story. Throughout the story Homeric parallels are being implied: Belinda's dressing-table, as she adorns herself for a visit to Court, becomes an altar where the "rites of pride" are performed; her lady's maid is "th'inferior priestess"; and the vases of ointments, puffs and powders have a strict ritualistic order. Similarly, when Petre burns the *billets-doux* of his former ladies, he is represented as making a burnt offering to the Gods to win their aid before he enters the lists of love. The game of cards in canto III becomes an heroic combat of medieval romance between crusading knights and Moors.

When the lock has been cut, the lamentations of the ladies resemble those of the women of Troy in Euripides' tragedy, and the bag of "sobs, sighs, and tears" that the Goddess of Spleen gives to Umbriel is reminiscent of the bag of winds that the God of the Winds gave to Odysseus. The final conflict in canto V is on a Homeric scale, but its weapons are bodkins and snuff, and the armour is whalebone petticoats. Finally the mock-heroic climax is reached when the lock is raised to the sky and given a place among the stars.

Almost every couplet contains some literary allusion or echo. There is a complete social scene in the poem, from the ladies' boudoirs to the colourful pageantry of state barges on the River Thames, and the glittering scene at Hampton Court where a reputation dies at every word and

> "Snuff, or the fan, supply each pause of chat,
> With singing, laughing, ogling, *and all that*." (III 17)

The passages that describe the sylphs reveal the most delicate flights of fancy that Pope's imagination ever made. Word music floats as lightly as the sylphs, and fragile imagery really persuades us that we are looking upon the invisible:

> "Some to the sun their insect-wings unfold,
> Waft on the breeze, or sink in clouds of gold.
> Transparent forms, too fine for mortal sight,
> Their fluid bodies half dissolved in light.
> Loose to the wind their airy garments flew,
> Thin glitt'ring textures of the filmy dew." (II 59)

Variety of Pope's Style

It might be thought that the succession of detached couplets would become monotonous to the ear, but Pope avoids this by superimposing many variations upon the essential similarity of their make-up. The verse assumes a heavier tone to describe the gnomes of mischief and the cave of Spleen:

> "Umbriel, a dusky, melancholy sprite,
> As ever sully'd the fair face of light." (IV 13-14)

The balance given to the divided line by antithesis is seen in Pope's description of Belinda's tactics in retaining her suitors and yet holding them at a distance:

> "Favours to none, to all she smiles extends;
> Oft she rejects, but never once offends.
> Bright as the sun, her eyes the gazers strike,
> And, like the sun, they shine on all alike." (II 11-14)

Here the satire is playful, but it can bite deeper:

> "On her white breast a sparkling cross she wore,
> Which Jews might kiss, and Infidels adore." (II 7-8)

Another figure of speech favoured by Pope to convey his satire is anticlimax, sometimes achieved by a word or phrase:

> "Here thou, great Anna! whom three realms obey,
> Dost sometimes counsel take—and sometimes tea." (III 7-8)

The roundabout style of the eighteenth century lends itself readily to burlesque. Thus the fatal pair of scissors is "a two-edg'd weapon," and a telescope is "Galileo's eyes" (a nice inspiration making the image more vivid).

Pope's Poetical Essays

The philosophic bent and intellectual habit of Pope's mind are seen in *An Essay on Criticism* and *An Essay on Man.* In the first he deduces principles of poetic art in the manner of the *Ars Poetica* of Horace: a poet must follow nature, as Greeks and Romans did, so they are the guides to poetic practice. Pope does, however, realize that the inventive genius of a poet is not confined within laws; but what in a poet's inspiration goes straight to the heart must be endorsed by the reason. From generalizing he proceeds to give a wealth of examples, illustrating with the flexibility of his couplets the style he is describing. Thus he illustrates a poet's power to make sound echo sense by lines that are in themselves onomatopoeic:

> "When Ajax strives some rock's vast weight to throw,
> The line too labours, and the words move slow:
> Not so, when swift Camilla scours the plain,
> Flies o'er th'unbending corn, and skims along the main." (ll. 370-3)

In the sound of the words, we see the dipping flight of the bird. Again, the laboured alliteration of

> "The bookful blockhead, ignorantly read,
> With loads of learned lumber in his head." (ll. 612-3)

points the pedantry of the learned dunce; and the poverty of the sentence

"And ten low words oft creep in one dull line," (l. 342)

is self-illustrated by the words.

Many proverbs in daily use owe their origin to Pope; for example:

"The proper study of mankind is man." (I 2)

These words state the topic theme of the *Essay on Man*, which is an analysis of human nature, often ironical and sometimes bitter:

"If parts allure thee, think how Bacon shined,
The wisest, brightest, meanest of mankind:
Or ravished with the whistling of a name,
See Cromwell damned to everlasting fame!" (IV 281-4)

In both these essays there is an over-riding principle of moral purpose which, Pope insists, must be present in the work of both artist and mankind in general. In this aspect his work presents a counterpart in verse to Addison's *Spectator* essays.

Other Works by Pope

In his translations of the *Iliad* and the *Odyssey*, Pope transforms the primitive vigour of Homeric gods and heroes into the polite refinement of the Augustans. The translations were so popular that the financial rewards made Pope the first independent man of letters.

In the *Epistle to Dr. Arbuthnot* Pope attacked Addison, who had expressed doubts about the wisdom of adding gnomes and sylphs to *The Rape of the Lock*; Pope thought these doubts sprang from jealousy. Addison had also sponsored a translation of the *Iliad* that was a rival to Pope's version. Pope's attack on Addison in his *Epistle to Dr. Arbuthnot* has the gleam of polished steel:

"Should such a man, too fond to rule alone,
Bear, like the Turk, no brother near the throne;

Like *Cato*, give his little Senate laws,
And sit attentive to his own applause." (ll. 197-210)

John Bunyan, the Tinker

In this period two English prose-writers emerge, Bunyan and Defoe, each isolated in his individuality. The unique quality of their work springs from the individual circumstances of their lives and the special conditions that determined their style.

John Bunyan (1628-88) was born in Bedfordshire, the son of a tinsmith. He fought in the Parliamentary army and later, in Commonwealth times, underwent a religious conversion and became Pastor of a sect of Baptists.

His literary work was stimulated by persecution in the reign of Charles II, when he was twice imprisoned for several years for preaching, which was forbidden by the Conventicle Act. The world treated him harshly, and his two outstanding works were both written in prison; so he had a kind of nostalgia or home-sickness for a better world, which he proceeded to create in his books. *Grace Abounding* is an account of his religious conversion, one of the most intimate autobiographies ever written. There is nothing mystic about his experience, no deep searchings of his soul in the manner of a modern psychologist: simple but profound thoughts that pass through his mind are conveyed in the outward drama of the simple circumstances of his life. While playing Tip-cat after hearing a sermon denouncing indulgence in pleasures on the Sabbath, he thus describes his sudden misgivings:

> "But the same day, as I was in the midst of a game at Cat, and having struck it one blow from the hole, just as I was about to strike it the second time, a Voice did suddenly dart from Heaven into my soul, which said, *Wilt thou leave thy sins and go to Heaven, or have thy sins and go to Hell?* At this I was put to an exceeding maze. Wherefore, leaving my Cat upon the ground, I looked up to Heaven, and was as if I had, with the eyes of my understanding, seen the Lord Jesus looking down upon me, and as if He did severely threaten

The Moot Hall and village green at Elstow, where Bunyan was converted.

me with some grievous punishment for these and other my ungodly practices. . . . Thus I stood in the midst of my play, before all that then were present; but yet I told them nothing."

The Pilgrim's Progress

The Pilgrim's Progress, the work popularly associated with Bunyan's name, is inspired by the same qualities of style. The theme is a Christian's search for salvation, presented in visible dramatic form as a journey from the City of Destruction to the Celestial City, across a tract of country characterized by a variety of features and beset with hazards, amidst which the traveller encounters all manner of adventures.

The story of *The Pilgrim's Progress* is so simply written that a young child can read it and be absorbed by it, yet so profound that a deep religious experience emerges from it that transcends all creeds and appeals by its simple humanity and sincerity. Much of the story is told in dialogue form. The book is an allegory in which all detail has the quality of symbols: there is By-path Meadow where the pilgrims lose their way and fall into the clutches of Giant Despair of Doubting Castle; there is Vanity Fair, the Valley of the Shadow of Death and the Delectable Mountains. The host of characters that figure in the story have evocative names and represent abstractions or qualities of mind and temperament—Faithful, Hopeful, Mr. Greatheart, Mr. Worldly Wiseman, Ignorance, Talkative, and so on—but all are vitally alive and convincing as men and women. *The Pilgrim's Progress* is perhaps the greatest of English allegories because it convinces as a story, and a reader responds emotionally to the events. The characters spring from Bunyan's direct and penetrating observation of his fellow-men: they are not caricatures or travesties of humanity.

The countryside is the landscape of rural Bedfordshire in Bunyan's time, as he himself knew it, with meadows, marshes and broad sluggish rivers; and the less normal features, such as mountains with fire breaking from them, giants, dragons and demons, are English too, deeply embedded in popular tradition and figuring in the broadsheets of sensational story and adventure that were sold by pedlars up and down the country. *The Pilgrim's Progress* thus belongs to the literature of the people. Bunyan is an instinctive artist: in his genius as a storyteller he is self-taught by the single source of his inspiration, the Bible. *The Pilgrim's Progress* is basically a commentary upon the Bible, particularly the Gospels; Bunyan is continually quoting the Bible, and his object is to explain it to simple minds. His style is that of the Bible, with its simple diction, poetic cadences and direct statement; and so it is also the style of the vernacular or native idiom of the people. The Bible was in every household, the only literature of virtually illiterate folk. They also heard it read in church, and so it gave a standard to popular speech.

Robinson Crusoe, marooned on an island, has only a parrot for company.

Now they could add Bunyan to their book-shelf. In this way the book achieved an enormous vogue.

Defoe the Journalist

Daniel Defoe (*c.* 1660-1731) is another writer belonging to the middle class, and points to their growing importance in the community. He represents the Puritan element in English life, who were turning their minds from fanaticism to material prosperity. In a sense Defoe is the first journalist, employed by commercial patrons to collect information in various parts of the country regarding the condition of industry and commerce. This suited his inquiring mind, with its passion for facts and the utilitarian features that characterize so many of his writings. Later he was employed, in turn, by both Whigs and Tories, and seems to have regarded himself as a professional informer by the ease with which he changed allegiances. On this account he came to be regarded with distrust, and the devastating satire of his *The Shortest Way with the Dissenters*, in which he exposed with stark realism the methods and motives of persecution, offended the Anglican Church authorities and brought about his appearance in the pillory and his temporary imprisonment. His later works of fiction are an early appearance of the novel form, but they are documentaries rather than studies of a social setting. Defoe, with his insatiable curiosity, is investigating the way people behave, particularly in the criminal and less reputable world. *Robinson Crusoe*, by which Defoe is usually judged, is only superficially romantic in its story of shipwreck and a desert island. Defoe builds up a vast body of detailed facts to show a man thrown back upon meagre resources, improvising and adapting in the eternal duel between man and nature.

Perhaps indirectly, in Crusoe's struggle to survive, Defoe is reminding us of the painful and arduous process through which man must have passed in his efforts to civilize himself and to secure those commonplace amenities that we now take for granted. Some of his comments on savages can be construed in this light. Another element in the story is his insistence upon divine providence, and the effort of Crusoe to work out his relationship with God. This gives an ethical and moral element to the story which reflects his Puritan upbringing.

Addison and Steele

As Defoe is associated with the commercial prosperity of the middle class, so is the work of Steele and Addison in their publication of *The Tatler* and *Spectator* a response to a middle-class desire to link themselves socially to the lower fringe of aristocracy, and to acquire something of the classical culture. The contribution that the middle class made to this social tendency was to effect a reform of manners and morals, after the laxity of the Restoration period. Indirectly this represents a return to Puritanism, but shorn of religious fanaticism and now accompanied by elegance and manners, humour and wit. The note sounded was of broad-minded toleration and compromise.

Though Addison became the greater contributor to the partnership, Steele was the pioneer in his publication of *The Tatler* (1709-11). Richard Steele (1672-1729) was the less stable character of the two: an Irishman by birth, he had seen military service, and there are qualities in his earlier character that smack of the Restoration rake or dandy. When he settled down after 1700 as a writer in the moral crusade, he was writing as much to convince himself as his readers, which gives his essays a spontaneous quality that Addison's, in their more studied and polished elegance, often lack. Steele can rise higher and sink lower than Addison's more consistent level of quality.

Joseph Addison (1672-1719) occupies a position of more assured elevation, which at times gives him a condescending air, especially to ladies. He had a university education, and was attached to the Whig interest in politics. In later life he became Secretary of State. Addison was also a poet and dramatist. His poem *The Campaign* pays tribute to Marlborough's genius in his victory at Blenheim. He also wrote a number of hymns, of which "The Spacious Firmament on High" is best known. In it he first traces the glory of God in physical laws of the Universe and then correspondingly the moral law in the heart of man. His hymn is a paraphrase of Psalm 19. In later life, Addison's classical tragedy *Cato* was an immense success in the theatre, though possessing little merit as a play.

Steele had also written plays without any conspicuous success. Both writers realized their genius in establishing the essay as a literary form of classical prose. Fluent, balanced and refined, their style gives a standard to English prose: whenever a note of urbanity has since been struck, there will be found some echo of the manner of Steele and Addison.

The Tatler and *The Spectator*

The Tatler appeared three times weekly and contained several essays and articles; *The Spectator*, its successor, was published daily and contained only a single essay. A loose unity was given to the essays by introduction of fictitious characters who appeared with more or less frequency. The presiding genius in *The Tatler* was Isaac Bickerstaff, whom Steele had borrowed from Swift; he was a magician who had insight into the minds of others, and so could present various types of the town in his comment on and correction of manners and fashions. Jenny Distaff tended to appear whenever the theme was married or domestic happiness. The plan of *The Spectator* was more ambitious: the Spectator Club was formed, consisting of a few representative types of society. Thus Sir Roger de Coverley is a country-gentleman; there is a lawyer from the Inner Temple who, however, prefers literary arts to law; Sir Andrew Freeport is an eminent merchant of the City; Captain Sentry, heir to Sir Roger, is an army officer of extreme modesty; Will Honeycomb is an elderly wit and rake of the town; and there is a clergyman of great integrity who seldom appears. Here is a broad cross-section of society; and the Spectator himself, who links them together, is a caricatured version of Addison, a shy and detached figure in sober black, who flits in and out of social clubs and coffee-houses, unobtrusive but observing.

The coffee-houses of London were meeting-places where members of this new middle-class society gathered, and they served the same purpose as the salons of the aristocracy. Each coffee-house became associated with a certain interest or taste; the literary men tended to gather at Will's, politicians at the St. James', and lawyers at the Grecian.

Sir Roger de Coverley

Sir Roger is the most prominent of Addison's characters, and a sequence of essays presents him to us with all his oddities of behaviour and geniality of disposition. He is the Don Quixote of the Augustan age; for almost every period in literature throws up its Don Quixote whenever the springs of goodwill need to be renewed. Sir Roger joins company with Fielding's Parson Adams and Dickens' Mr. Pickwick. He is unconsciously humorous in his eccentricities, old-fashioned but warmly generous. His servants are all elderly because they have grown old in his service; he exercises a benevolent despotism over his tenants; he hunts the hare but always calls off the dogs before the kill and lets the hare live the rest of its life in his orchard; he takes his place on the Bench at Assizes, and has a whispered word with the Judge to please his self-importance. When he comes to town his old-fashioned simplicity inspires mirth: some youths on the Thames, when he is on his way to Spring Gardens, disrespectfully call him "the old put"; and his loud and naïve criticism at the theatre embarrasses his friends. Nevertheless his unfailing dignity and good humour defeat all attempts to make a laughing-stock of him. Addison's humour is sly and ironical: he is very fond of what he laughs at.

Topics of the Essays

The presentation of these characters by Addison and Steele in a series of loosely-connected incidents is the first appearance in embryo of the novel of character and social values. There are social themes such as family-life (*Tatler* 79; *Spectator* 261), and the changes and vanities of fashion (*T.* 116; *Sp.* 98, 435). Upon politics the Spectator discourages excesses of party-spirit (*Sp.* 81, 125). Again, on religion, the Spectator emphasizes tolerance and the quality of Christian living rather than aspects of dogma. Sometimes, in more imaginative flights, he indulges in tales and allegories with a moral or mildly philosophical bearing; *The Vision of Mirzah* (*Sp.* 159) is perhaps the best example. There are also essays on literary criticism dealing with such topics as wit, humour and taste (*Sp.* 35, 58, 409). Addison recommends to his readers such diverse works as *The Ballad of Chevy Chase* (*Sp.* 74) and Milton's *Paradise Lost*. On the latter poem, Addison's criticism and valuation have usually been upheld, and at the time they assisted a wide range of readers to appreciate Milton's epic.

The tone of the essays is one of mannered conversation. The informal manner of their presentation conceals the skill and deliberate art that has gone to their making. Sometimes Addison will state a theme plainly and emphatically in the opening sentences. At other times he will commence with an anecdote, a conversation or an incident, from which the essay will develop into reflections or moralizings which revolve round the topic theme, usually returning neatly to re-state and affirm it at the conclusion. Thus the essay has described a circle, which is a very good form because it is obeying an instinctive law. The style is never laboured or merely abstract: even when the thought is abstract, the style is enlivened with terms of visual imagery. In his essay on *The Royal Exchange* (*Sp.* 69) he thus conveys the prosperity that merchants bring to a country and the interdependence of nations in trade:

> "Our English Merchant converts the tin of his own country into gold, and exchanges his wool for rubies. The Mahometans are clothed in our British manufacture, and the inhabitants of the Frozen Zone warmed with the fleeces of our sheep."

Swift, Creator of Gulliver

The personality of Jonathan Swift (1667-1745) is mysterious and baffling. Writers and critics have been asking questions about his formidable genius ever since he died, and still the mystery persists. Born in Ireland but probably of Yorkshire descent, his origin is obscure. In childhood he was virtually an orphan, and under the guardianship of an uncle he eventually graduated at Trinity College, Dublin. Coming to England, he gained the rather precarious patronage of the Temple family, to whom he was probably related by birth. Swift's moroseness and bitterness must have been temperamental, but no doubt they were accentuated by his failure to obtain, in a world dominated by patronage, an adequate outlet for his intellectual powers. He took Holy Orders and was given a living in Ireland, but spent most of the years 1704-13 in England. His Anglican position led him to distrust the Whigs, and he attached himself to the Tories under Harley, writing valuable pamphlets for them, such as *The Conduct of the Allies*, which established the Tories in power and ended the wars of Marlborough. Queen Anne, however, distrusted Swift owing to the devastating religious satire of his *Tale of a Tub*, and so the most that he could obtain in the way of preferment was the Deanery of St. Patrick's in Dublin. When the Whigs triumphed on the death of Queen Anne, he retired to Ireland, a disappointed and embittered man.

Swift, in an age so favourable to the development of satire, was the most uncompromising and courageous of the satirical writers. His satire, unlike Pope's, was never personal. His sensitive mind penetrated behind all the shams and self-deceptions of human intellect in matters of religious belief and of political institutions and loyalties. With ruthless frankness he exposed intellectual dishonesty and all the intrigue, bribery and corruption that went with it. The gloom of the picture fed his morose and pessimistic nature.

Gulliver's Travels

Gulliver's Travels is the culminating work of this satirical view of life. Since the story is an excursion into a fantastic world, Gulliver, like Dante before him and the Ancient Mariner after him, must tell his own story. This assists the reader to suspend his disbelief and makes the story credible; a fantastic story must convince: we say to ourselves that Gulliver was there, so he ought to know. The allegory in *Gulliver's Travels* is political: as the Lilliputians are afraid of Gulliver and tie him down, so the average politician fears the great man and hampers him with all manner of restrictive practices; but when the country is in great danger, politicians forget their lesser fears and appeal to the great man to save them, as Gulliver saves Lilliput by towing the fleet of Blefuscu into their harbour. In the first two stories of Gulliver's adventures, in Lilliput and Brobdingnag, the allegory clearly depends upon the size of his captors relative to Gulliver himself. In the story of Lilliput, the human littleness that Swift is satirizing is illustrated by the Lilliputians themselves: their party politics are frivolous, unrelated to real issues, but determined by such trivialities as whether they crack the big or the little end of their eggs; delicate manoeuvres of politicians are likened to balancing tricks on a tight-rope, which often result in a fall; and the palace is a hot-bed of intrigue and scandal in which Gulliver finds himself involved.

Gulliver in Brobdingnag

When, however, Gulliver comes to Brobdingnag, the creatures of superior size are also of superior mind, and Gulliver is made to feel his human inferiority. Brobdingnag is not a Utopia or ideal state, but the giant race lives within the simple dictates of common-sense and reason. The king is horrified by Gulliver's account of his country's institutions and the men who work them:

> "It doth not appear, from all you have said, how any one perfection is required towards the procurement of any one station among you; much less that men are ennobled on account of their virtue, that priests are advanced for their piety or learning, soldiers for their conduct or valour, judges for their integrity, senators for the love of their country, or counsellors for their wisdom. . . . And he gave it for his opinion, that whoever could make two ears of corn or two blades of grass to grow upon a spot of ground where only one grew before, would deserve better of mankind, and do more essential service to his country than the whole race of politicians put together."

The Flying Island and the Houyhnhnms

Gulliver's visit to the Flying Island in Book III is a satire upon the progress of science under the auspices of the Royal Society, and upon the scholastic pedantry of philosophers. Swift has no faith in the power of science to improve the moral stature of man (which to him is the essential positive value in life), and he does not think that moral philosophy has added anything of value to what the Greek philosophers propounded. This and the concluding Book IV are unrelieved in their pessimism. As if despairing of humanity, he finds perfection in his philosophic race of horses, the Houyhnhnms, who live, guided by nature and reason, in a state of innocence. In this story, Swift gives us the term "Yahoos" for creatures living in primitive bestiality whom the Houyhnhnms have enslaved to do the lowest

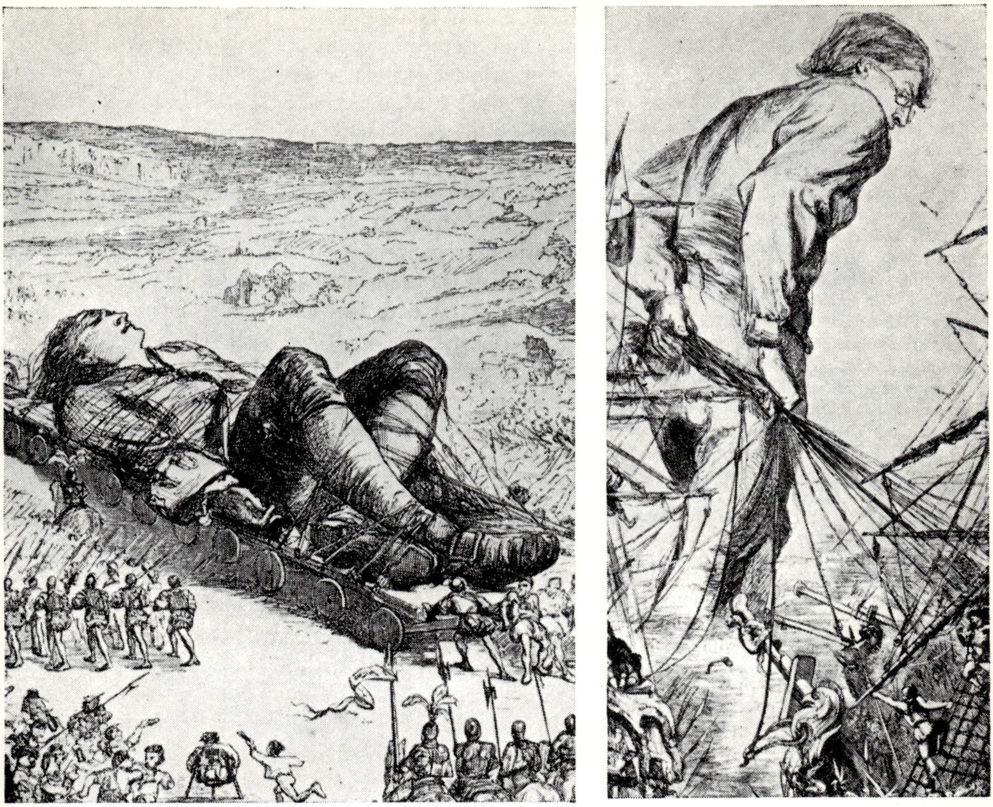

Gulliver, tied down by the Lilliputians, later tows away their enemies' fleet.

tasks. In the Yahoos, to our discomfiture, we are forced to recognize some characteristics of the human race.

To many, the pessimism of Swift's satire springs from a diseased state of mind, but this must not conceal from us its truth. When he threw off the burden of his vision, he could be gay in human relationships; he inspired the love of two women, "Stella" and "Vanessa," and his *Journal to Stella* shows the kindlier and more sympathetic side of his sensitive mind. Perhaps it is significant that one of his most pessimistic satires, *Gulliver's Travels*, joins company with *The Pilgrim's Progress* and *Robinson Crusoe* to provide enthralling reading for the early years of childhood.

QUESTIONS

1. From your reading of *Absalom and Achitophel* describe in some detail and *in your own words* the characters of (*a*) the Earl of Shaftesbury (Achitophel) and (*b*) *either* the Duke of Buckingham (Zimri) *or* King Charles II (King David).

2. Select *two* of the following passages from *The Rape of the Lock*, re-write them freely in your own words so as to bring out the meaning, and make brief comment on any features of Pope's style *or* satire that they illustrate:

(*a*) "As now your own, our beings were of old,
And once inclos'd in Woman's beauteous mold;
Thence, by a soft transition, we repair
From earthly Vehicles to these of air.
Think not, when Woman's transient breath is fled,
That all her vanities at once are dead;
Succeeding vanities she still regards,
And tho' she plays no more, o'erlooks the cards." (Canto I 47)

(*b*) "There Affectation, with a sickly mien,
Shows in her cheek the roses of eighteen,
Practis'd to lisp, and hang the head aside,
Faints into airs, and languishes with pride;
On the rich quilt sinks with becoming woe,
Wrapt in a gown, for sickness, and for show.
The fair ones feel such maladies as these,
When each new night-dress gives a new disease." (Canto IV 31)

(*c*) "How vain are all these glories, all our pains,
Unless good sense preserve what beauty gains:
That men may say, when we the front-box grace:
'Behold the first in virtue as in face!'
Oh! if to dance all night, and dress all day,
Charm'd the small-pox, or chas'd old-age away,
Who would not scorn what housewife's cares produce,
Or who would learn one earthly thing of use?" (Canto V 15)

3. Describe *either* Robinson Crusoe's efforts to provide himself with cooking and eating utensils and with clothing, *or* his educating of Man Friday. What purpose does Defoe serve by these features of his story?

4. Show by some detailed reference to *two* incidents in *The Pilgrim's Progress* how Bunyan relates landscape or settings very closely to his story.

5. Select an essay by Addison or Steele that you have enjoyed reading, briefly state the topic or theme, summarize the essay, and make some brief comment on the writer's style.

6. Describe the mind and outlook of *either* the king of Brobdingnag *or* Gulliver's Houyhnhnm master.

REVISION SUMMARY OF AUTHORS BORN BY THE END OF THE SEVENTEENTH CENTURY

EARLY AUTHORS (Before 1350) *Page*

Beowulf: An anonymous heroic poem of Scandinavian origin, transcribed and added to in Anglo-Saxon times. 28

The Venerable Bede (673-735): Northumbrian priest and scholar whose writings in Latin, notably ***The Ecclesiastical History of the English Race***, influenced Anglo-Saxon literature. 28

Alfred (*c.* 848 - *c.* 900), King of Wessex: scholar, soldier, lawgiver. Patron of scholars, inspired ***The Anglo-Saxon Chronicle.***

Geoffrey of Monmouth (1100-1154): A Latin chronicler who collected the Celtic legends of King Arthur. 29

Sir Gawain and the Green Knight (*c.* 1350): An anonymous poem in alliterative verse but in the spirit of the French Romances. Allegorical and symbolic. 30

William Langland (*c.* 1330-1400): A humble priest, author of ***Piers Plowman,*** a poem written in alliterative verse to trace the purpose of God in human life. Vivid description of human scene, and visions in which allegorical figures appear. 30-1, 19

BALLADS (Fourteenth and fifteenth centuries) 54-8

Anonymous and traditional folk-songs, originally linked with dancing, and dramatically reproducing local incident. Usually written in four-line stanzas (A B C B). Themes cover popular taste: love (***The Gay Goshawk***); war (***Chevy Chase***); violent death (***Edward, Edward; Binnorie***); magic (***Wife of Usher's Well***); fairy lore (***Thomas the Rhymer***); history (***Sir Patrick Spens***).

GEOFFREY CHAUCER (*c.* 1340-1401) 32-53

The son of a London wine-merchant, he became a page in a noble household, and was later promoted to Valet at the Court of Edward III. Taken prisoner in the Hundred Years' War and

Page

ransomed, he was sent to France and Italy on trade missions by the King. Here he tapped Renaissance influence a century before it reached this country. In later life he became J.P. for Kent, and represented Kent in parliament. Chaucer's experience thus covered a wide range of national and European life.

After writing early works in the manner of allegories and dreams, he adopted the modern direct portrayal of convincing men and women, revealing character in action and dialogue.

Troilus and Creseyde: The love of Troilus, son of Priam, for Creseyde, a Greek refugee, is frustrated by the circumstances of the siege of Troy in which the story is set. Pandarus, busybody and go-between, is a product of Chaucer's genius in creating comic character. 34-5

Prologue to the Canterbury Tales (Begun 1386): An original and entirely English work. The choice of a pilgrimage as the setting within which the Tales are told enabled Chaucer to present a wide cross-section of contemporary social types: 35-40

(*a*) The Army: Knight, Squire, and Yeoman compose the military unit. Chivalry survives in crusading zeal: its ideals persist in the Knight, and courtly love in the Squire. 36

(*b*) The Church: Demoralized by wealth left in wills or paid as fees for absolution. Monk lax, Friar, Summoner and Pardoner immoral and greedy for gold. Poor Parson alone conscientious. 37, 351

(*c*) Town Life and Trade: Wealthy merchants thriving on export of wool; prosperous Guildsmen displaying snobbery. 37-8

(*d*) Country Life: Comfortable freehold farmers performing local administration (Franklin); dishonest manorial officials (Miller and Reeve). Plowman honest and hardworking.

(*e*) There are also professional men, not very strongly individualized (Doctor, Lawyer, Manciple).

The characters present both social types and convincing individuals. Chaucer reveals their characters by dress and ornament (Knight, Lady Prioress), by physical features (Miller, Cook), some by what they say (Monk, Friar), some by their actions (Knight, Poor Parson). These methods overlap in many characters. Chaucer uses irony to imply ridicule (Lady Prioress, Friar, Pardoner). He does not avow moral purpose, but this is implied. 369

The Host of the Tabard Inn leads the company and devises the scheme for the journey. The journey is dramatized by passages which form links between the stories. Each story

Page

further illustrates and amplifies the character of the narrator.

The Knight's Tale: A tale of chivalry and courtly love in the rivalry of Palamon and Arcite for the hand of Emily. The scene at the court of Theseus is of spectacle and pageantry. 40-5

The Nun's Priest's Tale: Burlesque of medieval learning set within the fable of the Cock and the Fox. Background gives a picture of medieval village life. Ingenious blend of human and animal in the portrayal and behaviour of the birds and animals. The domestic life of Chanticleer and Pertelote is a humorous picture of wedded bliss. The learned digressions give a mock-heroic character to the tale: they introduce medieval theories of dreams, allusions to the Bible and Classical literature, medieval authors, and philosophy of free-will. 45-7, 356

The Pardoner's Prologue and Tale: The Prologue is a frank and impudent self-confession, showing the technique by which he imposes on the credulity and fears of simple folk with bogus relics to gain money. The Tale consists of a sermon denouncing the sins of Blasphemy, Gluttony (including Drunkenness) and Gambling with illustration from medieval life, and a morality story, a masterpiece of condensed and patterned drama. The three "riotours," setting out to kill Death, have a strange encounter with an old man, who in response to their inquiry after Death, directs them to a heap of gold beneath a tree. In their covetousness each plots the death of the others with such ingenuity that they all die. 47-50, 380-1, 425

SIR THOMAS WYATT (*c.* 1503-1542) and THE EARL OF SURREY (*c.* 1517-1547) 59

Poets at the Court of King Henry VIII, both employed on diplomatic missions to France and Italy. Their lyrical forms, notably the sonnet, are concise and personal in emotion, and introduce the Continental influence of the Renaissance. Surrey introduced Blank Verse in his translation of the *Aeneid.*

EDMUND SPENSER (1552-1599) 60-2

Of humble origin, he depended on Court patronage. He was given a Government post in Ireland, but his house was burnt by rebels. He returned to England and died shortly afterwards in poverty. A major poet. His work is distinctive for the beauty and clarity of imagery and the liquid smoothness of rhythm.

The Shepherd's Calendar (1579): Pastoral poetry of shepherd 60

Page

life adapted to themes of love, elegies and religious debate.

Prothalamion (1596): A poem written before a marriage, showing the poet's dependence on patronage. 60

The Faerie Queene (Begun 1589): A poem on epic scale in six cantos (unfinished). The adventures of Una and the Red Cross Knight constitute a two-fold allegory: the hazards and temptations of a Christian life, and the duty of an Englishman in his service to Queen Elizabeth. The Spenserian nine-line stanza is employed: ABAB, BCBC, C. The landscape has an enchanted Irish quality: fantastic settings mingle with domestic scenes, and allegorical abstractions with real people. 60-2

SIR PHILIP SIDNEY (1554-1586) 59-60

An Elizabethan poet, scholar, soldier and courtier, he died after being wounded at the Battle of Zutphen.

Astrophel and Stella (1580-4): An Elizabethan sonnet sequence showing the progress of a love suit. 59

Apology for Poetry (1580): The first considerable prose work of English criticism. 71-2, 12, 24

FRANCIS BACON (1561-1626) 72-3

One of the intellectuals of his age: as philosopher he propounded new methods of reasoning; as scientist he established the experimental method; and he was also statesman, diplomat and lawyer. He derived his precise accuracy from Latin, in which he wrote many of his books. He is a master of the concise, epigrammatic sentence; his style employs antithesis and other forms of word-pattern. 65

Essays (1597): Bacon submits human behaviour to the scientific method, deriving maxims of (mainly) worldly wisdom from his observations of human nature. 72-3

CHRISTOPHER MARLOWE (1564-1593) 81-4

Educated at Canterbury and Cambridge, Marlowe belonged to the University Wits. He led a wild life and dabbled in heretical religious views, which brought him into conflict with the Church. He died in a tavern brawl. He established the Elizabethan romantic drama of heightened passions and exaggerated incident; the splendour of his blank verse lifted stage diction. His plays revolve round a single character. 64

Tamburlaine the Great (two parts, 1587): Hero's lust for power; melodramatic incident and exotic splendours. 81

Page

Doctor Faustus (1588): Here the thirst for power is through unlimited and forbidden knowledge. With trivial comedy scenes (perhaps by another hand) the play is very uneven, but there is real dramatic conflict in the mind of Faustus arising from his defiance of God. The blank verse of Faustus' soliloquies anticipates Shakespeare's tragedies. Morality element in appearance of devils, angels and abstractions. 81-3

Edward II (1593): A rather mechanical historical drama significant in preparing the stage for Shakespeare's histories. Rapid dialogue achieves effective interplay of character. 83-4

WILLIAM SHAKESPEARE (1564-1616) 90-130

Born at Stratford-upon-Avon, Shakespeare probably attended the local Grammar School. He married Anne Hathaway, and possibly had some experience as a lawyer's clerk. He left Stratford about 1586, and may have joined the Gentlemen Adventurers in sea or land expeditions. In 1592 he was writing for the theatre, first in Moorfields, later at the Globe on Bankside. He prospered as a playwright, actor (secondary parts) and poet, and became a shareholder in the theatre. He returned to Stratford, bought a gentleman's residence, and eventually died there in 1616. 63-4, 364, 367, 390-1

A Midsummer Night's Dream (*c.* 1596): Five elements in plot all related to the marriage of Theseus and Hippolyta. Love is fancy, a trick of the eyes. The fairies, themselves capricious, manipulate events mischievously. The Rude Mechanicals are contemporary London craftsmen with their leader, Nick Bottom, supremely self-confident, whether in fairyland or at Court: an early example of the unconscious humour of many of Shakespeare's comic characters. 91

The Merchant of Venice (*c.* 1596): The melodramatic story of Shylock and the romantic theme of Bassanio's suit to Portia are linked by Portia's intervention in the Trial Scene. The Jew is greedy, cunning and cruel, but proud of his race, a strict Puritan, and a victim of persecution. The Belmont scenes have the character of a fairy story, with the Casket scheme as a test of character. Portia outwits Shylock, after an appeal for mercy, by encouraging him to insist on the letter of his bond. The poetry of the Belmont scenes is rich in imagery and allusions, particularly in the Garden Scene, Act V. 91-3, 372-8, 425, 363-4

As You Like It (*c.* 1599): Shakespeare gathers a medley of characters into the Forest of Arden (Warwickshire in dis- 93-4

Page

guise), where they have taken refuge from the sordid realism of the Court. The Duke cherishes idealistic notions; Jaques is melancholy and sentimental; Silvius and Phebe pastoral and Arcadian. All are exposed to the correctives of Touchstone's wit and the sanity and high spirits of Rosalind's love for Orlando. 369-71

Twelfth Night (*c.* 1600): Another high-spirited comedy set in the Illyria of Shakespeare's imagination. The love story is one of disguises and mistaken identity. The characters are ridiculed with light irony: Orsino is in love with love, Olivia emotionally dramatic but uncontrolled. Only Viola is practical and restrained. 94-8

In Olivia's household are: Sir Toby Belch, care-free and dedicated to the "cakes and ale" of life; Sir Andrew Aguecheek, Sir Toby's dupe, comic in his stupidity; Feste, a clever and professional fool; and Maria, a witty lady-in-waiting ready for any mischief. The antics of this group culminate in the mock duel between Sir Andrew and Viola, when the intervention of Sebastian complicates but ultimately resolves the comedy. 386-9

The gulling of Malvolio is more bitter in its satirical comedy. Malvolio is a good steward, valued by Olivia, but "sick of self-love," lacking in humour, and self-righteous, which brings him into collision with Sir Toby's midnight frolics. The letter joke develops into cruelty.

King Richard II (*c.* 1596): In the early scenes Richard is the impulsive and selfish centre of a luxurious, extravagant court; but in his downfall he displays the mind of a poet, dramatizing his own despair, and acquiring tragic greatness in his fall. Weakness is his cardinal fault. By contrast, his rival Bolingbroke is practical and unimaginative, a calculating politician. Political wisdom is spoken by John of Gaunt, a patriot, and by the Duke of York, a weaker, compromising character. The women characters are victims of political disorder, the young Queen being especially pathetic. The theme of failure is relieved by many patriotic passages. 99-102, 351, 365-6

King Henry V (*c.* 1598): The spirit of the play is patriotic and Elizabethan. Henry V is Shakespeare's ideal king: religious, decisive, ruthless or merciful as circumstances demand, a born leader, modest, and with a sense of humour. By contrast the French Dauphin is lazy, boastful and inefficient. In the play history and invention mingle: the commoners in Henry's army are portrayed in comic vein. Fluellen, in spite of Welsh 102-7, 360-1, 367-8

Page

oddities of behaviour and speech, is conscientious and efficient; he clashes with Pistol and his group of "hangers-on" 371-2
whose cowardice and rogueries contrast with the heroic theme. The King's visit to his troops on the night before battle is the most valuable part of the play, with reflections on kingship and its burdens and responsibilities. There are passages of sustained oratory and spectacular pageantry.

Shakespeare, impressed by the limitations of his stage 399-400
("This wooden O"), introduces a Prologue who appears before each Act to indicate the movement of scene and passage of time. Some fine word-pictures are in these passages.

A Shakespearean tragedy is an action passing through a 107-8
central climax which is brought about by the hero, but which creates circumstances which inevitably draw the hero to his ruin. In his resistance to this Fate the hero displays resources of character which lift him above normal human dimensions, and so he acquires greatness in his fall.

Julius Caesar (*c.* 1599): The tragic hero is Brutus, a political 108-14
idealist who, after much inward conflict of mind, murders Caesar to preserve the political liberty of Rome; but Antony by his oratory persuades the mob of Rome to avenge Caesar's murder. Brutus flees to Sardis, where he and Cassius raise an army but are defeated by Antony and Octavius at the Battle of Philippi.

There are sharp contrasts of character in the play. Caesar is a great man in his dotage, pompous, superstitious and easily 359-60
influenced. Cassius is an artful politician with personal 398-9
motive. Antony is an opportunist with the arts of a demagogue, swaying the people by emotional appeal. Brutus, in his failure to read character, misjudges both these men. The wives of Brutus and Caesar, directly contrasted, emphasize their husbands' characters by their behaviour towards them.

The mob of Rome, incapable of exercising freedom, is the 425-6
background influence determining the issue between the parties.

Macbeth (*c.* 1606): Macbeth, a loyal and victorious general of 114-22
King Duncan, is nevertheless ambitious. Tempted by the witches and persuaded by Lady Macbeth, he determines after much inward conflict of mind to murder Duncan. Imaginative and sensitive to horror and any suggestion of the supernatural, he suffers acute mental anguish. He succeeds to the throne, but for his own security is forced to murder

Page

Banquo. Gradually he becomes hardened to crime. He again visits the witches, who promise him deceptive security. Failing to trap Macduff, he murders Macduff's wife and children. Malcolm and Macduff lead an avenging army from England; the witches' promises are revealed to be equivocal; and Macduff slays Macbeth. 381-3

Lady Macbeth, in contrast, is unimaginative and literal (Act II, Sc. 2); she is single-minded in pursuing Duncan's murder. Realizing the horror after the event, her mind gradually breaks under the strain.

Banquo is cautious, first in his reaction to the witches, and later in disguising his hostility to Macbeth. This brings him 391-2
to his death. Contrariwise, Macduff is an open enemy, who 426
avenges Duncan.

The three witches are a background influence in the play, representing the temptations that come to men's minds, and seeming to imply satanic forces in the universe. They induce in our minds a sense of Fate.

The Tempest (*c.* 1611): Shakespeare's last play is a tragi-comedy. A great wrong has been committed in the past, Antonio's usurpation of Prospero's dukedom, assisted by Alonso, King of Naples. The tempest links past and present, bringing Prospero's enemies into his power by shipwrecking them on the island. However, Prospero's purpose is not revenge but reconciliation and forgiveness, after his enemies have been brought through suffering to repentance. Reconciliation is aided by the love of Miranda, Prospero's daughter, for Ferdinand, son of Alonso. 122-30

The murder theme is triplicated, by the plot against Alonso and by Caliban's conspiracy with Stephano. This generalizes murder as inherent in the human mind, but is counteracted by Prospero's moral purpose.

The setting on the magic island, with its scenery, spirits, music and songs, gives a masque-like quality to the play. Ariel, a spirit of air, loves freedom but is benevolent in nature. Caliban, half-demon, half-human, is a creature of earth and evil. On his human side, however, he is intelligent, and loves nature and music, and he is therefore redeemable (unlike Stephano).

In construction, the play observes the classical unities of time and place: the past is drawn into the play by dramatic narration and the entire action takes place on the island.

Page

THOMAS DEKKER (*c.* **1572-***c.* **1632**) 87-8

A Londoner of little education, in whose plays Londoners saw themselves presented in a mixture of romance and realism.

The Shoemaker's Holiday (1600): The shoemakers' fraternity at work and play, with vigorous Cockney speech, independence and pride in their craftsmanship. Simon Eyre, who rises to be Lord Mayor and gives the holiday, shows characterization rich in comedy. Rowland Lacy, an Earl's son, becomes an apprentice to win the Lord Mayor's daughter; and love triumphs after trials in the story of Ralph and his Jane. 88

BEN JONSON (1572-1637) 84-6

A scholar and critic, he advocated a classical restraint which he did not always follow in his plays. His quarrelsome nature often involved him in brawls, and sometimes with the law. In most of his plays he is a satirist. His early comedies present eccentric oddities of London life, type characters known as "Humours." Two Roman plays, ***Sejanus*** and ***Catiline,*** are his nearest approach to classical tragedy. 67

Volpone the Fox (1606): Reminiscent of Italian drama in the extravagant and almost incredible roguery of Volpone, miser and sensualist. The victims of the ingenuity of Volpone and his parasite Mosca are also exaggerated, but behind the fantastic quality of character and incident lies essential truth to life. 85-6

The Alchemist (1610): A similar story of imposture by a group of servants who set up as alchemists in their master's absence. The comedy is robust and the best satire is that directed against their credulous and puritanical victims. 84

Lyrical Poems: Influenced the metrical forms and temper of later Cavalier poets. Jonson's verse is classical in inspiration, but avoids the artificiality of earlier Elizabethans in use of mythology and pastoral settings.

JOHN DONNE (1573-1631) 65-6

He held the persecuted Catholic faith, but later took Anglican Orders and became Dean of St. Paul's. His ***Sermons*** enriched the tradition of English prose. In early life he wrote satires and love poetry, in later life religious verse. He established the Metaphysical school of poetry. His metres are often irregular and cumbrous, moulded by the urgency of his thought. His

Page

deep feeling and fine intellect employ paradox, strange images and obscure metaphors. His intellectual metaphors and precise Latinized words, and the way his mind moves by association of words and images, have appealed strongly to twentieth-century poets. His later religious sonnets are more regular, and achieve the deep harmonies of his prose.

JOHN WEBSTER (*c.* 1580-*c.* 1625) 86-7

A writer of revenge melodramas reminiscent of Italian Renaissance drama of the family feud, he satisfied a taste for horror and sensation. Examined critically, his plays lack tautness in construction, and character is often crude in motive. Nevertheless his plays grip by the power of their verse and by the pity and fear which Webster raises in his audience; but he 64
can also play on gentler emotions.

The Duchess of Malfi (1614): The virtuous widowed duchess 86-7
is persecuted by her two brothers; the play ends in slaughter.

FRANCIS BEAUMONT (1584-1616) and JOHN FLETCHER (1579-1625) 88-9

Wrote plays in partnership.

The Knight of the Burning Pestle (1613): A burlesque 88-9
presenting the artless citizens of London and their literary tastes, by which they project themselves into the adventures of knights errant. The play is a medley in both incidents and styles of writing.

ROBERT HERRICK (1591-1674) 68

The master of the short lyrical poem. His earlier poetry of love and wit links him with the Cavalier poets, but later he took Holy Orders and retired to Devonshire, where he wrote delightful lyrics of nature and country life.

GEORGE HERBERT (1593-1633) 67

A writer of metaphysical and religious verse which reflects the spiritual qualities of his personal religion. His collection of poems, ***The Temple*** (1633), caused him to be regarded as a saint by contemporaries. His poems are often used as hymns.

JOHN MILTON (1608-1674) 133-49

A Londoner who, after coming down from Cambridge in 1632, lived at Horton in Buckinghamshire until 1638, when he went

Page

on a Grand Tour of Europe. On his return he became involved in the politics of the Civil War, and was Latin Secretary to Cromwell during the Commonwealth. In 1652 he went blind, but was able to begin writing *Paradise Lost*. At the Restoration, after suffering short imprisonment, he lived obscurely in London writing his later works. Milton is isolated from other poets of his time. A Classical scholar, his mind was sensitive to the beauty of the pagan mythology of Greece and Rome (which he is constantly adapting to Christian themes), to the power of music, and to the beauty of nature; but the thought and ideals of his poetry are Puritan.

Ode on the Morning of Christ's Nativity (1629): The humble Babe of Bethlehem is Almighty God, Creator of the world and Controller of princes. His coming, heralded by music, anticipates the triumph of peace over war and good over evil. Pagan gods are banished. Milton's learning, philosophical, Classical and biblical, fills the whole poem. 135-7

L'Allegro and ***Il Penseroso*** (*c.* 1632): Two lyrical poems written at Horton and conceived as a pair to portray the pursuits of a light-hearted man and a melancholy or studious man; really one man in two moods, Milton himself. *L'Allegro* is a poem of daytime and sunlight, simple interests, comedy and romance, and light airs of music. *Il Penseroso* celebrates night-time and moonlight, shady groves and clouded skies, indoor studies (Philosophy), tragedy, Gothic architecture and organ music. Each poem has a mythological preamble introducing the mood; short rhyming couplets give buoyancy to the verse. 137-9

Lycidas (1637): An elegy mourning the death of Edward King, a college friend drowned at sea. The poem follows the Pastoral Convention, by which characters are represented as shepherds; and the natural background is closely linked with the thought of the poet. There are transitions to varying themes—one autobiographical, showing Milton's sense of God's purpose in his life, and one introducing religious controversy—but unity is maintained by the theme of the tragedy of death in youth. 139-42

The Sonnets are reflective autobiographical poems. Milton adopts the Petrarchan model, with the sonnet divided into octet and sestet—ABBA, ABBA: CDE, CDE. All the sonnets are characterized by very condensed thought and stately utterance. 142-4

On His Being Arrived to the Age of Twenty-three: Shows Milton's Calvinistic sense of God's purpose in his life. 134

Page

On His Blindness: Deep religious faith prevailing over doubt. 144

To Cyriac Skinner and ***To Mr. Lawrence***: Cultured pleasures. 144

On the Late Massacre in Piedmont: Shows Milton's Puritan zeal. 143

Paradise Lost, Books I and II (completed 1667): An epic poem on the scale of Homer's *Iliad*: the story of Satan's revolt in Heaven and his fall into Hell, the creation of the world, and the fall of man. This poem reflects the thought and outlook of Puritan England. Books I and II take place in Hell and show Satan planning with the Fallen Angels to invade newly-created Earth and lure Man into sin. 144-9 427

Style: Blank verse varying from condensed Latinized diction to rich romantic passages of sustained rhythm. Unearthly scenery, connected to earthly reality by use of similes, which become poems in themselves and relieve the tension of the story. Constant allusion to future world history, mainly biblical. The building of Pandemonium, the Gates of Hell, and Satan's crossing of the Abyss of Chaos show the imaginative quality of Milton's mind. Satan is the hero of the poem, a tragic character, indomitable in defeat. The Debate in Pandemonium reflects parliamentary oratory of Milton's time, with statesmen of varying types. The story of Sin and Death introduces allegory. 383

JOHN SUCKLING (1609-1642) 67

A Cavalier poet who wrote easy natural lyrics in which are mingled love, wit and cynicism. He died in exile during the Civil War.

RICHARD CRASHAW (*c.* 1612-1649) 67

A writer of mystical religious verse, devotional in character. He was converted to Roman Catholicism when driven from Cambridge by Puritans.

RICHARD LOVELACE (1618-1658) 67-8

Unequal in achievement, he wrote two perfect lyrics, ***To Lucasta, on Going to the Wars*** and ***To Althea from Prison.*** Lovelace has the courtly wit and sense of honour of the Cavalier. Ruined by the Civil War, he died in poverty.

ANDREW MARVELL (1621-1678) 68-70

A cultured, polished Puritan without fanaticism, he served in governments under both Cromwell and Charles II, seeking only

Page

to defend liberty. His mind and outlook closely reflect the England of his day.

An Horatian Ode upon Cromwell's Return from Ireland (1650): A patriotic poem. 68

To His Coy Mistress: Lyrical power, and metaphysical wit. 68-9

The Garden and ***Song of the Emigrants in Bermuda***: Convey Marvell's feeling for nature. 69

HENRY VAUGHAN (1622-1695) 67

A Welsh poet influenced by Herbert, he conveys his mystical religious thought through a feeling for nature. His poem ***The Retreat*** (1650) influenced Wordsworth. 67

JOHN BUNYAN (1628-1688) 158-61

Of humble birth in Bedfordshire, Bunyan underwent religious conversion and became a Baptist minister. Suffering persecution after the Restoration, for preaching without a licence, he wrote his books in Bedford gaol.

Grace Abounding (1666): Autobiography; intimate, simple yet profound. 159-60

The Pilgrim's Progress (1678): A Christian's search for salvation dramatized as a hazardous journey from the City of Destruction to the Celestial City. The story is an allegory, but characters, scenery and events reflect the Bedfordshire of Bunyan's day, including fabulous wonders of the broadsheets, in biblical style. The book had an enormous vogue. 160

JOHN DRYDEN (1631-1700) 150-4

He was educated at Westminster and Cambridge. In the new age introduced by the Restoration (1660) Dryden established moulds in which the literary developments of the Classical period were to be set, notably the Heroic Couplet. His poetry shows the restraints of classical form. He wrote on public events rather than on a personal note.

Annus Mirabilis (1667): Describes naval war against Dutch, and Great Fire of London, in picturesque but formal verse. 151-2

Absalom and Achitophel, Part I (1681): Dryden uses the biblical story of Absalom's revolt against David to expose a plot to bring about the succession to the throne of the Duke of Monmouth. Characters on both sides of the struggle are represented in satirical portraiture (e.g. the Earl of Shaftesbury). The verse employed is the Heroic Couplet: two rhyming 152-3, 19

Page

ten-syllable lines, the sense-pause falling on the second rhyme so that each couplet becomes a verse. Lines are given epigrammatic force ("Brevity is the soul of wit"), or divided to give antithesis of sharply contrasted notions. These proved effective devices for the poetry of ideas in an Age of Reason.

Odes: Two of these, the ***Song for St. Cecilia's Day*** and ***Alexander's Feast,*** provided models for eighteenth-century poets. 154

Dryden also wrote several successful plays, including:

Marriage à la Mode (1673): Amorous intrigues. 151

All for Love (1678): A version of the Antony and Cleopatra story. 150

The Spanish Friar (1681): An attack on the Roman Catholics.

DANIEL DEFOE (*c.* 1660-1731) 161-2

The son of a London butcher, he took part in Monmouth's rebellion. Employed as an early journalist to collect facts for the new middle-class, he was imprisoned and put in the pillory for various political writings.

The Shortest Way with the Dissenters (1702): A fierce satire which brought Defoe to the pillory. 161

Robinson Crusoe (1719): Superficially a romantic chronicle of adventure, is really a factual survey of man's duel with Nature and his dependence on the providence of God. 161-2

A Journal of the Plague Year (1722): Vivid account of the Great Plague of 1665.

JONATHAN SWIFT (1667-1745) 165-7

Of obscure birth, probably related to the Temple family, he went to Dublin University and was given a parish in Ireland when he took Holy Orders. In England from 1704-14, he wrote political pamphlets for the Tory party which brought about the fall of the Whigs, and the end of the wars of Marlborough. Upon the fall of the Tories he was made Dean of St. Patrick's, Dublin, where he lived in virtual exile for the rest of his life. The deadly effectiveness of Swift's satire sprang from a powerful intellect and a bitter realization that he had never met with his deserts.

The Battle of the Books (1697): Vindication of Classical literature.

A Tale of a Tub (1704): A satire on religious strife. 165

Gulliver's Travels (1726): A satirical allegory developed in four imaginary voyages, to Lilliput, Brobdingnag, Laputa 165-7

Page

and the Land of the Houyhnhnms. In the first two, qualities 166
of mind relate to physical size: the Lilliputians represent
little-minded humanity, but the giants of Brobdingnag are a 20
superior race. The story of the flying island of Laputa is a
satire on the development of science, and the Houyhnhnms
are an ideal race of horses guided by nature and reason (the
foundations of Swift's philosophy). In this tale human nature
is represented by the depraved and bestial Yahoos.

JOSEPH ADDISON (1672-1719) 162-5

Educated at Oxford, Addison was an occasional poet and
playwright, attached to the Whig interest in politics and rising
to high office in later life; but he found his true genius in
collaboration with Steele in the conduct of ***The Tatler*** and ***The*** 163-4
Spectator. These journals were addressed to the newly prosperous middle-class, who wished to acquire manners and culture, and who gathered in the coffee-houses of London.

The essays were given a loose unity by the introduction of fictitious characters: the Spectator Club consisted of a few representative types of London society with Addison himself as the unobtrusive Spectator. Pre-eminent among these was Sir Roger de Coverley, an elderly and eccentric but warm-hearted country gentleman. In this way the essays anticipated the eighteenth-century novel of character and social values.

Topics include the caprices of fashion, politics, religion, tales and allegories, and some literary criticism. The tone is one of mannered conversation. Humour and wit are ironical but kindly. The aim is to cultivate tolerance and broad-mindedness. Addison introduced urbanity into English prose style.

RICHARD STEELE (1672-1729) 162-5

An Irishman of rather unstable early life, he established ***The Tatler*** (1709) and was joined by Addison, the partnership persisting in the later ***Spectator*** (1711). Steele showed more imagination as a writer, and the initiative was his. He created Isaac Bickerstaff, the Wizard of the *Tatler*. Addison was the more consistent writer and gave stability to the venture.

ALEXANDER POPE (1688-1744) 154-8

Born in London of middle-class parents, he was a sickly and deformed child, and belonged to a Catholic family, which debarred him from University. These handicaps in a sensitive

Page

mind stimulated aggressiveness in personal quarrels, and encouraged a natural bent for satire. Wide reading of the Classics and a natural instinct for rhythm made him pre-eminent among poets of the Classical period. He almost invariably employed the Heroic Couplet (see DRYDEN). He was the first poet to gain independence by his writing.

The Rape of the Lock (1712-14): A poem in five cantos inspired by a social scandal, describing with good-humoured satire the social vanities of beaux and ladies of fashion at the court of Queen Anne. The poem is given the quality of the mock-heroic by introduction of Homeric allusions and parallels from the *Iliad* and *Odyssey* in treatment of character and incident. The supernatural was introduced into the later version in the form of Sylphs and Gnomes, who inhabit the elements of air and earth and are akin to Good and Evil; they influence the behaviour of mortals. Pope describes these spirits in delicate and colourful imagery. The style of the poem shows the variety of rhythms that Pope can introduce into the superficially uniform couplets. His copious use of antithesis, epigram, anti-climax and circumlocution assists the sparkling wit that characterizes the whole poem. 155-7 365

Essay on Criticism (1711) and ***Essay on Man*** (1734): Two philosophic poems, on the art of poetry and on human nature. The abstract nature of the themes is relieved by copious examples presented in concrete imagery. Both poems abound in aphorisms (epigrammatic proverbs): Pope can give novelty to an obvious truth by the way he expresses it. 157-8 19

The Dunciad (1728): Pope's most sustained satirical work: his rivals and detractors are dismissed with withering sarcasm and irony.

Epistle to Dr. Arbuthnot (1735): Another satire, modelled on the Augustan writers; contains a slashing criticism of Addison. 158

SAMUEL RICHARDSON (1689-1761) 205

A master printer whose stories, written in the form of a series of letters, established the social novel of the eighteenth century as a literary form, blending romance and realism.

Pamela (1740): The story of a domestic servant whose virtue was besieged but triumphant. 205

Clarissa Harlowe (1747-8): Characters are more convincingly portrayed, and the moral purpose of the novel less avowed.

Sir Charles Grandison (1753-4): A later study of character.

CHAPTER 9

THE SECOND HALF OF THE EIGHTEENTH CENTURY

MARLBOROUGH'S wars in the reign of Queen Anne were followed by peace for three-quarters of the century; this peace, by giving scope for profitable trade, such as was conducted by Sir Andrew Freeport in the *Spectator* essays, led to wealth and leisure and these in turn to the spread of education and the rapid growth of a substantial middle class and a reading public. In any random group of readers, most will prefer prose to poetry, and, whereas the quality most needed to appreciate poetry is a responsive imagination, that most needed for prose is good sense. As appreciation is the climate in which most writers thrive best, it was natural that, although the greatest production of the adventurous sixteenth century was drama, and that of the contentious seventeenth was the epic, the eighteenth century, at least until publication of Wordsworth's and Coleridge's *Lyrical Ballads* in 1798, developed as "an age of prose and sense," distinguished chiefly by its novels, essays and biographies; popular plays, too, when they came from Sheridan and Goldsmith in the last quarter of the century, were in prose. But, as poetry is in itself a higher form of expression than prose, it is best to look first at the successors of Pope and Dryden, and later at those of Swift, Addison and Steele.

Poetry in the Eighteenth Century

In the first half of the century, poets aimed rather at wit than imagination, at how a thing was said rather than what its value was in itself. Pope, the chief exponent of this ideal, has himself defined it as producing "what oft was thought, but ne'er so well expressed," and it must be admitted that there are limits to our enjoyment in reading what oft was thought. Though it may be, as Lytton Strachey in a cynical comment on Pope's *Pastorals* points out, delightful to know that we are going to understand so very, very easily everything that will be said, it is also delightful to realize that the apparent ease with which it is said shows the highest degree of skill.

At the other end of the century came five great romantics, Wordsworth, Coleridge, Byron, Shelley and Keats; but as their first important work came only three years before 1801, they belong to the nineteenth rather than the eighteenth century.

The fifty years before are best represented by seven notable poets, Gray,

Collins, Goldsmith, Cowper, Crabbe, Blake and Burns, born between 1716 and 1759, of whom only Blake outlived the century. Their importance lies both in their choice of and attitude to their subjects, and also in their manner of expressing ideas, by which they showed that they were gradually moving away from the restrictions of the Augustans and opening the way towards their greater successors.

These poets, pre-eminently humanitarian, stir in the reader an awareness of his surroundings and earth-born companions, more vital and more enriching than Pope and his followers could arouse; their outlook on their home in time and space and on three subjects in particular, the poorer classes, animals and nature, gives the reader a feeling that a window is being opened in a well-ordered but rather airless eighteenth-century drawing-room.

Attitude to the Poor

Although in the plays of Sheridan and Goldsmith the "lower classes" are represented as content, either servants of the well-to-do (such as Fag, Lucy and Diggory) who can eat pig and prune sauce daily in their employers' kitchens, or able to pursue independent trades, the often desperate condition

The poor people of London watch Tom Jones on his way to the scaffold, in a scene from the film based on Fielding's novel.

of the poor seeps through the poetry. This poverty was not a result of sheer callousness. It was not the evils so much as the disturbing knowledge that such evils existed that the comfortable upper and middle classes avoided.

The century on the whole accepted "the rich man in his castle, the poor man at his gate," as a divinely appointed law. Wordsworth's lines, "High Heaven rejects the lore of nicely calculated less or more," were not written till 1821; such charitable projects as took shape often had their basis in the wish to have an easy conscience rather than any actual love of their objects, and a good deal of nice calculation must have lain behind any reforms. Even in 1847 Lowood, the charitable institution to which Jane Eyre was relegated, could flourish. By the end of the century, however, workhouses were established, and though in *The Old Cumberland Beggar* Wordsworth attacks political economists as:

> ". . . Ye
> Who are so restless in your wisdom, ye
> Who have a broom still ready in your hands
> To rid the world of nuisances,"

at least some of them were attempting to secure that no man in England needed to starve. But that disinterested kindness was still rare is witnessed by his story of old Simon Lee, whose overwhelming gratitude for a small service grieved him more than ingratitude would have done.

William Cowper (1731-1800), in *The Task*, draws no romanticized picture; he describes from his own observation, "the taper soon extinguish'd, which I saw dangled along at the cold finger's end." To the poor even conversation, an inexpensive recreation, is an impossible luxury:

> "Sleep seems their only refuge; for, alas,
> Where penury is felt the thought is chain'd
> And sweet colloquial pleasures are but few."

The Deserving Poor

So long as the poor were hard-working and honest, and no nuisance, they were admitted as objects of a good man's sympathy:

> "Poor yet industrious, modest, quiet, neat;
> Such claim compassion in a night like this,
> And have a friend in ev'ry feeling heart."

Cowper knew of their wants, that they were often "ill-clad and fed but sparsely," huddled round a fire so small that the mother must shiver while

> "Her infant race, with outspread hands
> And crowded knees, sit cow'ring o'er the sparks."

These are laudably independent poor, "whom famine cannot reconcile to filth," and who, as their children grow up to "find their hands, and labour too," may look for easier times; meanwhile Cowper does not stop at sympathy alone;

"Ye shall not want
What, conscious of your virtues, we can spare."

The Undeserving Poor

But all the poor are not deserving; poverty, in his experience, is too often "self-inflicted woe, th' effect of laziness or sottish waste." Village craftsmen gather at the inn to drown their griefs:

"Smith, cobbler, joiner, he that plies the shears,
And he that kneads the dough; all loud alike,
All learned and all drunk."

Nor will the Government check a useful source of revenue:

"Vain th' attempt
To advertise in verse a public pest, . . .
Th' excise is fatten'd with the rich result
Of all this riot."

Reform cannot be the work of reformers or reformed separately, but of co-operation, nor can it be kept alive by doles of charity. We have to go back behind the observer, Cowper, to the prophetic Blake. The worst, because unconsciously hypocritical, type of reformer is addressed by Blake:

"O'er my sins thou sit and moan;
Hast thou no sins of thy own?
O'er my sins thou sit and weep
And lull thy own sins fast asleep."

But there were many men of genuine goodwill who, like him, recognized that the cure lies not in repressive laws, but in the human heart that knows that harm to one is harm to all:

"For Mercy has a human heart,
Pity a human face,
And Love the human form divine,
And Peace the human dress."

William Blake (1757-1827) often gives us contrasting pictures of the ideal and the real. In his *Songs of Innocence* he presents an idealized picture of orphans supported by public charity; the grey-haired beadles carry "wands as white as snow," the aged men who sit behind them are "wise guardians of the poor," the "thousands of little boys and girls" themselves are innocent and clean, flowers of London town, multitudes of lambs. This is how it pleases the public mind to think of them, but in *Songs of Experience* Blake's indignation at a wealthy society that can with complacency accept such a state of things breaks through:

"Is this a holy thing to see
In a rich and fruitful land—
Babes reduced to misery
Fed with cold and usurous hand?"

Effectual Provision

Even if we discount both as views of a visionary, we cannot so discard the evidence of the novelist Henry Fielding (1707-54) in his *Proposal for Making an Effectual Provision for the Poor*, written in 1753. Fielding, who was by profession a magistrate with practical experience of the crime that poverty produced, recognized that the poor were indeed "a very great burden and even a nuisance," but showed that the heavy tax on property for their relief was so misapplied as to leave many in bitter woe, of whom numbers were reduced to "stench, vermin and want." Our ancestors, he saw, were not so much heartless as ignorant: "That such wretchedness as this is so little lamented arises therefore from its being so little known," and nothing much was or was likely to be done.

Those whom Fielding called "the better sort," by which he meant the upper and middle class who had the natural kindliness, the means, or even merely the practical motive of protecting their own property, which would lead them to attack these evils, did not do so because they remained unaware of them.

He went further, and held that, as not every man suffered from the consequences, "it is not every man's business to suppress them," but here the magistrate is only stating the disease, and pointing out what is not done to cure it. It is Blake who shows that it would be cured only by becoming "every man's business," whether he personally suffered from it or not.

The two are, in fact, complementary; a seer who formulates the natural law of the heart and a magistrate who applies the practical law of his country are mutually necessary, though the second law must be the product of the first.

Blake's is a more authentic voice even than Fielding's because he is "the bard that present, past and future sees." He was not concerned with the age-old argument as to which came first, poverty or crime; they were contemporaneous, and the answer was in the heart first and the law-court and charitable institution second.

Education and Class Distinction

Even where difference in material wealth did not produce a cleavage between classes, difference in education did. Thomas Gray (1716-71) in his *Elegy*, though contemplating with profound and sympathetic understanding the lives of poor country labourers, looked on a weary ploughman as of a

Burns was born in this cottage, and lived here until he was eight.

different world from himself, "unlettered," and it is astonishing enough that a man who could read should think of him at all. But in the last quarter of the century the ploughman, in the person of Robert Burns (1759-96), was writing songs no less widely known than the *Elegy*. Burns' chief quality lies in the way in which his love-songs sing themselves:

"Yestreen, when to the trembling string,
The dance gaed thro' the lighted ha',
To thee my fancy took its wing,
I sat, but neither heard nor saw;
Tho' this was fair, and that was braw,
And yon the toast of a' the town,
I sigh'd, and said amang them a',
'Ye are na Mary Morison'."

The Use of Dialect

It is not only that music runs under the words in every line; the very metre and rhymes depend on the fact that the verse is written in the Scottish tongue. We cannot substitute "yesterday evening," "hall," or "brave," without ruining both, and Burns, by naming particular localities and using words of actual speech, was doing for Scotland what, to some extent, William

Barnes did later for Dorset and its dialect. But Burns could and did use the English of polite circles whenever a moral consideration or a solemn occasion called for him to be, poetically, on his unnatural best behaviour. For example, the second verse of *To a Mouse* seems to be hardly in the same language as the first:

"I'm truly sorry Man's dominion
Has broken Nature's social union."

What would a "wee, sleekit, cow'rin, tim'rous beastie" of Scottish breed make of so carefully expressed a sentiment?

Both Gray and Burns include a description of the homecoming of the labourer, Gray in Augustan diction that almost needs paraphrase to a modern ear, Burns in the Scottish tongue that almost needs interpretation to a Southern ear. The two forms of expression lie equidistant from the plain prose of the matter; children who are almost too young to walk or speak run to meet their father. In the *Elegy*, Gray laments that no more shall

"Children run to lisp their sire's return,
Or climb his knees the envied kiss to share."

North of the Border this becomes,

"Th' expectant wee-things, toddlin', stacher through
To meet their Dad, wi' flichterin' noise an' glee."

Attitude to Slavery

Another unhappy class of the time was the slaves. Toleration of the slave trade, taken for granted at the beginning of the century, was gradually undermined. Cowper's sympathies were possibly quickened by his contact with the Rev. John Newton, himself at one time a slave-trader, who combined that profession with strongly religious feeling.

Among many grimly realistic verses in which Cowper describes, either directly or with trenchant sarcasm, the torments of the wretched cargo, the most telling are those in which he exposes two reasons why men who felt as he did took no steps to end the open abuse: first self-interest, and second the argument—the oldest and falsest in the world—that, as one nation or individual cannot alone cure an evil, it will do no good to come out against it; until everyone in the world does right, why should anyone?

"I pity them greatly, but I must be mum,
For how could we do without sugar and rum?
Especially sugar, so needful we see?
What? Give up our desserts, our coffee and tea!
If foreigners likewise would give up the trade

Much more in behalf of your wish might be said;
But while they get riches by purchasing blacks,
Pray tell me why we may not also go snacks?"

In fact Cowper realized clearly enough that a slave-owner, simply by being one, did himself more deadly harm than any that he could inflict:

"I had much rather be myself the slave,
And wear the bonds, than fasten them on him."

But why either? "We have no slaves at home—then why abroad?"

This was the attitude of a humanitarian; but to a lady of fashion, a small black page was a modish appendage, much as a pet monkey might have been, one of her "little elegant expenses."

Cowper, however, writes of the symptom, not the cause, which lay in lack of common humanity with the coloured man; for a recognition of this we must turn to Blake. In *The Little Black Boy*, the mother taught her son that:

" These black bodies and this sunburnt face
Is but a cloud and like a shady grove."

He loves the English child, "white as an angel," and longs for a life where the accidental and meaningless difference of colour does not divide them. We can see, in passing, that Blake is here attributing to the little black boy a sense of the natural desirability of being white which an actual black boy might be very far from feeling. To Blake's black boy, angels are white; in the twentieth-century play *Green Pastures*, in which the characters are coloured people, angels are black.

Children as Chimney-sweeps

Nearer home we find Blake invoking the same sympathy for English children who were to all intents black slaves, the unhappy chimney-sweeps. Again the victim of oppression pleads his own cause:

" When my mother died I was very young,
And my father sold me while yet my tongue
Could scarcely cry, 'Weep! Weep! Weep! Weep!'
So your chimneys I sweep, and in soot I sleep."

The guilt he lays not only on their brutal masters but on the nation; "the mind-forged manacles" of men's callousness and laziness bind them from doing the good that they might. Though Lamb in his essay *In Praise of Chimney-Sweeps* extols these "innocent nigritudes," whimsical twists of language do not hide his genuine sympathy.

By 1817 a Parliamentary Committee explored the abuse, and in 1832 the practice was forbidden by law, surely a case in which poets were, in Shelley's phrase, "unacknowledged legislators."

The trial scene from the opera Peter Grimes, *based on Crabbe's poem.*

It is, however, from George Crabbe (1754-1832), not a great poet but an exact observer who troubled to inform himself, that we get the most direct picture of abuses against the young and helpless. His Peter Grimes, wicked by nature and made more brutal by poverty, buys three orphan boys, one after another, to serve as apprentices on his fishing-boat, and causes in turn the deaths of all three. What was the law doing to allow it? Magistrates doubted his story that one boy, whom he had killed by a blow, had fallen down an open hatch, but could do no more than warn him to bring a different excuse next time.

The Common Man at War

As to the condition of men in the services, in a period when the press-gang supplied the navy, and a common soldier had neither opportunity nor education to understand the cause for which he was forced to fight, Cowper set responsibility for war on the monarchy, though the nation was at fault for putting up with it:

"War's a game which, were their subjects wise,
Kings would not play at."

It was Crabbe's avowed intention to present the life of the poor stripped of all romantic adornments, "As truth will paint it and as bards will not," and he avoids any artificial pictures of idyllic joys; but Blake's visionary metaphors pierce deeper into the imagination, and so have a profounder influence on the minds of men. The protests of all these inarticulate victims against conventionally respectable and established institutions that crush them rise from a metaphor of terrifying vividness:

"How the chimney-sweeper's cry
Every blackening church appals,
And the hapless soldier's sigh
Runs in blood down palace walls."

In the Elizabethan *Spanish Tragedy*, mad Hieronimo, commissioning an artist to depict the murder of his son, asks him, "Can'st thou paint a cry?" This is exactly what Blake has done.

Attitude to Pet Animals

To pass from consideration of the poor, illiterate and oppressed, human beings without voices, to that of animals, there are, until the last decade of the century, few examples of genuine affection or even respect for animals, though those which do appear charm the more by their rarity.

Gray, indeed, did compose what promised by its title to be a sad and simple little lament for *A favourite Cat, drowned in a Tub of Gold Fishes*, but he could not really have cared much; the elegized cat was one of two which belonged to his friend Horace Walpole, and though Gray calls her "the pensive Selima" it was actually Jemima who "tumbled headlong in." Indeed, the whole purpose of the poem is not to give a voice to affectionate grief but, in substance, to moralize that all that glitters is not gold, and, in style, to contrast poetic diction with that of prose. Except in the title, which gives the facts of the matter in hard, common-sense monosyllables, the word "cat" is used in one line only, "What cat's averse to fish ?" In the verse itself Selima is "demurest of the tabby kind," a "hapless nymph," a "presumptuous maid"; the "tub" becomes a "lofty vase" with a "slippery verge"; and gold-fish are "the genii of the stream." Before poor puss surrendered her last life,

"Eight times emerging from the flood
She mewed to every watery god
Some speedy aid to send."

Lycidas could have done no more.

But Cowper's cat and her kittens were personal friends, as were his spaniel Beau, and his hares, Bess, Puss and Tiney. It is true that in *The Retired Cat* he describes his heroine in her favourite "old empty wat'ring pot" as

"Wanting nothing, save a fan,
To seem some nymph in her sedan;"

but he does so because this poem is only half recounting a true domestic anecdote and also half using the cat as a means of demonstrating a moral, this time,

> "Beware of too sublime a sense
> Of your own worth and consequence."

We go a step further, however, in *The Dog and the Water Lily*, in which Cowper is chiefly concerned to tell the world how cleverly Beau had "puzzling set his puppy brains" to swim out and crop the water-lily that his own walking-stick could not reach; the actual lesson, to be more "awake at duty's call," is tacked on as a proper thing to say. In *The Colubriad*, which records how he rescued a cat and her kittens from a viper, there is indeed a moral at the end and an impressive one, but it is the viper who gets it this time. When he saw one of the kittens watching the snake's darting tongue and "projecting with attention due her whiskered face," Cowper fetched a garden tool and, in his own heroic language and capital letters:

> "With outstretched hoe I slew him at the door,
> And taught him NEVER TO COME THERE NO MORE."

Fables on bees, ravens and glow-worms with a talent for improving rhetoric are a different affair, and any reader who tackles one of them must expect to be done good to, but when Cowper describes the woodman's dog:

> "Close behind his heel
> Now creeps he slow; and now, with many a frisk
> Wide-scamp'ring, snatches up the drifted snow
> With iv'ry teeth, or ploughs it with his snout,"

we are doing no more than going for a winter morning's walk.

Cowper felt hunting to be a detested sport, "that owes its pleasures to another's pain"; he confessed of his hare, "I kept him for his humour's sake," and lovingly recorded in his diary:

> "This day died poor Puss, aged eleven years eleven months. She died between twelve and one at noon, of mere old age, and apparently without pain."

No moral is here, no lesson for fashionable beauties, just the mutual cheer and comfort of man and beast.

Attitude to Wild Animals

Wild creatures also have claims on man's regard and kindness. Mice and men are equally mortal, equally vulnerable to disappointment, so Burns regrets the more that his unintentional destruction of its nest should justify even a field-mouse in looking on man as its enemy. To Blake, wildness is itself as innocent as meekness; his "Tiger, tiger, burning bright" and the lamb who wears its "clothing of delight" are neither of them individuals, as are all the creatures so far mentioned; both are aspects of divine power and beauty, and a world away from "pensive Selima" and the beau-monde towards whose moral improvement her end contributed.

Christopher Smart (1722-71), in his exultant *Song to David*, echoes the joy of strength in earth, air and sea, that belongs to creatures who afford little or nothing to man's domestic uses:

"Strong is the lion—like a coal
His eyeball—like a bastion's mole
His chest against the foes;
Strong the gier-eagle on his sail;
Strong against tide the enormous whale
Emerges as he goes."

Gray had heard about a particular cat, Cowper knew an actual kitten and a dog, Burns saw one mouse, once only; but Blake's tiger is every tiger, always, everywhere, and his lamb every lamb.

William Collins as a young man.

Respect for Life

This feeling for animals is not vitiated by false sentimentality; their use to supply human beings with labour, food or commodities is held to be moral so long as they are treated with respect. But complacent acceptance by a nation of deliberate or negligent cruelty is a sign of deadly spiritual disease:

"A dog starved at his master's gate
Predicts the ruin of the state,
The lamb misused breeds public strife
And yet forgives the butcher's knife."

It is only an extension of these various forms of sympathy with animals that makes the Ancient Mariner, who shot an albatross merely for the sake of killing, feel "a spring of love" for "the creatures of the great calm," not for any mortal thing that he can get out of them in the way of use, sport or pleasure, but just because they are "happy living things" and, by so feeling, save his soul.

Two years later, in the last year of the eighteenth century, William

Wordsworth clinched the matter in the poem *Hart-Leap Well* by his vow:

> "Never to blend our pleasure or our pride
> With sorrow of the meanest thing that feels."

Attitude to Nature

In their attitude to nature, if we take one aspect only on which almost every poet tries his hand—evening—we see a similar change. Gray and Collins, trained to take personification and classical references as hallmarks of poetic competence, but themselves breaking through to a simpler and lovelier mode of expression, held out, each in his most famous poem, one hand to the past and the other to the future.

Gray's *Elegy Written in a Country Churchyard*

In Gray's *Elegy* the first twelve lines give, through gradations of light into darkness and sound into silence, a slow-motion version of Milton's five words, "Now came still Evening on." "Parting day" brings the last of the sunset before our eyes; light fades from glimmering fields until the moon strengthens overhead, and interwoven with these impressions the closing sounds of day, one after another, reach the ear: church bell, the lowing herd, homing footsteps, the drone of rising cockchafers, distant sheep-bells, and then, as silence becomes almost absolute, the strong and characteristic hoot of an owl takes possession of the night. There is nothing here unfamiliar to modern senses, nothing of Ben Jonson's *Hymn to Diana*:

> "Hesperus entreats thy light,
> Goddess, excellently bright,"

nor of Milton's Hesperus "that led the starry host," nothing but what we ourselves can see and hear and speak of.

But as soon as Gray begins to reflect how transitory are human lives and ambitions, and to picture himself as an educated gentleman in this simple country setting, the ploughman whom we know is replaced by "some hoary-headed swain," grassy hill slopes are "the upland lawn," the local tombstone-maker is directed by "th' unlettered Muse" and Gray's own classical knowledge is personified as "fair science" smiling on her poet.

Collins' *Ode to Evening*

Collins also has these two threads, personification and natural description, twisted together throughout his *Ode to Evening*. In the first two verses the close of day is "pensive Eve," a "nymph reserved," but by the third he too is putting into words familiar effects of the hushed air and a beetle's "heedless hum." The evening star wears a "paly circlet" and carries a warning lamp to summon attendant elves and personified pleasures to prepare her car; next

Collins in familiar words evokes a familiar scene, as the reader perceives

> "... Wilds and swelling floods,
> And hamlets brown, and dim-discovered spires,
> And hears their simple bell,"

though it is a personified evening whose "dewy fingers draw the gradual dusky veil." Then, after brief pictures of the four seasons we are back with "Fancy, Friendship, Science, smiling Peace," clearly symbolic figures.

Cowper welcomes peaceful evening in, with the cups "that cheer but not inebriate" in the affectionate company of Mary Unwin, reading the newspapers brought by the postboy, that "herald of a noisy world, with spatter'd boots, strapped waist and frozen locks," whose contrast more endears "the silence and the warmth enjoyed within." It is all very comfortable:

> "Now stir the fire, and close the shutters fast,
> Let fall the curtains, wheel the sofa round."

Even his pet hare, Tiney, shares the fireside enjoyments.

Many poets seem to have a favourite adjective; for Chaucer it is "fresh," for blind Milton "bright," for unsatisfied Keats "rich," for Shakespeare "sweet." Cowper's must surely be "snug"; his cat seeks repose "within her master's snug abode," and Tiney, at his death, was "in snug concealment laid." No part of "God's bright and intricate device of days and seasons" can have offered him better opportunity to be snug than "the hours of long uninterrupted evening" in the depth of an English winter. Writing in 1784, Cowper was enough of his own century to follow up this homely scene with a conventional description of Evening, with "matron-step" and "sweeping train," but the thread is wearing thin, and he is soon back in his "parlour twilight," seeing pictures in the fire.

Blake's Evening Poems

Blake keeps his two threads apart, and writes separate contrasting poems in two different manners, conventional and natural. When he directly addresses the evening star, he is committed to the earlier style: the "fair-haired Angel of the Evening" wears a radiant crown, carries a torch, draws "the blue curtains of the sky," and protects the flock; but no verse in the English language brings us to bedtime with more childlike security than

> "The sun descending in the west,
> The evening star does shine;
> The birds are silent in their nest,
> And I must seek for mine."

Over such a scene, when the sun is gone down, it seems utterly easy to

Blake, trained as an engraver, illustrated many of his own poems.

accept that there will pass not a personification of Evening as an Angel, but angels themselves:

> "Farewell, green fields and happy groves,
> Where flocks have took delight.
> Where lambs have nibbled, silent moves
> The feet of angels bright."

Farewell till the sun comes again, and then "such a day tomorrow as today."

Whether, with Gray, we are scholarly intruders in a country churchyard, molesting the owl's time-honoured solitude, or with Collins viewing an evening storm, or winning, with Blake's children, an extra timeless hour's play in slowly deepening summer twilight, or sitting with Cowper in undisturbed retirement to watch shadows "dancing uncouthly to the quivering flame," we are in the company of men who felt it incumbent on them occasionally to conform to the poetic diction of their predecessors, but whose natural instinct was drawing them away towards the great nature poetry to come. There is therefore, at the turn of the century, something inevitable in the reverence with which, to Wordsworth, "a beauteous evening, calm and free" is a "holy time," and the unaffected magic with which Coleridge invests

> "The journeying Moon, and the stars that still sojourn, yet still move onward, and everywhere the blue sky belongs to them, and is their appointed rest,

and their native country, and their own natural homes, which they enter unannounced, as lords that are certainly expected and yet there is a silent joy at their arrival."

Town and Country

In many poems of the century a false contrast between the vices and miseries of the town and the innocent joys of the country is emphasized. Pope, who had no intention of living anywhere but in or near London, declared,

"Happy the man whose wish and care
A few paternal acres bound,
Content to breathe his native air
In his own ground;"

and Samuel Rogers echoes the same wish in "Mine be a cot beside the hill." But every man of sense knows that the means to satisfy hunger, enjoy leisure and keep clean do not necessarily produce crime and misery, nor lack of them give happiness and peace of mind; and, by the middle of the century, poets said so.

The romantic attitude of Lydia Languish, who had never undergone an hour's want in her life, was exposed by Sheridan through Jack Absolute when he bade her consider that "A little comfort may be endured." Cowper established the false antithesis in "God made the country and man made the town," a line whose easy balance makes it memorable rather than true, and at one time indulged in an imaginary picture of a peasant's simple blisses. "Oft," he wrote, "have I wished the peaceful covert mine," but the difference between his wish and that of Pope and Rogers was that he meant it, and examined conditions from a practical point of view.

Crabbe, who knew and drew the matter as it was, admitted that life in the country was all right if one owned cattle and property, but that "poor laborious natives" suffered from real ills which all the "tinsel trappings of poetic pride" could not conceal. Two centuries earlier, Dekker accepted it as an axiom that the poor have golden slumbers and the rich "a mind perplexed"; his imaginary honest labourers can "drink the waters of the crisped spring." But not so those who actually inhabited Buckinghamshire in Cowper's time; he observed that a peasant, instead of drinking the "sweet waters of the crystal well," had often to "dip his bowl into the weedy ditch" and wait for his bread,

"Dependent on the baker's punctual call,
To hear his creaking panniers at the door,
Angry and sad, and his last crust consumed."

Romantic fancy itself is perhaps a pleasing mental indulgence, but dirty water and sour bread are certainly not its best nourishment, and with refreshing honesty Cowper decides that he will make the best of the matter:

> "So farewell envy of the peasant's nest!
> If solitude make scant the means of life,
> Society for me!—thou seeming sweet,
> Be still a pleasing object in my view;
> My visit still, but never mine abode."

The way was now clear for Wordsworth's realistic approach and genuine sympathies. His own status was that of a professional man, living in a cottage but not a hut, knowing and feeling the deprivations of a leech-gatherer and an old Cumberland beggar without any attempt to present them as picturesque.

Landscape Gardening

The country estates of wealthy men, however, were influenced by the artificiality of town in a strange vogue for landscape gardening, whereby for a time an uneasy compromise was attempted between the corrupt taste of a townsman for contrived picturesqueness and the disposition of a countryman to let Nature take her own way so long as it did not interfere with him. The Elizabethans, whose clothes declare their love of patterns, delighted in the geometrically arranged flower-beds of their knot-gardens, and Milton in the seventeenth century had given such a detailed description of the Garden of Eden that it is possible to draw a plan of it. "Capability" Brown gained his nickname from his capacity to see and take advantage of the capabilities of an estate, with much felling of avenues, opening of prospects and diverting of streams; but Cowper, though himself enjoying and writing of the lawful "occupations of a retired gentleman in his garden," would have nothing to do with such artifice, and as a genuine countryman he mocks at the grandiose and discomfortable alterations by which the owner of many a modest estate ruined his fortunes and exiled himself to town.

> "Th' omnipotent magician, Brown, appears!
> Down falls the venerable pile, th' abode
> Of our forefathers,—a grave, whisker'd race,
> But tasteless."

The improver issues his orders.

> "He speaks. The lake in front becomes a lawn;
> Woods vanish, hills subside, and vallies rise . . .
> Ev'n as he bids! Th' enraptur'd owner smiles.
> Tis finished, and yet, finished as it seems,
> Still wants a grace, the loveliest it could show,
> A mine to satisfy the enormous cost."

The fashion persisted into the early part of the next century, when

Capability Brown was followed by Humphry Repton; in *Mansfield Park* (1814) Mr. Rushworth determines to "have Repton" to improve his place at Sotherton, feeling sure that "anybody of that sort would certainly have the avenue at Sotherton down." The difference between artificial and genuine simplicity here illustrated is comparable to that between the affected love of nature shown in Pope's *Pastorals* at the beginning of the century and the deep passion that inspired Wordsworth at its end.

Social Implications of Laughter

In one point, however, rules of conduct in town and country did differ, and differed profoundly: laughter. To a well-bred citizen the lack of restraint implied in allowing oneself to make any noise other than that required for speech linked laughter to shouting, jeering and other such offences against the correct taste of being quiet. Lord Chesterfield, arbiter of good manners, in his letters of instruction to his son Philip Stanhope, warns him that there is nothing so vulgar as audible laughter, but Blake's child on a cloud was laughing, and the nurse knows laughter as the accompaniment to heart's peace:

> "When the voices of children are heard on the green,
> And laughing is heard on the hill,
> My heart is at rest within my breast
> And everything else is still."

Perhaps this difference is a sign of a deep distinction between two aspects of the same thing. Wit was an ideal of the city, and wit, H. G. Fowler reminds us, is concerned with expression and addressed to the intelligent who can assess it; the pleasure of judging does not call for any actual sound. But humour is concerned with feeling, and is addressed to the sympathetic; the pleasure of fellow-feeling must be communicated and, though eyes can laugh silently, sound is the most immediate way of making such communication.

Characteristics of Eighteenth-century Poetry

Throughout the work of these poets, two characteristics recur: their poetic diction, and the moralizing of their songs.

Poetic diction is a fashion by which an object familiar in common speech, such as fish or birds, becomes "the finny tribe" or "the feathered songsters of the grove." Francis Thompson calls a similarly specialized vocabulary "praetorian cohorts of poetry, whose prescriptive aid is invoked by every aspirant to the poetic purple"; but this invoking is a deliberate process by which an author often seems to be translating his natural meaning on purpose to assure a reader that, as it is not the normal mode of speaking prose, he must be reading poetry. This is false reasoning, but there are entertaining parallels in support of it.

In a light-hearted dispute between a pipe and a snuff-box, Cowper calls pipe and tobacco by these exact names, though even here he supplies a synonym of "the sweet-smelling Virginian weed," but in *The Morning Walk* this directness will not do; we are in for description, and the woodman pauses,

> "Now and then with pressure of his thumb
> T' adjust the fragrant charge of a short tube
> That fumes beneath his nose; the trailing cloud
> Streams far behind him, scenting all the air."

In other words, he fills, lights and smokes his pipe, but we have lost something by translation into prose, not the fact but its importance.

Not only does poetic diction mark the eighteenth century for her own, but the habit of drawing a lesson from the most engaging or trivial occasions

Thomas Gray is best remembered for his Elegy in a Country Churchyard.

Cowper, though often unhappy, wrote the amusing poem John Gilpin.

particularly recommended itself to the period. The danger is that a poet may value the moral so highly that he forces into its service "a gift God gave for other ends," and to this danger the eighteenth century was especially prone. Fortunately, no great work of art can exist divorced from a power to do good, whether explicitly stated as its moral or not, so no great harm is done so long as the work is great. Of the seven poets under consideration, not one fails to state his moral purpose; but of all, Cowper was most weighed down by his responsibility to do so, even on apparently unsuitable occasions. He had, as his portrait by Romney shows, a mouth ready to break into a humorous quirk, and on his winter morning walk was delighted to record that his lengthened shadow,

> "Spindling into longitude immense. . . .
> Provokes me to a smile."

But the pleasure of this preposterous sight must not be its own justification; he inserts between the two lines a conscientiously depressing thought,

> "In spite of gravity and sage remark
> That I myself am but a fleeting shade,"

and then he is free to joke again.

It is the same with the Empress of Russia's palace of ice; a reader cannot help being better for knowing that the world contained something so lovely:

> "Ice upon ice, the well-adjusted parts
> Were soon conjoined, nor other cement ask'd
> Than water interfused to make them one."
> "A watery light
> Gleam'd through the clear transparency, that seem'd
> Another moon new risen."

But "the wonder of the North" must serve a moral as well as an aesthetic purpose; it was a scene:

> "Of evanescent glory, once a stream
> And soon to slide into a stream again,"

and by so doing to deal on the Empress herself

> "A mortifying stroke
> Of undesign'd severity, that glanc'd,
> (Made by a monarch) on her own estate,
> On human grandeur and the courts of kings."

In effect, so long as the Empress is made sufficiently miserable by thoughts of the transitory nature of human life and glory, she may be happy in its loveliness; "It smiled, and it was cold." When in *Kubla Khan* Coleridge described his "miracle of rare device, a sunny pleasure-dome with caves of ice," he drew no lesson, but made one lovely thing the source of another:

> "Could I revive within me
> Her symphony and song
> To such a deep delight 'twould win me
> That with music loud and long
> I would build that dome in air,
> That sunny dome, those caves of ice!
> And all who heard should see them there."

Deep delight is the inspiration of such a building, and it is moral enough.

A second agent of reform was satire, still a popular medium, though it had been more expertly practised by Pope and his school. When Cowper tries his hand at reforming vices of his age, the gentler his gibe the more effective; a mole is a great conqueror who

> "Disfigures earth, and, plotting in the dark,
> Toils much to earn a monumental pile
> That may record the mischiefs he has done."

His picture of "the paralytic who can hold her cards but cannot play them" is less annihilating than Pope's "a youth of folly, an old age of cards," but neither conqueror nor card-player really affects Cowper.

The town dandy rouses his indignation because "there is a public mischief in his mirth," and folly has achieved "what enemies could ne'er have done," the ruin of England; he feels an implacable disgust for an affected cleric, brother to Chaucer's self-indulgent Friar:

> "Constant at routs, familiar with a round
> Of ladyships,—a stranger to the poor."

A yokel turned soldier returns "to be a pest where he was useful once."

At these and many other anti-social types Cowper would willingly snipe "through the loopholes of retreat," but his weapon does not, like Pope's, shoot to kill.

The Rise of the Novel

In prose, the outstanding event was the rise of the novel as a popular form of literature. It may in some ways be compared with the rise in our own century of the cinema; in both cases popularity was immediate and immense, earlier examples dealt with events and obvious emotions rather than with psychological analysis, and characters were of instantly recognizable innocence or villainy, presented firmly in white or black.

In this new genre the chief authors were Richardson, Fielding, Smollett and Sterne, born between 1689 and 1721, and dying between 1754 and 1771. Between 1740 when Richardson published *Pamela* and 1771 when Smollett published *Humphry Clinker*, the works of all four authors established the novel in public favour, and constructed an incomparably varied picture of their own times.

In *Pamela* and Fielding's companion to it, *Joseph Andrews* (1742), the authors adopted the convention of telling their stories through a series of letters, a method which, in spite of its rather slow movement, recommended itself to a leisured and polite public so well that Smollett used it in *Humphry Clinker*, and Fanny Burney, seven years later, in *Evelina*. Letters are still freely used in Jane Austen's *Pride and Prejudice* (1813), but rather to reveal character or explain past events than as a framework for straightforward narrative. In all these novels, interest varies between events and conversation; things happen, heroes and heroines experience occasions, and then talk about them, or write if the author is committed to letters, but even in letters conversations are copiously recorded.

Each of the two great figures of the central years of the eighteenth century shows in a different way the importance of good talk; Dr. Johnson established himself at the centre of a brilliant circle as an unrivalled exponent of the game; and Goldsmith, reduced to being inarticulate in his presence, presented as his hero in *She Stoops to Conquer* a young man of fashion, Marlow, who can chatter wittily enough with a barmaid, but is overawed into stammering and speechlessness by a companion of his own social level.

Hazards of the Times

The things that happen in novels of this period range over the contemporary scene, from the world of fashion in London and Bath to the then practical terrors of highway robber and press-gang. To modern readers the everyday violence and callousness seem almost incredible until we realize that, in absence of effective controls, the well-to-do looked on the poor as their natural enemies, threatening loss and disease at every contact.

In the country Joseph Andrews is attacked, robbed, beaten, stripped and

A scene from Oliver Goldsmith's comedy, She Stoops to Conquer.

left for dead by two highway ruffians armed with pistols, and, when the postilion of a passing coach draws attention to his groans, the coachman at first refuses to stop on the grounds that "we are confounded late, and have no time to look after dead men." A young lawyer persuades the inhuman passengers to take him into the coach only to protect themselves from being implicated in a murder. The only kindness that he receives is from the postilion, "since transported for robbing a hen-roost," and it is with genuine satisfaction that the reader finds that a little later the same two rascals stop the coach and ransack its cowardly and selfish occupants.

Matters are no better in the city; at Tower Wharf Roderick Random, though carrying a weapon, is seized by a press-gang, whose leader, "a squat, tawny fellow, with a hanger by his side and a cudgel in his hand," delivers him to a pressing tender where he might well have bled to death.

A Visit to the Theatre

Meantime in London the comfortably off who frequented the theatre could foster their capacities for appreciating fine art and forming just opinions. Tom Jones was one of a party attending Garrick's performance of *Hamlet*, taking with them Partridge, up from the country on his first visit. Few criticisms could more skilfully emphasize the difference between Garrick's superb art and the barn-storming exaggerations that passed for acting in country districts than his honest and uninformed comments.

On first seeing the Ghost, he stoutly refused to give it credence, but when he saw Garrick in his scene with it he "fell into so violent a trembling that his knees knocked against each other," for, said he, "if that little man there upon the stage is not frightened, I never saw any man frightened in my life." The art that conceals art completely deceived him, and he chose as best actor "the King, without doubt." When his more sophisticated London hosts objected that Garrick was held to be "the best player who was ever on the stage," Partridge thought they must be joking, for

> "though I was never at a play in London, yet I have seen acting before in the country; and the King for my money; he speaks all his words distinctly, half as loud again as the other. Anybody may see he is an actor."

Ranelagh Gardens, Chelsea

Lydia Melford, travelling among fashionable circles, describes Ranelagh as

> "the enchanted palace of a genie, crowded with the great, the rich, the gay, the happy, and the fair. While these exulting sons and daughters of felicity tread this round of pleasure, or regale in different parties, and separate lodges, with fine imperial tea and other delicious refreshments, their ears are entertained with the most ravishing delights of music, both instrumental and vocal."

The pleasures of these exulting sons and daughters of felicity sound to us woefully restricted; Lydia confesses,

> "I could hardly find patience to be put in a condition to appear, yet I was not above six hours under the hands of the hair-dresser, who stuffed my head with as much black wool as would have made a quilted petticoat."

Manners, even among those who prided themselves upon knowing the code, were often strangely impertinent; the heroine takes it as a great sign of condescension that fashionable Lady Griskin "sometimes adjusts my cap with her own hands," foreshadowing Lady Catherine de Bourgh.

Bath, a Fashionable Spa

Bath, though less formal, is equally delectable.

> "At eight in the morning, we go in dishabille to the Pump-room. Right under the Pump-room windows is the King's Bath; a huge cistern, where you see the patients up to their necks in hot water. The ladies wear jackets and petticoats of brown linen, with chip hats, in which they fix their handkerchiefs to wipe the sweat from their faces."

In the coffee-house for ladies, young girls were not admitted, "inasmuch as the conversation turns upon politics, scandal, philosophy, and other subjects above our capacity." Indeed, capacity for scandal was the passport to Lady Teazle's London circle.

That Bath drew impecunious Irish fortune-hunters such as Sir Lucius O'Trigger or Lydia Melford's suitor, Captain O'Donaghan, with his light-grey eyes, Roman nose, and "a certain boldness in his look and manner that puts one out of countenance," was only to be expected: that her gouty uncle, on the first day of their visit, "beat two black-a-moors" was accepted as natural behaviour. The more refreshing it is to find Laurence Sterne's Corporal Trim telling Tristram Shandy's Uncle Toby, although doubtingly, that "A negro has a soul? an' please your Honour," and though Uncle Toby refuses to venture on a theological argument, he shows sense and humanity in advance of his time in his comment,

> "Tis the fortune of war which has put the whip into our hands now—where it may be hereafter, Heaven knows!—but be it where it will, the brave, Trim, will not use it unkindly."

At two hundred years' remove, readers of these novels may often be aghast at the cruelty based on fear, and the vice engendered by wretchedness.

The Novel of Horror

One strange outcrop from this fertile soil was the novel of horror, of which, though many inferior authors met popular demand for Gothic ruins, ghosts,

Lady Teazle and her friends, from Sheridan's School for Scandal.

skeletons, mysterious friars and fatal casques, the most significant are Horace Walpole's *The Castle of Otranto* and Mrs. Radcliffe's *The Mysteries of Udolpho.* In such tales, heroines peruse half-obliterated manuscripts and drop senseless to the floor, preferably of a dungeon, heroes pace and brood, planning, one cannot help thinking, how to become Lord Byron, arras waves, shades beckon and dislimn. Even so we get an occasional glimpse of eighteenth-century common sense. In *Otranto* Bianca, terrified that "the hand, the giant," has returned to destroy her, cries out to her master, "I will not sleep in the castle tonight!" but prudently adds, "My things may come after me tomorrow." Bianca, however, is only a serving-wench who attends Matilda, and is thus allowed a strain of that "frugal mind" which the middle-class linen-draper John Gilpin approved in his spouse, but which would be unbecoming to the sensibility of Bianca's high-born mistress.

But a taste for supernatural terrors was a natural outlet for a century bred to worship reason; somewhere in the minds of readers was an unsatisfied desire for something beyond what they could explain, some suggestion that existence entitled them to more than a world limited by their five senses. This awareness, an essential part of the human spirit and a prerequisite for reading such poems as *Christabel* and *La Belle Dame Sans Merci*, was at that time fed only by the vulgarities of mere sensation. Their crudeness is easy game for a modern mind, more impressed by intimations of immortality in M. R. James' *Ghost Stories of an Antiquary*; it was also a target for those of Mrs. Radcliffe's own time whom rational thought satisfied.

Northanger Abbey

Jane Austen, born only eleven years after her, found such novels more irritating than stimulating. In *Northanger Abbey*, written less than three years after *The Mysteries of Udolpho*, the ingenuous Catherine Morland, misled by the bad taste of her friend Isabella Thorpe, is launched, after she has finished reading *Udolpho*, on a series of "ten or twelve more of the same kind," and is anxious only to be assured that they are "all horrid." Unable to relegate such fiction to its proper place in her mind, "the well-read Catherine" applies its rules to a respectable household, and lets herself in for a merited rebuke from her host:

> "What have you been judging from? Remember the country and the age in which we live. . . . Dearest Miss Morland, what ideas have you been admitting?"

The conclusion that she draws, on behalf of all readers of such tales, is inevitable:

> "Charming as were all Mrs. Radcliffe's works, and charming even as were the works of all her imitators, it was not in them perhaps that human nature, at least in the midland counties of England, was to be looked for. . . . Among the Alps and Pyrenees, perhaps, there were no mixed characters. There, such as were not as spotless as an angel might have the dispositions of a fiend. But in England it was not so. Among the English, she believed, in their hearts and habits, there was a general though unequal mixture of good and bad."

This verdict, though not published till 1818, was arrived at shortly before the end of the eighteenth century, and clears the way decisively enough for the picture of English character, a "mixture of good and bad," which was to inform the great novels of the nineteenth century.

Villainy in the Theatre

Shakespeare's chief villains are murderers and usurpers who cause death and are punished by death. Those of Sheridan and Goldsmith commit less irrevocable sins and their punishments are less drastic. For what is their ultimate fault? Simply that they are not socially desirable, that they make other people uneasy when they are around, and spoil pleasure. But their authors will not allow them to do any permanent harm. Lady Sneerwell may complain that she was wounded in her youth "by the envenomed tongue of slander," but the ruin of her happiness occurred before *The School for Scandal* begins, and Snake, who plans the same disservice to the innocent, has his fangs drawn by the Muse of Comedy.

If it is objected that it is uneasy to live in the company of murderers and usurpers, the answer is that none of their victims does so, at least not for long; but a dullard, bully or scandalmonger may accompany, while destroying, the whole of a heroine's young womanhood. Even Joseph Surface, a would-be seducer, is unmasked before he can act his villainy. His real fault is that he is untrustworthy as guest or host; his real punishment is that he is laughed at.

Johnson and Goldsmith, Men of Letters

Looking back over the eighteenth century, we see two authors of supreme genius, Dr. Samuel Johnson (1709-84) and Oliver Goldsmith (1728-74), who justly represent it, having achieved excellence or importance in each department of literature. They were personal friends, though Johnson, born in 1709, was nearly twenty years older than Goldsmith and died ten years later than he; they came (from Lichfield and Ireland respectively) to London, where they succeeded in establishing the profession of "man of letters" in a double way.

First, they succeeded not in a single literary form only, as did Steele in essays, Pope in poetry, Richardson in novels and Sheridan in plays; each, though in differing degrees, succeeded in all four. Johnson has to his credit a play in classical tradition, *Irene*; a story, *Rasselas*, though rather a vehicle for philosophical argument than a narrative; a poem, *The Vanity of Human Wishes*; and his papers in *The Rambler*. Even though none of these is known to modern readers as well as his *Lives of the Poets*, his *Dictionary* and his daily conversation recorded in Boswell's *Life*, all succeeded in their day.

Goldsmith was equally various, but more successful in attracting readers in later centuries. A well-read man must still be familiar with his novel *The Vicar of Wakefield*, his poem *The Deserted Village*, his play *She Stoops to Conquer*, and his essays presenting Beau Tibbs, that shabby dandy, and the Man in Black.

On the other hand, Dr. Johnson far outstripped Goldsmith in direct utterance, and is more familiar to most readers for what he said than for what he wrote. In his judgments on life and letters, common sense is raised to the status of a grace (witness the last word to be said on lectures, "I cannot see that lectures can do so much good as reading the books from which the lectures are taken," or the use of wit to express prejudice, "The Irish are a fair people; they never speak well of one another.")

Secondly, while many of their predecessors wrote as an elegant pastime but relied for daily bread on private means, help of friends or the salary of some other occupation, these two established and practised the art of writing as a profession, and earned their living, however precariously at times, by their pens. In so doing they put an end to the bad old system of patronage by which a poor author must rely chiefly on the casual generosity of some wealthy noble. There are many contemporary evidences of the evils of the system. In his *Elegy*, Gray writes of crimes which their ignorance debarred country labourers from committing; among the more dramatic ones of being murderous usurpers or merciless judges, he shows that an illiterate hind can never be tempted to:

> ". . . heap the shrine of luxury and pride
> With incense kindled at the muse's flame,"

to use his heaven-sent genius in flattering poems to the undeserving rich.

The better educated hack-writer, however, could and did; Goldsmith gives a comically shameful picture of a wretched Grub Street rhymester, debased and disappointed, telling a club of authors of his experience:

> "You must know, gentlemen, some time ago, upon the arrival of a certain noble duke from his travels, I set myself down, and vamped up a fine flaunting poetical panegyric, which I had written in such a strain, that I fancied it would have even wheedled milk from a mouse. In this I represented the whole kingdom welcoming his grace to his native soil, not forgetting the loss France and Italy would sustain in their arts by his departure. I expected to touch for a bank bill at least; so, folding up my verses in gilt paper, I gave my last half crown to a genteel servant to be the bearer."

His Grace, however, after considerable delay, returned him

> "no bank bills, but six copies of verse, each longer than mine, addressed to him upon the same occasion."

A Wider Reading Public

It was time the system stopped, and, as peace and prosperity produced a rapidly growing reading public, the position of patron shifted from an individual to the nation. An author could look for his money no longer to Lord Chesterfield and his like, but to a publisher, expanding lists of subscribers, establishment of

Lydia Languish enjoyed library books.

circulating libraries and finally to the thousands who would pay for his book because they could and would get entertainment from it. Of this audience women formed an important part. It is true that when Lydia Languish showed want of duty to her aunt, Sir Anthony Absolute was sure that it came of her reading, but he must not be blamed too much for such an old-fashioned attitude towards the education of girls; nearly a century later Tennyson was still urging Lady Clara Vere de Vere to "teach the orphan boy to read, or teach the orphan girl to sew."

If, however, the system of patronage had thus contracted a wasting disease, it was Dr. Johnson who dealt it the death blow. Of Goldsmith's sordid picture his own experience of patronage provided some corroboration; but, far from putting up with being ignored, Dr. Johnson turned the tables. He had, in 1749, published *The Vanity of Human Wishes* in which he noted the chief misfortunes that can befall a man who aspires to literary fame:

> "There mark what ills the scholar's life assail,
> Toil, envy, want, the garret and the jail."

In later editions for "garret" he substituted "patron," as a greater evil. Downright poverty was less intolerable than such a relationship, and a debtor's prison equally likely to be the result of either.

He went further. He had been recommended to the notice and patronage of Lord Chesterfield, had twice waited on him without result, and had withdrawn in proud independence. When, by his own gifts, Dr. Johnson had written himself into fame and fortune, the noble lord awoke to the fact that Johnson's great *Dictionary* was on the verge of publication and that it would redound to his own credit to be known as patron of its author; with some haste he published two papers recommending it to the public.

The Final Blow to Patronage

This was too much for Dr. Johnson. Neglect he had been forced to accept, but help from the same source he need not and would not accept; and in his famous reply he rejected all offer of it. He had one technical difficulty to overcome; contemporary forms of courtesy exacted that he should sign himself Lord Chesterfield's "most humble, most obedient servant" at the foot of a letter the whole purport of which was to prove that he was the exact opposite. Even this difficulty, however, contributed to the finality of the death-blow. After recording the plain fact that he had never received from Lord Chesterfield "one act of assistance, one word of encouragement or one smile of favour," he adds:

> "Such treatment I did not expect, for I never had a patron before. . . . Is not a patron, my Lord, one who looks with unconcern on a man struggling for

> life in the water, and, when he has reached ground, encumbers him with help? The notice which you have been pleased to take of my labours, had it been early, had been kind; but it has been delayed till I am indifferent, and cannot enjoy it; till I am solitary and cannot impart it; till I am known and do not want it. I hope it is no very cynical asperity not to confess obligations where no benefit has been received, or to be unwilling that the public should consider me as owing that to a patron, which Providence has enabled me to do for myself."

In conclusion of his letter, and indeed of the whole matter, he tells the man who could have been entitled to his gratitude,

> "I have been long wakened from that dream of hope, in which I once boasted myself with so much exultation,
>
> My Lord,
>
> Your Lordship's most humble,
>
> Most obedient servant, Sam. Johnson."

Had Lord Chesterfield realized that within seventeen years of his death Boswell would have published this immortal snub to a world that has ever since associated his name with it, he would hardly have been tempted to indulge in the vulgarity of audible laughter.

Johnson's *Dictionary*

The same magnificent independence appears in Johnson's attitude towards his responsibilities as lexicographer, a word which he defines as "a harmless drudge"; and surely in return for his toil, his staggeringly wide scholarship and his giving our language such a local habitation the harmless drudge may have a little fun and indulge an occasional prejudice. It may not be true that a pension is "pay given to a state hireling for treason to his country," but his definition has the charm of personality and his book is, in every sense, "Johnson's" *Dictionary*.

Relationship Between Art and Literature

The greatest artists of the earlier part of the century, such as Sir Joshua Reynolds and Raeburn, were portrait-painters; brown trees and stormy skies are subdued to a background for gleaming satin and scarlet uniforms, as in the portraits of Lady Arabella Stewart or Captain Ralph Schomberg in the National Gallery. But to Turner and Constable at the end of the century, landscape or seascape is an object in itself, in which the human figures, as in *The Hay Wain* or *Girl Crossing a Brook*, mark the proportion of man to his natural surroundings.

It is the same with the poetry: Gray's country scene is a setting for the "rude forefathers", and the "flowery banks o' bonnie Doon" are flowery to contrast with a deserted lover, but in Wordsworth's greatest ode cataracts and mountains have their own voices—"Land and sea give themselves up to jollity"—which the happy shepherd boy shares but does not dominate.

The Pindaric Ode, like the great houses raised by Sir John Vanbrugh, is based throughout on the architectural virtues of elaborate design, elevated style and correspondence of parts. Gray's *The Progress of Poesy* has three equal sets of three verses, the first two on the same plan, the third differing; and the pleasure of reading it, like that of roaming through Blenheim Palace, comes from appreciation of its construction and recognition of its classical allusions, for which the reader must train his ear as the visitor must study a ground plan. The matter could undoubtedly be put in a less elevated manner but more concisely and intelligibly in prose; but the manner is the poem, nor could it have been written in any century except the one which valued how a thought was expressed more than the thought itself. The small Scots boy who paraphrased Scott's lines, "Now yield thee or, by Him who made the world, thy heart's blood dyes my blade," to, "If you don't give in, by God I'll kill you," did the original couplet no disservice, for he was expressing in prose what was better expressed in prose; but to paraphrase *La Belle Dame Sans Merci* is not possible, for the meaning is in the poetry; and to paraphrase a Pindaric ode, or reduce it to a summary, is to reduce a noble building to its ground plan.

Dr. Samuel Johnson, a man of letters.

A Period of Transition

The eighteenth century holds a balance between the violence and civil strife of the seventeenth and the social securities of the nineteenth. Its middle position is illustrated by two circumstances; during it, tea came and swords went. Though tea had, as a rare commodity, been introduced into England before the Restoration, and though Queen Anne at Hampton Court would "sometimes counsel take and sometimes tea," it was still so expensive that some decades passed before it replaced chocolate, such as Pope's Belinda dispensed in her drawing-room, as a normal drink in polite circles. Meantime in Bath Beau Nash, as a step towards checking duels, forbade wearing of swords; in *The*

Sheridan's play, The Rivals.

Rivals, set in Bath in 1775, Sir Lucius tells Bob Acres, whom he is urging to challenge his rival to a duel, "We wear no swords here, but you understand me." London and other centres of fashion followed suit. But in 1741, in the same letter, Lord Chesterfield warns his son of two dangers, that

> "When an awkward fellow first comes into a room, it is highly probable that his sword gets between his legs, and throws him down,"

and that the same incompetent gentleman, if he drinks tea or coffee,

> "certainly scalds his mouth, and lets either the cup or the saucer fall, and spills the tea or coffee in his breeches."

Before that century there would have been no tea to spill, and after it no swords to trip over; only as we move from early to late Hanoverians can a single drawing-room offer both hazards at once.

QUESTIONS

1. What do you learn of conditions of life in the country from Cowper and Crabbe?
2. Illustrate the importance of pattern in the verse scheme of three poems of this period.
3. For what qualities would you consider Blake the greatest poet of the second half of the eighteenth century?
4. What pictures of high and low life do novels of the period present?
5. Illustrate the range of the profession of man of letters from the works of either Goldsmith or Dr. Johnson.
6. With reference to two of his plays, show how Sheridan gives pattern to the plots of his social comedies.

CHAPTER 10

THE FIRST HALF OF THE NINETEENTH CENTURY

Of the five great poets in the Romantic Revival, beginning at the end of the eighteenth century and profoundly affecting the whole of the nineteenth century, Wordsworth was born in 1770, Coleridge in 1772, Byron in 1788, Shelley in 1792 and Keats in 1795, and they died in reverse order, Keats at the age of twenty-five in 1821, Shelley at twenty-nine in 1822, Byron at thirty-six in 1824, Coleridge at sixty-two in 1834 and Wordsworth at eighty in 1850. Poets do not all die young, but three of these did. During the twenty years after Trafalgar in 1805, the three youngest wrote all their immortal poetry, and died; the working lives of Wordsworth and Coleridge extended roughly from ten years before these three had begun to write to a quarter of a century after they had ceased.

Though all five must be understood together, it is natural to find in the last three a quality of eternal youth, for indeed none of them was ever old, and in the first two qualities of originality, since they inaugurated the Revival, and of wisdom, since they achieved the "years that bring the philosophic mind." It is also natural to think of Wordsworth and Coleridge together, because they were personal friends, intimate with each other's poetical thought and practice and sharing a common ideal; and of Shelley and Keats together, since they met, corresponded and exchanged comment on each other's writing.

William Wordsworth, the Poet of Nature

It gives something of a shock to a reader who labels Wordsworth "the poet of nature" and sets him against an unvarying background of daffodils, lakes and lonely clouds, to realize that in his lines, "Never did sun more beautifully steep in his first splendour valley, rock or hill," the sun was not steeping some wildly natural scenery in Cumberland, but the "ships, towers, domes, theatres and temples" of London; and that if, at thirty-two, he said "never," he had enough experience of both town and country to mean it.

Nevertheless his title of nature poet was well earned, for, whereas eighteenth-century poets who described the country scene at all are praised for transferring into words with the exactness of a painter's brush the externals of shape, light and colour, Wordsworth not only noted but pierced through these externals to spiritual qualities of which they were an outward sign.

The Rashfield at Rydal, planted by Wordsworth for his daughter, Dora.

Herbert's hymn points out that

"A man that looks on glass
On it may stay his eye
Or, if he pleaseth, through it pass
And then the heaven espy."

Wordsworth indeed saw the visible world, but did not stay his eye on it; in almost every case he passed through, to become aware of, and to respond to, a world beyond.

From his earliest years he was conscious of this power to pierce through limitations of a world of the senses; and in the first book of his autobiography *The Prelude*, after an objective description of a boy's delight in "silver wreaths" and "leagues of shining water" that gave notice of the rising moon, he records:

"Even then I felt
Gleams like the flashing of a shield;—the earth
And common face of Nature spake to me
Rememberable things."

Deeper Perception

After almost every passage of external description we are led gently on until "we see into the life of things." Daffodils are first merely flowers; they speak joy and present themselves as "a jocund company"; but later, by exercising it, they lead him to recognize heaven's gift of imagination, "that inward eye which is the bliss of solitude." In another poem, the cuckoo's "twofold shout," while it excites the poet's ear, also transforms the earth on which he is passing his manhood till he sees it as "an unsubstantial faery place" in which his spirit can recapture its "golden time."

Such lines are not morals tacked on to the end of an experience as guides to future conduct; they rise from a deeper part of man's nature, and answer a question more implicit in human life, the question not of what we must do but of what we must be.

Far from being unconcerned with public affairs of his times, even after he withdrew his practical support from the French Revolutionaries, Wordsworth constantly shows (by such sonnets as that to Toussaint L'Ouverture, a champion of liberty imprisoned by Napoleon, or those on the threatened invasion of 1802) that every event that affected mankind, and especially that affected his country, was of deep concern to him.

Above all, in *Lines on a Picture of Peele Castle in a Storm* he repudiates the idea that men can ever find satisfaction in escapism, for though he had formerly known the castle only in halcyon weather, he would rather not be spared the knowledge that storms exist.

"Farewell, farewell, the heart that lives alone,
Housed in a dream, at distance from the kind;
Such happiness, wherever it be known,
Is to be pitied, for 'tis surely blind.
But welcome fortitude, and patient cheer,
And frequent sights of what is to be borne,
Such sights, or worse, as are before me here.
Not without hope we suffer and we mourn."

"Welcome fortitude"; "not without hope"; like the song of the soldier in *St. Joan*, such phrases "keep you marching."

The Unity of Life

It is a common mistake to divide life into compartments, to disconnect one stage from another, to speak of "when he was a boy" and "when he was a man," or of this life and the next, as if we were speaking of different people. The terms have uses, but may obscure the fact that identity is, by definition, oneness and life indivisible. A sense of this unity of mortality and immortality indissolubly mixed in the fact of being underlies many of Wordsworth's most significant poems. In *Composed Upon an Evening of Extraordinary Splendour:*

"An intermingling of Heaven's pomp is spread
On ground which British shepherds tread,"

and is here and now, not postponed beyond some impenetrable barrier.

Far from constantly shedding an old self and becoming someone different, Wordsworth assimilates each experience, and is at any moment the sum of what he has been; nothing is irrelevant or lost to one who realizes that what has been "must ever be," that tenses such as past and future are merely a convenient way of dealing with the present circumstance that we are in one aspect "dwellers all in time and space."

This is the position of one who feels, like the Lady in *Comus*, a "sober certainty of waking bliss"; who chooses not the intoxicated song of a nightingale who sings "as if the God of wine had helped thee to a Valentine," but that of the stock-dove, of "serious faith and inward glee"; who loves his wife not only as "a phantom of delight," but more deeply as:

> "A being breathing thoughtful breath,
> A traveller betwixt life and death. . . .
> And yet a Spirit still,"

who knows that the only division is between being and not being; and that if we can think so we exist, and are indestructible.

One point on which Wordsworth, Coleridge, Shelley and Keats agree, which indeed they take for granted, is the necessity and naturalness of being happy. This principle is implicit in all Wordsworth's poetry. From boyhood he knew "a grandeur in the beatings of the heart," nor did his fellowship with nature depend on seasons of the year or times of day;

> "In November days,
> When vapours rolling down the valley made
> A lonely scene more lonesome,"

or "in the frosty season, when the sun was set," it was equally a happy time. No season lacked this quality; happiness was eternal and inalienable.

Because, like Keats, he was one to whom "the miseries of the world are miseries and will not let them rest," Wordsworth never lost sight of its importance. To be happy is a positive state and unhappiness its absence, as, in Milton's angels, to be evil was a ceasing of the positive state of being good.

One kind of joy passes into another. If the mere physical delights of a boy who "made one long bathing of a summer's day" are over, he nevertheless has "abundant recompense." On the "first mild day of March" he finds:

> ". . . a blessing in the air
> Which seems a sense of joy to yield
> To the bare trees, and mountains bare,
> And grass in the green field."

Keats, in a similar mood, wrote of the thrush's song:

> "O fret not after knowledge—I have none,
> And yet my song comes native with the warmth.
> O fret not after knowledge—I have none,
> And yet the Evening listens."

Shelley instinctively knows, as Keats and Masefield know, that "the days that make us happy make us wise," and the bareness is no enemy.

But though a happy man is capable of being alone, he cannot be entirely self-absorbed. His hold on life must include every creature. In *Lines left upon a Seat in a Yew-tree*, Wordsworth laments the fate of a proud youth, eating out his heart from a "sense of injured merit," since:

> "... he who feels contempt
> For any living thing, hath faculties
> Which he has never used."

Such a man is made more wretched by gazing at natural beauty, which increases his inability to live at ease with himself. "He then would gaze on the more distant scene," until "his heart could not sustain the beauty."

Natural Dignity and Joy

Wordsworth saw the poverty of the Old Cumberland Beggar and the Leech-Gatherer with sympathy, but realized that they too fulfilled a purpose which gave them natural dignity, since:

> " 'Tis Nature's law
> That none, the meanest of created things,
> Of forms created the most vile and brute,
> The dullest or most noxious, should exist
> Divorced from good—a spirit and pulse of good,
> A life and soul, to every mode of being
> Inseparably linked."

These men gave to human life as much as they received and more. Even naughty little beggar-boys who have wreathed their hats with flowers, "the gayest of the land," and told "the Gentleman" barefaced lies, call forth love because they themselves love life, and when they see that their tales are not accepted:

> "In the twinkling of an eye,
> 'Come! Come!' cried one, and without more ado
> Off to some other play the joyous vagrants flew."

The Idiot Boy's delight in the hooting of owls on a moonlit night transcended his power to express it; all he could stammer was, "The cocks did crow to-whoo, to-whoo, and the sun did shine so cold," but he could convey it to Wordsworth, who says of the poem, "I never wrote anything with so much glee."

The human spirit should be uplifted by the natural majesty of our home in space; and if this merely abashes us, something is wrong. In *The Star-Gazers* a showman with a telescope invites the crowd to view the starry heavens; "What an insight it must be," and yet each viewer comes away as if dissatisfied. What is wrong? Wordsworth will not admit that the poor spectators are incapable of rising to such heights: "No, no, this cannot be; men thirst for power and majesty." But it is disturbing that each turns away less happy than before. Someone, somewhere, expects them somehow to live up to something; and when, in Keats' phrase, they have made "the homeward journey to habitual self," the thought troubles them. They are wasting themselves, and waste is the essence of "that which is at enmity with joy.'

Coleridge, Poet of the Supernatural

This world, in which we must "find our happiness or not at all," reaches us first through our five senses. Wordsworth enriches "the light of common day," but Samuel Taylor Coleridge (1772-1834) adds a possibility of perceptions which we must develop a sixth sense to achieve.

Three of his poems, *Kubla Khan*, *Christabel* and *The Ancient Mariner*, have this magical power to capture the imagination, a power that defies analysis.

We can work out that there is alliteration in each of the first five lines of *Kubla Khan*, that the ten syllables of the line, "Ancestral voices prophesying war," are made up of four words of one, two, three and four syllables (as in Marlowe's line, "To entertain divine Zenocrate"); we can make the line "Tu whit, tu whoo" into four feet, each of one elongated syllable and thus just as long as the eleven syllables of "Tis the middle of night by the castle clock"; but all these technical details will not take us a step nearer to understanding why no mind can ever shake off the spell cast by the lines,

"But oh! that deep romantic chasm which slanted
Down the green hill athwart a cedarn cover!
A savage place! as holy and enchanted
As e'er beneath a waning moon was haunted
By woman wailing for her demon-lover!"

In *Christabel*, under a moon "both small and dull," the outlines of the castle, its clock and courtyard, its great entrance and mastiff bitch, loom up out of the middle of night, of magic, of the thin grey cloud that "covers but not hides the sky." In the leafless wood—no, not leafless; there is that "one red leaf, the last of its clan," demoniacally possessed, that now hangs still at this midnight hour as if the very night wind held its breath at the evil about to be—on the other side of the tree Christabel hears a sigh. She may fold her arms to the sign of a Cross beneath her cloak, but nothing can save her from the shock of wildly glittering jewels and the witch's beauty:

"I guess 'twas frightful there to see
A lady so richly clad as she,
Beautiful exceedingly."

The strange story is never finished, but enough queer things happen in

Coleridge, whom Lamb described as "an Archangel a little damaged."

the poem to set our thumbs pricking.

Though in *The Ancient Mariner* Coleridge introduces a Spirit of Ice and Snow, this is a natural being, and there is no evil except the callousness of men. A sinner kills an innocent and happy creature for sheer love of using his power of death, and so breaks the circle of life; he sins against the spirit which "rolls through all things," and includes both him and his victim; and his punishment is a logical result of his deed, that he is put outside the circle, becalmed in the Pacific without a living thing with which he can communicate. Any form of being that has companionship and a home, and that is amongst its fellows, is to him an object of passionate envy.

When by his love of God's creatures the relationship is restored, and he can come home to his "own countree," he must use his own suffering to awaken the heart that is nearly dead to feeling, the "one of three" still accessible. He has his orders:

"The moment that his face I see,
I know the man that must hear me:
To him my tale I teach."

Not all Coleridge's poems derive their power from the supernatural. In *Frost at Midnight* he determines that the natural joy denied to him in his boyhood shall be free to his little son:

"For I was reared
In the great city, pent 'mid cloisters dim,
And saw nought lovely but the sky and stars.
But thou, my babe, shalt wander like a breeze
By lakes and sandy shores,"

and he grieves for those misled to waste their chance in hot theatres and ballrooms, and "lose the deepening twilights of the spring."

In his political outlook, too, the power of joy is paramount, and in *Ode on France* he hopes that "conquering by her happiness alone shall

France compel the nations to be free." Happiness will bring liberty, not the other way round.

Byron, a Romantic Poet

Though to English critical judgment the least of the five, to other European countries George Gordon Byron (1788-1824) is most impressively representative of the qualities that make a romantic poet. Such a poet must write introspectively of his own emotions, joys and sorrows, but preferably sorrows; an air of mystery and loneliness must surround him, and his endowments of mind and soul, by rendering him capable of more powerful feeling, must set him above and apart from his fellows.

If he is also well-born, or alternatively of unknown parentage, handsome and inconsolable, his self-revelation is more engaging and his challenge more irresistible.

Whatever the actual circumstances of Byron's life had been, the character of Childe Harold presented a more dramatic combination of these essential qualities than even his closest rivals could achieve; and since it was impossible not to identify Byron with Childe Harold, creator and created shed romantic lustre on each other.

Byron had immense and obvious advantages in capturing sympathy; a proud, reserved, misunderstood spirit withdrawn from an insensitive world is calculated to appeal to every generous and undiscriminating heart. In his descriptions of "self-exiled Harold," Byron presented himself: "where rose the mountains there to him were friends" (to Wordsworth's integrity, Byron's assumption of a sentiment which he himself genuinely felt was intolerable); "apart he stalk'd in joyless reverie"; "his was not that open, artless soul that feels relief by bidding sorrow flow." He is "the wandering outlaw of his own dark mind," one "who fain no more would feel, secure in guarded coldness," "a wild-born falcon with clipt wing."

But the portrait is no more truthful than self-portraits are liable to be. To such natures a fault is like a dog; to own it entitles them to keep it. Dr. Johnson was nearer truth when he remarked that "all censure of a man's self is oblique praise. It is in order to show how much he can spare."

Byron's Public Image

To anyone enchanted by the music of Byron's lyric verse and repulsed by the falsity of his public image there must recur the words of G. B. Shaw in *The Doctor's Dilemma*, that "The most tragic thing in the world is a man of genius who is not also a man of honour."

At a safe distance the good, true and pure commanded his reverence, though not his allegiance. In *Don Juan* he describes the chapel of an old Norman abbey, then in ruins:

MODERN EUROPEAN WRITERS WHO INFLUENCED ENGLISH LITERATURE

The Russian novelist Leo Tolstoy (1828-1910) wrote many novels and short stories. In this scene from *Anna Karenina*, Anna visits her son Sergei secretly on his birthday, against her husband's orders.

The Russian Anton Chekhov (1860-1904) wrote many stories, but is chiefly famous for his plays. In this scene from *The Cherry Orchard*, Gaev promises Anya and Varya that the estate will not be sold.

The Norwegian Henrik Ibsen (1828-1906) has had a profound effect on literature, through such plays as *A Doll's House*. Here, Nora Helmer arrives home laden with Christmas parcels for her children.

August Strindberg (1849-1912) wrote many plays and novels in the Swedish language. In this scene from *Miss Julie*, the heroine talks to the man-servant Jean while he cleans her father's boots.

The French novelist Marcel Proust (1871-1922) describes his own infatuation with Marie de Benardaky in his book *Jean Santeuil*, where she is portrayed as Marie Kossichef, whom Jean meets in the park.

The Austrian novelist Franz Kafka (1883-1924) changed the form of the modern novel. In *The Trial*, a bank official is arrested but no charge is disclosed. He visits many offices in search of justice.

The German playwright Bertholt Brecht (1898-1956) wrote *St. Joan of the Stockyards*, set in Chicago. Here, Joan Dark, a selfless Salvation Army girl, is seen making a plea to prevent mass unemployment.

Samuel Beckett (1906-   ), although an Irishman, writes his novels and plays in the French language. In this scene from *Waiting for Godot*, two tramps talk while waiting for Godot, who never comes.

Newstead Abbey, Lord Byron's romantic home, influenced his poetry.

"But in a higher niche, alone, but crowned,
The Virgin Mother of the God-born Child,
With her Son in her blessed arms, looked round,
Spared by some chance when all beside was spoiled;
She made the earth below seem holy ground.
This may be superstition, weak or wild,
But even the faintest relics of a shrine
Of any worship wake some thoughts divine."

This passage reminds us of Dr. Johnson's friend whom he called a "religious" man because, although he had not been into a church for thirty years, he never passed one without raising his hat.

Byron's Language

Yet it is impossible not to be overwhelmed by the force of Byron's language, swept along by the incantation of his verse. Storm rather than tranquillity evoked his powers, but both were at his command. The beauty of a night "of cloudless climes and starry skies," the lovely light "of a dark eye in woman" can be matched by the verses on the Lake of Geneva:

"Far along
From peak to peak the jagg'd crags among
Leaps the live thunder, not from one lone cloud,
But every mountain now hath found a tongue,
And Jura answers through her misty shroud
Back to the joyous Alps, that call to her aloud."

When he was not writing of himself, and so had no compelling need of insincerity, Byron used his searching wit to see through the characters of others, and his power of epigram, developed through his admiration of Pope, to put them in easily memorized and quotable summaries. He was lucky in his close predecessors and contemporaries: Napoleon, Gibbon, Voltaire, Rousseau, George III, all lent themselves to such treatment.

"Conqueror and captive of the earth art thou,"

"Sapping a solemn creed with solemn sneer,"

"This old, blind, mad, helpless, weak, poor worm,"

all summarize their subjects. His line on Napoleon, "but quiet to quick bosoms is a hell," is applicable to himself; by "quick bosoms" he meant the living spirit in a man, and the truth of the words depends on the quality of that life.

Wordsworth lived with a far intenser passion of being, and of him it simply is not true; in quiet, the opposite of an unpurposed restlessness, he found his most heavenly converse.

"Think you, mid all this mighty sum
Of things forever speaking
That nothing of itself will come,
And we must still be seeking?"

Silent, not doing, he was doing most. But of Byron it is quite true that, however much he was able to enjoy his life of fame, travel, lovemaking, rank and wealth, he was

Byron, said Macaulay, "had a head which statuaries loved to copy."

unable in the strict sense of the words to enjoy himself. There are few emotions that he cannot express with a force and beauty that charm a young heart, few in which he does not seem by the touchstone of experience to be a poseur.

Some of the finest lines on actual fighting are his, written on his thirty-seventh birthday at Missolonghi, where he had betaken himself in support of the Greek War of Independence:

"If thou regret'st thy youth, why live?
The land of honourable death
Is here:—up to the field, and give
Away thy breath!
Seek out—less often sought than found—
A soldier's grave, for thee the best;
Then look around, and choose thy ground,
And take thy rest."

He died of fever.

Shelley, the "Sun-Treader"

Browning, whose youthful enthusiasm for Percy Bysshe Shelley (1792-1822) lasted a lifetime, exclaims in *Memorabilia*:

"Ah, did you once see Shelley plain,
And did he stop and speak to you?
And did you speak to him again?
How strange it seems and new!"

It is easier to see Shelley plain if we do not try to justify or condemn the steps, often apparently mistaken, which he took in pursuit of his idealistic theories, but let the generosity of his spirit glow in every line he wrote. Many of his actions were quixotically generous; he refused to return to a comfortable home and behave as his father thought befitted the heir to a baronetcy; he left England rather than live trammelled by convention. Before the great period of social reforms, he championed the cause of the voteless working man:

"Men of England, wherefore plough
For the lords who lay ye low?"

The subjects that attracted him were those of revolt against established tyranny. In *The Revolt of Islam* Cythna tells Laon that the world's benefactors are "Heroes, and Poets, and prevailing Sages."

Prometheus Unbound

At the end of *Prometheus Unbound*, Prometheus has successfully resisted, on behalf of humanity, the temptation to betray to the oppressor, Jupiter, the source from which his destruction threatens, and has even disclaimed his curse. To find that "the rarer action is in virtue than in vengeance" is his triumph:

"To hope till Hope creates
From its own wreck the thing it contemplates,
Neither to change, nor falter, nor repent;
This, like thy glory, Titan, is to be
Good, great and joyous, beautiful and free;
This is alone Life, Joy, Empire and Victory."

The spirits who console Prometheus while he is under Jupiter's power represent the four types of human being who raise life to its highest, the fighter against out-worn creeds and tyrants, the one who gives his life for his enemy, the philosopher who plans for the future of mankind and, most powerful influence of all, the poet:

"He will watch from dawn to gloom
The lake-reflected sun illume
The yellow bees in the ivy-bloom,
Nor heed nor see what things they be,
But from these create he can
Forms more real than living man,
Nurslings of immortality."

Shelley's Nature

In *Alastor* a wandering poet is presented as "gentle and brave and generous"; and though in *Adonais* Shelley describes himself as "neglected and apart, a herd-abandoned deer struck by the hunter's dart," and in *Ode to the West Wind* as "tameless and swift and proud," the three adjectives in *Alastor* best sum up his own nature.

Through Leigh Hunt, Shelley met Keats, less happily endowed than himself with health, position and riches; and with his utmost endeavours he encouraged one whom a less generous man would have regarded as a rival. From Italy he wrote several times to urge Keats to visit him, and in a letter to Mrs. Leigh Hunt in November 1820, he tells of his intention to keep Keats warm and teach him Greek, adding,

> "I am aware, indeed, in part, that I am nourishing a rival who will far surpass me, and this is an additional motive and will be an added pleasure."

The words shine; but in less than four months Keats had died in Rome, and in less than twenty months Shelley himself was drowned. In his pocket were a volume of Aeschylus and another of Keats' poems; he died as he lived, in the company of great minds.

Of all the romantic poets, Shelley had the most adventurous spirit. To an

Elizabethan Englishman, adventure meant the physical dangers of seafaring with an added risk of encountering foes; in the seventeenth century adventures of the mind enlarged the world's horizons by scientific discoveries such as those made by Newton, whose statue in Trinity College, Cambridge, Wordsworth has described:

"With his prism and silent face,
The marble index of a mind for ever
Voyaging through strange seas of thought, alone."

The early nineteenth century saw exploration into original thought and expression, with risks of opposition in some ways greater than the physical and mental ones of previous adventures.

Shelley knew these risks, and in *Adonais*, the loveliest personal elegy in our language, he rejoices that Keats escaped them:

"He has outsoared the shadow of our night;
Envy and calumny and hate and pain,
And that unrest which men miscall delight
Can touch him not and torture not again."

But for himself, in the last verse, he accepts them:

"The breath whose might I have invoked in song
Descends on me; my spirit's bark is driven
Far from the shore, far from the trembling throng
Whose sails were never to the tempest given."

In *Ode to a Skylark* he writes of:

"A poet hidden
In the light of thought,
Singing hymns unbidden
Till the world is wrought
To sympathy with hopes and fears it heeded not."

The risk of being despised and ignored must itself be ignored and despised.

Poems of Despair

This mood of exultation does not exclude the opposite end of the scale. Much of Shelley's most melodious poetry seems to rise from a mood of despair; his "sweetest songs are those that tell of saddest thought." In *Stanzas written in Dejection near Naples* he confesses:

"I could lie down, like a tired child,
And weep away the life of care
Which I have borne and yet must bear."

In *Hymn of Pan* the destiny of men is that of gods also, the heartbreak of unsatisfied love, as Pan changes his happy pipings to a sad minor key:

"Singing how down the vale of Maenalus
I pursued a maiden and clasped a reed;
Gods and men, we are all deluded thus!
It breaks in our bosom and then we bleed."

In recalling tranquil hours he ends on a sudden note of despair:

"Less oft is peace in Shelley's mind
Than calm in waters seen."

As Ariel, the name which he chose for himself, he feels that

"The poor sprite is
Imprisoned, for some fault of his,
In a body like a grave."

And yet no purer delight sparkles in the verse of his contemporaries than that which dances through *The Cloud*:

"I bring fresh showers for the thirsting flowers,
From the seas and the streams;
I bear light shade for the leaves when laid
In their noonday dreams,"

A scene from Shelley's The Cenci.

A portrait of Percy Bysshe Shelley.

or in Shelley's joyous song written to invoke the very Spirit of Delight itself:

"I love snow, and all the forms
Of the radiant frost;
I love waves, and winds, and storms.
Every thing almost
Which is Nature's, and may be
Untainted by man's misery."

In his twofold nature, capable of extremes of joy and despair alike, Shelley shows the truth of Keats' *Ode on Melancholy*:

"Ay, in the very temple of Delight
Veiled Melancholy has her sovran shrine,
Though seen of none save him whose strenuous tongue
Can burst Joy's grape against his palate fine."

Keats, a Courageous Poet

If generosity is implicit in Shelley's choice of, and attitude to, his subjects, a courageous idealism marks the poetry of John Keats (1795-1821). His letters show his exalted idea of poetry in the abstract, his self-criticism and right estimate of the criticism of others. To his brother George he wrote of "the high idea I have of poetical fame," and to his friend Taylor, "I think poetry should surprise by a fine excess." Idealism armed him against the adverse criticism he often met; "Praise or blame has but a momentary effect on a man whose love of beauty in the abstract makes him a severe critic of his own works," and "I was never afraid of failure; for I would sooner fail than not be among the greatest." Such an ideal did not daunt his spirit or disable his judgment; it was no mistaken valuation that enabled him to say, "I think I shall be among the English poets after my death."

But by the end of 1818 he had seen his brother Tom die of consumption; by the end of 1819 he was no nearer to marriage with Fanny Brawne whom he had met over a year before; by February 1820 he realized that he too had contracted consumption and wrote, "How astonishingly does the chance of leaving the world impress a sense of its natural beauties on us"; and by the end of the year this had become a certainty. Within two months he died.

The two sonnets in which Keats expresses his sense that time is running him down, which seem as if they must have been produced during the last few months of his life, were in fact written some time before. It was still three years before his death that he wrote:

"When I have fears that I may cease to be
Before my pen has glean'd my teeming brain,"

and probably over two when he made a first version of *Bright Star, would I were steadfast as thou art,* of which he wrote the final one in his Shakespeare as he went down the Channel on his last journey to Italy.

What kind of poetry did he write against this background of ill-health, anxiety, discouragement and passionate but frustrated love? It is the poetry of a brave man. A sonnet to his brothers shows the warm affection he felt for his family:

> "This is your birthday, Tom, and I rejoice
> That thus it passes smoothly, quietly.
> Many such eves of gently whisp'ring noise
> May we together pass."

He can ignore the coldness of winter in the affection of his friends, "For I am brimfull of the friendliness that in a little cottage I have found."

Endymion, the Shepherd-Prince

The opening lines of *Endymion* are a rising spring of joy in every shape of beauty:

> "Therefore, on every morrow, are we wreathing
> A flowery band to bind us to the earth,
> Spite of despondence, of the inhuman dearth
> Of noble natures, of the gloomy days,
> Of all the unhealthy and o'er-darkened ways
> Made for our searching."

He knows which conquers which:

> "The passion poesy, glories infinite,
> Haunt us till they become a cheering light
> Unto our souls."

The story of *Endymion* will therefore be one of "full happiness." Its scenes of loveliness are "a constant rebuke" to heavy thoughts:

> "Apollo's upward fire
> Made every eastern cloud a silvery pyre
> Of brightness so unsullied that therein
> A melancholy spirit well might win
> Oblivion, and melt out his essence fine
> Into the winds."

Of his four other great narrative poems only *Lamia* is sad.

The Eve of St. Agnes

This poem is a romantic love-story with a happy ending made the more so by a family feud, "hyena foemen," dangers from "dim espial," "sleeping dragons," a wakeful but sagacious bloodhound and the final escape "o'er the southern moors." Over all presides St. Agnes; Madeline, her "charmed maid," is safe in her care, and only when "St. Agnes' moon hath set" is it time to flee.

The movement to both eye and ear is unbroken, or only momentarily suspended, from beginning to end. We are in a leafless copse with an owl shivering in the branches; we move over frozen grass to a sheepfold near the castle, and so into the Lady Chapel, down the north aisle and through a little door to a hall where a "prelude soft" draws us to "level chambers" prepared for a ball. We can see through open doors the "argent revelry" and "one Lady there." Into this hall steps Porphyro from behind the great portal, and here he is joined by Angela, who leads him "through a lowly arched way" to her little moonlight room. When she leaves him to fetch the "cates and dainties," we can go with her or stay with him, but together they make their way by dusky galleries to Madeline's room. Angela goes down the great stair, helped by Madeline who appears at its foot, and with her we return to her room to leave it only when the lovers do. "Down the wide stairs a darkling way they found," the ball by now being over and lights reduced to a "chain-droop'd lamp" flickering by each door, and through the hall to a porch, whose great door slowly opens until they are gone and we remain behind.

The Sounds of the Poem

With equal continuity we can hear the "sound track," the murmur of a beadsman's prayer, bare feet shuffling on stone, "music's golden tongue," the crescendo of trumpets, timbrels, a confused "sound of merriment and chorus bland," Porphyro's muted steps, the tap-tap of Angela's stick, their whispered exchange and her muttered exclamations, contrasting voices, old and young, and her feeble laugh, hobbling footsteps, conspirators' footsteps, quick light footsteps, and then a silence more eloquent than uttered syllable; the rustle of a dress, a "slumberous tenderness" of breathing that told the lover that his lady was asleep, the distant tones of clarion, kettle-drum and "far-heard clarionet" as someone opens and shuts the hall door, the hollow lute's "ancient ditty," Madeline's pleading accents and the quick pattering of "the flaw-blown sleet"; "in all the house was heard no human sound," but the wind made uproar in the arras and under the carpets; the watchdog's shake of his hide, the faint scrape of bolts drawn one after another, the clink of chains laid on stones, the grate of a key, the subdued groan of shifting hinges, and it is over. A blind man could see it; a deaf man could hear it. There is no story in the whole of English poetry that so takes the reader along with it.

Isabella or *The Pot of Basil*

This might be considered the counterpart of *The Eve of St. Agnes* as an unhappy love-story, if Keats himself had not expressly said that it is not one.

"Were they unhappy then?—It cannot be—
Too many tears for lovers have been shed,
Too many sighs give we to them in fee,
Too much of pity after they are dead,
Too many doleful stories do we see,
Whose matter in bright gold were best be read."

Ariadne's story is, he admits, sad, for she was deserted by Theseus:

"But, for the general award of love,
The little sweet doth kill much bitterness."

Lamia and *Hyperion*

Lamia has an unhappy ending, for one lover cheated the other, and at the killing touch of truth he must die of exposure, thrown out of his Fool's Paradise.

Although the Titans are dispossessed, *Hyperion* is however no tragedy; Oceanus shows that each defeat is a step towards greater perfection, and that the Titans are not the first nor the last but part of a process. As soil feeds the tree and the tree breeds a dove, so gods tower above Titans in their beauty, and

"... must reign
In right thereof; for 'tis the eternal law
That first in beauty should be first in might."

Hyperion is an answer to *Lamia*, for Lycius died of truth, but:

"... to bear all naked truths
And to envisage circumstance, all calm,
That is the top of sovereignty."

When men see another greater than themselves they can either kill or worship, and by doing the latter they have a share in that which is above them, and show their own greatness.

Keats' Note of Sadness

The note of sadness, when it is sounded, is for something lovely lost. Keats grieves for the passing of Greek legends; to Leigh Hunt he writes:

"Glory and loveliness have passed away;
For if we wander out in early morn,
No wreathed incense do we see upborne
Into the east, to meet the smiling day."

He grieves for Boccaccio's ghittern, now silent, and for the days of Robin Hood; "Gone the tough-belted outlaw." The heart of grief is:

At this house in Hampstead, Keats wrote many of his finest poems.

"To know the change and feel it
When there is none to heal it
Nor numbéd sense to steel it."

But this condition of constant loss can be recompensed by fancy:

"She will bring, in spite of frost,
Beauties that the earth hath lost . . .
Thou shalt, at one glance, behold
The daisy and the marigold;
White-plum'd lilies, and the first
Hedge-grown primrose that hath burst."

The delights of every season come together when imagination summons them.

The Five Great Odes

Four of the five great odes, written in 1819, reflect this sense of loss. In *To A Nightingale*, escape "on the viewless wings of Poesy" gives Keats a world of beauty and peace until with the word "forlorn" he loses that home of his imagination. In the *Ode on a Grecian Urn*, melodist and lover are happy because their music and their love cannot suffer any diminution.

A portrait of John Keats.

In *Ode to Autumn* the three verses are connected by a double thread of subject and of time. The first verse is concerned only with autumn as conveyed by the five senses; we can see the vines, taste the sweet kernel, smell the later flowers, touch the mossed cottage trees and hear the hum and buzz of bees in all the *m*s and *s*s of the last two lines:

"Until they think warm days will
never cease,
For Summer has o'er-brimmed
their clammy cells."

In the second verse we see through signs of autumn to Autumn herself, "thee amid thy store," and in the third, "while barréd clouds bloom the soft-dying day," there comes a diminuendo of sound, gnats in wailful choir, the bleat of full-grown lambs in the distance, hedge-crickets at hand, a robin in the garden and the almost imperceptible twitter of migrating swallows. The three verses take us through the three stages of day, morning with the bees at work, afternoon in "the half-reaped furrow" and evening in the "soft-dying day." But Keats grieves, even in the midst of Autumn's richness, for vanished spring: "Where are the songs of Spring? Ay, where are they?" and the tree in *Ode to a Grecian Urn* is happy because its boughs cannot "Ever bid the Spring adieu." Keats goes no further than the departing swallows, for the next step is winter, and to him wintry cold is death. For Shelley the west wind, "breath of autumn's being," may foretell winter because its prophecy includes the coming of spring at the far side of it; but for Keats there was no far side, and winter prophesied not spring but the end. In the *Ode on Melancholy*, where the capacity for luxuriating in sorrow must go hand in hand with that of savouring joy to the utmost, the loss is that mourned by poets of all ages, that of

"Beauty that must die,
And Joy whose hand is ever at his lips
Bidding adieu."

Keats once observed a field-mouse of whom he said, "The creature hath a purpose and its eyes are bright with it"; amidst all the uncertainties of his life he was "certain of nothing but of the holiness of the heart's affections and the truth of imagination," but this certainty gives a purpose to all that he writes, and his poems are "bright with it."

Scott, the Romantic Novelist

If, as has been said, Walter Scott (1771-1832) is for boys, at least a reader enjoys a boy's rightful satisfaction in knowing exactly where he stands. Hardy old virtues, loyalty, purity and physical courage, are unquestioned. Hardy old vices are equally well established: it is shameful for men to lie, for women's waxen hearts to suffer change, or for anyone, high or low, to alter his political opinions. Once it is accepted that none but the brave deserves the fair, a reader can be sure that in the end the brave will get the fair, and villains their deserts.

The supreme merit of Scott's thirty-two novels lies not so much in any one individual work, though the finest are still unmatched as pictures of their period, as in the sheer range in time, place and social grade. To choose only a few, the earliest in date, though one of the latest in composition, is *Count Robert of Paris*, set in the eleventh century, and *The Talisman* and *Ivanhoe* present the twelfth. The next two centuries proved less attractive to Scott's genius than the fifteenth with *Quentin Durward* and *Anne of Geierstein*; the best-known of three set in the sixteenth century is *Kenilworth*, and of the seven set in the seventeenth, *Woodstock*. The eighteenth century, his favourite, is background for a dozen, including *Waverley*, written in 1814, which gave its name to the whole series; only one, *St. Ronan's Well*, comes into the early nineteenth century, treading on the heels of contemporary fiction. As a background to historical studies and a means of entering into whatever century or country engages attention, the Waverley novels have no equal. Not a rank, profession, trade, occupation or service is omitted; three continents, seven centuries and over eight hundred characters—there's richness for you! The glorious game of "Go seek" is for him who chooses to play.

Scott's Poems

The narrative poems came first and seem, like Puck, "sent with broom before, to sweep the dust behind the door," to exercise his genius in those elements which were to come out most strongly in his novels. *The Lay of the Last Minstrel* experiments in the supernatural, *Marmion* (subtitled *A Tale of Flodden Field*) puts emphasis on combat, and *The Lady of the Lake* tells a love-story; but all three include love, war and villainy against a background of "Caledonia, stern and wild."

The chief difference is that the element of humour, strong in the simple wisdom of Scott's low-life characters, is absent from his poems, where there is no scope for it. The change from poetry to prose was to the advantage of Scott's reputation, because Byron, who in his satirical poem *English Bards and Scotch Reviewers* (1809) had laughed at Scott's poetry in the lines:

"Thus Lays of Minstrels—may they be the last!—
On half-strung harps whine mournful to the blast,"

was already outdoing him in heroic verse narrative, while in the province of the historical novel he was, and has remained, undisputed king.

But just as to the main body of some great cathedral there are often chapels lovely and complete in themselves, so Scott has left also a number of lyrics, some gay, some elegiac, that share the qualities of his other writings. We do not, in approaching them, need to stiffen the sinews and summon up the blood, and perhaps by their very persuasiveness they echo longer in our ears.

"Waken, lords and ladies gay;
To the greenwood haste away."

Yes, we will waken; it would be a pity not to rise with day and see those "springlets in the dawn" and "diamonds on the brake" when all is fresh and early.

"Come, read me my riddle! Come, hearken my tale,
And tell me the craft of bold Allen-a-Dale."

Yes, we will hearken, and contentedly remain baffled till Scott chooses to enlighten us.

"Soft is the note, and sad the lay,
That mourns the lovely Rosabelle."

It has it all, in about fifty lines: rock, oak and stormy firth, warning sprite and gifted seer, aged sire and lady-mother, Lord Lindesay's heir, graceful in dance and gallant at the ring, castle, chapel, battlement and rose-carved buttress, wondrous blaze, dead men's mail and the lordly line of high Saint Clair, chanted to the threnody of waters. Drop by drop it is romance distilled.

Rebecca and De Bois-Guilbert, from Sir Walter Scott's novel, Ivanhoe.

Jane Austen, an Exquisite Novelist

While from his northern eminence Sir Walter was surveying centuries and continents, a Hampshire spinster, Jane Austen (1775-1817), without deflecting her attention far from her own contemporaries, social circle and southern home, was producing in all six completed novels, two unfinished ones, and a couple of notebooks in which she had, in eighteenth-century phrase, "commenced author." The forty-two years of her life covered the French Revolution and the Napoleonic Wars; and her sailor brothers, Francis and Charles, must have given her much material about Napoleon, and her cousin Eliza, later her sister-in-law, whose husband had been guillotined, plenty about the Revolutionists, had she wished to use it.

Some references do, however, creep in; Captain Wentworth, in *Persuasion*, gains prize-money for the capture of a French ship, and in *Sanditon*, written in 1817, Mr. Palmer celebrates English victories over Napoleon in the names of his house and crescents, much as the Boer War was responsible for many a Mafeking Terrace. His new house he named Trafalgar House, but he later regretted it, "for Waterloo is more the thing now. However, Waterloo is in reserve, and if we have encouragement enough this year for a little Crescent to be ventured on . . . we shall be able to call it Waterloo Crescent."

Jane Austen's Villains

Jane Austen knew that vicious men existed, and frequently flourished. Wickham, Willoughby and Crawford are all seducers, but she warns us that we must not look for the satisfaction of seeing them ruined. Of Willoughby she expressly says,

> "That he was for ever inconsolable, that he fled from society, or contracted an habitual gloom of temper, or died of a broken heart, must not be depended on, for he did neither. He lived to exert, and frequently to enjoy himself."

Each had at some stage a prospect of gaining the heroine's affections, and each failed; Elizabeth looked first for Wickham at Netherfield ball, Fanny was softening towards a reformed Crawford, Willoughby held Marianne's heart in his hand. Their real crime is that they do not know a good thing when they see it, and their punishment that they miss their chance. And do they care? Not two ha'pence. Chastisement shall not give them a false importance. Frank Churchill, prepared to risk Emma's happiness to provide cover for his own, is let off with mere strictures; and Mr. Woodhouse, gentlest of rebukers, sums him up as "not quite the thing." Mr. Woodhouse may not be formidable, but his disapproval is.

Leisure-time Pursuits

Most of Miss Austen's gentlefolk of independent means and unrestricted leisure, however, passed those few hours not devoted to the pursuit of a suitable companion for life in blameless occupations. The men occupied themselves with fishing and shooting, and both sexes went for country walks, although even half a mile's walk betrayed an unescorted female to the possibility of being attacked by gipsies, as befell Harriet Smith.

Indoors men read aloud poetry or *Elegant Extracts* to the ladies; Marianne made a test of Edward's sensibility by giving him Cowper, a test which he signally failed to pass.

> "To hear those beautiful lines which have frequently almost driven me wild, pronounced with such impenetrable calmness, such dreadful indifference!"

The circulating library which Sir Anthony Absolute condemned as an "evergreen tree of diabolical knowledge" was now bearing a rich crop, and, even in sparsely-populated Sanditon, Mrs. Whitby presided over shelves full of "complete heroines," including Fanny Burney's *Camilla.* Mr. Collins, it is true, when invited to read to the Longbourn ladies, started back "on beholding the book offered (for everything announced it to be from a circulating library)" and substituted Fordyce's Sermons; but Henry Crawford, that suspiciously good actor, read himself into Fanny's good graces out of Shakespeare. Edmund complimented him: "To read him well aloud is no every-day talent." Alas, not even yet.

Acting was the next step, and a dangerously slippery one. The young Austens, encouraged by Eliza de Feuillade, got up plays amongst themselves in the barn or the dining-room; and Mansfield Park theatricals contained no essential harm except for Sir Thomas' known disapproval and the doubtful taste of *Lovers' Vows.* But when Mary Stanhope, "conditioning" with her suitor, demands that he shall build a theatre, "and I will do Lady Bell Bloomer," he promptly transfers his application to a younger sister.

Music, Dancing and Conversation

Since each group had to make its own, music was of great importance, though proportions of desire to please and to show off varied considerably. Mary Crawford, when she sent for her instrument which "she played with the greatest obligingness," was well aware that "a young woman, pretty, lively, with a harp as elegant as herself, and both placed near a window, cut down to the ground, and opening on a little lawn" was enough to catch any man's heart. Mrs. Weston and Anne Elliot were frequently pressed into service to play country dances. When Mary Bennet seized an opportunity, as Byron said of Southey, to "chant too often and too long," she was checked only by her father's comment, "Let the other young ladies have time to exhibit." Highbury had Jane, genuinely proficient, Emma and Frank, able to accompany a song with a second, "slightly but correctly taken"; and Mrs. Elton, having found what an accomplished society she had come into, was probably well advised to be "determined upon neglecting her music."

The entertainment dearest to the young, however, was dancing; and both private and Assembly balls provided unrivalled occasions for showing character. Darcy disgraced himself by being above his company; Willoughby and Marianne established an ill-mannered "particularity." On the other hand Mr. Knightley unselfishly saved Harriet from humiliation, and Emma Watson saved the little boy Charles from disappointment, when Miss Osborne, the belle of the ball, had deserted "her little expecting partner." Later she congratulated him, "You have got a better partner than me," to which "the happy Charles answered, 'Yes'."

Conversation was, however, the life-blood of social intercourse. Anyone who talked well was valuable, and thus "sensible" is a term of higher praise and "reserved" one of deeper condemnation than they are today. If, like Jane Fairfax, you were reserved, you would talk to no one; if, like Mr. Collins, you were not "sensible," no one could talk to you. It was like a game of ball, and there were various ways of failing. One must not play too obviously better than one's neighbours; when Emma imagines Frank as an ideal young man, able to "adapt his conversation to the taste of everybody" and to "follow the lead or take the lead just as propriety may require," Mr. Knightley indignantly protests that "if he turn out anything like it he will be the most insufferable fellow breathing."

Education and Class Distinction

Education of boys and girls was widely different. It is noticeable that Edmund, hero of *Mansfield Park*, was Eton and Balliol, and Henry, its villain, Westminster and Cambridge; but Jane Austen's uncle was Master of Balliol for over fifty years. As to Mr. Collins, we hear only that "he belonged to one of the universities," and, as seven cities are said to have disputed for the honour of being Homer's birthplace, so two universities may contend for that of not having educated Mr. Collins.

Captain Harville, Captain Wentworth and Captain Benwick, from Persuasion.

The girls usually had governesses at home, and what they acquired of sound learning we can gather from Maria and Julia Bertram, who could repeat the names of "the Roman emperors as low as Severus; besides a great deal of the Heathen Mythology, and all the Metals, Semi-Metals, Planets, and distinguished philosophers."

What was superimposed in the way of futile "accomplishments" Miss Bingley's conversation with Darcy reveals: "The word is applied to many a woman who deserves it no otherwise than by netting a purse or covering a screen." Governesses, with the glad exception of "poor Miss Taylor," had a wretched time, and schoolmistresses worse. Emma Watson declares romantically, "I would rather be teacher at a school (and I can think of nothing worse) than marry a man I did not like," to which her eldest sister replies, "I would rather do anything than be teacher at a school; I have been at school, Emma, and know what a life they lead."

Class distinctions were regulated first by possession of land and second by exercise of a profession; Bingley's sisters, conscious that their fortune had been acquired in honest trade, were anxious that their brother should buy an estate and "commence country gentleman" as soon as possible. Miss Austen favoured the Navy, "that profession which is, if possible, more distinguished in its domestic virtues than in its national importance"; the Army is gay and untrustworthy, and the Church of less prestige than the services.

Apothecaries such as Perry and Wingfield were liked and trusted by the landed gentry, but not invited to dinner; country attorneys and their clerks were below notice, as when Lady Catherine included Elizabeth's "broad-faced, stuffy uncle Philips, breathing port wine" on her long charge-sheet.

These firmly-established distinctions reflect no snobbery; they were part of the eternal scheme of things, and Jane Austen marks the degrees of favour with which she regarded the five Miss Bennets by the status of the husbands she assigned to them. Elizabeth married the hereditary owner of Pemberley; Jane, next in favour, married a man who by purchase of a neighbouring estate would soon blend with his background; Catherine, of whom no harm is known but a cough, married a clergyman, one of a profession traditionally inured to the fact that coughing drowns a parson's saw; Lydia, herself disgraced, married the son of a bailiff; and Mary, a blue-stocking of a most unbecoming shade of blue, must needs accept one of her Uncle Philips' clerks or become an old maid.

It was a truth so "universally acknowledged" that every young woman's first object was to secure a husband, at worst as a provision for old age, that Fanny Price's refusal of eligible Henry Crawford is, to her guardian, inexplicable.

Charles Lamb, Essayist of Charm

During the period when Miss Austen and Sir Walter Scott shared pre-eminence as novelists, though in such contrasting provinces, several other writers contributed to polite letters through a less demanding but more intimate form, the essay. Lamb and Landor (both born in 1775), Hazlitt (1778), Peacock and De Quincey (1785) each staked out a

Jane Austen died at this house in College Street, Winchester, in 1817.

claim, and each attracts readers in proportion as they like him personally.

There have been English authors, and fine ones too, whose books we can like better than we like the writers themselves. Young people can generally get on to terms with *Paradise Lost* more easily than they can with John Milton. But no one could fail to find Charles Lamb lovable. It is not only the fortitude with which he surmounted the tragic circumstances of his life, but the warmth of his affection for the diversity of creatures who shared it with him. He loved old leather-bound books, the front row of the gallery, good talk, the eccentricities of friends, "old familiar faces," and London. But, genuine as was his many-sided pleasure, there was much that it served to conceal; a writer whose shyness compelled him to disguise himself under the name of Elia was not likely to wear his heart upon his sleeve, and the sincerity when the mask must for a moment be dropped tells us more about him than all his cheerful pretence of taking us into his confidence. From the depths of family tragedy, he wrote to his childhood friend Coleridge, "Write as religious a letter as possible, but no mention of what is gone and done with," and, "Mention nothing of poetry." How much those few words say.

He accepted the imperfections of human beings for the delight that he took in their infinite variety. When his family was cheated of a considerable sum he could still feel richer for "the idea" of the specious old rascal who defrauded them; to chimney-sweeps, those little "nigritudes," he could afford a laugh at his expense; to S. T. C. he could afford a cherished book borrowed and never returned; to his brother James he could afford the satisfaction of going off whistling to a picture sale while he himself proceeded to work songless.

His charities were bottomless because he saw what made up the good of life to each of them.

Lamb's Affection for London

As to his own good, as far as was in his power to compass it, he was never in doubt; it was centred on London. And though he acknowledged Skiddaw to be "a fine creature," it was with London's "multitudinous moving picture" that he felt "unutterable sympathies." Here were his delights; the theatre was an appetite and a passion from the moment of his first visit, at the age of five, when, unable to bear the suspense until the curtain lifted, he reposed his "shut eyes in a sort of resignation upon the maternal lap" and knew his bliss. The china closet was a source of exquisite humour:

> "Here is a young and courtly Mandarin, handing tea to a lady from a salver—two miles off. And here the same lady, or another—for likeness is identity on tea-cups—is stepping into a little fairy boat, moored on the hither side of this calm garden river, with a dainty mincing foot, which in a right angle of incidence (as angles go in our world) must infallibly land her in the midst of a flowery mead—a furlong off on the other side of the same strange stream."

He may pretend that he is pointing out "horses, trees, pagodas, dancing the hays . . . a cow and rabbit couchant, and coextensive" to his cousin Bridget (self-protective disguise for his sister Mary), but he is sharing it with us all.

Only those insipid souls who "couldn't care less" were his abomination; even over food people must know what they liked, and he applauds Coleridge's dictum that no man with a pure mind ever refused an apple-dumpling. Nor did he narrow his friendships to those who shared his own tastes; at his Thursday evening parties, surely the best company in London,

> "If a person liked anything, if he took snuff heartily, it was sufficient. He would understand, by analogy, the pungency of other things, besides Irish blackguard, or Scotch rappee."

Hazlitt, a Vigorous Essayist

This "liking" is also the charm exercised by Lamb's friend, William Hazlitt (1778-1830). Hazlitt was quick to recognize that "books are a world in themselves, but they are not the only world"; and of course he liked other things and could say, on looking back, that he had enjoyed his life. He can communicate his pleasure in hearing Coleridge preach, ("I could not have been more delighted if I had heard the music of the spheres"), in going a journey, ("How fine it is to enter some old town, walled and turreted, just at approach of nightfall"), or in watching a fight. "Reader," says he, tucking an arm comfortably into his, "have you ever seen a fight? If not, you have a pleasure to come." No, thinks the reader, I haven't, but oh, I will; it is only some time after he has finished the blow-for-blow account of the blood-thirsty match in which Bill Neate vanquished the Gasman that he wonders if he would have enjoyed being there as much as he has enjoyed Hazlitt's being there.

Hazlitt makes everything fun, even trying and failing to paint, even hearing the letter-bell that reminds him to write a letter, even feeling humiliated at seeing the perfection of skill achieved by Indian jugglers, ("It makes me ashamed of myself. I ask what there is that I can do as well as this? Nothing.").

De Quincey, the Opium Eater

Thomas De Quincey (1785-1859), whose titles such as *Confessions of an English Opium-Eater* or *On Murder Considered as one of the Fine Arts* offer an allurement to curiosity, was of sufficiently eccentric habits to claim a special province. His method was often to observe his own impressions and seek an explanation, as of the abnormally dramatic effect of the knocking in *Macbeth*. The ideas that haunt the mind of a drug-addict or a murderer have special attraction for him, and in his imagination, as in that house in Greek Street which he visited only by twilight, "the noise of the rats made a prodigious uproar on the staircase and hall"; but it cannot have been in the first case as it was in the second, "from want of furniture," for he was a widely read scholar, an acute observer, and a critic of men and affairs. The dramatic effect of rats in an empty house cannot be denied, and at his best De Quincey feels and passes on the stimulus given by a symbol. In *The English Mail Coach* the flash of guns that have gained a victory for English arms on the Continent passes into and becomes the flash in the eyes of gallant horses that carry the news through England.

Nab Farm, the home of De Quincey, and later of Coleridge's son Hartley.

Peacock, a Satirical Novelist

The novels of Thomas Love Peacock (1785-1866) and the *Imaginary Conversations* of Landor are in effect specialized forms of essay, for their purpose is not so much to tell a story or present conflict in action, the stuff of drama, as to provide a vehicle for contemporary satire and philosophical conclusions. To take corruption in Parliamentary elections, a subject then ripe for criticism, such satire can equally be presented directly, as through Hogarth's pictures, or by implication through an episode in a novel, as in Dickens' account of the election at Eatanswill.

Peacock has his fling at bribery and drunkenness, but on the whole he starts from the assumption that in the arrangement of classes all is in its proper place and had better be kept there. Change connotes decay rather than reform. In *Nightmare Abbey* the new note in poetry is ridiculed in a caricature of Shelley; in *Crotchet Castle* Dr. Folliot, an accomplished scholar, takes it for granted that if the lower orders learn to read their betters will suffer for it:

> "Here has my house been nearly burned down, by my cook taking it into her head to study hydrostatics, in a sixpenny tract, published by the Steam Intellect Society, and written by a learned friend who is for doing all the world's business as well as his own . . . My cook must read his rubbish in bed; and as might naturally be expected, she dropped suddenly fast asleep, overturned the candle, and set the curtains in a blaze."

Peacock's wit has at times a bitter taste, but his songs are jolly:

> "Ednyfed, King of Dyfed,
> His head was borne before us;
> His wine and beasts supplied our feasts
> And his overthrow our chorus."

Landor and his *Imaginary Conversations*

Walter Savage Landor (1775-1864) strikes his sparks by putting against each other characters who would certainly not have held such debates in life, but the device enables him to reach and express a general principle:

> "The present, like a note in music, is nothing but as it appertains to what is past and what is to come."

Landor's accomplishment in epigram served him well in the flawless simplicity of one lyric:

> "Ah, what avails the sceptred race?
> Ah, what the form divine?
> What every virtue, every grace?
> Rose Aylmer, all were thine."

His better-known summary of his own life stirs less sympathy:

> "I strove with none, for none was worth my strife;
> Nature I loved, and next to nature art.
> I warmed both hands before the fire of life;
> It sinks, and I am ready to depart."

It makes rather a dreary business of life; was there nothing worth striving with during nearly ninety years of it?

Cobbett's *Rural Rides*

One man, at least, thought that there was. William Cobbett, at the age of forty, began in 1802 to produce his *Political Register*, continuing it until his death in 1835, to cry out against the injustices suffered by working-men. At fifty-nine, he began a series of rides on horseback over the southern shires, leaving in his *Rural Rides* a witness to the wretched state of agriculture and the miserable conditions of labourers. Other Members of Parliament thought kindly about the poor, but they did not get on a horse and ride about, as he did. As de Stogumber says in the Epilogue to *St. Joan*, "If you only saw what you think about, you would think quite differently about it."

The drive of a mind that believed with blazing passion every word he wrote gives Cobbett the status of a modern St. George, riding England on behalf of her weaponless sons, to fight every dragon that threatened the well-being of the common man. If John Bull slept, he must be awakened. The beauty of the countryside caught his eyes and is reflected in his descriptions, but the beauty that his spirit adored was plain justice.

To Cobbett, London was "the Wen," where lived those beyond reach of want, whose greed drove them on towards further material gain, with its accompanying need for bureaucratic power to protect it; the "Thing," a term suggestive of some formless, bloodsucking monster, was the name under which he hated this greed in print. Local tyranny which gagged appeal, swollen taxation and tithes which forced farmers to sack their labourers, inhuman hours of overwork in factories, and the crimes of fire-raising, machine-smashing, informing and theft which flourished rankly in such an atmosphere, were "all our woe, with loss of Eden," that Eden which England should be for a people of "industry perfectly unparalleled."

William Cobbett, self-educated crusader.

Against these he fought, in and out of Parliament, in and out of prison, in and out of his native country, when he had to flee for safety to America. Whether his political theories were always sound is not here the point; his heart was. He rode a horse because "in any sort of carriage you could not get into the real country places," and it was into the real country places that he intended to get, and got. First, the facts: "The more purely a corn country the more miserable the labourers." Next, the cause: "The great, the big bull-frog grasps all. In this beautiful island every inch of the land is appropriated by the rich." Then, the appeal: "All of you who are sixty years of age can recollect that bread and meat, and not wretched potatoes, were the food of the labouring people; you can recollect that every industrious labouring man brewed his own beer and drank it by his own fireside." But his faith rested in his cause: "I knew well that the seeds must lie long in the ground . . . but I knew also that the growth of them would be sure." Solid English monosyllables, aimed straight.

G. K. Chesterton, who, in our own century, was always swinging his great cross-handled sword against some dragon or other, loved him as a brother-in-arms, and in *The Old Song* he sees him both as the man he was and as a symbol of a fight not yet won:

"I saw great Cobbett riding,
The horseman of the shires:
And his face was red with judgment
And a light of Luddite fires;
And south to Sussex and the sea the lights leapt up for liberty,
The trumpet of the yeomanry, the hammer of the squires."

QUESTIONS

1. Which of the five great poets of the Romantic Revival tells you most about himself, and by what means?
2. Use *Lines amongst the Euganean Hills* and *To the West Wind* to show how Shelley blends imagery and lyrical quality with thought and feeling.
3. What are the qualities that make an historical novel interesting to the reader? Illustrate from two novels by Scott set in different countries and centuries.
4. Give a considered appreciation of the pictorial quality of Keats' poems of 1820, using varied reference.
5. Elizabeth Bennet says, "I hope I never ridicule what is wise or good. Follies and nonsense, whims and inconsistencies do divert me, I own, and I laugh at them whenever I can." How far can this be said of Jane Austen herself?
6. Discuss the comment that Jane Austen can give delight by representing characters who would be annoying or intolerable in real life.

REVISION SUMMARY OF AUTHORS BORN BETWEEN 1700 AND 1840

Page

HENRY FIELDING (1707-1754) 189

Of a well-established south-country family, Fielding was educated at Eton and Leyden. He wrote comedies and burlesques which were produced in London theatres. He was called from the Middle Temple to the Bar. He wrote miscellaneous works and journalism on topical subjects and on proposals for social reform. As a magistrate from 1748 he saw the lower side of human nature, and this is reflected in his later novels and pamphlets.

Joseph Andrews (1742): A parody of Richardson's *Pamela.* 205-7
Jonathan Wild (1743): An ironical account of a criminal hero.
Tom Jones (1749): Good and bad in human nature. 207
Amelia (1751): Social evils exposed.

SAMUEL JOHNSON (1709-1784) 211-4

The son of a Lichfield bookseller, Johnson became a Sizar of Pembroke College, Oxford. He became an usher at Market Bosworth School, and later unsuccessfully set up a school near Lichfield. At twenty-seven he settled permanently in London, establishing the profession of man of letters by the scholarship and variety of his writings: plays, parliamentary reports, lives and criticism of the poets, bibliographical catalogues, poems in *The Rambler* and *The Idler*, a philosophical novel, political tracts, an account of his tour in the Western Isles of Scotland and an edition of Shakespeare. His great *Dictionary* occasioned a breach with his patron, Lord Chesterfield, which ended the system of patronage by individuals. Boswell's *Life of Johnson* 25 has preserved many of his letters and his unrivalled powers of debate and conversation.

Irene (1737): A tragedy containing moral discussions. 211
The Vanity of Human Wishes (1749): Shows the emptiness of various ambitions. 213
A Dictionary of the English Language (1747-55): Still a classic, despite great advances in lexicography. 213-4

Page

Rasselas, Prince of Abyssinia (1759): Philosophical speculations on a slight plot. 211

Journey to the Western Isles (1775): In Boswell's company.

Lives of the Poets (1779-81): English poets of the two previous centuries. 211

LAURENCE STERNE (1713-1768) 205

Educated at Cambridge, Sterne became vicar of various Yorkshire parishes, and prebendary of York. He developed the sentimental and humorous elements in his novels, gaining immense popularity.

Tristram Shandy (1767): Uninhibited individual opinions and discursive episodes. 208

A Sentimental Journey (1768): Inspired by a four-year tour in France and Italy.

THOMAS GRAY (1716-1771) 189

Gray was educated at Eton and Cambridge. After brief periods in London and Stoke, he settled in Cambridge, continuing his leisurely legal studies. In 1768 he became Professor of Modern History at Cambridge. His poems and copious letters reflect the thoughtful mood which caused him to call himself "Il Penseroso."

Ode on a Distant Prospect of Eton College (1742): Pensive foreboding of ills.

Ode on the Death of a Favourite Cat (1748): Self-parody. 194

Elegy in a Country Churchyard (1751): Contemplation of humble lives. 197

The Progress of Poesy (1754): The great ages of poetry.

The Bard (1757): Love of Welsh scenery.

The Fatal Sisters and ***The Descent of Odin*** (1760): Norse myth.

TOBIAS SMOLLETT (1721-1771) 205

Of a respected Scottish family, Smollett attended Glasgow University, later becoming a naval surgeon under Admiral Vernon. He set up as a doctor in London and Bath, but with little success. He made a living by writing, chiefly popular novels, but also history books.

Roderick Random (1748): Episodic adventures of a hero at sea, unrestrained by moral purpose. 207

Peregrine Pickle (1751): Lively, often humorous, record of a

Page

swashbuckling rascal imbued with his century's callousness.

Humphry Clinker (1771): Gentler narrative, conveyed 205
through letters, of a servant's travels, chiefly in Scotland. 207-8

WILLIAM COLLINS (1721-1759) 196-8

Collins was educated at Winchester and Oxford. In later years he declined in mental powers. Of his few poems the best show an appreciation of quiet scenery, especially Southern England.

How Sleep the Brave. A lyrical elegy written in 1746.

Odes (1747): On abstractions such as ***Liberty, The Passions.***

Ode to Evening: Unrhymed; varied metre; characteristic 197-8
eighteenth-century diction.

OLIVER GOLDSMITH (1728-1774) 211

The son of an Irish clergyman, Goldsmith became a Sizar of Trinity College, Dublin. Rejected from ordination, he became temporarily tutor, law student, medical student and usher. He toured Europe, and turned his varied education and experiences to account as literary critic for the *Monthly Review*. He became a member of the literary club which included Dr. Johnson.

The Vicar of Wakefield (1766): A vehicle for its author's 211
opinions.

The Deserted Village (1770): A poem depicting the with- 211
drawal of the peasantry to manufacturing towns and to America.

She Stoops to Conquer (1773): A comedy based on an early 206
adventure.

WILLIAM COWPER (1731-1800) 187-8

Educated at Westminster, Cowper was called to the Bar, but 191-2
did not practise. He was prevented from accepting a clerkship 194-5
in the House of Lords by diffidence, which drove him to retire- 198
ment with the Unwins in Huntingdon and later in Olney. 200-1
Depression deepened to religious melancholy and occasional 203-4
mania. Cowper wrote, to distract his mind, descriptions of 205
familiar rural scenes, and lyrics and letters warmly testifying to
his love for relatives, friends and animals.

Olney Hymns (1779): Written at the suggestion of the Rev. 191
John Newton; many are still sung today.

The Task (1785): Six autobiographical books. 187-8

The Diverting History of John Gilpin (1785): A humorous
contemporary ballad, first published anonymously.

Page

RICHARD BRINSLEY SHERIDAN (1751-1816) 210-2

Educated at Harrow, at twenty-five he became joint lessee of Drury Lane theatre. Though ridiculing sentimentality, he romantically eloped with Elizabeth Linley. He furbished up old comedy plots with the wit and manners fashionable in Bath and London. He became a Whig Member of Parliament. 200

The Rivals (1775): Confused identities exposing affectations. 216

The School for Scandal (1777): An old husband and his young wife are involved in a witty, scandal-mongering society. 210-1

The Critic (1779): Caricatures of contemporary playwrights and critics in a parody of excesses.

GEORGE CRABBE (1754-1832) 193

Apprenticed as a medical student, Crabbe returned to practise in his native Aldeburgh. At twenty-five he went to London to live by writing, finding a patron in Burke, who ensured his ordination. His voluminous verse narratives mingle detailed description and criticism of village life. He chiefly used heroic couplets, as his predecessors had done, but his revolt against the sentimental idealism of the poor showed a forward look. 200, 393-5

The Village (1783): Serious observation contrasts with Arcadian pastorals.

The Parish Register (1807): A country vicar recounts stories of his flock.

The Borough (1810): Pessimistic, occasionally humorous, studies.

Tales (1812): Based on events or people known to Crabbe.

Tales of the Hall (1819): Low and middle-class life.

WILLIAM BLAKE (1757-1827) 188-9

The son of a London hosier, Blake became an engraver, illustrating his own poems. His literary tastes were formed by the Bible and by poets of the sixteenth and seventeenth centuries. His lyrics show a spontaneous sense of joy, and indignation against all forms of restraint that would check it. 192, 194, 198-9

Poetical Sketches (1783): Delight in free natural forms.

Songs of Innocence (1789): Sense of Divine care. 188

The Book of Thel (1789): Symbolic narrative against repressive authority.

Songs of Experience (1794): Sense of evil power. 188-9

The Book of Urizen (1794): Attack on restrictions of moral law.

Page

ROBERT BURNS (1759-1796) 190-1

After a hard-working youth on the family farm, he gained fame by his first volume of lyrics. He sought his fortune in Edinburgh, where he prospered in literary and social circles. He returned to unprofitable farming and small Government commissions. Though influenced by his immediate predecessors, he drew his most valuable inspiration from old Scottish ballads, his most congenial subjects being rural manners, his smoothest language the vernacular and his best lyrics adapted to music, often with choruses.

The Kilmarnock Volume (1786): Early lyrics.

The Cotter's Saturday Night: Rural humour and festivities.

The Jolly Beggars (1799)**:** A vigorous portrayal of tramps.

Hallowe'en (1786)**:** High-spirited account of local superstitions.

Tam o' Shanter (1788): An exciting ride through a storm, and witches' revelry.

Scottish Airs with Poetry (1792): Burns contributed the lyrics.

WILLIAM COBBETT (1763-1835) 251-2

The son of a farmer, after service in the army he went to America, and returning to England in 1800, he instituted his influential *Political Register*. He lost a fortune by farming, but regained it by writing. He was an M.P. from 1832 to 1835, and toured southern rural England, producing deductions from first-hand observation.

Political Register (1802-35): A weekly newspaper changing its complexion from Tory to Radical. 251

Rural Rides (1830): A close factual description of the countryside, and the conditions of labourers. 251

WILLIAM WORDSWORTH (1770-1850) 217-22

Born at Cockermouth, the son of a solicitor, Wordsworth lost his mother at eight and his father at thirteen. Educated at Hawkshead Grammar School, he lodged in Ann Tyson's cottage, spending holidays unhappily with his grandparents. At seventeen he went to Cambridge, but after gaining a degree he undertook no regular profession. From 1790 to 1792 he spent much time in France, at first sympathizing with the Revolutionaries, but later alienated by their excesses. In 1795 he settled at Racedown, Dorset, with his sister Dorothy; they moved in 1797

Page

to Somerset where Coleridge became an intimate friend, collaborating in the *Lyrical Ballads*. In 1799 they moved to Dove Cottage, 25
Grasmere; and in 1802 he married Mary Hutchinson. They moved to Rydal Mount in 1813. Frequent visits to Scotland and the Continent furnished material for poems. Southey, Coleridge and De Quincey were neighbours or visitors. In 1843 Wordsworth succeeded Southey as Poet Laureate. He died on St. George's Day.

Lyrical Ballads (1798): A break with the Augustan tradition.

Lines Written above Tintern Abbey (1798): Tracing the stages in his love of nature.

Lucy Poems (1799): A series of love poems.

The Prelude (1799-1805): Tracing the growth of a poet's mind. 218

Michael (1800): Moving picture of rural affections. 383-5

Sonnets (*c.* 1802): Love for England.

Ode on Intimations of Immortality (1807): Greatest philosophical ode in the language.

SIR WALTER SCOTT (1771-1832) 241-2

The son of an Edinburgh attorney, he worked in his father's office. Early conversant with Scottish history, he imbibed Jacobite sympathies. In 1799 he was appointed sheriff of Selkirkshire, on the Border. For a time his popularity as a narrative poet was supreme. When outrivalled by Byron he turned, at over forty, to gain supremacy in historical novels. As he estab- 12
lished his fortune, he acquired Abbotsford, entertaining widely; but on the bankruptcy of his firm of publishers, he gave it up, making himself largely responsible for the firm's debts.

The Lay of the Last Minstrel (1805): Romantic border legends. 241

Marmion (1808): Feudal warfare, culminating in Flodden. 241

The Lady of the Lake (1810): A love-story in verse, set in wild scenery. 241

Waverley (1814): An English officer's adventures in 1745. 241

Lord of the Isles (1815): A verse account of Bruce's fortunes.

The Antiquary (1816): A treasure-hunt by an eighteenth-century professor.

The Heart of Midlothian (1818): A Scots girl's journey to London to save her condemned sister.

Ivanhoe (1819): The clash between Norman and Saxon. 241

Kenilworth (1821): Queen Elizabeth and Amy Robsart in rivalry for Leicester's loyalty and love. 241

Page

The Fortunes of Nigel (1822): A Scotsman's adventures in James I's London.

Quentin Durward (1823): A Scots youth's adventures in Louis XI's bodyguard. 241 13-4

The Talisman (1825): Richard I's adventures in Syria. 241

SAMUEL TAYLOR COLERIDGE (1772-1834) 222-4

He was a schoolfellow of Lamb, at Christ's Hospital. While at Cambridge, Coleridge was influenced by Southey to support the French Revolutionaries and to develop the scheme of pantisocracy. In 1795 he married Sara Fricker. Close companionship with Wordsworth at Stowey and Grasmere developed his deeper powers. By his early thirties he had contracted the opium habit; from 1816 till his death he was in the care of Dr. James Gillman at Highgate, struggling with some success against it.

The Ancient Mariner (1798): A crime against life and its expiation. 223 426

Kubla Khan (1816): A visionary's enchanted dream. 204, 222

Christabel (1816): Evil magic underlying familiar experience. 222

Biographia Literaria (1815-17): Literary criticism establishing a new era of interpretations and canons.

WALTER SAVAGE LANDOR (1775-1864) 250

A contemporary of De Quincey and Leigh Hunt, Landor wrote essays, verse and drama which mingled classical and romantic features; his skill is most apparent in his epigrams.

Imaginary Conversations (1824-9): Widely-ranging series of scholarly discussions between famous characters arbitrarily brought together. 22

JANE AUSTEN (1775-1817) 242-7

The daughter of the rector of Steventon, Hampshire, she later lived in Bath, Southampton and Chawton (near Winchester) with her family.

Sense and Sensibility (1811): Contrast between sisters. 243-5

Pride and Prejudice (1813): The gradual overcoming in hero and heroine of the faults named in the title. 18, 206, 243-6

Mansfield Park (1814): Shows the value of a well-ordered household and well-principled behaviour. 243-6

Emma (1816): A match-making heroine's own romance. 243-6

Northanger Abbey (1818): Exposes the exaggerations of the contemporary horror novel. 12, 210, 355

Page

Persuasion (1818): The ill effects of yielding to persuasion are overcome. 243-5

CHARLES LAMB (1775-1834) 246-8

Educated at Christ's Hospital, Lamb became a clerk in South Sea House (1791-2) and East India House (1792-1825). He shared a home with his sister Mary. From 1809 to 1834 they settled successively at Inner Temple Lane, Covent Garden, Islington, Enfield and Edmonton. Lamb wrote for several periodicals, and contributed essays under the pseudonym of Elia to the *London Magazine*.

Tales from Shakespeare (1807): Summaries of the plots of twenty plays, making them familiar to a wide audience.

Specimens of English Dramatic Poets (1808): Excerpts with comments, from *Gorboduc* to Shakespeare's contemporaries.

Essays of Elia (first series, 1822; second series, 1833): Humorous and pathetic reflections of his experiences. 247-8

Album Verses (1830): ***The Old Familiar Faces*** is most characteristic.

WILLIAM HAZLITT (1778-1830) 248-9

The son of a Unitarian minister of radical persuasions who, after many years in Ireland and America, settled at Wem, near Shrewsbury, he enjoyed walking and talking, but adopted no profession seriously until his meeting in 1798 with Coleridge, and through him with Wordsworth, when he abandoned painting and began to write. In 1808 he married Sarah Stoddart, a friend of Mary Lamb, and settled at Winterslow. He lectured and wrote reviews and essays on men of letters, especially the Elizabethans and his contemporaries. He also wrote for journals.

A View of the English Stage (1818): Criticism of widely various plays and actors seen in London.

The Spirit of the Age (1825): Criticism of contemporaries.

Essays: On his own hobbies, pleasures and experiences. 248-9

THOMAS DE QUINCEY (1785-1859) 249

Educated in Manchester, he wrote biographies and critical articles in elaborate prose on a wide variety of subjects.

The Confessions of an English Opium-Eater (1821): A sombre record of dreams induced by the drug. 249

On Murder Considered as one of the Fine Arts (1827): 249

Page

Intellectually skilful discussion of a serious subject in a pseudo-serious vein.

THOMAS LOVE PEACOCK (1785-1866) 249-50

He produced a series of novels in which he devised no plot, but used the country-house framework to give an opportunity for discussions on social abuses, topical cant and critical opinions.

Headlong Hall (1816): Satire on opposed personified points of view.

Nightmare Abbey (1818): Notable for the burlesque of Shelley. 250

Crotchet Castle (1831): Exposing eccentrics. 250

Gryll Grange (1860): Satirical comment brought up-to-date after a lapse of nearly thirty years.

GEORGE GORDON BYRON (1788-1824) 224-31

He inherited the title of sixth Lord Byron, and the estate of Newstead Priory. Brought up by his mother in Scotland, he was educated at Harrow and Cambridge. In 1815 he married Anne Milbanke, an heiress; but they separated in 1816. He spent his remaining years on the Continent, chiefly in Venice, Ravenna and Pisa, inspired by Countess Guiccioli. As the romantic school gained influence, Byron achieved wide popularity in Europe. He enlisted in support of the Greek War of Liberation, and died of fever at Missolonghi.

Hours of Idleness (1807): Youthful lyrics ridiculed by the *Edinburgh Review*.

English Bards and Scotch Reviewers (1809): A retort to the *Review*. 241-2

Childe Harold's Pilgrimage (1812-17): Autobiography. 224

Manfred (1817): Characteristic melancholy hero.

Don Juan (1818-23): Satirical comments on social scenes. 229

A Vision of Judgment (1822): Cynical comment occasioned by Southey's elegy on George III.

PERCY BYSSHE SHELLEY (1792-1822) 231-5

The son of Sir Timothy Shelley, baronet, he was educated at Eton and Oxford. He refused a conventional life and an allowance from his father, embracing the tenets of the revolutionary philosopher, Godwin. In 1811, when nineteen, he married Harriet Westbrook; after her suicide in 1816 he married Mary Wollstonecraft Godwin. He was accidentally drowned in the Gulf of Spezia, while sailing home from Leghorn. 361-2

		Page
Alastor (1816): Allegory of an idealist in conflict with reality.	232
The Revolt of Islam (1817): Fight against degrading evils.	231
Prometheus Unbound (1820): The triumph of man's spirit over repressive tyranny.	231-2
Adonais (1821): An elegy on Keats.	233
Defence of Poetry (1822): (prose) Order won out of chaos in life and literature.	

JOHN KEATS (1795-1821) 235-41

The son of a London livery-stable keeper, Keats made friends at school in Enfield with his master's son, Charles Clarke, who introduced him to poetry. Through Leigh Hunt at Hampstead, he met Shelley. Hunt fostered his love of Greek mythology and Elizabethan literature. Apprenticed to a surgeon, Keats qualified as an apothecary, but gave up further professional training and devoted himself to poetry. On tour in Scotland he developed tuberculosis, and in September 1820 he left England for Rome, where he died in February 1821.

Endymion (1818): The poet's search for ideal beauty, symbolized in a shepherd's search for the moon-goddess.	236
Hyperion (1818): (unfinished) Gods displace the Titans.	238
Isabella (1818): Love-story with a sad ending.	237-8
The Eve of St. Agnes (1819): Medieval love-story.	236-7
Lamia (1819): The touch of truth destroys a fool's paradise.	238
Odes (1819): An unequalled group, predominantly on the permanence of beauty amid transience.	239-40 389-90

THOMAS CARLYLE (1795-1881) 297

The son of a Scottish stonemason, Carlyle was educated at Edinburgh University. From 1814 to 1818 he taught in Annan and Kirkcaldy. He studied law, and became a professional writer. He married Jane Welsh. In 1834 they moved to Chelsea. In 1865 he became Rector of Edinburgh University. The death of his wife in 1866, and his own ill-health, checked production.

Life of Schiller (1825): Showed the influence of German thought and literature.

Sartor Resartus (1834): The philosophy of clothes.

History of the French Revolution (1837): Facts interpreted by intellectual bias.

On Heroes, Hero-Worship and the Heroic in History (1841): Originally given as lectures, on the importance of individual character in leadership.

Page

Past and Present (1843): The integrity of the past contrasted 297
with contemporary standards.

Letters and Speeches of Oliver Cromwell (1845): Portrait of an heroic character, of the type praised in *Heroes*.

Frederick the Great (1858-65): Based on long research on the Prussian monarch.

ELIZABETH BARRETT BROWNING (1806-1861) 285-7

The eldest child of a West Indian planter, she spent her youth near Malvern and at Sidmouth, before settling in London at Wimpole Street. When fifteen, she injured her back and became an invalid under her father's mistakenly repressive care. She
and Browning admired each other's writings, and in 1845 he 277-85
obtained an introduction. After their marriage in 1846 she left 264
England for Florence, returning only for visits and unable to effect a reconciliation with her father. From 1859 her health declined. She was buried in Florence, whose citizens erected a memorial.

Sonnets from the Portuguese: Forty-four poems on aspects 286-7
of love, written during Browning's courtship.

Aurora Leigh (1856): Vehicle, through the heroine's narrative, 286
for its author's own opinions.

ALFRED TENNYSON (1809-1892) 269-77

The son of a Lincolnshire rector, he was educated at Louth
Grammar School and Cambridge. On leaving his childhood home 24
at Somersby in 1837 he lived near, and frequently visited, London. In 1850 he married Emily Sellwood, and succeeded
Wordsworth as Poet Laureate. He moved in 1853 to Farringford 271
in the Isle of Wight, and in 1869 Aldworth in Sussex was completed. Tennyson spent his remaining years between these two
homes. In 1884 he accepted a peerage. 395-6

Poems (1832): Early lyrics with the germ of future development.

Poems (in two volumes) (1842): Containing many of permanently popular quality.

The Princess (1847): Forecast of a women's university.

In Memoriam (1833-50): Reflections on death and immortality, 270
occasioned by the death of his friend Arthur Hallam.

Maud (1855): Lovers divided by class distinction. 276

Idylls of the King (1842-85): Chivalrous adventures of the 271-3
Knights of the Round Table.

Ballads and other Poems (1880): Vigorous narratives.

Page

MRS. GASKELL (1810-1865) 295-6

Elizabeth (*née*) Stevenson was the daughter of a north-country minister, and spent her youth chiefly at Knutsford in Cheshire (Cranford) and in London. In 1832 she married a minister in Manchester. She established sympathies with the poor in her first novel, and gained the support of Dickens, to whose *Household Words* she contributed.

Mary Barton (1848): Contemporary social problems.

Cranford (1853): Women's social sphere in a country town. 295

Life of Charlotte Brontë (1857): Based on personal knowledge.

Sylvia's Lovers (1863): Strong pictures of a press-gang.

Wives and Daughters (1865): (unfinished) Published in serial form.

WILLIAM MAKEPEACE THACKERAY (1811-1863) 294

The son of an East India Company official, Thackeray lived till the age of six in India. He was educated at Charterhouse and Cambridge, where he met Tennyson. He spent some time in Weimar and Paris, where he developed talents for caricature and satire. In 1837 he settled in London, and contributed to journals, literary reviews and articles weighted with social comment. He produced most of his great novels in monthly numbers. He edited the *Cornhill Magazine* from 1860.

The Book of Snobs (1846): Satirical portraits.

Vanity Fair (1847-8): A large canvas of London society, culminating in Waterloo. 294-5

Pendennis (1848): Partly autobiographical, describing Devon and Cambridge.

Henry Esmond (1852): A historical novel of the early eighteenth century. 294

The Newcomes (1853-5): Sequel to *Pendennis*.

The Virginians (1857-9): Sequel to *Henry Esmond*. 294

ROBERT BROWNING (1812-1889) 277-85

The son of a Bank of England clerk in Camberwell, who encouraged his taste for many arts, Browning was devoted to Shelley. When twenty-six, he travelled widely in Italy and came deeply under its influence. In May 1845 he achieved an introduction to the poetess, Elizabeth Barrett; sixteen months later 285-7
they married, and lived in Florence till her death in 1861. He 263
returned to London where, from 1863 onwards, he was a public

Page

literary figure. He died in Venice, while visiting his only son there.

Pauline (1833): Record of youthful poetic growth. 285

Paracelsus (1835): Record of intellectual ambition.

Pippa Passes (1841): Unconscious influence of one life on others, through four scenes of one day.

Dramatic Lyrics (1842): Aspects of love.

Dramatic Romances (1845): Men with a cause to serve.

Men and Women (1855): Real or fictional characters through whose mouths Browning speaks.

Dramatis Personae (1864): Men and women facing a choice.

The Ring and the Book (1868-9): A seventeenth-century murder and trial illuminated from nine points of view. 281-2

Asolando (1889): Last lyrics proclaiming Browning's faith in life.

CHARLES DICKENS (1812-1870) 293-4

His education was early sacrificed to supplement his family's income; but he continued it by his own wide reading. He became a reporter of parliamentary debates. From his middle twenties onwards Dickens gained fame, a considerable fortune and national popularity among all ages and classes by a series of world-famous novels, mostly in serial form, depicting English life in town and country, especially in London. Between 1858 and 1868 he gave readings from his works in America and in England. 362-3

The Pickwick Papers (1836): Commissioned as a serial, to illustrate a set of pictures. 275

Oliver Twist (1839): A small boy's experience of London's underworld.

Nicholas Nickleby (1839): Notable for its description of infamous Dotheboys School.

The Old Curiosity Shop (1841): In the Victorian tradition of pathetic sentiment.

A Christmas Carol (1843): Most universally beloved of Dickens' Christmas books.

Martin Chuzzlewit (1843): Experiences in America.

David Copperfield (1850): Partly autobiographical.

Bleak House (1853): The law's delays.

Little Dorrit (1857): Based on his father's imprisonment for debt. 294, 13

A Tale of Two Cities (1859): His only novel set in the past abroad. 293

Great Expectations (1861): The making of a gentleman. 379-80

Page

ANTHONY TROLLOPE (1815-1882) 294

He earned his living as a civil servant and an author. He studied life in cathedral cities and made the imaginary county of Barsetshire his own province.

The Warden (1855): Good, and less good, aspects of clerical life and character.

Barchester Towers (1857) ***Doctor Thorne*** (1858) ***Framley Parsonage*** (1864) ***The Last Chronicle of Barset*** (1867)	Social portraiture, ranging from local aristocracy to lower middle class, presented with affection and critical comment.

CHARLOTTE BRONTË (1816-1855) 296

The daughter of an Irish clergyman who settled at Haworth in Yorkshire, Charlotte was educated at two boarding-schools, the earlier of which suggested Lowood in *Jane Eyre;* to the second she returned for three years as a teacher. To qualify to set up a school with her sisters, she went to a *pension* in Brussels in 1842-3. She married her father's curate, but died soon after.

The Professor (1846): Reflecting its author's experiences in Brussels.

Jane Eyre (1847): Powerful, melodramatic romance. 296

Shirley (1849): A love-story full of observation of character.

Villette (1852): Further reflections of the visits to Brussels.

EMILY JANE BRONTË (1818-1848) 296

A younger sister of Charlotte, with whom she visited Brussels in 1842, Emily spent most of her life in Haworth Parsonage, on the Yorkshire moors.

Poems, by Currer, Ellis and Acton Bell (1846): (pseudonyms adopted by Charlotte, Emily herself and Anne Brontë).

Wuthering Heights (1847): A strange, powerful love-story, wild in character and setting. 296

GEORGE ELIOT (1819-1880) 296-7

Mary Ann (*née*) Evans spent a happy youth in Warwickshire, keeping house for her father. After the death of George Henry Lewes, the companion of her chief years of literary production, she married in May 1880 John Walter Cross. She died in London, in the following December.

Page

Scenes of Clerical Life (1857): A simple plot, based on observation.

Adam Bede (1859): Religious revivals of the period.

The Mill on the Floss (1860): The struggles of a youthful and passionate nature towards integrity. 296

Silas Marner (1861): Development and regeneration of a miser. 297

Romola (1863): Historical romance in medieval Florence.

Felix Holt (1866): Based on contemporary politics.

Middlemarch (1872): A noble character struggling against social conventions.

Daniel Deronda (1876): Jewish character and problems.

JOHN RUSKIN (1819-1900) 298

Educated at Oxford, Ruskin became a disciple of Carlyle, sharing his love for the Middle Ages. He encouraged William Morris and the Pre-Raphaelites, and wrote aesthetic criticism and works advocating social and economic reform. From 1854 he fostered the Working-men's Institute in London. He became Professor of Art in 1870. He gave his considerable fortune to charitable and educational causes. He has been called "the apostle of spiritual beauty."

Modern Painters (1843-60): Five volumes expanded from a defence of Turner. 298

The Seven Lamps of Architecture (1849) and ***The Stones of Venice*** (1851-3): Laws of constructive art.

Sesame and Lilies (1864-9): Books, reading and education.

Praeterita (1886-8): Autobiography.

MATTHEW ARNOLD (1822-1888) 287-91

The son of the famous Headmaster of Rugby, Arnold was educated at Rugby and Oxford. Elected a Fellow of Oriel, he later became Professor of Poetry at Oxford. He was a school inspector till 1886. He studied education on the continent, and toured America as a lecturer. 297

Empedocles on Etna (1852): Shows its author's classical bent in theme and control. 291

Poems (1853): Chiefly distinguished for ***Sohrab and Rustum*** 287-8
and ***The Scholar Gipsy***. 289

Balder Dead (1853): Scandinavian mythology. 288

New Poems (1867): ***Thyrsis*** and ***Dover Beach*** are notable.

Essays in Criticism, 2 volumes (1865 and 1888): Independent valuations of a wide range of authors.

Page

DANTE GABRIEL ROSSETTI (1828-1882) 292

Rossetti was born and lived in London. In 1848 he formed the Pre-Raphaelite Brotherhood with Millais and Holman Hunt. He published his first poems in 1850. In 1860 he married Elizabeth Siddal, often the model for his paintings.

The Blessed Damozel (1850): His most famous mystical poem.

Poems (1870)
Ballads and Sonnets (1881)
} Reflections of his own experiences, afterwards published as ***The House of Life.***

Sister Helen (1870): Dramatic narrative, combining romance with witchcraft.

WILLIAM MORRIS (1834-1896) 292-3

Educated at Marlborough and Oxford, he there formed one of a circle who developed his love of medieval and Scandinavian literature and art. He settled finally at the Red House, Bexley Heath, from which, as head of a firm, he produced a revolution in decorative household arts of two dimensions, such as stained glass, embroidery, tiles, textiles, wallpaper and painted decorations. He acquired Kelmscott Manor, near Hammersmith, in 1871, giving its name to the Press from which he issued, among other works, a beautifully printed edition of Chaucer.

The Defence of Guenevere (1858): Romantic themes in a youthful experiment.

The Earthly Paradise (1868-70): A classical story treated in the medieval manner.

Sigurd the Volsung (1876): An epic based on Norse legend.

The Dream of John Ball (1888): Social doctrines put forth in village romance.

ALGERNON CHARLES SWINBURNE (1837-1909) 292

Educated at Eton and Oxford, Swinburne spent his childhood near the sea. He was familiar with Greek and French literature.

Atalanta in Calydon (1865): A Greek story retold in blank verse with lyrical comments by the chorus.

Poems and Ballads (in three series, 1866-89): Themes chosen in defiance of convention.

Songs before Sunrise (1871): Notable for their harmony of expression.

Tristram of Lyonesse (1882): The chief poem is a love-story of epic quality, written in rhymed couplets.

CHAPTER 11

THE VICTORIAN ERA

IN 1812, nine years before the death of Keats (the first of the five great Romantic poets to die), Tennyson was three years old and Browning was born. By the death, in 1850, of Wordsworth, oldest and last of the Romantics, the two great Victorians were entirely established in fame and favour. Tennyson had followed his early volumes, containing *Oenone*, *The Lady of Shalott*, *The Lotos-Eaters*, *The Two Voices*, *Ulysses* and *Morte D'Arthur*, with *The Princess* in 1847, and *In Memoriam* in 1850, the year in which he married and was made Poet Laureate. Browning, having challenged public taste with such strange and massive works as *Paracelsus* in 1835 and *Sordello* in 1837, had found his most characteristic form in *Dramatic Lyrics* and *Christmas Eve and Easter Day* in 1850. Both lived to old age. Browning, going from strength to strength, added his chief works, *Men and Women* (1855), *Dramatis Personae* (1864), *The Ring and the Book* (1868) and *Asolando* (1889). Tennyson, who died in 1892 at the age of eighty-three, added *Maud* (1855), *The Idylls of the King* (1859), his plays (1875) and *Ballads* (1880).

This pair of Victorian giants dominated the reading public of the nineteenth century, one or other of them producing almost every five years from 1830, the year of Tennyson's first volume, to 1889, the year of Browning's last, a volume that contained lyrics, narratives, monologues or dramas in endlessly varying forms, as an immortal part of the English heritage. To them must be added a third great Victorian, though of shorter life and less achievement, Matthew Arnold (1822-88), whose collected poems in 1853 established his position with them, if not beside them.

Even before 1892, when all three were silent, the songs of the Pre-Raphaelites, Dante Gabriel Rossetti (1828-82), his sister Christina (1830-94), William Morris (1834-96) and Algernon Charles Swinburne (1837-1909), had given the end of the century a dying fall and a sunset glow.

Alfred Tennyson, English Laureate

The low-lying river meadows, sand dunes and long rolling edges of the North Sea which made up the landscape of Tennyson's childhood in Lincolnshire persist in his imagination throughout his poetry; his chosen home for nearly forty years, from 1853 onwards, was at Farringford, in the western corner of the Isle of Wight, within reach of downs and Channel. Something of the largeness, the sweep of sky and sea, the clear, heartening air, seems to have made the climate of his thought and language.

This largeness is nowhere more apparent than in his attitude to his own calling: the poet is "dowered with the hate of hate, the scorn of scorn, the love of love." With "one poor poet's scroll," freedom can shake the world. Song, since it must be true at heart, must be happy at heart. Matthew Arnold, though he called Tennyson "our wisest," concentrating on the more despairing passages of *In Memoriam*, found him pessimistic.

But *In Memoriam* is far more than a "store of sad experience"; and in *The Two Voices*, a full debate on Hamlet's dilemma, to be or not to be, Tennyson plays fair on both sides. The still small voice that counsels self-destruction has many a powerful argument on its side: for example, death brings relief from human misery; the marvel of man's creation does not connote immortality in him any more than in a dragon-fly; this world is only one of many and not the best; the human race will not perish or even be affected if he goes. Let him be a realist and recognize his own wretchedness. But at last the "I" who strives to meet each argument finds that argument is not the point; a second voice which has no dealings with deductions, fallacies or false conclusions removes the discussion to a different plane, of "a hidden hope" against which all argument is unavailing. This is what being a poet meant to Tennyson, an unswerving belief in life.

Attitude to Poets and Critics

Tennyson's generous sense of brotherhood with his fellow-poets comes through two channels. He greets many by friendly phrase and praise. He dedicated *Tiresias* to "my good friend Robert Browning, whose genius and geniality will best appreciate what may be best, and make most allowance for what may be worst"; Victor Hugo, even though he is no lover of England, is "lord of human tears"; Milton is a "mighty-mouthed inventor of harmonies"; Virgil is "wielder of the stateliest measure ever moulded by the lips of man."

A nature of such magnanimity could not endure mean rivalry between poets, or ungenerous lack of understanding among critics. Critics may be merely a chorus of "irresponsible, indolent reviewers," and even bibliographies may come between poet and reader; Virgil, Horace and Catullus should be jubilant that they flourished "before the love of letters, overdone, had swampt the sacred poets with themselves."

As years pass, changes in taste will reverse even a conscientious judgment, and the poet should write independently of both. Nor should irrelevant details of a writer's life have anything to do with enjoyment of his poetry. "Scandal-mongers" are "carrion vultures" who wait "to tear his heart before the crowd," itself "the many-headed beast." Here are two principles

Tennyson, who became Poet Laureate when Wordsworth died in 1850, lived for many years at Farringford in the Isle of Wight.

for a reader: first, let him allow that no critical judgment is absolute or final, and secondly, let him feel completely free to like what he likes, to enjoy any song that pleases him "from its worth," and not waste his time on that which cannot make a pennyworth of difference to such enjoyment. This is shining commonsense.

The Idylls of the King

What were Tennyson's favourite themes? To us today he stands as author of the *Idylls of the King*. Rudyard Kipling, in *Romance*, shows that each age thinks of itself as prosaic, and of romance as belonging to that just passed; Tennyson, as its "chosen bard," seems "to say, our king was with us yesterday," for he took as the theme of his chief work the exploits of the Knights of the Round Table under King Arthur, bound by an honourable code to a life of danger in pursuit of noble deeds. In the fifteenth century, Sir Thomas Malory collected the Arthurian legends in *Morte D'Arthur*.

Tennyson's plan is like that used by Spenser in his *Faerie Queene*; the centre is a sovereign who both shapes and personifies an ideal, and from whose Court the knights and their adventures radiate. It has these differences, that Tennyson gave one book to the Coming of Arthur and one to his "death," in the sense of his departure from earthly life, and that the figure of Arthur himself, making fallible decisions and vulnerable to human misfortunes, is involved in every tale. He is shown as a perfect man, too far removed from sinful humanity to engage our sympathies, which inevitably turn to Lancelot, "the warrior whom he loved and honoured most," invincible in tourney or fight, who served his honour in all points but one, and repented to bitter tears, "not knowing he should die a holy man."

Arthur, in contrast, is to his wife:

> ". . . the faultless King,
> That passionate perfection, my good lord,
> But who can gaze upon the sun in heaven? . . .
> The low sun makes the colour."

Even the most chivalrous of knights could not have it both ways, and Lancelot knew it; but had he been happy and faultless, he would not have been loved at sight by the faery Lady of Shalott and the mortal lily maid of Astolat. Many Victorians saw in the ideal character of Arthur a reflection of the Prince Consort. Tennyson emphasized this view in his dedication of the *Idylls* to his memory:

> "Since he held them dear,
> Perchance as finding there unconsciously
> Some image of himself."

There is help from another world by the sword Excalibur, and to another world it must be returned. This allegory is different in kind from that of Mr. Valiant-for-Truth in *The Pilgrim's Progress* who, as he goes from this life, leaves his sword "to him that shall come after me in my pilgrimage." Both allegories are sound; they are different swords.

It is significant that, when Tennyson wrote his first draft under the title *Morte D'Arthur* in 1842, the story ended with the words, "On the mere the wailing died away," but that when he incorporated it in *The Passing of Arthur* twenty years later, he fulfilled his own words, "The old order changeth, yielding place to new," and linked the legend with the next stage in the life of the world, by adding a passage in which Sir Bedivere, though he recognized that "the King is gone," climbed a hill from which he could see limitless vistas of the great deep, "and a new sun rose, bringing a new year."

The tales give glimpses of halls and gardens, shadowy towers, royal feasts and ceremonies. When, after Modred's treachery and the "last, dim, weird, battle of the west," Arthur tells Sir Bedivere:

> "I think that we
> Shall never more, at any future time
> Delight our souls with talk of knightly deeds,"

that "never more" echoes among the mountains of Lyonesse.

There is a handful of lovely lyrics, flung out from the same theme: first comes the magic of "remote Shalott," a faery island until reality breaks in upon it; Sir Lancelot, in a green poem, rode with his Queen "thro' the coverts of the deer"; Sir Galahad, in a starlit one, rode alone through dreaming towns, "by bridge and ford, by park and pale."

Tennyson did not limit himself, however, to the King who was with us yesterday. Arthur himself held the balance true between regret for the end and welcome to the beginning; and though to Sir Bedivere the word "new" was one of dread to find himself "among new men, strange faces, other minds," it became a word of hope as the "new" sun rose.

The qualities for which Tennyson particularly valued his race were its love of freedom and hatred of extremes. He would live in England rather than seek "the palms and temples of the south" as long as it remained the land where "a man may speak the thing he will"; but new ideas must have "time and space to work and spread." His love is far brought:

"From out the storied Past, and used
Within the Present, but transfused
Thro' future time by power of thought."

Tradition and principle must be no dead hand checking progress, but a guiding one to the world, as it adapts itself to the "ringing grooves of change." His central principle was England's contribution to human thought:

"Whatever harmonies of law
The growing world assume,
Thy work is thine.—The single note
From that deep chord which Hampden smote
Will vibrate to the doom."

Noble occasions in England's history furnished the basis of many narrative poems, such as *The Revenge*, *The Relief of Lucknow*, or, to go back to earlier times, *Boadicea* or *The Battle of Brunanburh*, with its jolly alliterative swing:

"Many a carcase they left to be carrion,
Many a livid one, many a sallow-skin,
Left for the white-tailed eagle to tear it."

Fairy-tales and Legends

Fairy-tales are put into rhyme with even less motive of teaching. *The Goose* may preach contentment, but its purpose is a glorious uproar. King Cophetua sees his beggar-maid, and *The Day-Dream* is romance distilled:

"Across the hills, and far away
Beyond their utmost purple rim,
And deep into the dying day
The happy princess followed him."

Enjoyment is moral enough for these poems; their true intent is our delight.

From Greek legends of the fall of Troy, Tennyson chose three: *Oenone* recounts the judgment of Paris that led to the siege, and *The Lotos-Eaters* tells one of the adventures of Ulysses, after Troy's destruction, on his way home to Ithaca through the Aegean; *Ulysses* in turn tells how the ageing leader rouses his comrades to one last adventurous voyage.

Ulysses decides to "drink life to the lees," since even in old age " 'tis not too late to seek a newer world"; his last determination, "to strive, to seek, to find, and not to yield," is fittingly inscribed on the memorial to Scott and his companions that fronts the Antarctic wastes. But it is not these lines that drift about the memory so much as the scenes in which the stories are set:

"The swimming vapour slopes athwart the glen,
Puts forth an arm, and creeps from pine to pine,
And loiters, slowly drawn."

By such images the mind, whether it achieves any "self-reverence, self-knowledge, self-control" or not, is imperishably enriched.

Occasional Poems

Though from this point of view Tennyson seems chiefly concerned with the past, he had also an alert interest in his own century, which shows itself mainly in two kinds of poem. Verse on topical events, that as Poet Laureate Tennyson was committed to commemorating, is a type of poetry which seldom produces anything first-rate, but which he dignified in 1852 by his *Ode on the Death of the Duke of Wellington*, great in its own right. With measured tread, the slow opening lines move unfalteringly forward; thought ranges over the Duke's own character, "whole in himself, a common good," and over the example of duty followed regardless of reward:

"Not once or twice in our rough island-story
The path of duty was the way to glory."

The quiet close is in sight of eternity :

"In the vast cathedral leave him;
God accept him; Christ receive him."

Such an occasional poem reaches greatness when it becomes "a people's voice."

In his *Ode on the Jubilee of Queen Victoria in 1887*, Tennyson celebrated, perhaps in a significant order,

"Fifty years of ever-broadening commerce,
Fifty years of ever-brightening science,
Fifty years of ever-widening empire."

Even when not called forth by a special occasion, some reflection of each appears. At the opening of the International Exhibition in 1862, Tennyson looked to rapidly-developing commerce to be the universal peacemaker:

> "Till each man find his own in all men's good,
> And all men work in noble brotherhood,
> Breaking their mailed fleets and armed towers."

Such a purpose exalts "growing commerce" from the mere acquisition of property, the ideal of the farmer, to be "a fair white-winged peacemaker."

Science and Religion

As to science, even before the publication of Darwin's *Origin of Species* in 1859, thoughtful men were faced with the difficulty of reconciling its discoveries with accepted tenets of religion. Already in *The Epic* (1842), college friends' conversation on Christmas Eve naturally led Parson Holmes to take:

> ". . . wide and wider sweeps,
> Now harping on the church commissioners,
> Now hawking at geology and schism."

There must have been thousands of such discussions in their cosy middle-class setting of solid mahogany, red plush and gilt frames; there were also forfeits and punch, skating and mistletoe as at Dingley Dell in *The Pickwick Papers*, but it is doubtful if conversation during Christmas festivities there ever turned on geology and schism.

The English landowner, however, as Tennyson presents him in the person of Sir Walter Vivian, felt it his duty to enlighten his tenants about scientific progress; typical of his peaceful time and established position, he was:

> "A great broad-shouldered genial Englishman . . .
> A patron of some thirty charities . . .
> A quarter-sessions chairman, abler none."

Solidly good as his own furniture, he annually invited his tenants, in pursuit of "an universal culture for the crowd," to Vivian-place, where they beheld "knobs and wires," clockwork steamers, electric shocks and an elementary telegraph, so that "sport went hand in hand with science," and his twilight thoughts that day were "upon the future man."

The progress of popular education did not, however, include in his mind the future woman; the distinction implicit in his charge to Lady Clara Vere de Vere:

> "Oh teach the orphan-boy to read
> Or teach the orphan-girl to sew"

is openly expressed in his mockery of Lilia's demand for college and a chance. There were in 1847 no great girls' schools, nor the remotest prospect of admitting women to universities; but since it is the business of education to make young minds hungry and show them what there is to eat, the women of a hundred years ago refused to starve, and nowadays undergraduates of both sexes crowd the lecture-rooms when term is in full swing and bicycles hang by the wall.

One social principle most firmly rooted in Victorian consciousness was the desirability in marriage of equality of class and fortune. It is the bitterness of *Maud* that the hero, of humble origin, suspects that the grace shown to him by the daughter of the Hall is a snare, a "silken net," and that her brother will oppose him as a suitor, as indeed he does, to the ruin of everyone's happiness. Lady Clara drives the foolish yeoman, young Lawrence, to suicide by heartless flirtation.

The Northern Farmer, on the other hand, warns his son against marriage with "Parson's lass," despising her descent from a "gentleman born" since it brings no shillings or pence. Even a love-match, if unequal, works out unhappily: the Lord of Burleigh's village bride fades away under "the burden of an honour unto which she was not born."

Tennyson had the supreme gift to distil into lyrics the qualities that, by association, remind us of his longer poems. The background of every Arthurian tale rises to the harmonies of

"The splendour falls on castle walls,
 And snowy summits old in story;
 The long light shakes across the lakes
 And the wild cataract leaps in glory."

Robert Browning and Elizabeth Barrett Browning, sketched in 1850.

The gracious peace and ordered loveliness of a Victorian country house lie behind the quiet of the lines:

> "Now sleeps the crimson petal, now the white,
> Nor waves the cypress in the palace walk,
> Nor winks the gold fin in the porphyry font.
> The firefly wakens; waken thou with me."

The sea, that rolls through so many of his poems, rocks the heart to rest almost inaudibly in the lullaby *Sweet and low.* Sight and sound are united in vision; twilight and evening bell bring us home.

Robert Browning, a Dramatic Poet

Robert Browning (1812-89), whose lifetime covered six years fewer than Tennyson's, was much less representative of his era, for three reasons. Firstly, his concern was with problems of conduct presented to and solved by men and women of any period or country, actual or imaginary, rather than with his own circumstances in time and space; secondly, his genius was essentially dramatic rather than lyric; and thirdly, he lived for many years out of England.

It is ironical that Browning's best-known poem is loved for its picture of an English spring, when:

> "Whoever wakes in England,
> Sees, some morning, unaware,
> That the lowest boughs and the brushwood sheaf
> Round the elm-tree bole are in tiny leaf,"

but the song was written because he was *not* in England, and he declares:

> "What I love best in all the world
> Is a castle, precipice-encurled,
> In a gash of the wind-grieved Apennine . . .
> Open my heart and you will see
> Graved inside of it, 'Italy'."

The Englishman in Italy gives a picture of drought, when

> "Pomegranates were chapping and splitting
> In halves on the tree,"

and shows the setting-out of the quail nets; round the fisherman from Amalfi bringing "pink and grey jellies, your sea-fruit" swarm "children as naked and brown as his shrimps." Then Browning paints a grape harvest, the feast of snails, "lasagne so tempting to swallow in slippery ropes," purple slices of gourd, olives and figs. Along comes a gipsy tinker, then the drummers and trumpeters of the religious festival. All this is as foreign as the scorpion that drops out of the plaster wall.

In *A Light Woman* Browning, having presented a situation involving three human souls, addresses himself:

"And, Robert Browning, you writer of plays,
Here's a subject made to your hand."

A writer of plays? This is not how we think of him first, but most of his poems are grouped under such headings as *Dramatic Lyrics*, *Dramatic Romances*, *Dramatic Idylls*, *Dramatis Personae*, *Men and Women*, all of whom speak in the first person, as do the nine characters of *The Ring and the Book*. Several of his longer works are in the actual form of a play, such as *Pippa Passes*, *King Victor and King Charles*, *Luria* and *A Blot in the 'Scutcheon*.

But none got off the page or on to the stage with enough force to earn Browning the name of playwright. His tragedy *Strafford* did reach the stage with a cast headed by Macready, but a series of misadventures baulked its success. In the practical sense he was a writer of poems, not plays, even when these are cast in dramatic form, but his dramatic instinct entitles him in two senses to the claim.

First, to gain their full effect, his poems must be read aloud. All poets suffer from the barriers between voice and ear, but especially those whose poems contain direct speech. For example, in *A Toccata of Galuppi's* Browning imagines two Venetians of the eighteenth century who whispered their love-making while the famous Italian composer "sat and played toccatas stately at the clavichord."

" 'Were you happy?'—'Yes.'—'And are you still as happy?'—'Yes. And you?'
—'Then, more kisses!'—'Did *I* stop them, when a million seemed so few?'
Hark, the dominant's persistence till it must be answered to!
So, an octave struck the answer. Oh, they praised you, I dare say!
'Brave Galuppi! that was music! good alike at grave and gay!
I can always leave off talking when I hear a master play!' "

There are four different voices here—his, hers, Browning's as narrator, and Galuppi's—four different pitches and tones, with their range from confidential whisper to hypocritical applause, from insincerity and oblique warning to the finality of the verdict. But they must be heard, either vividly by the ear of imagination or actually by the ear of the flesh. No poet's work better repays reading aloud, or has a wider claim to the right virtue of drama, to convey its meaning through many voices and varied tones.

Poems of Conflict

Secondly, Browning's instinct for drama drove him to choose for all his greatest works conflict of some kind; and conflict is the essence of dramatic, not of lyric, verse. The conflict may be military, political, spiritual, between forces of evil and good in a man's own soul, or between one principle of life and another, and Browning has no sympathy whatever with the half-hearted. A hero, to engage his interest, must know hope and refuse to evade or even count the cost. In *Prospice*, imagining himself within sight of death, Browning claims, "I was ever a fighter, so—one fight more, the best and the last"; and in *Asolando*, published on the day of his death, he describes himself as "one who never turned his back, but marched breast forward." He had the right, for in his own life, when faced with the decision whether to take the invalid Elizabeth Barrett from her father's care, or to refuse the risk and forgo their mutual love, he chose a positive rather than a negative way of life, and was in the outcome superbly justified.

Browning's sympathies were always with men and women who used their free will and span of life for positive ends; his contempt was for those who wasted it, and his pity for those on whom the burden of choice bore too hardly. On the other hand, his love and admiration were always at the feet of those who vowed themselves to a cause and served it with their whole being, undaunted and undeterred. His poems furnish examples of every degree in both kinds, as the following poems show.

The Statue and the Bust tells the story of a Duke and a Lady, the core of whose lives was their love for each other, but who were too indeterminate to put first things first, and so lost all. The point at issue was whether they would allow any secondary consideration to impede their lives' purpose. They did. Day succeeded day of hesitation and inaction, each with its insufficient reason. But there is only one day—today. Then came an end of all todays, and of all chance. And what next?

> "Still, I suppose, they sit and ponder
> What a gift life was, ages ago."

It hits us all:

> "So we resolve on a thing and sleep;
> So did the Lady, ages ago."

Soliloquy in a Spanish Cloister

The monk in this poem has done at least part of what he set out to do, stayed in his cloister and submitted to its discipline; but he has been wrong to set out on this particular path. In Brother Lawrence he sees one whose simple goodness has unconsciously achieved a true holiness, and he is faced with the world's decision—when we see someone else possessed of an art or a grace that we would give anything to have but have not, we can worship it or kill it; there is not anything else that we can do, for it cannot be ignored. The monk plans to damn Brother Lawrence's soul, unable to realize that, by owning its greater beauty and loving him for it, he himself could have a share in it. In this way he could have made his life what he had intended. He wasted his chance, not, as the Duke did, from not prizing anything enough, but from mistaking the way to fulfil his life's ambition.

My Last Duchess

There are others worse. To the Duke in this poem, conscious that there is no quality in himself to command respect above other men except his "nine-hundred-years-old name," for which he personally can take no credit, a distinguishing deference from his wife is essential. Beauty has no genuine value for him; the sunset and bough of cherries are not worth his notice because they are not exclusive to him, but a statue "thought a rarity" is, because no one else has one. He knows himself to be slow-witted, and any circumstance that confirms it, such as an argument with his wife, is a danger to his carefully fostered self-esteem. He is the antithesis of all "holy and humble men of heart," for he is neither holy nor humble nor a man of heart.

Another life used so wrongly as to lead to death is that of the heartbroken court lady of the *ancien régime* who, in *The Laboratory*, pours out all her wealth, even her gift of kisses for which she no longer has a use, to buy death for her rival. These two murderers have no value for the lives of others because within themselves they have already ceased to live. For those, however, who hated their own lives enough to refuse life altogether, Browning has a deep understanding and an unconquerable hope. In compassion he calls their failure "apparent," not actual, and withholds judgment on the youth of unsatisfied ambition, the "leveller" with clenched fist, the losing gamester. It is impossible to put oneself beyond the reach of mercy; even the worst criminal, Guido, after his just execution, must pass into

> ". . . that sad, obscure, sequestered state
> Where God unmakes but to remake the soul
> He else made first in vain; which must not be."

Fighting for a Cause

On the other hand, in a world such as this, there is never any lack either of causes powerfully demanding loyalty or of fellow-beings sorely needing help. Browning's heroes are those who immediately and unreservedly respond. Some of his most vigorous songs are those of uncomplicated partisans who are just getting on with the job by any means to hand; the bearer of good news clapped his hands, "laughed and sang, any noise, bad or good, till at length into Aix Roland galloped and stood." The word "galloped" echoes in almost every verse. We are never beyond the sound of horses' hooves till that "and stood"; and what the good news was that they brought from Ghent who knows or cares? In our own Civil War, "Kentish Sir Byng stood for his King," so naturally God was also for King Charles; and the other side, including Hampden, were "Noll's damned troopers" or carles of the Devil. He and his troop go "marching along, fifty score strong, great-hearted gentlemen singing this song." One cause of their vigour is that they never questioned the doctrine, "hold by the right, you double your might," nor that they themselves were holding by the right. It all sounds deceptively simple.

Leaders and Followers

But leaders could fail their followers. In *The Lost Leader*, the whole-hearted follower, reinforced by a sense that

> "Shakespeare was of us, Milton was for us,
> Burns, Shelley, were with us—they watch from their graves,"

finds it hard to understand how mere bribes of honours and wealth could ever lure away a trusted leader, but accepts that separation in this life is final. At the end of *A Soul's Tragedy* the Pope's legate, cynical Ogniben, is sure that the people's saviour, Chiappino, can be induced, as others have been, to forgo his ideals. He has had plenty of experience ("I have seen three-and-twenty leaders of revolts"), and his cynicism is justified. When Chiappino flies, he adds him to his bag with the words, "I have known four-and-twenty leaders of revolts."

Again and again Browning presents a man glorified by devotion to a woman, finding his highest self in serving. A face once seen will evoke a lifetime's devotion, a likeness will do it; an old bachelor feels his heart thump as he waits to hear if his friend will see what he himself sees in his cherished etching, will admit that

> "He never saw, never before today,
> What was able to take his breath away,
> A face to lose youth for, to occupy age
> With the dream of, meet death with."

An old huntsman finds the centre of his life in the moment when he helps his mistress to flight from the Duke, her hated husband; old as he now is, with wife and children dead, he remembers every detail of look and gesture in the empty courtyard, as when

> ". . . Her face looked down on me
> With a look that placed a crown on me."

Perhaps fifteen minutes out of eighty years were spent in service to one who knew how to accept it, but it restored her life and filled his.

The response is again immediate in *The Ring and the Book*. Caponsacchi, the young canon of Arezzo, receives an appeal from helpless Pompilia to rescue her from her murderously-minded husband, Duke Guido. (Dukes are not much good in Browning's poems, but this one was an historical character, and his crimes were actual events.) He believes the letter to be a forgery, and keeps the appointment merely to reject it; but to his intense surprise it is not. Pompilia appears:

> "So close above me, she could almost touch
> My head if she bent down; and she did bend,
> While I stood still as stone, all eye, all ear."

Without a word from him she recognizes his faith:

> "At no time, you with the eyes here
> Ever intended to do wrong by me,"

and recalls, as she is dying,

> "The first word I heard ever from his lips,
> All himself in it,—an eternity
> Of speech, to match the immeasurable depth
> O' the soul that then broke silence—'I am yours'."

The will to serve, unrecognized and unrewarded, is the basis of many a lyric. In *Pippa Passes*, the Queen hears the despair of a page who, because there is nothing she lacks, can give her nothing but the will to give.

Count Gismond seems to follow the Arthurian chivalric pattern; it accepts the convention of slandered heroine (this time a Queen), black villain (Gauthier), unknown champion (Count Gismond) who has worshipped from a distance, a combat in which he triumphs over the false knight who confesses and dies, and the marriage of the lady and her defender; and would seem as if it must be utterly stereotyped. Only somehow it contrives, by concentrating on the moment and the sense of absolute faith, to become alive.

> "This glads me most, that I enjoyed
> The heart of the joy, with my content
> In watching Gismond unalloyed
> By any doubt of the event."

Count Gismond was first published in 1842, when Browning was thirty, and *The Ring and the Book* not until 1868, over a quarter of a century later, but the figure persists in his imagination: "over my head his arm he flung against the world" might sum up either of them.

Browning took it for granted that life continued after death, or this life would be nonsense. When "Beautiful Evelyn Hope is dead" he is ready to wait for her love to reward his:

> "Delayed it may be for more lives yet
> Through worlds I shall traverse, not a few . . .
> But the time will come."

The use of old age is summarized in *Rabbi Ben Ezra* as a time for judging and absorbing experience: "Young, all lay in dispute; I shall know, being old."

As to the moment of death itself, in *Childe Roland* it is symbolized by the dark tower which comes as a stunning surprise even "after a life spent training for the sight." The thought of it did not inspire fear beyond that common to mankind called on to resign its familiar mode of being when

> ". . . the blasts denote
> I am nearing the place . . .
> Where he stands, the Arch Fear in a visible form,
> Yet the strong man must go."

On the other side of that temporary experience lay for him an absolute trust in reunion with his wife. Browning was content to wait, impatient and often unhappy, but certain that there would be nothing strange.

Heaven was to be a chance to carry into effect what eluded a man here; Andrea del Sarto, the faultless painter, satisfied with easily attained success, realizes it all too well:

> "Ah, but a man's reach should exceed his grasp,
> Or what's a heaven for?"

But he knows that he will not take it. To Browning himself heaven will afford

A scene from The Barretts of Wimpole Street, *a dramatized version of the romance of Robert Browning and Elizabeth Barrett.*

the joy of being a painter or a musician. In *One Word More* he tells his wife:

> ". . . I stand on my attainment.
> This of verse alone, one life allows me;
> Other heights in other lives, God willing."

It would give Abbé Vogler a chance to recapture and perfect his extemporized music, for "on the earth the broken arcs, in the heaven a perfect round." It would give the grammarian a chance to drink deeper of knowledge from which lack of time on earth had debarred him. It would establish a correspondence with the use made of this life; in it, the "soldier-saints" would "burn upward each to his point of bliss."

Honesty and Communication

Armed with his own tremendous mental energy, Browning had no patience with intellectual trickery. Abuse of a good brain by plausible argument is treachery to reason, and Bishop Blougram, who "believed, say, half he spoke," receives poetic justice when Gigadibs, his audience, captured by one of his over-elaborated similes, simply does not listen to any more of his sophistries. Sludge, the medium, is less detestable because he at least thinks straight, knows when his arguments are fallacious and takes in only those who ask to be duped. When he plans lies, he knows that they are lies.

The mind that thinks straightly and independently, however, must from time to time question and revalue ideas accepted from of old.

The Epistle of Karshish shows a scientist glimpsing an incredible truth because his mind is open not merely to the scientific possibilities of spider-life and blue-flowering borage, but to the unscientific fact that a dead man has returned to life. Karshish gives up the struggle to fit it into the limits of received knowledge, and makes the dangerous crossing into an uncharted realm of thought.

In the old story of the glove and the lions, in which a lady tests the sincerity of her lover's vows by dropping her glove amongst the beasts for him to recover, and he accepts the challenge but repudiates her, popular opinion agreed with the king's estimate of "rightly done," but in Browning's *The Glove*, the poet Ronsard will not accept the obvious judgment; he must think the thing out for himself and examine her motives, for this was his proper business:

> " 'For I'—so I spoke—'am a poet;
> Human nature,—behoves that I know it'."

As a result he reassesses her action.

The arts also are a means of communication, and would say something if man would listen. In playing the fugue of Master Hughes of Saxe-Gotha, a complex form, Browning finds that elaboration of a plain theme, as it becomes involved, may overlay the music, just as spiders' webs hide the gilt of the roof above him, and he gropes his way to the conclusion:

> "Is it your moral of life?
> Truth's golden o'er us although we refuse it."

To him, as to Fra Lippo Lippi,

> "This world's no blot for us,
> Nor blank; it means intensely, and means good:
> To find its meaning is my meat and drink,"

and so in looking at pictures he is equally alert to what they say. But the beauty of the world, however deeply loved, must not be all-absorbing or it fails in its purpose. Where is its use, "unless we turn, as the soul knows how, the earthly gift to an end divine?" The Bishop who found such aesthetic ecstasy in "peach-blossom marble" and the blue of lapis lazuli that he made of their beauty a barrier, not a stepping-stone, to his bliss must remain for ever where his heart and treasure were, earthbound through the ages.

Browning responded to the same vital quality in things, such as the old yellow book which he bought for a lira in a Florentine square and found "restorative i' the touch and sight." Most vital of all touch was contact with other great poets; even at second-hand, poetic experience irradiated him. In *Pauline*, his earliest poem, he wrote of Shelley the "Sun-treader":

> ". . . I would have thrown to dust
> The wreaths of fame which seemed o'erhanging me,
> To see thee for a moment as thou art."

Twenty-two years later he did meet someone who had done so, and enthusiasm burst forth as fiery as ever:

> "Ah, did you once see Shelley plain,
> And did he stop and speak to you?
> And did you speak to him again?
> How strange it seems and new!"

That verse was first printed over a century ago; yet today the shining moment which it commemorated seems as strange and new to us as when it occurred, for it is not only the life of the body but that of the mind and heart that can renew itself from one generation to another.

Elizabeth Barrett Browning

Much has been written of the oppression of Elizabeth Barrett (1806-61) by her father, presenting him as the archetype of Victorian tyrant; but up to the age of thirty-eight she was deeply attached to, and profoundly dependent on, him. In 1844, in a dedication of her poems to him, she writes of his "belovéd image" and deliberately associates "with the great pursuit of my life its tenderest and holiest affection." In a poem on his birthday, she wrote:

"No name can e'er on tablet shine,
My father! more beloved than thine!"

Here she was wrong. In May 1845 she first met Robert Browning. Each had already been attracted by the published poetry of the other; in September of 1846 they married secretly, to avoid the inevitable opposition of her father, she being forty and Browning thirty-four. For the sake of her precarious health, they spent most of their fourteen years of married life in Italy. Among their contemporaries her reputation was earlier and more steadily established than his, owing partly to what readers found obscure in his longer poems, such as *Sordello,* and partly to what they found advanced in her own long novel in verse, *Aurora Leigh.* Later judgments have firmly reversed the positions.

The mid-century's romantic tone and taste found an appeal in many of her stories, such as *The Romaunt of the Page* or *The Rime of the Duchess May,* neither of them far from the pictorial quality and musical balance of the Pre-Raphaelites.

Though poets are, by their influence on public opinion, "the unacknowledged legislators of the world," it does not often befall one author, through one work, to affect one definite issue. Mrs. Browning in *The Cry of the Children* stirred national indignation to a pitch which led directly to reform of the employment of children in factories, for whom

"Turns the sky in the high window blank and reeling,
Turns the long light that drops adown the wall,
Turn the black flies that crawl along the ceiling,
All are turning, all the day, and we with all!"

It is a heart-warming achievement for a woman without a vote, who spent her years from fifteen to forty as an invalid in the seclusion that she herself called "my prison."

Sonnets from the Portuguese

Her hold on the public, however, now rests almost entirely on forty-three sonnets written to her future husband during his courtship, though he saw them only some months after their marriage. Although she chose to limit herself "within the sonnet's scanty plot of ground," this record of undisguised feeling, published under the title *Sonnets from the Portuguese* and not made public until three years later in 1850, is the freest expression of her powers, freest because uninfluenced by prevailing literary fashions and mature in her power to direct those emotions which her earlier poems had foreshadowed. The first of the series speak naturally of doubts; she, being, like Rosalind, one "that could give more but that her hand lacks means," felt the inequality of the exchange. Of Browning, the "chief musician," she asks:

> "What hast thou to do
> With looking from the lattice-lights at me,
> A poor, tired, wandering singer?"

Others end or begin with phrases such as, "Go," "Go from me," "Go farther." But she soon learned that the unique gift in her power was that of giving him the power to give, to draw on her behalf "a blade for a knight's emprise."

Arnold, a Stoical Poet

The third great Victorian, Matthew Arnold (1822-88), like the other two, employed his powers on copious narratives. His range was wide: *Sohrab and Rustum* is set in Persia, *Balder Dead* in a Scandinavian Valhalla, *Tristram and Iseult* in Cornwall and Brittany, *Empedocles* on Etna and *The Strayed Reveller* beside the gods, surveying the world.

They present, as comprehensively as the length of the poem allows, a way of life distant from nineteenth-century England in time and place, using its events for descriptions of scenes, often through similes characteristic of it, much as a medieval illuminator would fill a capital O or Q with a miniature scene of the countryside. The interest of *Sohrab and Rustum* lies in pictures

Matthew Arnold lived at Rugby School, where his father was headmaster.

such as those of Persian and Tartar tents, "clustering like bee-hives on the low flat strand." We can see inside an oriental house the poor drudge

> "Who with numb blacken'd fingers makes her fire—
> At cock-crow, on a starlit winter's morn,
> When the frost flowers the whiten'd window-panes."

There is an unskilful gardener who scythes down hyacinths, and a "cunning workman, in Pekin":

> ". . . at early morn he paints,
> And all day long, and, when night comes, the lamp
> Lights up his studious forehead and thin hands."

Best of all is that journey as a troop of pedlars from Cabool cross underneath the Indian Caucasus:

> "That vast sky-neighbouring mountain of milk snow,
> Crossing so high, that, as they mount, they pass
> Long flocks of travelling birds dead on the snow,
> Choked by the air, and scarce can they themselves
> Slake their parch'd throats with sugar'd mulberries."

In *Balder Dead* we are in golden-roofed Valhalla, feasting on boar-flesh, drinking (actually, quaffing, I suspect) from gold-rimmed skulls and silver-rimmed horns. We can play a kind of divine darts, construct a funeral pyre of lichen-bearded pines, and ride "towards the northern ice through valleys deep-engulphed, by roaring streams."

Through age after age, we can stray in scene after scene: Tristram's "old sea-side knightly hall," the deep forest-glades of Broceliande, "sand-strewn caverns cool and deep," "still glistening beaches"; and it is only natural that "the gods are happy," for "they turn on all sides their shining eyes," and can take their choice of the Scythian steppe or the "lone Chorasmian stream" with its ferry-boat astern of which

> "The cowering merchants, in long robes,
> Sit pale beside their wealth . . .
> Of turquoise-earth and amethyst."

But we can choose thus too.

And we can always come home to "the stripling Thames" and the darkening fields round Oxford, less strange but no less magical, cool, dewy, beset with corn, convolvulus and drenched bluebells, or roam the "green-muffled Cumner hills." It seems as if there should be loveliness and variety enough in the world to make anyone happy.

But when it comes to a consideration of the spirit of man in this home of his, the light fades. Men are evil and, what is worse, indifferent. Faith has died, an "exploded dream"; no one minds anything much. Matthew Arnold did not enjoy his century, and neither would he have liked ours. England

> "Stupidly travels her round
> Of mechanic business, and lets
> Slow die out of her life
> Glory and genius and joy."

It sounds a very modern utterance.

Arnold longs for certainty, without knowing how to get it; and, like Tennyson's Lotos-Eaters, he doubts the value of man's life because he thinks of the gods as indifferent mockers:

> "The gods laugh in their sleeve
> To watch man doubt and fear,
> Who knows not what to believe
> Since he sees nothing clear."

He distrusts a world which, although it seems:

> "So various, so beautiful, so new,
> Hath really neither joy, nor love, nor light,
> Nor certitude, nor peace, nor help for pain."

This is not cheap pessimism, but the doubt of an unsatisfied idealist.

The heart of darkness is that one being cannot fully communicate with another, but each is eternally alone, as islands are divided by "the unplumbed, salt, estranging sea." Men who "never deeply felt . . . languidly their lives to some unmeaning task-work give," year in, year out, till death reaches them in their prison.The adventurer, a freed prisoner, is little better off, since he has no chart by which to guide his ship on life's incognizable sea, "still standing for some false impossible shore."

If it is man's destiny to be unhappy, it is a part of manliness to conceal the hurt; Arnold loved Wordsworth because, though

> "He too upon a wintry clime
> Had fallen—on this iron time
> Of doubts, disputes, distractions, fears,"

he brought freshness and healing power. But for such ills there is no cure: even philosophers, "comfortable moles," merely drug suffering.

In choosing the seventeenth-century tale of the Scholar-Gipsy, Arnold finds a man whose complete escape he envies, for, if we ourselves attempt to fly for refuge to past times, we cannot escape the contact of reality which will "pluck us back." He warns the Scholar-Gipsy to avoid a return to such nineteenth-century reality with "its sick hurry, its divided aims," and his own generation "who fluctuate idly without term" and half live "a hundred different lives." There is a fallacy at the root of such a view of life, and it seems to lie in the demand for certainty. As we cannot attain certainty, says Arnold, we cannot know what to aim for. But what would one do with certainty if one had it? First of all one would lose the opportunity of choosing freely.

To such a nature, in contrast with Browning's, old age must be merely loss, death merely annihilation, and peace of mind merely oblivion. In *Thyrsis*, as age creeps on, Arnold writes:

> "I feel her finger light
> Laid pausefully upon life's headlong train,—
> The foot less prompt to meet the morning dew,
> The heart less bounding at emotion new."

The foot less prompt does not particularly matter, but the heart less bounding is serious. In *Growing Old* he is more explicit; old age is not merely to lose bodily powers, but a grim reversal of the benign *Il Penseroso* that youth had imagined.

> "It is to spend long days,
> And not once feel that we were ever young;
> . . . Deep in our hidden heart
> Festers the dull remembrance of a change,
> But no emotion—none."

But this is not true. Old age is a relative term, and Matthew Arnold did not live to experience it.

Even more disheartening is Arnold's attitude to the place of sorrow in human life. He presents Cadmus and Harmonia as lucky to have reached complete forgetfulness:

> "They had stay'd long enough to see,
> In Thebes, the billow of calamity
> Over their own dear children rolled."

Therefore the gods, in mercy, changed them to "two bright and aged snakes," and placed them in the Illyrian brakes. There, wholly forgetting "their first sad life and home," they stray "for ever through the glens, placid and dumb." Who would not reject such mercy if it cost such a price? What sort of beings do the gods think mortals are?

No wonder that Arnold finds his mood one of "sadness at the long heart-wasting show." If we have known that:

> "Soon will the high midsummer pomps come on,
> Soon will the musk carnations break and swell,
> Soon shall we have gold-dusted snap-dragon,
> Sweet William with his homely cottage smell,"

we should be content and not deceive ourselves with hopes of "a bliss of doubtful future state."

It is a delight to find in Arnold's later poems on household pets the simplicities of affection and humour exercising their natural functions.

Of his dachshund, Geist, who died at the age of four, Arnold wrote:

"We see the flaps of thy large ears
Quick raised to ask which way we go;
Crossing the frozen lake, appears
Thy small black figure on the snow."

Nor can it now ever disappear. He moralizes on the death of Matthias, a canary who must have been ailing unnoticed for some time but who, alas, could not communicate with his master; even so, brother-man calls in vain.

Where, in such predicaments, does the poet stand? It is useless for him simply to cut himself off from the despicable race of men, for this is death-in-life. Empedocles challenges Apollo:

"The jars of men reach him not in thy valley—
But can life reach him?"

If being apart is the price of being a poet, Empedocles will not pay it, and rejects Apollo's laurel bough. Once again Arnold seems to be tormented by taking as mutually exclusive what must be complementary, solitude and companionship. Although he knows that "the lightnings of wit, the thunders of scorn" will not win an audience to the poet's way, he dreads lest he should win the wrong kind of audience to whom beautiful poetry becomes:

". . . not wisdom,
But drugs to charm with
But spells to mutter"

—mere incantation. It is only when far from the "black, rushing smoke-bursts" of contemporary life that the poet finds his home.

There follows, in the song of Callicles, an exquisite picture of peace, and of the god of music and his train, moving like moonlight up the glen. In such a setting the soul of poetry is free and finds its right subjects, the Immortals, the life of men, the beauty of the universe:

"First hymn they the Father
Of all things, and then
The rest of immortals,
The action of men,
The day in his hotness,
The strife with the palm;
The night in her silence,
The stars in their calm."

The Pre-Raphaelites

Empedocles discarded the poet's singing-robes, but the three Pre-Raphaelites joyfully assumed them as their natural wear. Rhythm, verbal music, repetition, refrain, all that underlies the art of spell-binding, was theirs to command. In revolt from the ugliness and materialism of their century, they plunged back to the Middle Ages, or further to Greece.

They shared amongst themselves aesthetic principles, and expressed them more widely than in song alone. Rossetti painted; many a theme seems to offer equal opportunities for a poem or a picture, and in some cases, as in *The Tune of the Seven Towers*, he both wrote and painted his idea. William Morris applied his gifts also to printing, weaving, making glass and other household furnishings. The poems of both these authors cry out at almost every stage for pictorial illustration.

Swinburne, the Melodious Poet

Algernon Charles Swinburne (1837-1909), the most melodious, can enchant by sheer power of sound. The pleasure of a rhyme is that it fulfils anticipation; to this Swinburne often adds anticipation of the second of a pair of lines, or the second half of a single balanced line, or the second initial letter of an alliteration; and if a reader has absorbed the one, he may supply the other himself.

"The sun burns sere and the rain dishevels
One gaunt bleak blossom of scentless breath.
Only the wind here hovers and revels
In a round where life seems barren as death."

The swing of such phrases as "an inland island," "winter's rains and ruins," "remembrance fallen from heaven, and madness risen from hell," underlies so much of the construction of a verse that each part seems to have its counterpart, and the first to necessitate the second, but when it is not too obtrusive it sweeps a reader along with it. The beauty of the way in which it is said often blinds us to what Swinburne is, in fact, saying, to the insufficiency of passion rather than love, remorse rather than repentance, sound rather than sense.

William Morris, the Craftsman

William Morris (1834-96) found one province in verse which he made his own, that of the knight defeated. Knights, good or bad, go riding through our literature, but we see the story from the good knight's point of view and he always wins. Spenser's champions may have partial failures by the way, but the upshot is never in doubt; to Morris, being in the right did not ensure freedom from mishap, disaster or defeat, however unmerited.

Tennyson's bad knights were overthrown and sent to Arthur's court for justice; Browning allowed Childe Roland's heart to find "failure in its scope"; but Morris went further. His "good knight in prison" has failed; things can go wrong. "Wearily, drearily, all the day long," his enemy's flag

Dickens at the age of twenty-six.

The hero of A Tale of Two Cities.

flutters over his cell, and he cannot console himself with any hope of release.

Again, what about the story from the bad knight's point of view? Morris wrote the thoughts before a trial by combat of the guilty man himself, a man with no right on his side to sustain him, and with little hope of victory. The villain, hitherto a lifeless block whose sole purpose seemed to be to give a good knight a chance to earn his title, is suddenly a living man, capable of guilt and fear, and of being hurt.

Dickens, Novelist of Humanity

The vast output of the novelists of first rank makes it impossible here to give a comprehensive list even of names and dates; there is only one way of possessing them and that is to read them. In the case of at least eight, four men and four women, we can see what position they occupy by considering to what audience they appeal.

Charles Dickens (1812-70), born in the same year as Browning, was greatest in genius, widest in scope and most representative of his age. From his first published works, *Sketches by Boz* and *The Pickwick Papers* in 1836, a year before Victoria's accession, until his death in 1870, which left *Edwin Drood* unfinished, he produced, at steady intervals of two to three years, the succession of novels that will always represent and clearly portray his period.

The numberless aspects of London's underworld, its business houses, law-courts, prisons, inns and lodgings, shops and back streets, middle-class homes and slums of sordid and grinding poverty, were all familiar ground to him. The pattern is intricately interwoven; crime is never far from respectability, humour from pathos, innocence from selfishness; and, though country industries and sports produce jolly interludes, his scene is the City.

Throughout his life, Dickens viewed the world of grown-ups through the eyes of a boy, observing and treasuring small deviations from normality that beset us all, and that give to the adjective "Dickensian" its special meaning of "engagingly unusual." It often reconciles us to troublesome realities to think, "What a character Dickens would have made of him"; at any rate, the trick is worth trying. Some of his models are known; his own father, for instance, provided material for Micawber, and for the debtors' prison in *Little Dorrit*. So keen was his gusto for humanity in all its forms that his characters are personal acquaintances and his readers are personal friends.

Thackeray and Trollope

William Makepeace Thackeray (1811-63) and Anthony Trollope (1815-82) displayed a more critical attitude to their fellow-men; each author was an accomplished man of the world and a connoisseur, more diverted by humanity's failings than disturbed by its sins.

Thackeray's field of observation was the Europe of his time, the social world of London, besieged by Becky Sharp, and the Paris of his *Sketch-books*. In his excursions in *Henry Esmond* and *The Virginians*, into the 18th century and across the Atlantic, he still took his quizzing-glass, in the use of which his study of English humorists had instructed him. His most interesting women, Beatrix and Becky, are intelligent and unscrupulous, while Amelia is calculated to make the word "good" equivalent to "dull." The readers to whom he appeals are those whose taste is educated to appreciate the salt savour of a critical wit.

Trollope, no less acute an observer, staked out his claim to the English cathedral town with its hierarchy of churchmen, from detestable Slope up past worldly-minded Archdeacon Grantley to the well-meaning but henpecked Bishop and the beloved Mr. Harding; his audience is of those who enjoy recognizing a revealing study of their friends while keeping well out of the picture themselves.

Robert Louis Stevenson

Just before the half-century came Stevenson (1850-94), deriving his "Yo-ho-ho and a bottle of rum" from Kingsley, and passing on the wicked Master of Ballantrae to Sir James Barrie, to cast a gleam of malevolence round the head of Captain Hook. Stevenson made up for a life-time of ill-health by all the adventures in which any Lord Jim imagined himself playing a leading part. Black arrows whizz through the pages, we climb the rigging with knives in our teeth, fight unequal duels by candlelight in the snow, buy the bottle imp, live gladly and travel hopefully. His audience are those who, as he did, keep up to any age the heart of youth that looks for "such a day tomorrow as today, and to be boy eternal."

Mrs. Gaskell

Of the four women, Mrs. Gaskell (1810-65), author of several books, including a life of Charlotte Brontë, is now known almost exclusively for *Cranford*, and largely misjudged by it. It is generally accepted as a feminine, indeed a spinster's, world, though Miss Pole assures the other ladies, "My father was a man, and I know the sex pretty well." Miss Matty, however, though now chiefly important as the arbiter of manners, had in her youth a suitor (less than determined though he might be), a dominant father and a high-spirited brother, and knew well enough what a mess men could make of life. When the little village shop is the setting for genuine disaster and financial ruin, Miss Matty faces it with the quiet invincibility of a gentlewoman in the right. Readers should be restricted to those who are prepared

Becky Sharp gambling, in a scene from Thackeray's novel, Vanity Fair.

to ponder the question with which Galsworthy closes *The Skin Game*: "What's gentility for if it can't stand fire?"

The Brontë Sisters

Of the Brontë sisters, Charlotte (1816-55) and the stormier Emily Brontë (1818-48) have left two monuments to the power of the human spirit to compensate itself by an inner life for restrictions to its natural development. Charlotte Brontë found her outlet in the immensely masterful picture of Rochester, resisted and defeated by the small, plain governess, Jane Eyre.

Charlotte Brontë.

A scene from Jane Eyre.

In Emily Brontë's *Wuthering Heights* it is difficult at times to tell whether the ruggedness is more in Heathcliff or in the moorland scenery, but in neither is any trace of softness admissible. The lover of fine English, the reader in search of events and the psychiatrist are equally engaged.

George Eliot

George Eliot (Mary Ann Evans, 1819-80), in her more serious and less read novels, showed the conditions of the poor in rural districts or small industrial towns. Women characters are more subtly varied than her fairly uncomplicated men. Maggie Tulliver in *The Mill on the Floss* shows the superior attraction of a dark and passionate heroine to that of gentle Lucy, and the infinite richness of her nature compared with that of her brother Tom.

In *Silas Marner*, Dolly Winthrop's homely wisdom makes her more "in the round" than the brothers Godfrey and Dunstan, both weak in different ways; sympathy is concentrated on Silas, but interest on the social changes that have overtaken Lantern Yard by the time he returns. No social historian can afford to ignore George Eliot.

Victorian Minor Prose

As the intellectual horizons of the average educated reader expanded, writers of various aims directed his interest to other countries and other times, to Holland's seventeenth century and the Middle Ages, the East, the West, Elizabethan and contemporary England. All the following seven authors except Carlyle (1795-1881) and Prescott (1796-1859) were born and died in the nineteenth century.

Interest in other European countries was fed by Motley's voluminous *Rise of the Dutch Republic*, with his concise and simple picture of its hero, William of Orange:

> "As long as he lived, he was the guiding star of a brave nation, and when he died the little children cried in the streets."

Matthew Arnold, on the other hand, found in his spiritual home, Oxford, a retreat from "the fierce intellectual life" of his century; and even though he refused to sail on "that huge Mississippi of falsehood," history, he loved Oxford for "whispering from her towers the last enchantments of the Middle Age."

Kinglake's *Eothen* left a picture of his travels in Greece and Asia, of dragomen and Bedouins, sailors, merchants, rulers and cheats, of that notable fugitive from Victorian convention, Lady Hester Stanhope, and of a whole ageless and inscrutable region, fit setting for an Arabian night.

Prescott's *Histories* of the conquests of Mexico and of Peru dramatically contrast South America as it was and as it is. He glories in the landscape of valleys, forests and lakes, in the midst of which stands:

> ". . . like some Indian empress with her coronal of pearls—the fair city of Mexico, with her white towers and pyramidal temples."

Carlyle, holding that "whoso belongs only to his own age must needs die with it," applied his creative imagination to the task of seeing vividly and accurately into the past. In *Past and Present* he bids us:

> "Behold therefore, this England of the year 1200 was . . . a green solid place, that grew corn and several other things. . . . Cloth was woven and worn; ditches were dug, furrow-fields ploughed, and houses built."

Froude, in his *History of England*, grieved at the end of the age of chivalry:

> "Only among the aisles of our cathedrals, only as we gaze upon their silent figures sleeping on their tombs, some faint conceptions float before us of what these men were when they were alive."

But in his picture of Elizabethan seamen in the *Pelican* pursuing a Spanish treasure-ship, the years are rolled away.

As the sun's "rosy light faded from off the snows of the Andes . . . the night wind rose, and the water began to ripple under the *Pelican*'s bows. . . ."

Where are we? Is this a boyhood tale by R.L.S. of a pirate ship with her booty of silver bullion, gold nuggets uncounted and "great store of pearls, emeralds and diamonds"? Not a bit of it. She is a real English ship, with her captain on board, a seaman called Drake, who "dined alone with music."

Ruskin gives not so much a distant horizon as the eyes with which to see what is near. "The greatest thing a human soul ever does in this world," he wrote in *Modern Painters*, "is to see something and tell what it saw in a plain way." Just looking comes first; interpretation may follow.

The Victorian Theatre

The nineteenth century, though it saw a well-established stage free from the competition of cinema or television, and though many of London's most famous theatres were built in the reign of Victoria, did not produce much drama of lasting merit.

Apart from the poetic dramas of Tennyson, given added prestige by the fact that Henry Irving played in some of them, and those of Browning, less often presented, the most significant play was *Caste* by T. W. Robertson (1867). As brother of the actress Dame Madge Kendal, Robertson was familiar with backstage life, cleared of its accustomed romantic haze; and, being impatient of the exaggerations and artificiality of most contemporary plays, he aimed at presenting human beings as they are, in stage settings of credible rooms. Even before the century ended, the break with romanticism had become theatrical history; Pinero's *Trelawny of the Wells* (1898), based on stage life in the early sixties, represents Robertson in the character of Tom Wrench, member of a troupe of the old school, who declares:

> "I tell you, I won't have doors stuck here, there, and everywhere; no, nor windows in all sorts of impossible places! . . . Windows on the one side, doors on the other, just where they should be, architecturally. And locks on the doors, real locks to work; and handles—to turn."

His dialogue, too, approaches natural conversation.

In *Caste* comes the meeting of the waters; the well-born hero, George, proposes in defiance of "the inexorable law of caste" to marry an actress. Hawtree, his prudent friend, who divides the human race into "people" and "common people," warns him, "All those marriages of people with common people are all very well in novels and in plays on the stage," where they do no harm, "but in real life, with real relations, and real mothers, and so forth . . . it's utter social and personal annihilation and damnation." George's rejection of this point of view opened a way of escape for the playwright.

The Popularity of Melodrama

Spectacle and melodrama were, however, the chief delight of pit and gallery, whose faithful support was essential to the run of a play. Two plays of the early 1860s represent many similar ones. A playbill of just over a hundred years ago of *The Colleen Bawn* lures its audience in by promising scenes on the Lake of Killarney, Macgillicuddy's Reeks and the O'Donoghue's Stable; finally, in the Water Cave,

> ". . . a rejected lover of Eily's happens to be on the spot when Danny throws the girl into the lake, although he does not see the deed itself. He only fires at and wounds Danny, whom he takes in the doubtful light for an otter; but presently he sees the body of Eily in the water, plunges in, and rescues her. . . . Nothing can be more precise and complete than the manner in which the young girl is dashed into the water; while the way in which Mr. Boucicault takes what is called in the dialect of bathers a tremendous 'header' into the lake is astounding for its agility and naturalness."

It must have been well worth four guineas for a box holding twelve persons to see a real girl thrown in a precise and complete manner into real water, let alone the agile header which followed; a sixpenny gallery was cheap.

Irish peasantry, however, had not a monopoly of melodrama. In *Lady Audley's Secret*, dramatized in 1863 from a novel of the previous year, wicked Lady Audley neatly disposes of George, who threatens to expose her, by striking him from behind with the iron handle of the old well, and pushing him down it. When her sins find her out, she dies to maniacal cachinnations; there is a "tableau of sympathy," while gentry and villagers remove their hats—in strict order, we may be sure, of social precedence.

The Bells, produced in 1871, telling the story of Mathias who murdered a Polish Jew and was haunted by his sleigh-bells into madness and self-betrayal, is in essence equally melodramatic, but has attained a special place in the history of the stage through Irving's superb acting, another proof that genius shows itself not in its material but in the use made of it.

> "Irving was buckling his second shoe, seated, and leaning over it with his two long hands stretched down over the buckles. We suddenly saw these fingers stop their work; the crown of the head suddenly seemed to glitter and become frozen,—and then, at the pace of the slowest and most terrified snail, the two hands, still motionless and dead, were seen coming up the side of the leg."

The effect was mesmeric, the audience spellbound.

An opening scene from Oscar Wilde's brilliant play, An Ideal Husband.

Oscar Wilde, the Witty Playwright

Themes of social reform, so long as they were sufficiently melodramatic, attracted some authors, such as Douglas Jerrold in *Fifteen Years of a Drunkard's Life*, and historical ones inspired others, such as Bulwer Lytton in *Richelieu*; but no play reached front rank until Oscar Wilde's four period pieces in the last decade of the century. *Lady Windermere's Fan* (1892), *A Woman of No Importance* (1893), and *An Ideal Husband* and *The Importance of Being Earnest* (1895) have more claim to a place in literature than his stories, poems or essays, and were entirely suited to society's taste for triviality in theme and wit in expression. So much do they now represent to us, in setting a narrow circle of the idle rich, in theme a self-conscious refusal to be serious, and in dialogue a single-minded pursuit of the witty phrase, that it takes a modern reader aback to realize that Wilde was born less than two years before another Irishman, Bernard Shaw; in genuine originality the two seem a century apart.

Oscar Wilde's type of epigram relies upon taking a commonplace accepted truth or principle and giving its contradiction, a kind of reflection in a mental looking-glass where right hand appears left. There is for a time a pleasant sense of freedom in discarding all copybook maxims, the only bother being that they are true.

G. B. Shaw and Oscar Wilde shared one quality, independence of mind that comes rebelliously into the open against conventional morality; the difference is that Shaw, when he rejects an idea, does so because he has examined it and finds the opposite to be true, whereas Wilde rejects it simply because his contemporaries accepted it. His style becomes at times such a slave to the trick of saying the opposite of what is expected that we can confidently expect what he will say. While his witticisms are tossed off with apparent ease, the audience delights in them: "This is the whole truth pure and simple—The truth is rarely pure and never simple." As soon as they become contrived the audience grows mentally restive: "We in the House of Lords are never in touch with public opinion. That makes us a civilized body."

Neat intricacies of plot, the glitter of epigram and the Olympian Lady Bracknell, whose Christian name should be Boadicea, make her play a first-class example of a type less than first-class, and as such it has been uninterruptedly successful since its first production. Three years earlier Shaw's first play, *Widowers' Houses*, dealing with the canker of the slums, was produced, and failed. But the twentieth century was on the doorstep.

QUESTIONS

1. Support Tennyson's right to be considered an essentially English poet by reference to two poems in each case:
(*a*) describing English scenery;
(*b*) commenting on contemporary events and conditions;
(*c*) recounting events in England's past history.

2. Illustrate the view that Browning's chief interest lay in the choices made by men and women when faced with making a difficult decision about their own conduct.

3. What ideas have Matthew Arnold's poems given you of (*a*) Greece, and (*b*) the East?

4. "Dickens' power as a novelist is that, whatever his theme and whoever his reader, he is supremely readable." What elements chiefly give his work this "readable" quality?

5. "*The Mill on the Floss* is George Eliot's classic work."—Do you agree? Give your impressions of the qualities of this novel, and make some comparisons with others of her novels.

6. *Cranford* is often accepted as the presentation of a narrow, genteel world, almost exclusively inhabited by spinsters. What have you found in it to show that it is wider in experience and deeper in feeling than this description suggests?

CHAPTER 12

THE TWENTIETH CENTURY

In the first few years of the twentieth century the poetic dramas of Tennyson and Browning and the witty drawing-room comedies of Oscar Wilde soon became unfashionable. For a time Stephen Phillips drew audiences to His Majesty's Theatre with his blank verse tragedies but, fine as his turn of phrase often was, his manner looked backward rather than forward. When Ulysses told Calypso that he longed:

> "To look into the eyes of her who bore me,
> And clasp his knees who 'gat me in his joy,"

the audience rightly concluded that, if this meant in effect "I want to go home to my parents," the twentieth-century theatre was not the place for such elaborations, and turned to seek the fresh air of plain truths plainly said.

Shaw, the Crusading Irishman

Already over thirty-five before he wrote his first play in 1892, George Bernard Shaw was beginning to utter such truths. Having trenchant comments to make on social conditions, he had earlier written two novels, *An Unsocial Socialist*, attacking the slums, and *The Irrational Knot*, attacking the stringency of marriage laws which A. P. Herbert later satirized in *Holy Deadlock*. From the lack of success of these two novels, Shaw deduced that a reformer's voice would reach the public ear more audibly from a stage than from a library, a platform or a tub in Hyde Park, and he later used both themes in dramatic form, in *Widowers' Houses* and *Getting Married.*

Each of his earlier plays exposed some abuse, but with so much dramatic force, natural speech and genuine humour that audiences who came for an inspiriting laugh left with a mental questioning of which they could not free themselves. Naturally in over half a century many of those abuses which Shaw attacked have been at least partly remedied, and his first plays have suffered the fate of all satire, losing their grip as conditions have changed; but one still sometimes feels towards him as the seventeenth-century bishop Richard Corbett felt in taking farewell of rewards and fairies: "O, how the Commonwealth doth need such Justices as you!"

Widowers' Houses exposed the rent racket by which a slum landlord could, by letting single rooms to separate families, extract rents equal to those of Park Lane from almost uninhabitable property, and the means by which local councillors in the know could buy, decorate and sell at immense profit buildings already condemned. In *The Philanderer* he mocked the prevailing false worship of Ibsen, whose plays he himself greatly admired. In *Mrs. Warren's Profession* the heroine, Vivie, refuses even for a good purpose to use money made by immoral means, and finds time for a sidelong blow at profitable betting, "meaner than stealing." In *Major Barbara*, however, the champion of the Salvation Army is offered a large donation out of money made from the sale of arms or of drink, and realizes that in a modern civilization we are all financially members one of another, and it is impossible to ensure that the good done by charitable institutions is not paid for by the very evil that they are fighting. In *Misalliance* Shaw showed the futility of an idle aristocracy, that did nothing to support itself and could not pay its way because it never made anything.

Plays About Social Conventions

In *Man and Superman* Shaw reversed the romantic convention that man pursues and woman flies; and in *You Never Can Tell* he presented the New Woman, independent, educated and within sight of the vote. In *Arms and the Man* another romantic convention was exploded, that of a military hero charging recklessly at the head of his men, a convention that underlay the thunders of Tennyson's poem, *The Charge of the Light Brigade.*

Pygmalion showed that the most immediately obvious barrier dividing

George Bernard Shaw.

A scene from Saint Joan.

class from class is the accent in which people speak, but that even when this is broken down there lies behind it the stronger one of what they think and how they express these thoughts, and that this barrier is often erected on a basis of finance. Doolittle rejects the middle class code of morals on the grounds that he "can't afford 'em," and his status is fixed more by his lack of money than by his lack of *h*s. Each idol is in turn taken out of its shrine, dusted, examined, stood on its head, presented in a new light, turned round and joyfully hailed as having on the other side a human countenance. Shaw's later plays followed the same process of casting the light of common-sense on the ideas which events brought forward; increased expectation of life gave rise to some of the speculations in *Back to Methuselah*; in *Geneva* he mocked Hitler, Mussolini and the English diplomat, representative of public school standards, who was stirred to passionate protest only by an unaccustomed pronunciation of a Latin name. *The Apple Cart* put the case for monarchy and foreshadowed abdication. *Heartbreak House* gave the country a solemn warning, all the more to be heeded because it came from a licensed jester.

Saint Joan, Shaw's Masterpiece

But however much time may minimize the effects of these topical themes and battles long ago, Shaw's greatest play, *Saint Joan*, is also the greatest play of this century. There are again many old conventions turned inside out; the old method of fighting for ransoms gives way to the new method of fighting for causes; the old idea of the Inquisition as an organization of intense cruelty gives way to the new one that it is the heretic's best defence against it. The two central ideas, however, essential elements in Joan's behaviour, are both concerned with single-heartedness: the subject is led to appeal directly to his king without intervention of the barons, and the individual soul to appeal directly to God without intervention of the Church, from which rise the ideals of nationalism and protestantism. The common quality is directness for the common man: "The unpretending praise thee."

This clear, straightforward singleness of purpose and refusal to be deflected, which is the central quality of his saint, is the same as that which Shaw himself showed in his attacks on each contemporary foe. At the trial of Joan

> ". . . the truth was told; the law was upheld; mercy was shewn beyond all custom; no wrong was done but the final and dreadful wrong of the lying sentence and the pitiless fire."

This statement is, as Browning wanted his language to be, "fit and fair and simple and sufficient." What is wrong in itself cannot be justified by the rightness of any preceding argument or motive; if the answer to a sum is wrong, the working-out cannot be right. In proportion as we apply it to problems of today, it makes *Saint Joan*, set in the fifteenth century, a reconstruction of an historical event or the most modern of all modern plays.

For topical themes Shaw's medium was necessarily prose, but not merely that of daily speech. He shows the highest skill in hitting on the head a nail in the coffin of some false dogma. Although he was no poet, and indeed Eugene Marchbanks in *Candida* utters little beyond a reference to stars and shallops and archangels with purple wings to substantiate his claim to be one, the greatest passages in his finest plays, such as the Epilogue in *Saint Joan*, rise in music and clarity to fulfil the main purposes of poetry—delight and communication.

Galsworthy, Social Historian

The social dramas of John Galsworthy (1867-1933) have the same seriousness of purpose, but are less tied to contemporary conditions; the situation in each presents a conflict which might arise in any period.

Strife works out the mutual misunderstanding of capital and labour in which the strikers sincerely believe capital to be a monster that says, " 'I'm very sorry for you, poor fellows—you have a cruel time of it, I know,' but

A scene from John Galsworthy's play, The Silver Box.

"The Admirable Crichton" takes command when wrecked with his employers.

will not give one sixpence of its dividends to help you have a better time," whereas the Chairman of the Board of Directors sincerely believes that, "When you have given way here, and given way there—you will find you have parted with the ground beneath your feet, and are deep in the bog of bankruptcy; and with you, floundering in that bog, will be the very men you have given way to."

In *The Silver Box* the son of a rich man and the out-of-work husband of a charwoman both possess themselves of objects not their own; the influence of his father gets the first off with a magisterial warning, but the out-of-work husband is called "a nuisance to the community" and receives a sentence of one month with hard labour. His protest of "one law for the rich and another for the poor" is not altogether fair; but the essence of the argument—that an illegal action is sometimes judged by the social position of its perpetrator—though increasingly less true, is worth keeping before the eyes of the public.

In *Loyalties*, the conflict is between a Jew, De Levis, and an Englishman, Captain Dancy, whom he accuses of stealing money from his bedroom. The audience is predisposed to agree with Dancy's friends that such an action is impossible for a soldier and a gentleman; and racial prejudice induces even the man in the street to take sides. But De Levis is in the right, and imminent disgrace drives Dancy to suicide. Each side has shown what it calls loyalty, which is in effect prejudice and, like patriotism, "not enough";

and we are left to ask little Peterkin's unanswerable poser, "What good came of it at last?"

The Skin Game presents a fight between not races but classes; in many ways the situation is parallel with that between the nations in 1914. Hornblower, seeking "a place in the sun" like that enjoyed by the Hillcrists for three centuries, quarrels with them over the Jackmans, humble people whose right to remain in their cottage he had guaranteed, but whom he evicts when they are in his way. The German invasion of Belgium was the origin of Britain's entry into the war, but the bitterness engendered caused most people by 1918 to forget it in larger issues. "What is it that gets loose," asks Hillcrist, "when you begin a fight, and makes you what you think you're not? What blinding evil?"

Only in *Escape* does Galsworthy not seem to play quite fair. An escaped prisoner, after a series of narrow squeaks, hides in a vestry, and the clergyman, who knows that he is there, is asked directly by the pursuers if he has seen the prisoner. Shall he tell the truth and betray a man who has claimed sanctuary, or shall he protect him by a lie? From the horns of this dilemma the convict rescues him by giving himself up, with the reflection, "It's one's decent self one can't escape." The conclusion is satisfactory; but it is hardly fair that Galsworthy has made his convict a charming, well-mannered gentleman, sentenced for manslaughter which had been largely a matter of bad luck, and has made all the people who help him charming and well-mannered too, while all those who chase him are vulgar and unkind.

Galsworthy's sympathies are always on the side of the underdog, of all captives such as Falder, the defaulting clerk in *Justice*. His training as a barrister induced him to give an impartial summing-up for each side, but he generally plays so fair that one is inclined to believe that Justice is blindfold lest she should get a legal squint from seeing both sides at once.

Barrie, Creator of *Peter Pan*

The comments implicit in the plays of Sir James Barrie (1860-1937) are some of them so topical as to be now old-fashioned and some of eternal application. The immense popularity of *Peter Pan* was a marked feature of the century's early years. Why, then, has the second half of the century grown a little impatient with this play, in spite of annual revivals at Christmas, and a little diffident about owning its enchantment? The trouble seems to be with the hero: Peter Pan himself declared, "I want always to be a little boy and to have fun," and his first audiences could not have agreed more; but since most of the little boys in those audiences had after 1914 to grow up straight from sixth form or university into war, always having fun seemed, as an ideal of life, unsubstantial enough.

The pre-war years are also reflected in *The Admirable Crichton*, in which

Lord Loam, a Liberal peer (strange phenomenon in 1905), exhibits his democratic attitude by once a month having to tea the servants of his town establishment (over twenty of them for himself and three daughters) on terms of equality in the drawing-room. When a small party is wrecked on a desert island, he finds that the butler and tweeny are infinitely more capable and desirable members of their little society than the other six, most of them effete aristocrats, and Crichton becomes their natural leader.

Dear Brutus, however, is not of its age but for all human beings who let themselves off the bitter business of self-contempt by pleading that if they had taken a different road in life they would have turned out differently. In Lob's magic Midsummer wood, each of eight assorted characters has a second chance, and all find out exactly how much they will turn out the same. Barrie runs no risk over his moral: Purdie quotes from *Julius Caesar*:

> "The fault, dear Brutus, is not in our stars,
> But in ourselves, that we are underlings,"

and Joanna hands it across the footlights by adding, "For 'dear Brutus' we are to read 'dear audience,' I suppose?"

One aspect of the times which drew Barrie's sympathy without engaging his support was the natural and widespread desire of those who had lost loved ones to establish communication with them. When Mary Rose returns home after many years' disappearance her parents are aged, her husband grey-haired, her baby grown up, but she herself is unchanged. They cannot communicate, for they are of a world where time goes on, and she of one where it does not. "Do you think," asks her father in despair, "she should have come back?"

Irish Playwrights

The Irish dramas of this century are either avowedly poetic plays of Celtic legend, such as Yeats' *The Countess Cathleen*, or avowedly realistic pictures of Irish character working in modern conditions, such as Synge's *Playboy of the Western World* and later the plays of Sean O'Casey.

In *The Countess Cathleen*, in a time of famine, the devil's merchant-men buy souls for money with which the peasants can buy food. The Countess, whose holiness of spirit commands a high price, deliberately sells her soul to save her people from starvation. When she comes to die, instead of going to hell in settlement of her debt, she is carried by angels to heaven on the grounds that her motive was pure and that:

> ". . . the Light of Lights
> Looks always on the motive, not the deed,
> The Shadow of Shadows on the deed alone."

The cadences of Yeats' verse sing in the mind, stifling the whisper of reason.

In *The Land of Heart's Desire* the world of the supernatural, this time of the fairies, is still a source of dread. These are not the fairies of glittering wand and granted wishes, and they would certainly never be accepted as godmothers; their seas are perilous, their lands forlorn. Up the airy mountain, down the rushy glen, we daren't go a-hunting. Beware; have no dealings; keep to the path.

The Resurgence of Poetic Drama

One of the most notable aspects of the theatre has been the resurgence between the wars of poetic drama which, though vastly different in content and form from any that had preceded it, drew its audiences from ordinary theatre-goers.

For a Canterbury Festival in 1935, T. S. Eliot wrote *Murder in the Cathedral*, about the martyrdom of St. Thomas Becket, an historical event which also attracted Jean Anouilh in *Becket* and Christopher Fry in *Curtmantle* (Henry II's nickname), both produced in 1961. Eliot's title recognized the contemporary vogue of detective drama, and his play was kept in touch with our times by deliberately modern speech and the ingenious casuistry of the four murderers.

The three dramatists deal with historical fact in very different ways. T. S. Eliot begins on 2 December and ends on 29 December, 1170, the day of Becket's murder; Henry II does not appear, and the quarrel that set him at enmity with his Archbishop, already ripe to bursting point, is reflected principally in the speeches of the knights after the event. The titles of Eliot, Anouilh and Fry show where the emphasis lies, on one of the two "mighty opposites," or in T. S. Eliot's play on the deed itself, the sin of murder, on guilt and expiation involving all men and worked out in one instance.

Murder in the Cathedral

This theme of sainthood in action, of a sin committed and to be expiated, both inevitably involving the daily lives of ordinary people on the fringe, is one that persists in T. S. Eliot's later plays; in *Murder in the Cathedral* it is powerfully expressed in the Chorus of cleaners and scrubbers. First comes their disclaiming cry:

> "We do not wish anything to happen.
> Seven years we have lived quietly,
> Succeeded in avoiding notice."

Their life has been one in which:

> "We have all had our private terrors,
> Our particular shadows, our secret fears,"

but when the Archbishop voluntarily returns from exile on the continent and the knights close in for the kill, they cannot escape the reality of sin:

"The forms take shape in the dark air:
Puss-purr of leopard, footfall of padding bear,"

and the lords of Hell are here with them. Although not actors in the drama, they foresee but cannot prevent the crime and martyrdom. Their "senses are quickened by subtle forebodings"; they "have smelt death in the rose," and find it is impossible to contract out of the sins of the world. The crime is with and within themselves "as well as in the plottings of potentates," and by being unresisting, they have consented to the murder and share its guilt. The priests have in vain tried to bar the door in protection of the Archbishop—in vain because he "will not have the house of prayer, the church of Christ, the sanctuary, turned into a fortress."

Eliot's Murder in the Cathedral.

While the knights are about their work of killing, the Chorus who "do not wish anything to happen" find that, simply by being alive, they are themselves involved in the "instant eternity of evil and wrong" that affects the whole world. Their cry is for cleanliness from the filth: the very air must be washed. In the end it is clear that the murderers have destroyed not the Archbishop but themselves, now "homeless in earth or heaven."

The women of the Chorus are at least partly living, but the doers are dead even while they are still going through the motions of being alive; and from the place where the martyrdom took place—martyrdom because the Archbishop could have avoided it—life perpetually rises; "From such ground springs that which forever renews the earth though it is forever denied."

The Cocktail Party

This central truth, that all are a part of everything, recurs in another guise in *The Cocktail Party*. Most of the characters gathered together for a casual social occasion are for one reason or another unfulfilled in their way of life, inwardly aware of a deep dissatisfaction, and betake themselves for a cure to the psychiatrist whose advice directs them into different channels. For one the right way of spending his life is to pursue a nobleman for permission to use his estate as background for a film; for others it is to give a cocktail party; for Celia Copplestone, who deeply feels a sense of some demand coming from somewhere and of guilt until she responds, the way leads to work amongst natives and finally to the sacrifice of her life in their service. If each lived utterly disconnected from everyone else, her service must appear to be greater than theirs; but if each form of service is necessary to the whole, then one cannot be greater than the other, for there can be no degrees of the adjective "essential." Once each has found the right way for him, he is a part of the whole, and there is no part of the whole that is not a part of him.

In *The Confidential Clerk* all nourish an inward wish, and to some degree gain it, but find that it does not bring the satisfaction they had anticipated; only Colby himself, finding the right line, can go forward instead of round and round.

In *The Family Reunion* old unhappiness, old evil willed, old curses never completely repented or retracted, are gathered together in the House of Wishwood, and descend as an inherited burden on the heir. To these he adds his own crime of willing the death of his wife; whether in fact he had, as he stated, pushed her overboard is a question of legal punishment and does not affect his predicament, which is concerned with his need to cleanse himself from a sense of guilt in his own will. He comes home, hoping to escape from the Furies, the Eumenides, who haunt by their presence the man of blood until his sin is purged. But they are there before him; he strives desperately to pretend that they are not, but they choose their moment and come through at him.

He realizes that, in fleeing from them, he is going the wrong way about expiation, that home itself is no refuge, and that he can attain peace of mind not by ignoring his sense of guilt but only by following and submitting to his tormentors, by confession and repentance. Once he knows this he leaves, sure that there is a way and that they will lead him in it. As soon as he can say, "Now I see at last that I am following you, and I know that there can be only one itinerary and one destination," he can add, "I shall be safe with them."

Christopher Fry

Fry, the other chief exponent of poetic drama since 1940, has been sometimes praised for "the rediscovery of language," and sometimes criticized on the grounds that, in spite of his rich and exciting flow of words, there is nothing special said by them. The second comment is less than just, for there is no play of his which does not say something definite and important; the lovely colours should not deceive us into thinking that the landscape is insubstantial. Each of his three chief plays represents a season.

The Lady's Not For Burning, set in the changing moods of April, presents a clash between love of life and desire for death; a soldier, Thomas, is so disgusted by the bestiality of human nature displayed in war and a witch-hunt that he seeks to be rid of life by getting himself hanged, while young Jennet, hunted as a witch, is nevertheless convinced that life is a positive good. In the opposition of their points of view, Jennet draws and reconciles Thomas to her belief, though not by any sentimental blindness to the wickedness of the human heart:

"Do you see those roofs and spires?
There sleep hypocrisy, porcous pomposity, greed,
Lust, vulgarity, cruelty, trickery, sham
And all possible nitwittery,"

but when she asks him, "Thomas, can you mean to let the world go on?" he accepts life in hope: "I know my limitations. When the landscape goes to seed, the wind is obsessed by tomorrow."

In *Venus Observed*, set in the gold of October, the Duke, having reached the autumn of his life, decides to settle down, but with such lack of passion that he asks his son to choose his own stepmother. When the eager and spring-like Perpetua crosses his line of vision, the emotions of youth revive in him and he becomes a rival, defeated in the end, of his own son.

The most moving of the three is the winter play, *The Dark is Light Enough*, set in the Hungarian Revolution of 1848. Its title is taken from an account given by the naturalist Fabre of the moths which by night cross a wood in complete darkness without damage to a single delicate wing. A similar directness of action and assurance of safety guides Countess Rosmarin, already an old woman; she does not delay through Hamlet's scruple of "thinking too precisely on the event," but acts, without complicated calculation, on the principle that, if it is right to do something, it is wrong not to do it.

She accepts responsibility for any results with the words, "I am always perfectly guilty of what I do, thank God"; and what she does is to respond to an appeal for help from a double traitor, Richard Gettner, and to shelter him even though to do so puts herself and her own house in danger. It is not that she mistakes his character but that she recognizes that:

"Harm to Richard is harm; and harm once done
Is harm to Peter, harm to everyone."

Like the circumnavigators of the globe in Noyes' poem who "came to their home in amazement simply by sailing on," she achieves her end without the dazzling and often confusing beams of reason, for the dark is light enough. When her friend Dr. Bellman, taking the natural view that there is no need to mourn when a traitor gets his deserts, protests, "I should more likely weep for stags or partridges," she does not argue the rights and

Jennet, Richard and Thomas, from Fry's The Lady's Not for Burning.

wrongs of retributive punishment, but simply rejoins, "Do then. Weep for what you can." No sentient being is outside the range of her protective pity, and thus she is never perturbed by the necessity of choice, for there is no choice; there is only the next step.

Just because she makes no attempt to influence the motives of others,

> "Lives make and unmake themselves in her neighbourhood
> As nowhere else. . . . If she should die, her gravestone would play havoc
> With the life of the mason who carved it."

In the end, just because she is there, though dead, Richard keeps faith with her even at the cost of letting in his enemies, and so saves his soul alive.

The Younger Dramatists

In considering the younger authors, whose observations seem tinged with hope, there may be a case for suspended judgment. It is easy to think that John Osborne's *Look Back in Anger* presents a common but undesirable type of young man, too cowardly to face the inherited difficulties of his time, disguising weakness under a show of blustering wrath; and that his *Entertainer* is a hollow man, past doing the only thing that he could ever do, and putting up a façade that deceives no one.

It is easy to think that Samuel Beckett's *Waiting for Godot* presents two cumberers of the ground on which they wait, with interludes on the relationship between capital and labour, and that the game is up with the title, for why accept instructions to wait instead of going out to seek?

It is easy to savour the bitterness in Pinter's *The Birthday Party*, with all its unhappy severance of family ties, or the nightmare futility of his play *The Dumb Waiter*, in which colleagues in murder, faithless even to each other, become aware of some kind of demand from what they took to be an empty restaurant above, and find themselves without means or grace to satisfy it.

It is easy to value Wesker's trilogy of *Chicken Soup with Barley*, *Roots* and *I'm Talking About Jerusalem* more for its truthful and sympathetic presentation of the circumstances that degrade life in the back streets than those that exalt it.

In all these instances it is impossible not to applaud the skill, attack and sheer technique with which the authors present their cases; but, though dustbins are useful articles in which to dump refuse, one cannot furnish a house with them: rightly to serve their purpose they must stand outside the place where we live. And where is this? Not in a world robbed of meaning or dignity or both, but, as one of the soldiers says in Fry's *A Sleep of Prisoners*,

> "In a sort of a universe and a bit of a fix.
> It's what they call flesh we're in.
> And a fine old dance it is,"

but a dance which gives importance to every quality that they possess.

Rupert Brooke in 1914 wrote, "Now, God be thanked who has matched us with His hour," and the thunder that cowardly despair takes for a prelude to destruction is to these prisoners "the thunder of the floes, the thaw, the flood, the upstart Spring." They too thank God that their time (though half a century later)

> ". . . is now, when wrong
> Comes up to face us everywhere.
> Affairs are now soul size."

Their last words before falling asleep are, "Rest you merry," and the bells of St. Mary's University Church at Oxford, where the play was first presented, chimed the exact notes of the answer, "Hope so; hope so."

Plays Reflecting the Status of Women

It was inevitable that the change in the position of women which has taken place since 1900 should make its way into drama. *The Twelve-Pound Look* by Barrie (1910) had already let the cat out of the bag, that work was fun. Kate, first wife of a newly-knighted businessman, Sir Harry Sims, deserted him, not for another man but to release herself from the suffocating effect of his success. She describes the means by which she earned £12 with which to buy the typewriter that spelt independence, and utters the warning: "If I was a husband—it is my advice to all of them—I would often watch my wife quietly to see whether the twelve-pound look was not coming into her eyes." To keep up his self-importance, Sir Harry congratulates his second wife, crushed by her position and possessions, on the difference between her luxury and the workaday life of a typist; she agrees, for she is too spiritless to do otherwise, but, as she goes out in obedience to his order, she asks inconsequently, "Are they very expensive—those machines?" The great Recording Angel in *The Zeal of Thy House* looks on a hatred of work as "one of the most depressing consequences of the Fall." For himself, he likes it.

In *The Silver Cord*, a possessive mother resents the fact that her son has married a woman with a career of her own, one who will therefore naturally not allow her husband to accept easy second-rate achievement. Christina says, "The third time I refused Dave he asked me for a reason. I told him I couldn't throw myself away on a big frog in a small puddle," and to his mother's shocked, "You don't mean that you want him to be a small frog, a mere tadpole, in a great ocean like New York," she rejoins, "I'm afraid that's just what I do mean." In the same play the opposite of the mother's attitude is

Alison and Jimmy Porter, from Look Back in Anger *by John Osborne.*

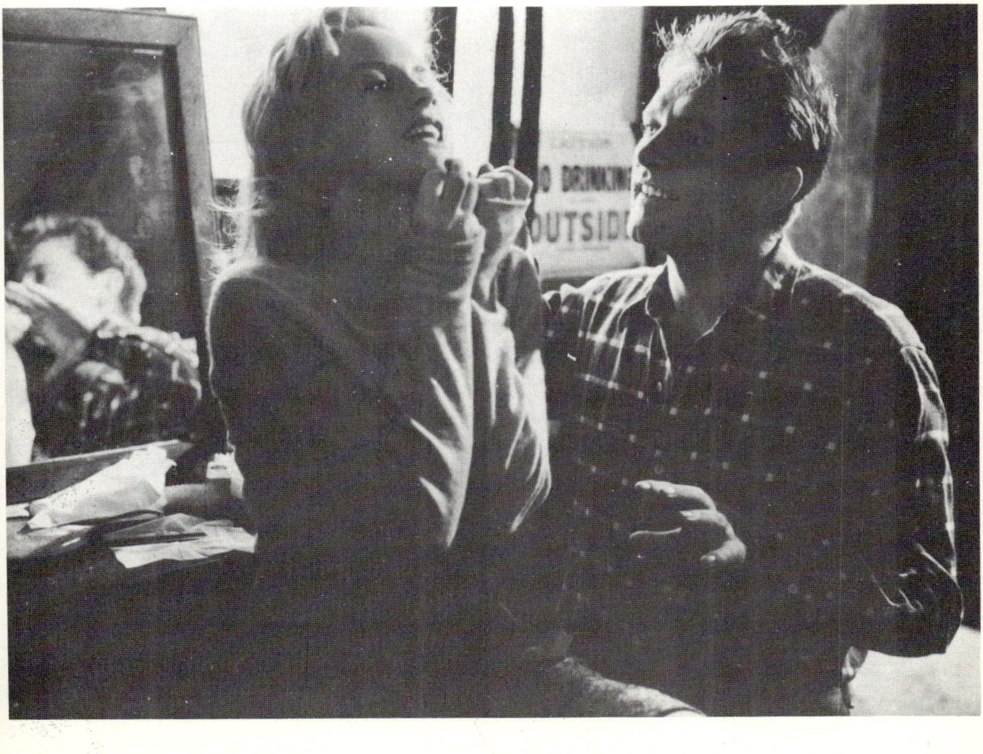

put in the words, "What I say about children is this. Have 'em. Love 'em and then leave 'em be."

But what is to happen when career and home duties are in conflict? *Robert's Wife*, by St. John Ervine, makes it clear that home comes first: when Robert gets his chance to move to a more difficult and demanding parish and his wife, a qualified doctor, must if he does so give up her own work at her clinic, she does not hesitate to put his fulfilment first, but even as she does so adds, "Don't waste me, Robert." And a career is not always an alternative to home life: on the contrary, in *Dear Octopus* the "grand toast" is the Family to which the professional daughters return. "It is, like nearly every British institution, adaptable. It bends, it stretches, but it never breaks"; and hence, though we grumble and "hear on every hand that the family ties are slackening . . . we pack the trains at Christmas, going home."

Plays Reflecting the Changing World

The century has been rich in single outstanding plays by different dramatists. Some look forward. *R.U.R.* (Rossum's Universal Robots), though written by Karel Čapek, a Czech, had a wide appeal in its English translation, being first to present the horrors of a mechanized world leading to one in which machines took command, and it has contributed to our dictionaries the word "robot," meaning an apparently human automaton, now in everyday use.

Some reflect legislation such as that which established the National Health Service, shown in *The Gleam*; the offer of places in public schools to boys from state schools, in *The Guinea-Pig*; or famous legal cases as in *The Winslow Boy*, in which a father, who believes in the innocence of his son expelled from Osborne, claims an ordinary citizen's right to sue the Crown by Petition of Right: he learns that "the custom is for the Attorney-General—on behalf of the King—to endorse the Petition, and allow the case to come to Court." On such occasions the words used are, "Let Right be done," and Sir Robert, the barrister in charge of the defence, comments, "It has a certain ring about it, has it not? 'Let Right be done'."

Historical Plays

The wars brought about a spate of fine plays—not those on aspects of warfare itself, which came afterwards, but on great characters in English history and literature. In Thornton Wilder's *The Cabala*, the dying Keats longs to hear good of England, being "hungry to hear things praised"; and those who were fighting for their country were hungry to know of her past. *Richard of Bordeaux*, *Viceroy Sarah*, *Clive of India*, *The First Gentleman*, *The Lady with a Lamp*, *Victoria Regina*, the names thunder past like the hooves of a cavalry charge. Many who never proposed to read or understand

Beatie Bryant talking to her mother, from Arnold Wesker's play Roots.

a verse of Browning's poetry thrilled to the rather exaggerated account of his courtship as told in *The Barretts of Wimpole Street* by Rudolf Besier.

Progress itself had its dramatic historians: in *Milestones* the three stages of 1860, 1885 and 1912 are presented, though the significant name in Act I is not that of a man but of a ship, the *Warrior*, first vessel of the British Navy to be built entirely of iron, with her champions and her opponents.

Plays About War

In retrospect, various aspects of the two wars were reflected in realistic pictures of the struggle above, on and under earth and sea: of these *Journey's End*, showing trench warfare, was much the most famous and far-reaching in its influence, but *Flare Path* (on the Air Force), *Seagulls Over Sorrento* (on the Navy), *Desert Highway* (on the African campaign), *Thunder Rock* (on isolationism) and numerous others informed the stay-at-home public. *X = O* showed the futility of mutual slaughter; in *An Inspector Calls*, Priestley warned his hearers against shuffling off responsibility; and in *Abraham Lincoln*, though ostensibly speaking about the American Civil War, Drinkwater's hero put the case for the use of force. To a sincere and heart-broken pacifist he says:

"Madam, I too believe war to be wrong. It is the weakness and the jealousy and the folly of men that make a thing so wrong possible. . . . But the best of us have an instinct to resist aggression if it won't listen to persuasion. You may say it's a wrong instinct. I don't know. But it's there, and it's there in millions of good men."

If it is the business of the stage to show "the very age and body of the time his form and pressure," our theatre today does not hesitate to present a rather dispiriting picture of the dangers, damps and difficulties of this our heritage. But another part of the business is to provide us with a lifting of the heart to meet its demands, and Graham Greene in *The Potting Shed* does just that. Anne, aged sixteen, an age at which certainty is the most desirable good, is, in common with her generation, denied this blessing. She dreads the laurel-walk "because if there were ghosts the potting-shed might be haunted." But one evening she wakes, sure of heart, after a dream, and tells her elders about it.

"Oh, I've had such a funny dream. I was going down the path to the potting-shed and there was a lion there fast asleep."
"What did you do?"
"I woke it up."
"Did it eat you?"
"No, it only licked my hand."

I woke my lion up and then it was friends with me—just as desperate and dangerous and simple as that.

Poetry and the Machine

The first business of the poetry of this century has been to keep in touch with the old while getting on to terms with the new. Some poets fear that the machine will master and ultimately destroy natural life. Gordon Bottomley gives a warning *To Iron-founders and Others:* "Your worship is your furnaces"; "Your vision is machines for making more machines." It is, however, too late to forgo the use of machines; we cannot uninvent our inventions; and Kipling shows that, while they remain our servants, we are better off for them. In *The Secret of the Machines*, however, they state:

"We can neither love nor pity nor forgive.
If you make a slip in handling us, you die."

This is saner than prophesying a world given over to robots, for we have got to live with them.

Nor is it enough that they should be useful; they have their own beauty, even for those who are most keenly awake to natural loveliness. In *Testament of Beauty*, Robert Bridges delights both in natural scenes, unchanged since sky spanned earth, and in the "new poetry of toil,"

"Whenas on frosty evenings neath its clouding smoke
the engin hath huddled-up its clumsy threshing-coach

against the ricks, wherefrom laborers standing aloft
toss the sheaves on its tongue; while the grain runneth out."

The Old Vicarage, Grantchester mirrors the serene, unaltered life of countryside and university; but in *The Great Lover* Rupert Brooke adds to his list of beloved natural objects "the keen unpassioned beauty of a great machine." In John Masefield's famous *Cargoes* the "dirty British coaster with a salt-caked smoke stack" is there to contrast with the quinquireme and the galleon, not as an enemy to beauty but as another form of it.

Stephen Spender in *The Express* traces the increasing speed of a majestic train from the moment when, with audible thrust and puff in the consonants,

"After the first powerful plain manifesto
The black statement of pistons, without more fuss
But gliding like a queen, she leaves the station."

But speed, idol of the century, merely for its own sake is not enough:

"'Speed and more speed,' the post-war children cry;
'Let not a moment of our lives slip by.'
Asked what their goal is they can only stare.
They have no goal, although they hasten there."

And a human being must protect himself against the tyranny of mechanical repetition. John Davidson's workers may grasp at a respite:

"Piper, play! Piper, play!
For a little we are free!
Foot it, girls, and shake your curls,
Haggard creatures though we be,"

but even in their dance the rhythm of wheels is in them. It will never be out of them.

Loss of Vision

Some get caught. Noyes' *Old Grey Squirrel*, who as a boy dreamed of voyaging to 'Frisco and fell asleep nightly to the tune of sailormen dancing on the quay, never got there:

"They caught him, and they caged him, like a squirrel.
He is totting up accounts, and going grey."

Vachel Lindsay laments the loss of vision in the new generations:

"Not that they serve, but have no gods to serve;
Not that they die, but that they die like sheep."

A factory increases material gocd; but if a worker is dulled by his job and "factory windows are always broken," there is some deadly disease in the state.

Even smashing things is not so killing as apathy, an apathy which is not just a result of having to earn one's living by "the trivial round, the common task," which should indeed also be earning what Agatha in *The Family Reunion* calls "a daily spiritual income," but of a sense that nothing is worth doing. The "twentieth-century blues," that deathly miasma of boredom and wanhope (Chaucer's word for despair) that smothers those who have "nothing to win and nothing to lose," colours Auden's *Funeral Blues*:

"The stars are not wanted now, put out every one;
Pack up the moon and dismantle the sun—
Pour away the ocean and sweep up the wood:
For nothing now can ever come to any good."

Nothing? Ever? This is the breeding-ground of disillusion with self that spreads to the rest of the world, of all the J. Alfred Prufrocks for whom T. S. Eliot's character stands as type, "Full of high sentence, but a bit obtuse"; and of his empty society woman bleating, "What shall we do tomorrow? What shall we ever do?"

But living men will not be content, or not for long, without some dignity of mind and nobility of heart. In Rupert Brooke's sonnet:

"Honour has come back, as a king, to earth,
And paid his subjects with a royal wage;
And Nobleness walks in our ways again;
And we have come into our heritage."

It is not absent today, and appears on the bookshelves in various guises, as records of gallant adventure, of daily work well done, of brotherly sympathies, of wonder at the world of our five senses, of the world that lies just outside them and of the world within.

In a modern epic of the air, C. Day-Lewis begins with a traditional epic opening, stating his subject:

"Sing we the two lieutenants, Parer and M'Intosh,
After the War wishing to hie them home to Australia,
Planned they would take a high way, a hazardous crazy air-way."

The wrath of Achilles I sing. Arms and the man I sing. A heap of scrap and the men I sing. The poem recounts in detail their cold courage and hair-breadth escapes, fire in the air, the spears of the Alps, failures in the desert, too many to tell. At the end, the applause of crowds was a minor recognition of an exploit which ennobled the human story:

". . . Them, whose meteor path
Lightened our eyes, whose great spirit lifted the fog
That sours a doubtful earth, the stars commemorate."

Rudyard Kipling (1865-1936) sings the songs of men with work to do among the five nations and on the seven seas, of the Roman legionary in Britain, the subaltern in India, ships and their crews, all who set their hand to a task.

John Masefield's stories in verse each recount some struggle of the human spirit: the conversion of Saul Kane in *The Everlasting Mercy*, the finding of manhood in *Dauber*, the terrible grinding of the wheels of justice in *The Widow in the Bye Street*, the partnership of man and beast in *Right Royal*, the enmity of man and beast in *Reynard the Fox*. Each originates in some deep stirring of pity.

James Elroy Flecker (1884-1915) evokes scenes of eastern magic: of the sea-lady in the Aegean; of the old ships that "sail like swans asleep beyond the village which men still call Tyre"; and of the four great gates of Damascus through which we can go eastward with Doom's caravan, north to Aleppo to sell the rotten and buy the ripe, westward to "the dragon-green, the luminous, the dark, the serpent-haunted sea," or south to the Mecca of the spiritual pilgrim. In *Hassan*, Flecker gives the richness of an Oriental story of love, jealousy and death.

Though Walter de la Mare (1873-1956) finds in the love and wonder that he feels for the world around him the "very proof" of his nature, he also finds and gives us eyes and ears for another world just beyond the boundaries of Earth's "live willed things"; his traveller is conscious of silent listeners.

Ishak, Jafar, Masrur and the Caliph, from Flecker's play Hassan.

D. H. Lawrence (1885-1930), in his poems on animals, on bats, toads, snakes or tortoises, directs our eyes to the strangeness which lives in the same world as we do, though beyond our daily experience.

Nearer home, Edmund Blunden illustrates the truth of Fra Lippo Lippi's comment, "Don't you mark? We're made so that we love first when we see them painted, things we have passed perhaps a hundred times nor cared to see." In this vein he paints in words and so makes us love the barn, "old, not strange":

"The smell of apples stored in hay
And homely cattle-cake is there.
Use and disuse have come to terms,
The walls are hollowed out by worms,
But men's feet keep the mid-floor bare
And free from worse decay."

Every reader has been into that barn.

Poems of the War

Poems on war vary much in tone between different authors and different wars. To some, as to Julian Grenfell, it offered a chance of fulfilment, of being indeed matched with the hour, for "who dies fighting has increase."

For Wilfred Owen, a sense of "doomed youth," of sheer waste, of all-embracing pity, overwhelms all other feeling, for his dead enemy laments "the undone years, the hopelessness," on both sides.

Siegfried Sassoon, by his bitter satire on the Armistice Day ceremonial at the Cenotaph, shows how easily lessons of the past are ignored:

"I saw the Prince of Darkness, with his Staff,
Standing bare-headed by the Cenotaph;
Unostentatious and respectful, there
He stood, and offered up the following prayer."

The devil's prayer is that men may so forget that the same incitements to war may bring the same results; and, as he bowed and turned away, he laughed.

John Betjeman, in satire of a more particular type, shows how hateful false patriotism can be; his shallow worshipper in Westminster Abbey prays:

"Think of what our Nation stands for,
Books from Boots' and country lanes,
Free speech, free passes, class distinction,
Democracy and proper drains.
Lord, put beneath Thy special care
One-eighty-nine Cadogan Square."

Wars do not end abruptly when the peace treaty is signed at the end of them. Auden puts poignantly the position of refugees and displaced persons:

"The consul banged the table and said:
'If you've no passport, you're officially dead';
But we are still alive, my dear, but we are still alive."

In *Flight of the Heart* Louis MacNeice suggests the natural shrinking of most people, already besieged by appeals for help and shouldering more than they can well manage, to take on any further responsibilities:

"Heart, my heart, what will you do?
There are five lame dogs and one deaf-mute
All of them with demands on you."

But evasion is impossible; even if we make ourselves all-powerfully immune from attack, even if we deliberately forget the whole business, the copper tower built for our protection will not stand, the cellar roof under which we can shut out the light will cave in, and the human race, bent to destroy by its own hand the civilization that by its own hand it has made, had better go back to its origins and begin the whole experiment over again. "If you will not come to me," says the trouble of the world, "I shall come to you." It is an open condition.

No poets of any previous war went as far as those of the 1939-45 war in accepting communal responsibility. In *A Song About Major Eatherly*, said to be the pilot who carried the second atomic bomb to Nagasaki, John Wain makes clear that "to take life is always to die a little," and that everyone is morally involved. So we have all invested in destruction and are drawing our dividends:

"And on the last day of the last year of Our Lord
The sun was blinded and died in darkness,
The earth was crippled and the rain dry death
On this the first day of the first year of Our Bomb."

We must either live with it or die from it. No wonder no poets of any previous war have had the same kind of thing to say.

The very elegies for the dead are shorn of their trappings; we must be starkly practical. The eighteenth century could luxuriate in all the pageantry of woe, drums, plumes and catafalque, arms reversed and the Dead March. Modern warfare doesn't afford time for it all; we must be quick with our elegies and get on with the next job. In *For Johnny*, John Pudney needs only fifty words to mourn his airman:

"Do not despair
For Johnny-head-in-air;
He sleeps as sound
As Johnny underground.

Fetch out no shroud
For Johnny-in-the-cloud;
And keep your tears
For him in after years.
Better by far
For Johnny-the-bright-star,
To keep your head,
And see his children fed."

The implications are uncomfortable enough. "Sin," as Christopher Fry has pointed out, "is so inconvenient." But we must have the chance to earn our bread and love our arts. Hardy, with his deep knowledge of country life, puts the old everlasting truths in their right proportion:

"Yonder a maid and her wight
Come whispering by;
War's annals will fade into night
Ere their story die."

Meantime, as Dylan Thomas observed in *Under Milk Wood*, "Isn't life a terrible thing, thank God?"

Galsworthy, Novelist of Social Change

During the first quarter of the century the names of five novelists stand out, each of whom marked out a territory for himself and reigns supreme in it.

The mightiest individual production is *The Forsyte Saga*, three novels and two long short stories, followed by *A Modern Comedy*, in which Galsworthy traced the fortunes of his widely-elaborated family of Forsytes and of their children and grandchildren. In this chronicle he has fixed for social historians of the future the way of life of middle-class Victorians, and has shown what they aimed at (safety of possession), what they feared (a social upheaval that would disturb values), what they avoided (the unusual or unreliable), and what they enjoyed (solid and assured comfort). The impact of the twentieth century on a world which for them consisted of the British Empire of which they were by established right owners and rulers threatened their central quality, possessiveness. In the first book, *The Man of Property*, the possibility that any force, even death itself, can loosen their hold on their possessions is brought home to them, and inly resented, by the death of Aunt Ann, born just within the limits of the eighteenth century. Later, artist challenges businessman, when the architect Philip Bosinney, to the Forsyte clan a "buccaneer", compels Soames Forsyte to let go his wife Irene; and, after "the waters of change" have come foaming in, the truth, that a man may not keep what is his own in the sense that he has bought and paid for it, is as shocking to their moral as to their material values.

Most typical of the Forsyte outlook is Soames, to whom "What I have I hold" is a creed; he is not, however, inaccessible to unprofitable emotions, and when the Armistice comes he finds himself insensibly turning his steps to St. Paul's and gazing at the Flag. In his daughter Fleur, even more unwilling to forgo possession than her father, he finds an object for selfless affection, and finally gives his life in trying to save hers. This is no unintentional softening on the author's part, for Galsworthy expressly states in the preface to *A Modern Comedy*, "Taking him for all in all he was honest anyway." In this story the White Monkey, symbolic of frustrated desire, holds "the rind of a squeezed fruit in its outstretched paw." Its dilemma is that of the post-war generations: "He won't be happy till he gets it; the only thing is, you see, he doesn't know what *it* is."

Maugham, Student of Character

W. Somerset Maugham, like Galsworthy, has established his fame in three departments, as novelist, playwright and writer of short stories. His interest is in the vagaries and capabilities of human nature, and he seeks his subjects in those fellow-beings who suddenly do the unexpected, whose lives hide strange secrets or flash into dramatic action. Such a principle of selection provides a series of uncommon characters, living out their problems against unfamiliar backgrounds far to the east or west of Europe, and though most of his stories have a tragic strain he gives a warning, "The reader must not suppose that the incidents I have narrated were of common occurrence." Most men and women are "good, decent, normal people," but, he adds, "they are not the sort of people I can write stories about. I write stories about people who have some singularity of character."

In his play *The Breadwinner*, the stockbroker father of a middle-class, tennis-playing, almost intolerably ordinary, family suddenly decides to leave them; the young ones have always taken him for granted, a harmless necessary provider, dull as ditchwater. That he in turn finds them boring is to them incomprehensible. But he is determined to up and go, and he ups and goes.

In *The Moon and Sixpence* Strickland, a city man, is "not in the least interested in literature or the arts"; and when he leaves his wife, his friends take it for granted that "he's gone off to Paris with a woman." But when the narrator appeals to him to return, he is up against an invincible rival.

> "Do you mean to say you didn't leave your wife for another woman?"
> "Of course not" . . .
> "Then, what in God's name have you left her for?"
> "I want to paint."

This compelling passion dictates all Strickland's future life, based in some aspects on the career of the painter Gauguin, up to his death from leprosy in Tahiti in a native hut whose walls he has covered with "a strange and elaborate composition . . . indescribably wonderful and mysterious." The doctor who finds him dead owes to it a new vision of the normal world. This is the true function of great art, and by achieving it Strickland "achieved what he wanted. His life was complete." It would not have mattered if he had not, in fact, found that he was a genius; he had exchanged the round silver sixpence of calculated material well-being for the round silver moon of his ideal. He had a centre to his life.

Wells, the Scientific Novelist

H. G. Wells (1866-1946) took for his province a much narrower territory, but one on which later discoveries are shedding a strange retrospective light, that of scientific prophecy. His method was to accept as data conditions not yet fulfilled and see where we went from there. It seems as if each discovery must bring advantages, but far otherwise. What happens if a man discovers how to make himself invisible? Surely he will be lord of the earth? Not at all. He is killed. In the country of the blind, surely a one-eyed man must be king? Not at all. He is faced with the choice between accepting voluntary blindness or dying in an attempt to escape. If a man has power to work miracles and can get anything he wants, surely he must be superbly happy? Not at all. His final wish is to be rid of so devastating a force. The conclusion in each case is that it is dangerous to be different, and better to have no more than our neighbours; which, however true in a practical sense, affords a rather dismal prospect.

However, scientists have never been deterred by danger and are catching up on Wells. His fantastic novel *The First Men in the Moon* will soon supply an engaging comparison with a factual account of the event, much as Kipling's prophetic short story *With the Night Mail* can already be checked by actual circumstance.

H. G. Wells did not limit his scope to science fiction; in *Mr. Britling Sees It Through* he recorded with tragic faithfulness the carefree mood of an average English family during the early summer of 1914. Even as they brush away any disturbing prospects of international trouble there is a loud explosion. One expects them all to be blown up, or anyhow shocked out of their complacency; but they do not even hear it, for it happened on the other side of the world, at Sarajevo, and set in motion the train of events that swept their old life away for ever. The ensuing war killed both the son of the house and his German friend; and at the end of the story Mr. Britling drags himself into writing to the young German's parents and sending them a photograph of both boys; "They are, as you see, smiling at each other very pleasantly."

In his transcriptions of daily life H. G. Wells keeps to the world he most intimately knew, and makes its joys, sorrows and adventures intensely moving; his Kipps and Mr. Polly, lovable in themselves, are most themselves and therefore most lovable amongst their own kind. They can be multiplied by thousands, but this does not imply any loss of significance, for each is an individual in his own right.

Bennett of the Five Towns

Arnold Bennett's province is the Five Towns, noisy, dirty, industrial, alive. His men and women rejoice to gain a foothold in the society of their equals, sound money, respected positions; but they are vastly different from the Forsytes, for they make all that they have, and most of them make good. They enjoy not so much getting as getting on; and this is no unworthy aim for men who begin with next to no advantages, and have always in their minds a vivid, personal realization of what happens to the workless and the shiftless who drift into the gutter. Their mental processes, like those of the Card, are directed by the pressure of their lives towards getting the better of circumstances and sometimes of their neighbours. They appreciate shrewdness rather than wisdom; their hands are occupied in making, their minds in evolving neat strokes of business and their hearts in the kindliness and fellow-feeling of men on the edge of a common danger.

Denry Machin, The Card.

Nor are their lives without dignity, though they may lack visible beauty: in *The Old Wives' Tale* Samuel Povey espoused the cause of the condemned man Daniel Povey, got up a petition to the Home Secretary, undertook journeys and interviews in icy weather, took one journey too many, and died of toxaemia, unable to sustain the spiritual and physical defeats which he had voluntarily endured. "He embraced a cause, lost it and died of it."

Conrad, a Seafaring Novelist

Joseph Conrad (1857-1924) takes as his special province the sea in all its moods, whatever coasts it washes: his greatest stories are of the men who use it and are tested by it. *Youth* tells of the heart-breaking delays and disasters that beset the *Judea* on her voyage to the East, and the exultant triumph of young Marlow in defeating the odds.

Lord Jim gives the terrifying experience of another young and generous heart, Jim, who had imagined himself the centre of so many courageous exploits and who, when tested, failed, and found that by jumping from the injured ship still full of sleeping pilgrims he had jumped into a bottomless pit of disgrace. His re-establishment of his personal honour is an adventure of more magnitude than any for which he had cast himself as hero.

The Nigger of the Narcissus, with the violent contrast of black and white in its title, admits us into the childish quarrels and childlike loyalties of sailors before the mast; and in *The Rover*, set in the years preceding Trafalgar, we meet the old pirate Peyrol, and follow the sacrifice of his life, by which he tricked Nelson into thinking that the despatches with which he seemed to be trying to escape were genuine.

After living among the natives, Kurtz, in *Heart of Darkness*, has lost his hold on civilization and has spiritually decayed. After all his power over life and death and his amassed riches of ivory, when he dies the end is announced with contemptuous brevity by the black man, "Mistah Kurtz—he dead," words that T. S. Eliot set at the head of *The Hollow Men*, that chronicle of men no longer men, but imitations stuffed with straw.

The Short Story

One literary form in which this century is especially rich is the short story. The adjective does not imply any inferiority, for "in small proportions we just beauties see"; the form, like the sonnet, has its limitations, but these, as in the finest sonnets, lead to its qualities. There is little or no room for development, so that characters may change but can hardly mature. The author is obliged to concentrate on one theme, and as far as possible to apply the unities of time and place, or at least not to dissipate interest too widely.

Kipling captured his public more by his short tales of Indian life in the army, the native quarters and the jungle, than by his novels *Kim* and *The Naulahka*. But it is of England that he writes best. The history of south country England round Pevensey, near which he made his best-loved home at Burwash, soaks through *Puck of Pook's Hill* and *Rewards and Fairies*.

The character who most belongs to him is old Hobden, lineal descendant of the Anglo-Saxons, the breed that endured successive conquest by Romans, Danes and Normans, and quietly went about its business of absorbing its conquerors into the island's life.

> "His dead are in the churchyard—thirty generations laid.
> Their names were old in history when Domesday Book was made."

The detective story is a branch of literature whose long-continued popularity is due partly to the fact that it is an intellectual exercise, and has not, or should not have, any more appeal to the emotions of love and pity than a crossword puzzle. Thus it is a form of escape for those who, for various reasons, would rather think than feel. In the Sherlock Holmes stories, its prototype, detection is based on observation and scientific deduction. As methods of causing death and misdirecting suspicion have, by mere variety, been gradually used up, authors have been deflected to a different type of clue and the psychologist has replaced the scientist. Chesterton's Father Brown relies on his knowledge of the human heart, and argues that this kind of crime could not have been committed by that kind of man. Its vogue is not exhausted. If "readers are getting cleverer and cleverer, authors are getting cleverer and cleverer too," and every new invention provides the author with a new chance.

Of ghost stories the chief practitioner is M. R. James, whose *Ghost Stories of an Antiquary*, though less subtle than Henry James' *The Turn of the Screw*, are still calculated to bring a chill to the spine in broad daylight and in the main street. If this could happen to him there and then, argues the reader, it can happen to anyone anywhere, to me here and now.

Finally three short stories stand out for a quality hard to define but relating them unmistakably to poetry. E. M. Forster's *The Celestial Omnibus* shows the growing response of an adolescent mind to the splendours of literature. Katherine Mansfield's *The Garden Party* makes an exquisite contrast between the noisy frivolities of a summer afternoon and the quiet serenity of the dead young carter's face. J. M. Barrie's *Farewell Miss Julie Logan* tells a story, of a Scots minister in his snow-locked glen, that steps imperceptibly to and fro across the boundary between this world and that of the supernatural which mortal men are forbidden to enter.

Hudson the Naturalist

W. H. Hudson (1841-1922), partly by his vivid descriptions of boyhood in South America but chiefly by his appreciation of simple honest country folk, takes the lead. Through *A Shepherd's Life*, his Caleb Bawcombe is known to thousands of readers:

> "Fifty years I've been on the downs and fields, day and night, seven days a week, and I've been told that it's a poor way to spend a life, working seven days for ten or twelve, or at most thirteen shillings. But I never seen it like that; I liked it, and I always did my best . . . I never left a place but I was asked to stay."

Of the chance to live his life again, such a man could say, "If 'twas offered to me and I was told to choose my work, I'd say, Give me my Wiltsheer Downs again and let me be a shepherd there all my life long." In *Hampshire Days* Hudson's old countrywoman deplores, as it is the privilege of age to deplore, the evils of modern times compared with the days of her youth. The very birds are not as well-behaved as they were. What would she have said to daylight-saving, when even the best of them go to bed an hour later than they used to do? She will no longer make elderberry wine, for greedy starlings take all her fruit:

> "We didn't have so many starlings when I were young. But things is very different now; and what I say is, I wish they wasn't—I wish they was the same as when I were a girl. And I wish I was a girl again."

Chesterton, Baring and Belloc.

Belloc and Chesterton

Hilaire Belloc (1870-1953), writer of verses and epigrams as well as of discursive essays, must by the same token have been a jolly fellow. His pilgrimages through Sussex were occasions for singing at the top of his voice. Even "the fleas that tease in the high Pyrenees" are part of the fun. As to the prospect of drowning in the North Sea, whatever could possibly be jollier? "I looked to windward and saw the sea tumbling and a great number of white waves. My heart was still so high that I gave them the names of the waves in the eighteenth *Iliad.*" The Nun's Priest quoted St. Paul as saying that all that is written is written for our good, and certainly Belloc would agree, for he ends with a flourishing admonition, "I have written for your correction. Read less, good people, and sail more." This advice, however, is not to apply to his own works: "When I am dead, I hope it may be said: 'His sins were scarlet, but his books were read'."

Belloc's friend, G. K. Chesterton (1874-1936), adopted the use of paradox, a trick of apparent contradiction which is as enlivening when it is fresh as irritating when use has staled it. His love of the melodramatic led him to some violence of expression; his prose is forceful in sound, vivid in colour and strong in taste. The biologist in his researches "would find the trail of monsters . . . groping and grasping and touching life with every extravagant elongation of horn and tongue and tentacle, growing a forest of fantastic caricatures of the claw and the fin and the finger"; this may not have the restrained exactitude with which the biologist would wish his researches to be recorded, but it fills the imagination with more daemonic creatures than lived in the pages of Tom o' Bedlam's Book of Moons. It has a nightmare's excitement. No critic has done more admirable justice to Browning, not by explaining away his love of the grotesque and his occasional obscurity, but by explaining them.

Lytton Strachey, Biographer

Lytton Strachey (1880-1932), on the other hand, draws his audience more by the hope that they will hear a neat joke at someone else's expense than that he will put himself out to entertain them at his own. Independence of judgment, recommended by a lively style, is his merit, when it does not decline into special pleading or attacking. In his essay on Pope he refuses to be dazzled by a great name. His life of Florence Nightingale not only gives an estimate of the importance of her work, but provides the basis of a popular drama. But elsewhere in *Eminent Victorians* he not only refuses, in his pursuit of independence, to make customary if insincere obeisance, nor does he simply stand upright; he bends over backwards in his effort to prove that he will not bend forwards. Can we not imagine, he asks, a conversation between the Pope and Newman before the latter became converted and a cardinal, and then he proceeds to suggest what he cannot assert, inventing what will best support his derogatory theory. The answer is that even if we can we will not, for it is no part of scholarship, biography or common fair play to do so. But we can share his enjoyment of Pope's *Satires* and *Epistles*.

> ". . . in which the verses, when they were written, resembled nothing so much as spoonfuls of boiling oil, ladled out by a fiendish monkey at an upstairs window upon such of the passers-by whom the wretch had a grudge against."

E. V. Lucas, Essayist

E. V. Lucas (1868-1938), in contrast, breathes a gentler strain. As a citizen of London, the "friendly town," he is the more persuasive because he invites the reader to walk beside him instead of dragging him along by the hair he has already caused to stand on end. A woman is arrested in Gerrard Street; but though E. V. Lucas is aware that he is witnessing a drama, we are never embarrassed in his company. The policeman, a necessary member of the cast, "takes his proper part as a London entertainer," and when he has uttered his opening lines, "That's enough of that. You come along with me," the play proceeds quietly enough. We join the procession, "merely to be in whatever is going on," and when the alley leading to Vine Street is reached we melt away. No fuss, no violence, no superlatives or paradoxes; we can return "to hunt books in the Charing Cross Road" or retire to a room over Bemerton's to handle those that we have already acquired.

There has never been a century in which inventions and discoveries have so changed man's way of life as that in the second half of which we now find ourselves. The internal combustion engine, cars, telephones, electricity, aeroplanes, wireless, television, nuclear fission and space travel were practically or completely unknown on the night when, in Noël Coward's *Cavalcade*, a young couple drank to the New Year, 1900. Today these innovations are commonplaces. What of tomorrow?

One mood which in life confesses defeat and in literature spells disaster is boredom. Those who are bored by what they read need not wait to be "bored to death," for they are dead already. The essential quality of life is that it perpetually renews itself, and it is the test of fine literature that it shares that vitality. Literature cannot always solve the riddles that life poses, but it can at least assure us that there are solutions.

There is in Argyllshire a hill, called "Rest-and-be-Thankful," from which an exhausted, exhilarated climber can see round him, through distances that he cannot calculate, to a horizon he may never reach. In *The Lady's Not for Burning* Thomas Mendip shows his companion a rose-hip, held in his hand; it may stand as a symbol of the written word:

"I can pass to you
Generations of roses in this wrinkled berry.
There: now you hold in your hand a race
Of summer gardens, it lies under centuries
Of petals. What is not, you have in your palm.
Rest in the riddle, rest; why not?"

Rest, and be thankful.

QUESTIONS

1. "Some of Bernard Shaw's plays are already outdated; some will never be." Discuss this comment, showing for what qualities any of his plays will last.

2. How far is each of Galsworthy's plays founded on a clash between two opponents or opposing classes? Illustrate his sense of justice to both sides.

3. "In T. S. Eliot's plays the drama is not in external events, but in the inner life of his characters; and the conflict is resolved not by external happenings, but by a change of heart." Illustrate this comment.

4. Give some estimate of the poetic achievement of any two of the following: Kipling, Masefield, Rupert Brooke, Walter de la Mare, Poets of the Great War. Give varied illustration from modern anthologies.

5. Give some account of the qualities of Joseph Conrad as a novelist. Illustrate his descriptive powers and his insight into character by making reference to at least two of his novels or stories.

6. "*The Forsyte Saga* is the most important prose work produced by a novelist in this century." Discuss this judgment.

REVISION SUMMARY OF AUTHORS BORN SINCE 1840

Page

THOMAS HARDY (1840-1928) 324, 384

Hardy was born in Dorset, and spent much of his life there; its scenery and rustic population provided the substance of his novels. Trained as an architect, in Dorchester and in London, he turned to literature. His writings are distinguished by a quick 427 response to the varying moods of nature, a sense of fatalism, and deep pity for the ironies, follies and sufferings of human life.

Under the Greenwood Tree (1872): A country romance. 385-6
Far from the Madding Crowd (1874): Rustic characters.
The Return of the Native (1878): Growing tragedy.
The Trumpet-Major (1880): Dorset threatened by invasion. 427
Wessex Tales (1883): Short stories, tragic and humorous.
The Mayor of Casterbridge (1886): Development of expiation.
The Woodlanders (1887): A sylvan pastoral set in Wessex.
Tess of the D'Urbervilles (1891): Struggle against fate.
Wessex Poems (1898): Rural episodes free from sentimentalism.
The Dynasts (1904-8): Epic drama of Napoleon's rise and fall.

W. H. HUDSON (1841-1922) 329-30

Born in Argentina, he developed a close love for its plant, bird and animal life. In 1870 he came to London and was naturalized in 1900.

Idle Days in Patagonia (1893)
Birds in London (1898)
Hampshire Days (1903)
} Personal experiences in South America and England, written with charm. 329-30

Green Mansions (1904): Presenting Rima, the bird-girl.
A Shepherd's Life (1910): Life on the Downs. 329
Far Away and Long Ago (1918): Autobiography of boyhood on the pampas.

ROBERT BRIDGES (1844-1930) 318-9

Educated at Eton and Oxford, Bridges trained at Bart's and practised for a year, but after 1882 he turned to authorship. He

Page

travelled widely, later settling at Boar's Hill, near Oxford. He became Poet Laureate in 1913. His style was based on experiment in metre and quantity.

The Growth of Love (1876-89).
Shorter Poems (1890 and 1893).
Milton's Prosody (1893): Critical study.
Demeter (1905): A masque on a classical theme.
Collected Poetical Works (1912): Justifying his Laureateship.
The Spirit of Man (1916): Anthology affirming belief in life.
The Testament of Beauty (1929): Elaborately varied metrical experiment in praise of nature. 318-9

ROBERT LOUIS STEVENSON (1850-94) 294-5

Born in Edinburgh, the son of a famous lighthouse engineer, Stevenson studied engineering at Edinburgh University, but at twenty-one gave it up for letters. His romanticism and zest for adventure, perhaps a compensation for illness, make him permanently a favourite with the young, his courage and sanity with their elders.

Travels with a Donkey (1879): In the Cevennes with Modestine.
Virginibus Puerisque (1881): Essays for lasses and lads.
Treasure Island (1883): The best tale of buried treasure.
A Child's Garden of Verses (1885): Rhymes of childhood.
Kidnapped (1886): A boy's adventures at sea.
The Master of Ballantrae (1889): Rivalry of two brothers.

OSCAR WILDE (1854-1900) 300-1

Educated at Dublin and Oxford, Wilde was distinguished for his wit, and for a deliberate affectation of disregard for moral principles, conveyed through nearly all his characters at the expense of their dramatic reality. After a period of great social success, Wilde was imprisoned for two years. He went abroad when released, and died in obscurity in Paris.

The Picture of Dorian Gray (1891): The tragedy of perpetual youth.
Lady Windermere's Fan (1892): Based on the bad woman with a good heart.
A Woman of No Importance (1893): A woman with a past reverses positions.
An Ideal Husband (1895): A politician's lapse from integrity. 300
The Importance of Being Earnest (1895): His finest comedy. 17
The Ballad of Reading Gaol (1898): Written in prison.

Page

ARTHUR WING PINERO (1855-1934) 298

Born in London, Pinero was trained for the Law, but decided to become an actor. He came to the London stage in 1876, and began to write plays. He was knighted in 1909.

The Squire (1881): Pinero's first important play.

Sweet Lavender (1888): A popular comedy, frequently revived.

The Second Mrs. Tanqueray (1893): Realistic drama.

Trelawny of the Wells (1898). 298

GEORGE BERNARD SHAW (1856-1950) 300-5

Shaw, the son of Irish parents, was educated privately and at various Dublin schools. In 1876 he went to London, tried various jobs, wrote five unsuccessful novels, and became a journalist. Between 1885 and 1899 Shaw was in turn reviewer, art critic, music critic and dramatic critic. Thereafter his success as a playwright induced him to devote himself to the stage. He received a Nobel Prize in 1925.

Widowers' Houses (1892): Exposure of slum rent racket. 301-3

Arms and the Man (1894): An attack on sentimentalizing war. 303

Candida (1894): Husband's success depends on wife's support. 305

Man and Superman (1903): The Life-Force in action. 303

Major Barbara (1905): Social context of the Salvation Army. 303

The Doctor's Dilemma (1906): Debate on the relative importance of art and morality.

Pygmalion (1912): Class cleavage in thought, not accent. 304, 354

Back to Methuselah (1921): Plays on the duration of life. 304

Saint Joan (1923): A study of the making of a saint. 303-5

The Apple Cart (1929): Monarchy in the modern world. 304

JOSEPH CONRAD (1857-1924) 327-8

Conrad was born in the Ukraine. With his Polish parents he was exiled in 1862, but later returned to Cracow, where he was educated. In 1874 he joined the crew of a French ship, and four years later he joined a British ship, qualifying as a Master in 1884. In 1894 he left the sea and settled in Kent, devoting himself to writing novels in English. 427

Almayer's Folly (1895): The results of observation.

The Nigger of the Narcissus (1897): Dominance of personality. 328

Lord Jim (1900): The recovery of personal honour. 328

Youth and ***Heart of Darkness*** (1902): Contrasting stories. 327-8

Page

Nostromo (1904): Set in a mythical South American country.
Mirror of the Sea (1906): Reminiscences of the sea.
Under Western Eyes (1911): Set against Russian background.
The Rescue (1920): Adventure in outlying parts.
The Rover (1923): A retired pirate tricks Nelson. 14, 328

JOHN DAVIDSON (1857-1909) 319

Of Scottish parentage, Davidson was educated at the Highlanders' Academy, Greenock, where he later taught. After some business experience, he devoted himself to literature. Though he tried other forms, his fame rests on his lyric poetry.

Fleet Street Eclogues (1893 and 1895): occasionally whimsical echoes of experience.
Ballads and Songs (1894): Of emotional beauty.

J. M. BARRIE (1860-1937) 307-8

The son of a Scots weaver, Barrie was educated at Dumfries 314-5
and Edinburgh. He was on the staff of the *Nottingham Journal* 329
in 1883, and later became a free-lance journalist and novelist in London, turning to drama at the beginning of the century.

The Little Minister (1891): Experiences of a young minister.
Quality Street (1902): Based on an earlier story.
The Admirable Crichton (1902): On a desert island. 306, 308
Peter Pan (1904): For children of any age. 307
What Every Woman Knows (1908): That her husband owes his success to her.
Dear Brutus (1917): Given a second chance, few change. 308
Mary Rose (1920): The futility of recalling to life those who have gone. 308

W. B. YEATS (1865-1939) 308-9

Yeats was born in Dublin, and educated there and in Ham- 397-8
mersmith. He was co-founder of the Irish National Theatre, director of the Abbey Theatre, and leader of the Irish literary renaissance. He was a senator of the Irish Free State from 1922 to 1928, and received a Nobel Prize in 1923. He edited the *Oxford Book of Modern Verse* in 1937.

The Countess Cathleen (1892): Sells her soul for her people. 308
The Celtic Twilight (1893): Essays on mystical element.
Deirdre (1907): On an Irish legend also used by Synge.
Plays for an Irish Theatre (1912): The Abbey Theatre.
Later Poems (1922): Haunting lyrical melody.

		Page
Collected Poems (1950) / ***Collected Plays*** (1952)	Author's love of Irish history and tradition.	397-8

RUDYARD KIPLING (1865-1936) 318

Kipling was born in India, and educated in England. He 320-1
returned to India at the age of seventeen, as assistant editor of 328
the *Lahore Civil and Military Gazette*, and later joined the 357
Allahabad Pioneer in which he first gained fame with short stories and sketches. After travelling extensively, he settled in Sussex, the history of which furnished the basis for his unrivalled stories of England's past. He received a Nobel Prize in 1907.

Departmental Ditties (1886): English life in India.
Plain Tales from the Hills (1888): Other men's work.
Barrack Room Ballads (1892): Verses on army life in India.
The Jungle Books (1894-95): Natural history in India.
The Seven Seas (1896): Swinging verse.
Stalky and Co. (1899): Schoolboy humour and reminiscences.
Kim (1901): The Secret Service in India. 328
Puck of Pook's Hill (1906): Short stories of England's past. 328
Rewards and Fairies (1910): Sequel to *Puck of Pook's Hill*. 328
Debits and Credits (1926) / ***Limits and Renewals*** (1932): The art of short story writing often raised to level of genius.

H. G. WELLS (1866-1946) 326-7

Wells, the son of a partly unsuccessful tradesman, was educated at Midhurst Grammar School, but left school at thirteen. After being apprenticed to a draper and to a chemist, he went to South Kensington Royal College of Science, and gained a B.Sc. He taught for a short time, but during a breakdown due to overwork he began to write. His novels were sometimes pseudo-scientific; others reflected his lower-middle-class background. Later he wrote historical and political surveys, showing a disillusioned intolerance of human stupidity. Wells' scientific fantasies are based on taking some impossibility for granted, and seeing what the results would be.

The Time Machine (1895): If we could put back the clock. . . .
The Invisible Man (1897): If we could become invisible. . . .
The War of the Worlds (1898): If the worlds engaged in war. . . .
The First Men in the Moon (1901): If men landed on the 24
moon and found life there. . . . 326
The Food of the Gods (1904): If a new food increased size. . . .

Page

Kipps (1905) / ***The History of Mr. Polly*** (1910): Social studies of lower-middle-class life. 353, 378
Mr. Britling Sees it Through (1916): The war and its effects. 326

ARNOLD BENNETT (1867-1931) 327

Born in Staffordshire, near Hanley (one of his Five Towns), Bennett was educated at Newcastle and was an external student of London University. In 1885 he abandoned a career as a solicitor, and began to undertake journalistic and free-lance work in London. From 1900 to 1908 he lived in France.

Anna of the Five Towns (1902) / ***Tales of the Five Towns*** (1905) / ***The Old Wives' Tale*** (1908) / ***Clayhanger*** (1910) / ***Hilda Lessways*** (1911) / ***The Card*** (1911): Stories of the inhabitants of the Potteries district, whose hard work, humanity and humour in surmounting obstacles Bennett much appreciates. 327, 327
Milestones (1912): Progress in a family over half a century. 317
Riceyman Steps (1923): Picture of lower middle class.
Imperial Palace (1930): Various aspects of a luxury hotel.

JOHN GALSWORTHY (1867-1933) 305-7

Born in Surrey, the son of an attorney, Galsworthy was educated at Harrow and Oxford. He read law, and was called to the Bar in 1890, but did not practise. He travelled widely, and met and encouraged Conrad. From 1897 he turned to writing novels and plays which reflect his own secure background. 324-5

The Man of Property (1906): First book of *The Forsyte Saga*. 324
The Silver Box (1906): One law for the rich and one for the poor. 305-6
The Country House (1907): Reflects the author's background.
Strife (1909): Clash between masters and men. 305-6
Justice (1910): Instrumental in abolishing solitary confinement. 307
In Chancery (1920): Further development of *The Forsyte Saga*.
The Skin Game (1920): A criticism of war. 307
To Let (1921): The end of *The Forsyte Saga*.
Loyalties (1922): The outcome of taking sides with one's kind. 306
Escape (1926): Pursuit of escaped convict, showing motives. 307
A Modern Comedy (1929): More about the Forsyte family. 324-5

E. V. LUCAS (1868-1938) 331

Lucas was born at Eltham in Kent, of a Quaker family. After seven years as a bookseller's assistant, he went to University

Page

College, London. He wrote pleasing verse for *Punch*, and worked for various publishing houses, becoming chairman of Methuen's. His essays on a wide variety of subjects, especially those on travel or artists, have literary charm.

The Open Road (1899): A personal choice in prose and verse.
Over Bemerton's (1908): A London bibliophile's experiences.
London Revisited (1916), ***Introducing London*** (1925), ***London Afresh*** (1936): Discursive accounts of charm and interest, showing him as an accomplished Londoner.

HILAIRE BELLOC (1870-1953) 330

Belloc was born in Paris, of a French father and an English 392-3 mother, and was educated in Birmingham and at Oxford. He wrote for journals and newspapers, and became a close friend of Chesterton. From 1906 to 1910 Belloc was a Liberal M.P. He wrote lives of Danton, Robespierre, Wolsey and Cromwell. Essays, novels and poetry reflect his skill in debate, his sympathy and rich enjoyment of life.

The Bad Child's Book of Beasts (1896): Delightful for all.
The Path to Rome (1902): Deep religious sense.
Cautionary Tales (1907): Antidote to *Struwelpeter*.
History of England (1925-27): A retort to H. G. Wells.
Anthology of Prose and Verse (1951): Fine craftsmanship.

WALTER DE LA MARE (1873-1956) 321

Educated in London, de la Mare wrote first under the pseudonym "Walter Ramal." He was a book-keeper to the Standard Oil Company, but later gave it up for authorship and reviewing.

The Listeners and other Poems (1912): Containing his best-known poem.
Peacock Pie (1913): Opening doorways in the imagination.
Memoirs of a Midget (1921): Prize-winning novel.
Come Hither (1923): Anthology reflecting delicate fantasy.
Broomsticks and other Tales (1925): Prose stories.
Early One Morning (1935): Other people's recollections.
Collected Rhymes and Verses (1944), ***Collected Stories for Children*** (1947): Distinguished by musical beauty.

G. K. CHESTERTON (1874-1936) 331

Born in London of English-Scots parents, Chesterton studied art and literature at the Slade School. He reviewed books, and wrote articles on artistic subjects. In 1922 he was received into

Page

the Roman Catholic Church. He edited *G.K.'s Weekly*, a vehicle for his political views, and presided over a weekly B.B.C. debate on literary subjects. He wrote voluminously: novels, short stories, verse, essays and criticism.

All Things Considered (1908), ***Tremendous Trifles*** (1909): Essays whose titles proclaim his range and love of paradox.

The Ballad of the White Horse (1913): Love of English history.

The Victorian Age in Literature (1913): Critical approach.

Wine, Water and Song (1915): Antagonism to teetotalism, etc.

The Innocence of Father Brown (1911), ***The Wisdom of Father Brown*** (1914), ***The Incredulity of Father Brown*** (1926), ***The Secret of Father Brown*** (1927): Psychological detective stories centred on a Roman Catholic priest. 329

GORDON BOTTOMLEY (1874-1948) 318

Born and educated at Keighley, Bottomley lived most of his life in Lancashire near the Lake District. He devoted his poetic gifts to reviving drama in verse suitable for fine verse-speaking, especially on Scottish themes.

The Riding to Lithend (1909): Verse-drama on heroic theme.

King Lear's Wife (1915): Imaginative reconstruction of the death of Lear's wife.

Gruach (1921): Imaginative reconstruction of circumstances leading up to *Macbeth.*

Poems and Plays (1953): Collection of his most significant work.

SOMERSET MAUGHAM (1874-1965) 325-6

Maugham was born in Paris, and educated at Canterbury and Heidelberg. He studied medicine at St. Thomas' Hospital, but left the profession for letters.

Of Human Bondage (1915): Reflects early hospital days.

The Moon and Sixpence (1919): Based on Gauguin's life. 325-6

East of Suez (1922): Close knowledge of the East.

The Painted Veil (1925): Chinese life in time of plague.

Ashenden (1928): Spy stories of distinction.

The Breadwinner (1930): Lack of sympathy between generations. 325

Cakes and Ale (1930): Vagaries of human nature.

A Writer's Notebook (1949): A harvest of wit and wisdom. 325

Page

Complete Short Stories, 3 vols. (1951): Seven of these were made into two films, *Trio* and *Quartet*.

JOHN MASEFIELD (1878-1967) 321

Born in Ledbury, Masefield served his apprenticeship on a windjammer, and later studied medicine in New York. From 1897 he settled in England, pursuing authorship as his profession. He became Poet Laureate in 1930.

Salt Water Ballads (1902): Swinging sea-faring lyrics.

The Widow in the Bye Street (1912): *Crime passionel.* 321

Dauber (1913): The making of a young artist. 321

Poems (1946): The chief collected edition.

E. M. FORSTER (1879-1970) 329

Forster was educated at Tonbridge and Cambridge.

A Room with a View (1908): Set in an Italian landscape.

Howards End (1910): Early work of mature subtlety.

A Passage to India (1924): Foreshadowing later political events.

ALFRED NOYES (1880-1958) 319

Noyes was born at Wolverhampton, and educated at Oxford. He visited America in 1913, and lectured at Harvard. He spent some years in California, and became professor of poetry at Princeton, giving lectures throughout Canada and the United States. Later, he settled in the Isle of Wight.

The Flower of Old Japan (1903): A collection of poems.

Drake (1908): A verse epic of Elizabethan seamen. 312

Collected Poems (1950): With additions to the 1927 edition.

Two Worlds for Memory (1953): An autobiography.

LYTTON STRACHEY (1880-1932) 331

Strachey was born in London, and educated at Cambridge. He reviewed books and, as his special province, adopted historical biography which aimed at debunking the over-reverent attitude of previous biographers; in some cases an element of malicious guesswork adds liveliness to his style, but impairs his value as an historian.

Eminent Victorians (1918) } His best-known works. 15

Queen Victoria (1921) } 331

JOHN DRINKWATER (1882-1937) 317-8

Born in London, Drinkwater was educated at Oxford High

Page

School. He became a clerk to the Northern Assurance Company at Nottingham and Birmingham, where he met Barry Jackson, who introduced him to literature. From 1910 he devoted himself to Birmingham Repertory Theatre, and from 1918 till 1925 a succession of his plays was produced there, securing fame and success.

Abraham Lincoln (1918): Reflects the first World War. 317-8

Mary Stuart (1921), ***Oliver Cromwell*** (1921), ***Robert E. Lee*** (1923): Serious in approach, these plays established his reputation as a dramatist.

JAMES JOYCE (1882-1941) 23

Born in Dublin, Joyce was educated at Jesuit schools and at the Catholic University. He studied theology, languages and medicine, and also trained as a singer. At first religious, he soon turned against the Catholic church. He went to live on the Continent, but always wrote about Ireland.

Dubliners (1914): A collection of fifteen short stories.

Portrait of the Artist as a Young Man (1916): First novel..

Exiles (1918): A play showing the influence of Ibsen.

Ulysses (1922): Eighteen hours in the life of three Dubliners. 15, 22

Finnegan's Wake (1939): Almost unintelligible.

ST. JOHN ERVINE (1883-) 316

Born and educated in Belfast, Ervine became manager of the Abbey Theatre at Dublin in 1915. He was a critic and novelist, but is now chiefly remembered as a playwright.

Jane Clegg (1911): Picture of north-country life.

John Ferguson (1914): Irish tragedy.

The First Mrs. Fraser (1928): Dramatized novel.

The Lady of Belmont (1928): Sequel to *The Merchant of Venice.*

Robert's Wife (1937): Clash between husband and wife. 316

JAMES ELROY FLECKER (1884-1915) 321

Born at Lewisham, Flecker was educated at Uppingham and Oxford. After attempts to teach, to live by writing and to qualify as an interpreter, he studied Oriental languages at Cambridge, and in 1910 was posted to Constantinople. He became ill with tuberculosis, and in 1913 went to Switzerland, where he died.

The Golden Journey to Samarkand (1913): Widely known for its echo of eastern music.

Page

Selected Poems (1918): Follows a 1916 collection.

Hassan (1923): Richly produced in London in 1923, set to music by Delius, with ballets by Fokine. 321

D. H. LAWRENCE (1885-1930) 322

Lawrence, the son of a miner, was born in the colliery area of Nottinghamshire. His mother, a teacher, fostered his talents, and Lawrence himself became a teacher. After some years on the Continent, he settled in Cornwall in 1916, and later moved to Derbyshire; but at the end of the war he again left England because of his health. He died in France.

The White Peacock (1911): Illustrates his personal style.

Sons and Lovers (1913): Shows developing command of medium.

Kangaroo (1923): Novel set in Australia.

Birds, Beasts and Flowers (1923): Close observation of life. 322

The Plumed Serpent (1926): Reflects Mexican experiences.

SIEGFRIED SASSOON (1886-1967) 322

Sassoon was educated at Marlborough and Cambridge, and became an Honorary Fellow of Clare College. He won an M.C. in the first World War, but adopted pacifism later.

Satirical Poems (1926): On themes suggested by the first World War.

Memoirs of a Fox-Hunting Man (1928): Country scenes.

Memoirs of an Infantry Officer (1930): Reminiscences of the first World War.

Sherston's Progress (1936): Further autobiography.

Collected Poems (1947): Powerful indictments of war.

RUPERT BROOKE (1887-1915) 319

Born at Rugby, Brooke was educated there and at Cambridge, and became a Fellow of King's College. From 1910 he lived at the village of Grantchester, made famous by his poem. With Drinkwater, Gibson and Monro, he edited *Georgian Poetry, 1911 — 1914.* He travelled widely from 1913 to 1914. In 1914 he joined the Royal Naval Division and went to Greece, where he died of septicaemia. 320

1914 and other Poems (1915): The most widely known poems of the first World War. 314

John Webster and the Elizabethan Drama (1916): The critical thesis which gained Brooke a Fellowship.

	Page
Letters from America (1916): A prose record of travels.	
Collected Poems (1918): With a memoir by Sir Edward Marsh.	
T. S. ELIOT (1888-1965)	309-11
Born in Missouri, Eliot was educated at Harvard, the Sorbonne and Oxford. He settled in England, and became naturalized in 1927. After posts as a teacher and in a bank, he became a director of Faber and Faber. He was awarded a Nobel Prize in 1948.	320 426
Murder in the Cathedral (1935): The murder of Thomas Becket, a verse drama first played in Canterbury Cathedral.	309-10
Collected Poems 1909-35 (1936): Including ***The Waste Land*** and ***The Hollow Men.***	328
The Family Reunion (1939): Modern drama of Greek furies.	311, 320
The Four Quartets (1944): Associated with places which have significance for the author.	
The Cocktail Party (1950): Individual response to demands.	310-11
The Confidential Clerk (1954): Submerged desires.	311
The Elder Statesman (1959): Unresolved guilt.	
KATHERINE MANSFIELD (1888-1923)	329
Born in New Zealand and educated in London, she became a proficient 'cellist, but turned to literature. In 1918 she married John Middleton Murry. She contributed many short stories and reviews to journals.	
In a German Pension (1911) ***Bliss*** (1920) ***The Garden Party*** (1922) ***The Doves' Nest*** (1923) } All collections of short stories and sketches, distinguished by psychological truth and sincerity of style.	329
WILFRED OWEN (1893-1918)	322
Educated at London University, Owen joined the Artists' Rifles in 1916. In 1917 he was invalided home, but returned to France, where he gained the M.C., and was killed a week before the Armistice. His poems were published posthumously.	
Poems (1920 and 1931): Pity at the waste of war.	
J. B. PRIESTLEY (1894-)	317
Born in Bradford and educated at Cambridge, Priestley is a prolific author of novels, plays, essays and criticism.	
The English Comic Characters (1925): Critical studies.	
The Good Companions (1929): Travelling actors.	

Page

Dangerous Corner (1932): Experiment in dramatic technique.
Laburnum Grove (1933): Comedy on life of respectable crook.
Time and the Conways (1937) / ***I Have Been Here Before*** (1937) } Plays on the theme of time, experimenting in flash-back.
Johnson over Jordan (1939): A dying man sees the significant moments in the past, and moves forward.
An Inspector Calls (1946): A warning against shirking responsibility for war. 317

NOËL COWARD (1899-) 332

Coward, who was born at Teddington, has written, directed and acted in many plays and revues.

The Vortex (1926): His first established success.
Hay Fever (1926): Comedy of manners in a theatrical family.
Cavalcade (1931): Outstanding events of the century. 332
Present Indicative (1937): Lively autobiography.
Blithe Spirit (1941): Light-hearted mockery of spiritualism.
This Happy Breed (1943): A middle-class family in wartime.
Future Indefinite (1954): Continuation of autobiography.

GRAHAM GREENE (1904-) 318

Greene was born at Berkhamsted, and educated at Oxford. He became literary editor of *The Spectator* in 1940. From 1944 to 1948 he was a director of Eyre and Spottiswoode, and he became a director of the Bodley Head Press in 1958.

Stamboul Train (1932): Lively adventure.
Brighton Rock (1938): A study of youthful degeneracy.
The Power and the Glory (1940): The spiritual struggles of a cowardly heroic priest in South America.
The Heart of the Matter (1948): A matter of conscience.
The Third Man (1950): Post-war conditions.
The Living Room (1953): Reactions of members of a middle-class household to their personal tragedies.
The Potting Shed (1957): Reactions to a miracle. 318
Our Man in Havana (1958): Satirical social comment.

C. DAY-LEWIS (1904-) 320

Educated at Sherborne and Oxford, Day-Lewis later taught at various schools. With W. H. Auden he edited *Oxford Poetry, 1927*. In 1946 he became a lecturer at Trinity College, Cambridge, and he also became a director of Chatto and Windus. He was

Page

professor of Poetry at Oxford from 1951 to 1956, and has worked at the Ministry of Information. Day-Lewis writes detective stories under the pseudonym "Nicholas Blake."

The Poetic Image (1947): Scholarly in approach and style.
Collected Poems (1954): Covering a period of 25 years.
Pegasus (1957) } Showing in practice the principles put
The Gate (1962) } forward in lectures and essays.

SAMUEL BECKETT (1906-) 228, 314

Educated at Trinity College, Dublin, Beckett became a lecturer in English at Paris and in French at Dublin. He has written poems, criticism and novels, influenced by modern French literature, but is chiefly known for his plays, some of which were first written in French. 15

Waiting for Godot (1954): Two down-and-outs rely on help from unknown outside source, with indeterminate results. 228 314
Endgame (1957): The approach of not-being to those who have given up belief in life.
Krapp's Last Tape (1959): The chief character reviews his past in flash-backs.
Happy Days (1961): Explores the necessity of communication and the stultifying effects of habit.

JOHN BETJEMAN (1906-) 322

Educated at Marlborough and Oxford, Betjeman is a writer of accomplished verse on familiar subjects, especially architecture. He is also the author of some of the Shell guide books to English counties.

Old Lights for New Chancels (1945): Criticism in verse.
Selected Poems (1948): Wide range of modern subjects.
A Few Late Chrysanthemums (1954): Later poems.
Summoned by Bells (1960): Autobiography in verse.

LOUIS MACNEICE (1907-1963) 323

MacNeice, born in Belfast and educated at Marlborough and Oxford, became a lecturer on classical subjects and on poetry at various universities abroad. He was made director of the British Institute, Athens, in 1950.

The Poetry of W. B. Yeats (1941): Interpretative criticism.
Christopher Columbus (1944): An historical play for radio.
Collected Poems (1949) } Showing lyrical command and
Eighty-five Poems (1959) } sympathy.

Page

W. H. AUDEN (1907-) 320, 323

Educated at Gresham's School and Oxford, Auden served with the Revolutionaries in the Spanish Civil War. He edited the *Oxford Book of Light Verse* in 1938, and the *Faber Book of Modern American Verse* in 1956. From 1956 to 1961 he was professor of Poetry at Oxford.

The Ascent of F6 (1936): Verse play written with Isherwood.
Selected Poems (1940)
Collected Shorter Poems (1950) } Stimulating poems based on his own experience.

CHRISTOPHER FRY (1907-) 309

Educated at Bedford Modern School, Fry became a theatre director at Tunbridge Wells (1932-5) and at Oxford. He has translated plays by Giraudoux and Anouilh. 311-3, 332

A Phoenix Too Frequent (1946): Based on a tale by Petronius.
The Lady's Not For Burning (1949): His spring play. 312-3
Venus Observed (1950): His autumn play. 312
A Sleep of Prisoners (1951): Imaginative throwback of soldiers imprisoned in a church to their Biblical prototypes. 314
The Dark is Light Enough (1954): His winter play. 312-3
Curtmantle (1961): Clash between Henry II and Becket. 309

STEPHEN SPENDER (1909-) 319

Educated at Oxford, Spender was a contemporary of Auden, MacNeice and Day-Lewis. He has travelled extensively in Europe. He became co-editor of *Horizon* in 1939, and of *Encounter* in 1953. He has held professorships at Cincinnati and California.

Ruins and Visions (1941)
Poems of Dedication (1946)
The Edge of Being (1949) } Chiefly expressing ideas roused by the second World War.

World Within World (1951): An autobiography.
Collected Poems (1955): The best of his previous work.
The Struggle of the Modern (1963): In conflict with present discontents.

DYLAN THOMAS (1914-1953) 324

Thomas, the son of a Swansea school-teacher, worked for a time as a reporter.

Portrait of the Artist as a Young Dog (1940): Autobiography.
The Doctor and the Devils (1953): About Burke and Hare.
Collected Poems (1952): Includes his well-known ***Fern Hill.***

Page

Under Milk Wood (1954): A day in a small Welsh village. 324

Adventures in the Skin Trade (1955): An unfinished novel.

JOHN WAIN (1925-) 323

Born at Stoke-on-Trent and educated at Newcastle-under-Lyme and Oxford, Wain became a Fellow of St. John's College and lecturer in English at Reading University (1947-55).

Living in the Present (1955): Reflections on contemporary themes.

A Word Carved on a Sill (1956): Collected poems.

Strike the Father Dead (1962): Modern youth in revolt.

JOHN OSBORNE (1929-) 313-4

Educated at Belmont College, Devon, Osborne gained his knowledge of stage conditions and techniques as an actor in touring and repertory companies.

Look Back in Anger (1956): The chief character, Jimmy Porter, was the original "angry young man." 313, 315

The Entertainer (1957): A study of music-hall tradition. 313-4

Luther (1961): Serious and effective historical drama.

HAROLD PINTER (1930-) 314

Pinter was educated at Hackney. His experience of London life and of the stage (repertory, wireless and television) is reflected in his plays which, essentially serious and challenging, take their place in the *avant-garde* Theatre of the Absurd.

The Birthday Party; The Room; The Dumb Waiter (1960): Three plays presenting the pressure of modern conditions. 314

The Caretaker (1960): Responsible and irresponsible elements.

A Slight Ache (1961): The necessity of communication.

ARNOLD WESKER (1932-) 314

Educated at Hackney, Wesker worked as furniture-maker, bookseller, plumber's mate and cook. His work shows close and sympathetic knowledge of Jewish life, and a deep love of the land.

Chicken Soup with Barley
Roots
I'm Talking About Jerusalem
} Published as a trilogy in 1960. 314

Chips with Everything (1962): Sympathetic study of the pressures of service life towards uniformity.

ANSWERING THE QUESTION

Aims of the Examination

A KNOWLEDGE of these aims will help you to see what kinds of question are likely to be set, and what kind of answer will be most satisfactory. In general, the examination has two purposes: first, to increase your enjoyment of literature, by widening your range of reading; secondly, to improve your powers of reading and writing. In reading, the examiners want to give you opportunities to see what an author is aiming at, and to distinguish between different kinds of writing; in writing, they want you to form opinions, express them clearly and briefly, and illustrate them by apt references.

Bearing these intentions in mind, you can see that you need to read carefully, to understand the author's meaning, and to think clearly about it. Mechanical reading of explanatory notes, learning by heart a few passages that textbooks say are important, or dutifully memorizing somebody else's phrases of admiration are not good ways of tackling the examination. Every examiner is dismally aware that such things are done; but no examiner can give high marks for dullness or insincerity. The first thing is to know your books, and to enjoy them as fully and personally as you can; the second thing is to be able to write answers in which your understanding and enjoyment are evident. These needs govern the choices which we are to consider next.

Choice

(i) CHOICE OF BOOKS. This choice is to some extent beyond your control: if you are at school the choice will be made for you. It is important, however, that the books should be within your range, and examining bodies recognize this by offering a fair choice of texts. Some candidates thrive on Shakespeare and Conrad; others do not, and will gain little from reading what they cannot enjoy, but they may be able to get real pleasure from tackling Chaucer and Dickens. Private candidates should ask for advice, or look quickly through some of the alternative texts to see which they like best.

You should never choose a book merely because it is considered a great work; all the books set are, one hopes, set because they are worth reading. A work of imagination makes its effect by pleasing the reader, and this necessity of enjoyment should be remembered by everyone concerned in the choice of books for examinations. To write with affection and understanding about the Wife of Bath or Joe Gargery is far better than repeating other people's opinions about Olivia or Duke Senior, or concealing one's own view about the Forsaken Merman.

(ii) CHOICE OF QUESTIONS. Most questions fall into one of four kinds, each requiring different treatment:

(*a*) Context questions.

(*b*) Questions on characters.

(*c*) Reproduction in detail, either of incidents or of the historical setting.

(*d*) Questions involving some aspect of literary criticism. These kinds will be considered separately and in detail below; for the moment, it is enough to note that (*a*), (*b*) and (*c*) are much easier to answer than (*d*), though they may look harder because they demand precise knowledge. Such a question as "Say why you have enjoyed reading this book" appears easy, but it demands just as much knowledge of fact as the others, *plus* a more mature critical appreciation and power to put one's personal opinions into persuasive language.

Questions of this kind are put in for the good candidates, but are most often answered, disastrously, by those looking for an easy way out. Candidates who feel doubts about their ability should read their books carefully, and stick to questions of types (*a*), (*b*) and (*c*).

(iii) CHOICE OF MATERIAL. This will be dealt with by examples in the following sections. You need reminding only that time is short, and the more you know, the more you need to select the material for your answers. Be brief; stick to the point; keep a sense of proportion. Many enthusiastic candidates, asked for a single detail about a character, tell the whole story, and never have time to answer later questions at all.

The Types of Question

(*a*) CONTEXTS. These are usually short passages of five or six lines, with specific questions to answer, but sometimes a longer piece is set for extended comment. This is a harder type of question, because not so much guidance is offered. Contexts demand close knowledge, and you must give detailed answers.

(i) First, be concise; sometimes a whole side is written as answer to a part of a question carrying only one or two marks. For instance, a question on the opening of *Henry V*, Act II, Scene 2 (the scene in which the conspiracy to kill Henry at Southampton is unmasked) might ask, "Who were the traitors, and what deed had they planned?" A correct answer would be, "Scroop, Cambridge and Grey were the traitors and they had planned to kill the king at Southampton." This would earn full marks, which would at most be two. A bad answer would include wholesale quotation from his long speech of reproach, because it had been learnt by heart. *Give only the details you are asked for; unnecessary details only waste your time, and earn no marks.*

(ii) Explanation of passages is sometimes asked for; allusions to mythology, literature or history should be briefly explained and the reason for their use made clear. For example, consider this passage, from *Richard II* (IV i):

"Though some of you with Pilate wash your hands,
Showing an outward pity—yet you Pilates
Have here delivered me to my sour cross
And water cannot wash away your sin."

Here you need to do two things: first, to explain the reference to Pilate and the cross, and secondly, to show how this reference fits the situation in which these lines are spoken. And, as always, you must be brief.

An explanation might go like this: "Just as Pilate tried to claim his innocence of Christ's death by calling for water and publicly washing his hands, so Richard's nobles are pretending to be sorry about the abdication; but they are as guilty as Pilate was: he executed God's Son; they are deposing God's representative."

(iii) Translation or paraphrase: the things to remember are that mere word-for-word substitution is not wanted, nor is a slavish following of sentence construction:

"What sholde he studie, and make himselven wood,
Upon a book in cloistre alwey to poure,
Or swinken with his handes, and laboure,
As Austin bit?"

should appear as

> What! Was he supposed to be a student, and send himself crazy, everlastingly hanging over a book in the cloisters, or to work hard with his hands—manual labour!—as Augustine orders?

(Note that the verse passage is turned into prose: line divisions have no meaning once the rhythm has disappeared. Also there has been an attempt to reproduce the Monk's shocked tone at the idea that he should work.)

Notes at the end are permissible, if a modern rendering cannot give a full explanation in fluent language: e.g. "the greet superfluytee of your rede choler" could be translated as "the great excess of red choler in your body," and a footnote added saying that choler was one of the four humours or liquids in the body believed to influence a person's constitution and character.

A metaphor is often best translated by expanding it into a simile, e.g.:

"My father hath a power; enquire of him,
And learn to make a body of a limb" (*Richard II*)

could be rendered as, "My father has an army; find out where he is, and try to make this smaller force serve as your main army, as if the strength of a part were to replace that of the whole."

(iv) Comment, in one form or another, on the poetic or dramatic effectiveness of a passage can be harder than the preceding types of question. "What do you find beautiful in this passage?" and "What is the poet's purpose in these lines?" give little guidance to a candidate, though a careful look at the passage will usually show you what the examiner had in mind. Provided that you talk sense and do not wander away from the lines set for discussion, you will do well enough, but you must be precise: vague sounds of approval such as "This is a beautiful poem, full of metre" (an actual answer once handed in) can convey nothing worth the trouble of writing or reading.

The description of Porphyro's preparations before waking Madeline is the kind of passage that might well be set for comment of this sort.

> "And still she slept an azure-lidded sleep,
> In blanched linen, smooth, and lavender'd,
> While he from forth the closet brought a heap
> Of candied apple, quince, and plum, and gourd
> With jellies soother than the creamy curd,
> And lucent syrops, tinct with cinnamon;
> Manna and dates, in argosy transferr'd
> From Fez; and spiced dainties, every one,
> From silken Samarcand to cedar'd Lebanon."

If asked about the poet's purpose, you would note the profusion of rich imagery: fruits, jellies, syrups, Oriental dainties and place-names, reminding us of the wealth of the Caliphs and of Solomon. This you would use to show that the poet intended to convey an impression of sensuous richness and luxury to correspond with the ardour of Porphyro's love. And then, noting the cool suggestions of linen, lavender, azure-lidded, the sharpness of quinces and of cinnamon, you would add that the rich impressions are carefully held in check by these other images, so that the final effect is one of controlled richness, not of excess or vulgarity.

This type of question needs a little patient reading, so that you can see precisely what is being asked; then answer that—and no more. Similar care is needed in the various types of essay question that we are to discuss next.

(*b*) CHARACTER QUESTIONS. The first point to note is that these are not usually narrative questions, of a kind that can be answered by straightforward reproduction of the story. Four main types can be distinguished:

(i) For the first, a likely wording would be, "Sketch the character of . . . , giving a close account of what he says and does, and of what others say about him." This is the most straightforward kind of character question, and is likely to be set about only a comparatively minor character who makes a few noteworthy appearances. You must take care not to stray outside the limits of the question by giving a full account of speeches or incidents in his scenes which do not directly affect or concern him. You are concerned with one person only, not with the whole story. Once launched, an unwary candidate may go straight ahead with a complete recapitulation of everything.

(ii) A question on a major character will probably be limited in some way, for instance, "Write an account of Mr. Polly's first visit to the Larkinses, and say what it reveals of his character." Look carefully at the question, and in particular at the second part. Only such indications of his character as the first visit shows are required. A candidate who has prepared Polly's character carefully, and learnt his notes, will be tempted to add many details such as Polly's irritability when suffering from indigestion, his failure to "buck up," or his resourcefulness in such unexpected crises as the fire or the war with Uncle Jim. Nothing outside the prescribed scene is wanted.

Such a question may ask for the development of a character as shown in certain specified scenes, or for an account of his motives for certain actions; or some critical comment about the character may be put up for you to discuss. In each case, you must look very closely at the aspects of character

Mr. Polly first meets his cousins, the Larkinses, at a funeral, and later visits them at their home.

Professor Higgins and Eliza Doolittle, from Shaw's play Pygmalion.

you are asked to deal with. Marks can be given only for what is relevant.

(iii) A question may be so worded that a particular approach is demanded, e.g. "Show how the Queen in *Richard II* is presented so as to command our sympathy," or "Describe the character in *Pygmalion* who seems to you to be the most amusing." Sympathy or amusement, or whatever response is to be considered, must be in the forefront of your mind in answering such questions, and details must be chosen accordingly. Above all, you must avoid vague or generalizing remarks. If you can remember nothing very amusing about *Pygmalion* at all, you should try to answer another question, because you will not do yourself justice on that one.

(iv) A character question is sometimes set in a different way, demanding attention to the book as a whole rather than to a character in isolation, e.g. "Select *two* of the following characters, and show their importance to the play: Duncan, Banquo, Lady Macduff." You should deal briefly with the main events in which these characters are concerned, showing why you think them important; for instance, you might say that the appearance of Banquo's ghost at the banquet makes Macbeth destroy the good order he is trying to recreate, or that the murder of Lady Macduff brings about an understanding and alliance between Macduff and Malcolm which is to overthrow Macbeth.

You should also think carefully how the dramatist has made use of these minor characters to arouse our feelings: Duncan as the embodiment of the goodness and life-giving generosity which Macbeth destroys, Banquo as a contrast to Macbeth, and Lady Macduff as an instance of the pathetic fragility of tenderness and family love in Macbeth's Scotland. Descriptive details should be chosen to bring out these points, and such aspects as the dramatic irony of Duncan's entry into Inverness should be made clear.

Preparation of questions on characters should be done with the following four headings in mind:

(*a*) What he looks like.
(*b*) What he says or does.
(*c*) Why he behaves as he does.
(*d*) Why the writer has put him in, i.e. his effect on the plot, on the behaviour of others, on the reader or audience, or as part of the meaning of the whole book.

Attention to (*c*) and (*d*) above is very important, as it often makes the difference between mechanical reading and real understanding. Such understanding will, incidentally, help to make the answer to the second part of an essay question easier.

For instance, a reader who has thought only about (*a*) and (*b*) will be well prepared for the first part of such a question as "Describe the changes in Catherine Morland's feelings about Isabella. How far do you think she is justified in changing?"; but that reader will be less able to deal promptly with the second part of the question than one who has thought about the contrast between Isabella and Eleanor, about Jane Austen's concept of "elegance," and about Catherine's gradual education by her companions.

(*c*) REPRODUCTION QUESTIONS. These are of two main kinds: (i) straightforward accounts, and (ii) reproduction with some added comment or with the aim of illustrating some specified points.

(i) Straightforward accounts. These offer little difficulty provided that you know the book well and can put plenty of relevant and important detail into your answers. You may be asked to give an account of an incident or of a scene, e.g. "Summarize the arguments used by Cassius to persuade Brutus to join the conspiracy," or "Describe Marlow's experiences in connexion with the *Judea* up to the time of the explosion on the ship." Or you may be asked for detail from the historical background used in the book: "What does the *Nun's Priest's Tale* show us of English country life in Chaucer's time?" or "What impression have you gained from *Quentin Durward* of court life in the fifteenth century?" Sometimes it is the author's own characteristics that are asked for: "Illustrate from the *Pardoner's Tale* the scope of Chaucer's reading and other interests, or his skill in describing people and scenes."

In all these questions, you must notice carefully the limits set on your answer. If you chose the questions given as examples above, you would, for instance, need to be sure that you included none of Marlow's experiences during the abandonment of the ship, because they took place *after* the explosion. You would not describe Cassius' speech about Brutus' noble nature, as it comes after Brutus has left the stage. You would leave out Chanticleer's dreams, though you would be right to include the detailed references to country medicines. You would have to take care that your account of the Courts of Louis and Charles did not turn into sketches of the rulers' characters.

This last fault is perhaps the commonest in reproduction questions: whatever is asked for, narrative is turned out, often at far greater length than the question demands, and including much that has no direct reference to the question. You need to think carefully about the whole book, and to arrange your material into orderly notes before you begin to write.

(ii) Reproduction with comment. Such a question is more usual than (i), and more interesting to answer: it means that you can show something of your understanding of the author's plan as well as your memory for his words. For instance, you might be asked, "Give an account, mainly in your own words, of Chaucer's descriptions (*a*) of the Widow and her cottage at the beginning of the *Nun's Priest's Tale*, and (*b*) of Chanticleer and Pertelote. What contrasts do you find between the two descriptions?"

The first part of the answer is a straightforward reproduction, using your own words; in the second part you can point out the contrast by showing how the Widow's simple life is described in homely language with rustic detail ("Three large sows; sometimes an egg or two; a yard enclosed with sticks"); then you can compare with this the grand vocabulary of heraldry, courtly life and love, and the high-sounding lines which introduce the cock and hen ("embattled like a castle; whiter than the lily-flower; the fair demoiselle"). You might conclude with a brief statement of the contrast between pride and humility which these differences seem designed to point out to listeners.

Another question of this type asks for an account of a scene or scenes and for their importance in the novel or play from which they come. Again, this gives you a chance to show that you have understood the author's scheme and intentions, and the second part of the question should be as carefully done as the first.

Suppose that you were asked to show how the meeting in *Macbeth* between the old man, Ross and Macduff is important in the development of the play. You could first point out that Ross and the old man discuss the King's murder in such a way that we feel it as a thing outrageous to the order of the universe. Macduff's first speech shows us that not everyone is satisfied with the explanation of Duncan's death. His description of Macbeth's movements makes us feel the indecent haste of the proceedings, and his final remark sounds a warning note about the future. More points can be made, but these four would show that you understand the play's construction.

It would not be enough to consider the scene merely for its contribution to the plot (we learn that Macbeth is to be king, and that Macduff will not be at the coronation), though this remark is not by any means irrelevant.

The second part of a question of this type may be so closely bound up with the first that they can be combined. Such a question is, "Describe the interview of the squire with the vicar in *Under the Greenwood Tree*, showing how Hardy makes it lively and amusing."

The main points in dealing with these "reproduction with comment" questions are:

(i) to notice what kind of comment has been asked for;
(ii) to remember that it may carry half the marks;
(iii) to answer it with plenty of illustrative detail.

(*d*) CRITICAL QUESTIONS. These, as we said before, are harder than the kinds discussed in (*b*) and (*c*) above. You should try them only if you feel that you are good at this sort of work. They are not easy ways out for those who cannot remember much about the book.

(i) Sometimes a whole poem or lengthy prose passage is printed in the question paper for you to comment on. Questions are usually in general terms such as, "Comment on the style and general effectiveness," or, "Write an appreciation of the poem, considering the figurative language, diction and rhythm." Sometimes questions are a little more specific: "Show how the piece conveys the atmosphere of the place described." Sometimes they merely invite you to, "Say why you have enjoyed the poem."

These questions, though they occur in the essay part of the paper, should be treated in the same way as those context questions which give a lengthy extract for comment; and the advice given under (*a*) (iv) above applies here also. Read the piece carefully, and make up your mind why it has been set. Confine your answer to points you think important, taking care not to go beyond the limits of the question. Illustrate by detailed reference.

(ii) Sometimes two poems are set for comparison, for instance, Kipling's and Untermeyer's poems about machines in *Rhyme and Reason*. There is usually a clear contrast between them: in the two mentioned, there is a sharp difference between Kipling's admiration for the machine's power, with his feeling that man is master, and Untermeyer's admiration for its beauty, with his feeling that the machine is master. Once this contrast has been noticed (probably during your reading of the book beforehand), contrasts in imagery, rhythm, vocabulary and tone can be used to illustrate it.

(iii) Sometimes you are given a freer hand: you are simply asked to give a detailed account of any poem that has attracted you. You may be asked to comment on its imagery, ideas or musical effect, making clear the nature of its appeal to you. "Making clear" is the phrase to attend to; you will only do this by detailed, frequent and apt quotation or reference. You would be wise to think over, in advance, some poems you have really liked; but unless you have a good knowledge, and can quote or refer closely, you should leave questions of this kind alone.

General Advice

(i) Read the question very carefully, and make sure you understand what you are asked to do.

(ii) Do not go beyond the limits of the question.

(iii) Even within these limits, keep to the point.

(iv) Keep an eye on the clock: unless you are told anything to the contrary, questions carry equal marks, and you can divide your time accordingly.

(v) Spell the names of books, authors and characters correctly.

(vi) Do not describe serious or dignified incidents and characters in trivial off-hand language: "Caesar was bumped off by Brutus"; "The knight had a go at all sorts of fighting"; "The Maid of Astolat made a pass at Lancelot." Such expressions only show that you have mistaken the tone of the book you are writing about.

(vii) *Most important:* Quote accurately whenever you can, and refer closely to the text if you cannot quote exactly. Remember, though, that your references must be to the point; several short apt quotations score far more, even if they are not word perfect, than a long passage evidently learned by heart for inclusion in any answer, whether appropriate or not. The examination tests understanding, not memory.

QUESTIONS CONSIDERED IN DETAIL

(A) Contexts

There is usually a choice of passages, of equal difficulty and carrying equal marks. Look at them all before you make up your mind. Note the time available, usually ten or fifteen minutes for each passage. The chief types are as follows:

(i) short passages with specific questions;
(ii) short passages with less exact questions;
(iii) pieces for translation;

Caesar's wife, Calphurnia, begs him not to visit the Senate.

(iv) pieces for critical comment.

In the specimens that follow, questions of all these kinds will be examined.

Question 1

> "The cause is in my will: I will not come;
> That is enough to satisfy the Senate;
> But, for your private satisfaction,
> Because I love you, I will let you know,—
> Calphurnia here, my wife, stays me at home." (*Julius Caesar*)

(i) Who is speaking, and to whom?
(ii) What has prompted Calphurnia to keep him at home?
(iii) What contrary explanation of her fears is given in this scene?

NOTES

Answers should be as brief as possible. Two or three details are usually wanted. Nothing but memory of the scene is here being tested.

SUGGESTED ANSWER

(i) Caesar is speaking to Decius Brutus. (No more need be said.)
(ii) She fears that he is in danger, because she has dreamt that his statue

spouted blood like a fountain, and that many smiling Romans came and bathed their hands in it. (Calphurnia's fear is mentioned first, and then the reason for her fear is given. Note that the dream contains two separate details.)

(iii) Decius suggests that the dream is a good omen: the blood means that Rome is to be revived by Caesar; the Romans bathing their hands suggest that he is to be courted by them. (A full explanation needs to be given; the two details quoted in (ii) are interpreted in the answer to (iii). It would not be enough to say that Decius says that the dream has been interpreted wrongly.

Question 2

"*Thou dost thy office fairly.* Turn thee back
And tell thy king I do not seek him now,
But could be willing to march on to Calais
Without impeachment." (*Henry V*)

(i) Who is speaking? Who is being addressed, and what "office" has he done?

(ii) Who is the king mentioned by the speaker? What has he sent to demand from the speaker?

(iii) Where did the speaker and the person addressed next meet, and on

Surrounded by his men, Henry V gives a message to the French herald.

what occasion? Give *briefly* two arguments from the speaker's answer on that occasion.

(iv) Explain the phrases in italics.

SUGGESTED ANSWER

(i) King Henry is speaking to Montjoy, who has come as a herald. (As before, keep your answer as short as possible. If the question will permit a one-word answer, give it.)

(ii) King Charles of France; ransom.

(iii) At Agincourt, before the battle. (Be careful; they also meet afterwards, but the question asks for the *next* meeting.) Many points are available to answer the second part of this question. Choose two which are not too long, but make complete sense. Any two of the following would do: A man who sold a lion's skin before he had caught the lion was killed in the hunt; even the dead English would be fighting the French, because their rotting bodies would breed a plague; though the English looked shabby, their hearts were high; they would soon have new clothes, by taking them from the French; Henry offered no ransom except his dead body.

(iv) "Thou dost thy office fairly" = You are carrying out your errand courteously.

"Without impeachment" = Without hindrance.

Question 3

"I met a traveller from an antique land
Who said: Two vast and trunkless legs of stone
Stand in the desert."

(i) What was the name of the man the statue represented? What other part of the statue remained?

(ii) Give three details describing the man's appearance and character.

(iii) Give the sense of the inscription on the pedestal. How does the poet intend us to take these words?

NOTES

The first two questions are simply tests of your knowledge. The third calls for understanding, both of the meaning and of the poet's intention.

SUGGESTED ANSWER

(i) Ozymandias; a shattered visage.

(ii) The face bore a frown, a wrinkled lip and a sneer.

(iii) I am Ozymandias, a king over all other kings. Those who think themselves powerful should look at what I have performed, and realize that they can never be so great.

By first describing the ruin of the statue, Shelley makes us feel that Ozymandias' words mock his own claim to be mighty. The question demands a paraphrase of the inscription, not a direct quotation. The explanation of how we are intended to take the inscription is backed up by reference to the structure of the poem.

Context questions on novels do not depend quite so much on exact memory of verbal detail. Instead they tend to concentrate on notable features of character, either mental or physical, and on your understanding of the significance of events, and how they affect the fortunes or feelings of people they concern.

Question 4

> "Standing at this table, I became conscious of the servile Pumblechook in a black cloak and several yards of hat-band, who was alternately stuffing himself, and making obsequious movements to catch my attention. The moment he succeeded, he came over to me (breathing sherry and crumbs), and said in a subdued voice, 'May I, dear sir?' and did."
>
> (*Great Expectations*)

(i) What had caused this meeting in the Gargerys' parlour? What did Joe and Pip think of the preparations and ceremonies carried out there?

(ii) Why is Pumblechook called servile? What does he mean by, "May I?"; when had he asked such permission before?

(iii) How had he treated Pip when they were both present in the parlour on Christmas Day?

NOTES

(i) is concerned with the funeral of Mrs. Joe, and demands an understanding of the feelings of the chief people there. The other questions are all about Pumblechook, and turn on the change in his behaviour when he realized that Pip was rich.

SUGGESTED ANSWER

(i) Mrs. Joe's death had caused the meeting. Joe thought it would have been pleasanter to have a simple funeral, but that it would not have seemed respectful in the eyes of the neighbours. Pip thought Trabb's arrangements were a horrible pretence and distraction. (This passage is an instance of the novelist's attack on judging by outward show, one of the main themes of the book.)

(ii) Pumblechook seemed servile to Pip because he became very humble when he found out that Pip had come into money. When Pip went to order his clothes for London, he had lunch with Pumblechook, who kept asking if he might shake Pip's hand.

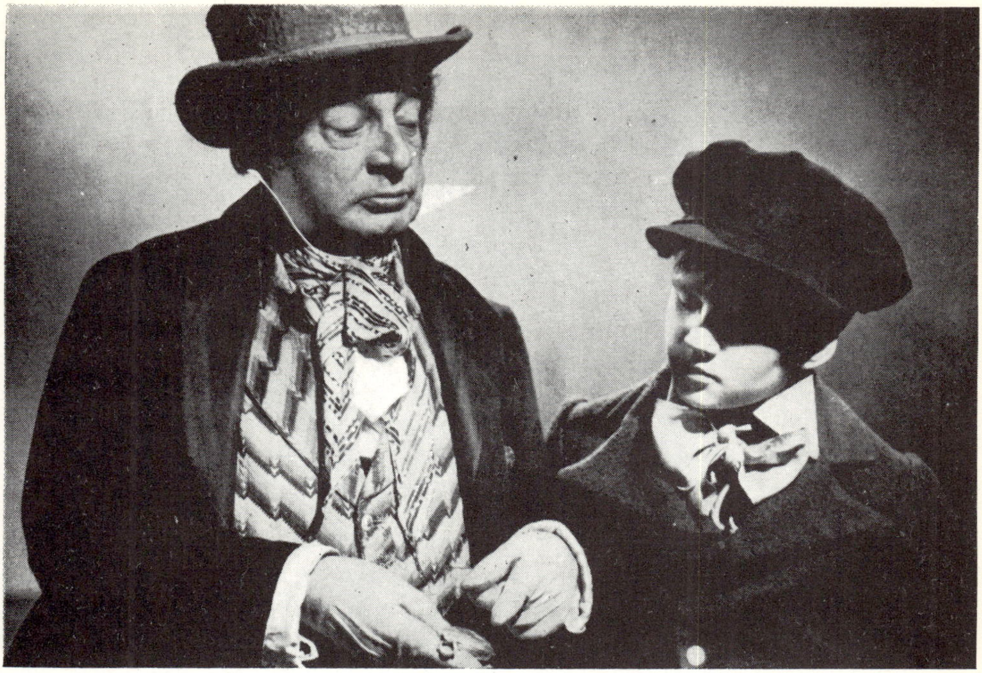

Pip and Uncle Pumblechook, from Charles Dickens' Great Expectations.

(iii) At the Christmas dinner when Pip was a child, Pumblechook told Pip in a bullying way to be grateful to "them which brought you up by hand."

Some Examination Boards do not ask specific questions on each passage, but instead give a large selection of passages, and ask you to choose three or four and then state briefly but exactly where they come from, showing their connexion with the immediate context, and explaining the parts in italics. As in the questions already considered, the first thing to remember is to keep to the point; "the immediate context" means the scene or passage in which the lines occur, and is not an invitation to talk about the whole story or scheme of the piece.

Question 5

"Now he goes,
With no less presence, but with much more love,
Than young Alcides, when he did redeem
The virgin tribute paid by howling Troy
To the sea-monster." (*The Merchant of Venice*)

SUGGESTED ANSWER

These lines are spoken by Portia about Bassanio, as he moves up to the caskets to make his choice. Alcides is Hercules, who rescued Hesione, daughter of the King of Troy, from a monster sent by the gods to ravage the city. Bassanio is as noble in appearance as Hercules, and less mercenary. Hercules acted for the reward, not for love of Hesione.

NOTES

In such a question, lines are identified by giving the speaker, the person spoken to or about, and the occasion. You should not write out the events of the whole scene, nor explain how the situation arose.

The italicized lines here contain three separate points: the identity and deeds of Alcides, and the two phrases, "no less presence" and "much more love." Details of the legend about Hesione are not needed; even her name is not essential, provided that you can show you understand why she is referred to.

Question 6

"Had I so lavish of my presence been,
So common-hackneyed in the eyes of men,
So stale and cheap to vulgar company,
Opinion, that did help me to the crown,
Had still kept loyal to possession." (*Henry IV*, *Part One*)

NOTES

The chief difficulties are the abstract nouns *opinion* and *possession*: they conceal a good deal of concentrated reference. The historical background will need explanation.

SUGGESTED ANSWER

These lines are spoken by Henry IV to the Prince of Wales in their reconciliation scene before Shrewsbury. Rebuking the prince for making himself cheap in the people's eyes by being friendly with Falstaff, King Henry says that if *he* had behaved so, the people would have chosen to remain faithful to Richard, who then held the crown.

Henry IV admonishes Prince Hal.

We turn now to the rather more difficult type of context question, in which you are asked for some explanation about the main effect of the passage.

Keep your answer short, but reinforce it with exact reference to the text.

Question 7

"First, robed in white, the nymph intent adores,
With head uncovered, the cosmetic powers.
A heavenly image in the glass appears,
To that she bends, to that her eyes she rears;
Th' inferior priestess, at her altar's side,
Trembling begins the sacred rites of pride." (*The Rape of the Lock*)

What is the poet's purpose in this passage?

NOTES

You are not asked to give the meaning of any words or phrases, and so should not attempt a paraphrase. Consider the passage as a whole, and put down the general intention as it appears to you. Then look for two or three detailed examples of how the effect has been made.

SUGGESTED ANSWER

Pope is here making fun of the absurdity of such devotion to one's appearance. He does this by describing making-up one's face as if it were a religious ceremony, reminding us here and there that the devout language is being misapplied: "*cosmetic* powers" are worshipped instead of heavenly ones; the maid becomes a priestess, the toilet-table an altar. But the image worshipped is Belinda's own, and pride is a sin. (A great deal more might be said, including comment on Pope's creation of a delicate beauty in the situation he is mocking, or on the firm moral basis from which he makes his attack; but you are told to be brief, and must pick out what seems to you the most important impression.)

Question 8

"I'll give my jewels for a set of beads,
My gorgeous palace for a hermitage,
My gay apparel for an almsman's gown,
My figur'd goblets for a dish of wood,
My sceptre for a palmer's walking-staff,
My subjects for a pair of carved saints,
And my large kingdom for a little grave,
A little, little grave, an obscure grave." (*Richard II*)

What do you learn about the speaker's character in these lines?

NOTES

In a play, the occasion when you say something may be as important as what you actually say. Think first of the situation (Richard's landing from

Ireland), and then of the language and sentiments. You will notice balance, contrast, elaborate detail and repetition at the end. All these tell us something about the speaker.

SUGGESTED ANSWER

Richard II has just learnt that he has no soldiers left to resist the usurper, Bolingbroke. After swinging between wild hope and abject despair, he says that he will give up his throne and become a hermit, an idea which appeals to his imagination. He lovingly and carefully works out in elaborate detail the contrast between king and hermit, making it all sound very beautiful; and ends with a self-pitying emphasis on the "little, little grave," all the land he can now call his own. The speech shows that he prefers words to actions, enjoys being unfortunate, loves playing with ideas, and is sorry for himself.

A prose passage would be treated in the same way. Consider the situation, and then examine the language closely.

Question 9

"I thought, however, that the pleasantest toys to play with during this interval were my pistols, and now and then, when I listlessly visited my loaded barrels with the swivel ramrods, or drew a sweet musical click from my English firelocks, it seemed to me that I exercised a slight and gentle influence on the debate." (*Eothen*)

What is the effect made by choice of words and phrasing in this passage?

NOTES

The general effect is of amusement at the casual way in which Kinglake describes his way of showing the Arabs that he will fight if they try to rob him. Words to note are "pleasantest toys to play with," "visited," "sweet musical click," "exercised a slight and gentle influence on the debate."

SUGGESTED ANSWER

The main words and phrases of this passage (here you would list those already noted) give an agreeable and friendly tone to the description, which is an amusing contrast to the actual situation. In fact, Kinglake is waiting while his guides dispute about robbing him; he amuses himself, and gives us an impression of his coolness in face of danger, by describing in these gentle terms how he showed that he would shoot them if they attacked. The passage is in a tone of casual irony.

Translation

Passages for translation are nearly always in verse. Instructions generally say, "Rewrite this passage in fluent modern prose," or, "Explain clearly the meaning of . . ." As we have already seen, you are not expected to translate the passage word by word, but to give a rendering which brings out the line of thought, and the feeling. You should take care to write continuous prose, and not break your answer up into lines.

Question 10

"I will redeem all this on Percy's head,
And in the closing of some glorious day
Be bold to tell you that I am your son,
When I will wear a garment all of blood
And stain my favours in a bloody mask
Which, washed away, shall scour my shame with it."
(*Henry IV*, *Part One*)

NOTES

There is a reference to the previous speech in the word "this." It should be made clear. References to a garment and mask of blood also need explaining.

SUGGESTED ANSWER

I will make up for all my past misdemeanours by overcoming Hotspur; and at the end of some victorious battle I will dare to tell you that I am indeed your son. I will fight so bravely that I shall be all covered in blood, and all my features will be obscured by blood. When it is washed off, it will wash away my disgrace at the same time.

Longer context passages are sometimes set, nearly always for comment on the way they are written, for an outline of the thought, or for an analysis of their humour, revelation of character, or creation of atmosphere. Examples of such critical comment have already been given when shorter passages were being examined. Here is a last instance—a question about the development of the speaker's thought.

Question 11

"And as our vineyards, fallows, meads and hedges,
Defective in their natures, grow to wildness,
Even so our houses, and ourselves and children,
Have lost, or do not learn for want of time,
The sciences that should become our country;
But grow, like savages—as soldiers will
That nothing do but meditate on blood—
To swearing, and stern looks, diffused attire,

And everything that seems unnatural.
Which to reduce into our former favour
You are assembled." (*Henry V*)

Trace clearly in your own words Burgundy's thought in this passage.

NOTES

A full paraphrase is not asked for. Run through the piece, noting the outline of thought, and especially seeing how one stage is linked to the next, and which lines are illustrations rather than main points.

SUGGESTED ANSWER

Our fields and countryside have all grown wild, against the nature of their proper growth. In the same way all our people, even children, are not living in a civilized way but turning savage, like soldiers whose fierce life brutalizes them. You, princes, have met to restore order in our country.

Essay Questions

The essay questions that follow are arranged in three sections: character questions, questions demanding reproduction of text in detail, and critical questions, which are harder than the other two kinds. Each question is followed by a short consideration of what the examiners had in mind; then come suggestions for an answer. Some of these are brief, to show an outline only, and how paragraphs should follow one another; some give detail which might be brought in, and discuss its use; some give complete answers, though these should be read more as indications of how an answer can be constructed than as guides to the books concerned.

The best form of preparation for such questions is not learning notes and critical opinions, nor learning long passages by heart. It is reading the books carefully and with understanding, trying to see what the author intended.

(B) Questions on Characters

(i) Straightforward accounts, usually of minor characters

Question 12

Some of Chaucer's pilgrims do not always act in the way expected in their profession. Describe *three* such characters, giving details by which their shortcomings are shown.

POINTS TO CONSIDER

Most of the pilgrims have shortcomings, but note that this question is limited to those who behaviour does not fit their profession; thus the Wife of Bath, the Gildsmen and the Squire are not the sort to be chosen. "Professions" included in the *Prologue* are the Church, Law and Medicine, and you should not go outside these. You have a free choice of three characters, which means that they will carry equal marks, and so you should try to choose three to whom Chaucer gives roughly equal attention. This will probably lead you to choose three connected with the Church, as the Lawyer and Doctor have not many *professional* failings. The Lawyer uses his great knowledge to evade restrictions on buying land, and the Doctor is very fond of money, but you will not find much more to say about them, whereas the Monk, Friar, Pardoner and Prioress give you plenty of scope for a detailed answer, and each falls short, in a different way, of the standards expected.

SUGGESTIONS FOR ONE PART OF AN ANSWER

THE PRIORESS: (i) should stay in her convent, ignoring the call of the world: (ii) dressing simply; (iii) she should not keep pets, but (iv) should pray for sinners. *But*

(i) She was out on a pilgrimage; she loved delicate table manners and courtly behaviour, and took trouble to behave like a fine lady. (The description of her manners comes from a book telling girls how to attract a husband, and the description of her face is that of a heroine of medieval romance.)

(ii) She had a pretty cloak, a neatly-pleated wimple, a forehead exposed in the very latest fashion, and a gaily ornamented rosary with the words "Love Conquers All" on a brooch that hung from it. (This could, of course, refer to Heavenly love: Chaucer leaves the question open to doubt.)

(iii) She kept little dogs, and was very upset if one died or was beaten.

(iv) We are told of her conscience, and tenderness of heart, but it was dogs and dead mice that she was sorry for: we hear nothing about her care for people. In short, she is a sweet woman, but in the wrong place.

Melancholy Jaques, from As You Like It.

Question 13

Write an account of the character of Jaques, with close reference to his speeches and what is said about him.

POINTS TO CONSIDER

Jaques has two functions in the play: (1) the Melancholy Man, a fashionable type of which Shakespeare is making fun; (2) he is used to comment on the life in Arden, to keep it from being insipid. Thus his character sketch must have two parts.

SUGGESTIONS FOR AN ANSWER

(1) The Melancholy Man:

(*a*) Before his actual appearance, he is described as weeping and commenting upon the sobbing deer. He makes a moral out of everything it does: its tears falling into a stream suggest legacies to men who already have more than enough; "abandoned of his velvet friends" suggests the world's treatment of misery; the deer's running past suggests rich merchants ignoring the distress of their bankrupt companion. He ends by calling the Duke a tyrant for driving out the natives of the forest, the deer: so Jaques is mocked for being sentimental and uttering common-places.

(*b*) He describes how he met Touchstone moralizing and uttering common-places about time. He does not realize, while laughing at Touchstone, that Touchstone is mocking his style of moralizing as shown in the speech about deer.

(*c*) He wishes for motley and the licence of a fool to mock whatever he pleases. The Duke tells him that as a sinner he cannot decently reprove others. He claims that his attacks will not be on individual men and women, but on universal faults. Shakespeare is making fun of those who claim that the world is in a bad way.

(*d*) He is easily outwitted when he tries to deride Orlando as a foolish lover; for example, he is caught about seeing a fool in the brook.

(*e*) He describes himself as having a special brand of melancholy, superior to that of scholar, musician or courtier. Rosalind laughs at his claim to have been a traveller, and to have brought melancholy back with him. She mocks him for his pose.

(2) The commentator on life in Arden:

(*a*) His moralizing over the deer comes immediately after the Duke's "sermons in stones," and makes one think again about their value. He says later of the Duke: "He is too disputable for my company. I think of as many matters as he, but I give heaven thanks and make no boast of them."

(*b*) His comment about the Duke usurping the animals' place shows another side to the pretty idea of country life held by his co-mates and brothers in exile.

(*c*) His passage with Amiens shows him as witty: "I do not desire you to please me; I do desire you to sing." His extra verse to "Under the greenwood tree" makes a sardonic comment on those who make themselves uncomfortable by abandoning wealth and ease.

(*d*) His cool remarks when Orlando tells them to eat no more, and that he will kill anyone who eats before his demands are answered, show up Orlando's melodramatics.

(*e*) His Seven Ages speech is a vigorous and concrete expansion of the

Duke's rather obvious image of woeful pageants. It is another sardonic comment on conventional ideas about life.

(*f*) He sees through Touchstone's mock-marriage.

His final appearance, introducing Touchstone's speech about the etiquette of quarrelling, and distributing farewell comments to all the chief characters, is little more than part of the machinery of the play; he is the man available to do these things, but the episode throws no particular light on him as a character.

Question 14

Sketch the characters of each of the following: Pistol, Nym, Bardolph, the Hostess. How are they joined to the main action of the play *Henry V*?

POINTS TO CONSIDER

(1) A sketch is short but vivid. The Boy's speech at Harfleur and their own first appearances show clearly what they are like.

(2) If you have prepared answers on the characters, remember that the second part of the question is important, as it tests your understanding of the play as a whole.

SUGGESTIONS FOR AN ANSWER

(*a*) Pistol. "A killing tongue and a quiet sword"; rants at Nym in absurd blank verse: "Solus egregious dog, O viper vile!"; uses long words without understanding them: "fracted and corroborate"; threatens Nym but stops at once when Bardolph threatens *him*; sounds brave at the bridge but is quickly found out. Bully and coward (French prisoner; Fluellen); thief.

(*b*) Nym. A man of few words: "scorns to say his prayers lest he should be thought a coward; few bad words matched with as few good deeds, for he never broke any man's head but his own, and that was against a post when he was drunk." Enemy of Pistol because he had hoped to marry the Hostess; full of obscure threats: "Men may sleep, and they may have their throats about them at that time; and some say knives have edges." Favourite phrase: "That's the humour of it." Coward and thief.

(*c*) Bardolph. "White-livered (i.e. cowardly) and redfaced (with over-drinking)." A convinced thief: he and Nym "will steal anything and call it purchase." More feeling than the other two: will "bestow a breakfast" to make them friends, and wishes he were with Falstaff whether in Heaven or Hell. Realistic view of life: "We must to France together: why the devil should we keep knives to cut one another's throats?"

(*d*) Hostess. Not much individuality: easily upset and flustered. Muddles her words: "We shall see wilful adultery and murder committed"; "Shaked of a burning quotidian tertian"; "A could never abide carnation." But affectionate: she speaks the great lament over Falstaff, full of feeling in spite of its absurdities.

(*e*) Links with the main action.

(i) The men are hangers-on of the army, and turn up as disreputable postscripts to the glories of war.

(ii) They remind us that the King, in freeing himself from his wild youth, has broken Falstaff's heart. They describe Falstaff's death immediately after Henry's long complaint that his friends have betrayed him.

(iii) Their first war-time scene is after, "Once more unto the breach," which Bardolph parodies with the overdone, "On, on, on, on, on, to the breach, to the breach!" after which they all stop and admit that they prefer safety to fighting.

(iv) Bardolph and Nym are both hanged because Henry has forbidden looting.

(v) Pistol quarrels with Fluellen because he will not intercede for Bardolph, and is forced to eat the leek he had made fun of.

(vi) He ends by saying that he will use his reputation as a veteran of Agincourt to make money at home.

Main use of the group is to show the less glorious side of war and of Henry's army, and by contrast to make us think a second time about various high sentiments expressed in the play.

(ii) Accounts of major characters, usually limited in some way

Question 15

Compare Shylock, as he appears on first meeting Bassanio and Antonio, with the Shylock of the Trial scene.

POINTS TO CONSIDER

(1) A limited answer, and you must concentrate on the two scenes named.

(2) All the chief points of Shylock's character can be seen in these scenes, however: it is simply a question of making sure that your illustrations come from the right places. If you have already made notes of his characteristics, you have only to run over the list and see how they appear in these scenes.

(3) Actors have interpreted Shylock in various ways. You may put forward any ideas about him that you can support *from the text.*

SUGGESTIONS FOR AN ANSWER

(*a*) First meeting

(i) Seems cautious; tantalizes Bassanio; enjoys keeping him waiting. (Repetition of Bassanio's words; hesitation and description of risks at sea; request to see Antonio.)

Henry Wadsworth Longfellow (1807-1882), the first well-known American poet, is now chiefly remembered for his long poem based on the life of the Mohawk chief Hiawatha, and Minnehaha.

Herman Melville (1819-1891) was almost ignored during his lifetime. Only recently has his novel *Moby Dick*, the story of Captain Ahab's long fight to capture a whale, been hailed as a masterpiece.

Mark Twain (1835-1910) wrote many humorous books, of which *Huckleberry Finn* is a well-known and well-loved example. Here Huckleberry is seen on a raft with Jim, an escaped Negro slave.

Henry James (1843-1916), a famous American novelist and short-story writer, spent much of his life in Europe. His book *The Turn of the Screw* has been made into a play entitled *The Innocents*.

Eugene O'Neill (1888-1953) wrote many plays, including a long one called *The Iceman Cometh*. Some lazy drunkards are joined by Hickey, a salesman, who soon threatens their pleasant dreams.

Ernest Hemingway (1898-1961) wrote many well-known novels. One of the last books he wrote was *The Old Man and the Sea*, about a man's struggle to catch a giant marlin and bring it back.

Tennessee Williams (1912-) is famous as a playwright, but he also wrote a novel, *The Roman Spring of Mrs. Stone*, about a middle-aged woman's infatuation for the poor young Italian boy, Paolo.

Arthur Miller (1915-), a modern American playwright, wrote *Death of a Salesman*, the story of a travelling salesman who has come to lose faith in his work and in his way of life in general.

(ii) Fiercely opposed to all Christians (refusal to dine with Bassanio).

(iii) Tells audience of hatred for Antonio (who brings down rate of interest, and rails at Shylock and his money-lending).

(iv) Deceitful (pretends he was considering how to raise the money; greets Antonio humbly and fulsomely).

(v) Justifies usury by reference to Jacob's bargain with Laban; refers to breeding of money, which Elizabethans thought unnatural.

(vi) Sudden change of key: deep-felt resentment of Antonio's treatment of him, expressed with bitter irony. Our sympathy aroused. N.B. This attack rouses Antonio to an angry answer, which gives Shylock a chance to make him feel ashamed and take the offer of friendship too readily.

(vii) Returns to friendly and deceitful tone, offers the bond as a joke, and ridicules the idea of claiming the forfeit. Urges Antonio to seal the bargain quickly.

General impression in this scene: dangerous, crafty, implacable.

(*b*) The Trial.

(i) Relies on the sanctity of law: he has sworn to have his legal due.

(ii) Confident of winning, and will not give any explanation except that he wants to satisfy his hate.

(iii) Refuses offer of twice the debt.

(iv) Says that he may do as he likes with his own, and refuses to consider mercy. ("What judgment shall I dread, doing no wrong?") N.B. The debate between law and mercy, in Old Testament and New, is here introduced.

(v) He eagerly sharpens his knife, brushing aside Gratiano's taunts.

(vi) When Portia speaks of mercy, he asks why he must be merciful, and (echoing the Jews at the Crucifixion) says, "My deeds upon my head! I crave the law."

(vii) Exults as Portia says that the law must not be perverted. "A Daniel come to judgment."

(viii) Offered three times the debt, he self-righteously refers to his oath. ("Shall I lay perjury upon my soul?") Murder is less shocking to him.

Shylock, from The Merchant of Venice.

(ix) Gleefully he points out that no surgeon is called for in the bond.

(x) He is horrified when Portia stops him: "Is *that* the law?"

(xi) Quickly he says he will take three times the debt; angry when told he can have only what he demanded.

(xii) Told the full penalty of the law, he suggests that he be killed:

> "You take my life
> When you do take the means whereby I live."

(xiii) His bold independence and reliance on the law collapse and he goes quietly away:

> "I am not well: send the deed after me
> And I will sign it."

Question 16

Why was Mr. Polly less happy in his shop at Fishbourne than he was later at Potwell Inn?

POINTS TO CONSIDER

(1) This is not a question asking for a great deal of memorized detail: you must select.

(2) Think of points in Polly's character which made him prefer one way of life to the other.

(3) Think of different circumstances which helped to make one life more agreeable than the other.

(4) Illustrate these points with a few relevant details, but keep your references short and to the point.

SUGGESTIONS FOR AN ANSWER

(i) Polly's character.

(*a*) Hated shop-work: loved the countryside.

(*b*) Hated dull and commonplace detail: loved wonder and romance.

(*c*) Disliked planning: liked to take life as it came.

(*d*) Disliked trying to get things, or *trying* to be good and happy: at the Inn, they did as they pleased and were content.

(ii) Circumstances.

(*a*) Indigestion: healthy life.

(*b*) Miriam (officious tidiness; bad housewife and cook; disliked his reading; nagged about his failure): the fat woman (good cook; contented; cheerful; needed his help).

(*c*) Failure and bankruptcy: success, especially with Uncle Jim.

(*d*) Neighbours: scenery and surroundings; the fat woman's niece.

(iii) General conclusion: his imagination was nourished at the Inn and starved in the shop.

Miss Havisham shows Pip her wedding-cake, in Great Expectations.

Question 17

Write an account of Miss Havisham as she appeared to Pip on his first two visits to her. Why did she live and behave as she did?

POINTS TO CONSIDER

The first part of the answer will demand more material; the second part should be a clear outline.

SUGGESTIONS FOR AN ANSWER

(*a*) The first visit.

(i) The dark passages and candle-lit room. (Important because they are expressions of her withdrawal from life.)

(ii) Her appearance: bridal dress, etc., but dressing never completed, and all withered and shrunken.

(iii) Her broken heart.

(iv) Her demand that Pip should play cards; later, Estella told to play 'Beggar my Neighbour' with him. "You can break his heart."

(v) She asks what Pip thinks of Estella.

(vi) Refusal to know about days and weeks.

(vii) She seems as though crushed by a heavy blow.

(*b*) The second visit.

(i) She sends him into the room with the decaying wedding-cake.

(There is no need to describe this incident at length.) She looks like a witch.

(ii) She makes Pip walk her.

(iii) She rebuffs the advances of toadying relatives.

(iv) She speaks of her birthday and of how she and the cake have worn away together.

(v) She again draws Pip's attention to Estella's beauty.

(*c*) The reason for her behaviour.

Compeyson, a rogue introduced to her by her ne'er-do-well half-brother, proposed marriage, and got a lot of her money, but jilted her on her wedding morning. She called in her lawyer, Jaggers, to lay Satis House waste, stopped all the clocks at twenty minutes to nine, the time when she received Compeyson's letter breaking off the engagement, stopped at the stage of dressing she had reached at that moment, and never looked on the light of day again. She later adopted Estella, and brought her up to torment men, in revenge.

Question 18

Give an account of the Pardoner's activities, as he describes them in his Prologue and Tale. What impression of him do they convey to you?

POINTS TO CONSIDER

(1) Nothing outside the Pardoner's self-description is asked for; this excludes Chaucer's account of him in the general Prologue, and also his attempt to sell pardon and display his relics to the pilgrims at the end of his tale.

(2) The second part of the question can be well answered by a commentary running through the reproduction; this will show that you understand the details as well as remembering them.

SUGGESTIONS FOR AN ANSWER

(*a*) His manner and grand vocabulary.

(*b*) Always the same theme: desire for money is the root of evil.

(*c*) His method.

(*d*) His claims for the relics.

(*e*) His pulpit manner.

(*f*) His intentions.

(*g*) His tale: melodramatic, eloquent and terrifying, and followed at once by an exhortation to come up and subscribe. He breaks off, however, to admit that it is all an act, and that Christ's pardon is best; he will not deceive the pilgrims. So the Pardoner ends on an unexpected note of sincerity, though he quickly turns to sell pardon to the Host, an offer which is roughly and coarsely rejected. The total picture is of a skilful salesman, playing on ignorant people's hopes and fears to make money, and delighting to use his skill. But the wild eloquence of the tale, and the moment of admission that he is a fraud at the end, suggest that he has other qualities as well, fear of sin and awareness of good and evil.

(iii) **Accounts of characters, demanding some particular line of approach.**

Question 19

"Macbeth always keeps some signs of nobility, although he is a murderer of the worst kind." Discuss this view of his character.

POINTS TO CONSIDER

(1) The way to treat this question is to think rapidly of the impression Macbeth makes at different points in the play, and to see whether nobility seems to you a constant quality in him. You should then outline your ideas about him, supporting them always by reference to the text, keeping the idea of nobility always in the foreground.

(2) "A murderer of the worst kind" need not be discussed at length; it can be dealt with briefly in your opening sentences. Constant nobility is the larger part of the question.

(3) Remember that there is no one "right" answer to a question about literature; you may put forward any view that you can support from the text. The suggestions that follow are only one such view, and you should attend more to how they are presented than to the opinion they indicate.

SUGGESTIONS FOR AN ANSWER

(1) "A murderer of the worst kind." Yes: he takes advantage of Duncan's love to kill his king, who is also a kinsman. He kills the grooms just to secure himself, and has Banquo killed treacherously because of the witches' prophecy. After that, he has Lady Macduff and her children killed for spite, and, according to Ross' account, is killing anyone who stands in his way.

(2) Nobility: at first, yes; later, no.

(*a*) References to Bellona's bridegroom; his valour and success against Macdonwald and Sweno; Duncan's praise, spoken in the scene where the battle is reported, repeated by Ross and Angus when sent to greet Macbeth, and spoken again by Duncan when Macbeth and Banquo meet him first. But these praises all have an ironic sound, because we know what Macbeth is contemplating, and can see how the new Thane of Cawdor resembles the old, "a gentleman on whom I built an absolute trust."

At this stage, his reputation and valour make him appear noble; his language is impressive and compels attention (e.g. the "supernatural soliciting" speech: we feel that this man is great, though not necessarily admirable). But his thoughts are already evil ("my black and deep desires").

(*b*) When he meets Lady Macbeth he seems to be trying to overcome temptation. Though his "face is as a book where men may read strange matters," he is not yet an accomplished hypocrite, and he does not jump at her ready acceptance of his thoughts, but will speak further.

(*c*) During the banquet for Duncan, his vision of the Last Judgment, although he makes out that he would "jump the life to come," leads him to say, "We will proceed no further in this business." Nobility is overcoming ambition. But he does not say that he is holding back because murder is wicked, but because he does not want to lose men's good opinion of him; and he quickly accepts Lady Macbeth's suggestion of how the murder can be done safely.

(*d*) His vision of the dagger, his imagination of the voice that cried, "Sleep no more," and his horror at the blood on his hands show him to be sensitive, conscience-ridden, and aware of the significance of his deed, but hardly noble. He compares himself to Tarquin, talks hysterically about not being able to say, "Amen," and is afraid to think what he has done, saying that every noise appals him.

(*e*) When the murder is discovered, he overacts (the "silver skin . . . golden blood" speech) and kills the grooms in a panic. If there is any nobility in this scene it is in the sad irony of "Had I but died an hour before this chance, I had lived a blessed time."

(*f*) Once established as king, he goes rapidly down: hypocrisy (" our bloody cousins . . . not confessing their cruel parricide") and treachery (the murder of Banquo) are followed by hysteria over Banquo's ghost, and the evil determination that "for mine own good all causes shall give way." Except for the vigour and power of his speech, all nobility has gone.

(*g*) When he visits the witches, he calls for chaos and destruction, provided that he can get his own way, and he determines to have no hesitation or remorse in crime: "The very firstlings of my heart shall be the firstlings of my hand." Again, except that his strength of language reminds us that he is a great man, there is no sign of nobility.

(*h*) The murder of Lady Macduff and her son, and the accounts of Macbeth and of Scotland under his rule by Macduff, Malcolm and Ross prepare us for

(*i*) The superstitious clinging to the witches' prophecies, the wild fury at bad news, the restless putting on and off of armour, and the once noble language degenerating to "I'll fight till from my bones my flesh be hacked."

(*j*) The reflective power of the speeches describing weariness ("The sere, the yellow leaf" and "Tomorrow and tomorrow and tomorrow") may be called noble, but his last fight is more desperation than courage.

(*k*) Our last impression is Malcolm's phrase: "this dead butcher." He was noble once, but is quite degraded by the end.

Question 20

What is there to admire in the character of Satan in Book One of *Paradise Lost?* Illustrate your answer by close reference to the text.

POINTS TO CONSIDER

A perfectly straightforward question, giving a particular aspect of Satan's character, and asking you to illustrate it.

SUGGESTIONS FOR AN ANSWER

(1) His situation.

(2) His speeches. Three to Beelzebub, one to rouse his followers from the lake, and one when they are formed up on shore.

(3) Milton's description of him:

- (*a*) comparison with the Titans and Leviathan
- (*b*) his shield and spear
- (*c*) the heathen gods who all obey him
- (*d*) his appearance before all his followers.

Epstein's Lucifer captures the spirit of Satan in Milton's Paradise Lost.

Question 21

Give a full account of the character of Michael, and show how the poet has made us feel sympathy for him.

POINTS TO CONSIDER

(*a*) Main points of character: strength, industry, simplicity, love of his son and of his land.

(*b*) Points to arouse sympathy: his story, his motives, Wordsworth's comments.

SUGGESTIONS FOR AN ANSWER

(*a*) Character.

(i) Outlined in first description: old, unusual strength, knowledge of mountains and weather, care for sheep, love of his surroundings, "pleasurable feeling of blind love."

(ii) Love of his wife (clean, frugal and industrious household) and still more of his son. Tenderness in nursing and bringing up Luke, mingled with loving sternness. Shearing and little crook. Daily companions since Luke was ten.

(iii) Love of his land, increased by Luke's companionship. Worked hard for twenty years to pay off mortgage.

> ". . . If these fields of ours
> Should pass into a stranger's hand, I think
> That I could not lie quiet in my grave."

(*b*) Sympathy.

(i) Good man brought down by faults of others (kinsman's failure and Luke's crime).

(ii) Patient industry all his life. Takes up extra burden at eighty-four.

> "Our lot is a hard lot; the sun himself
> Has scarcely been more diligent than I."

(iii) Simplicity. He is content with the frugal, hardworking life of the Evening Star. He remembered how he was indebted to his ancestors, and wished to hand on the same love and kindness to his son. Thought of the

Hardy was born in this thatched cottage near Dorchester, in 1840.

shared building of the sheepfold as a protection against the city's vices.

(iv) The strength of love. Michael endures for years, and goes on building the fold, although "many and many a day he thither went and never lifted up a single stone."

(v) Work never finished. He died; Isabel died; the cottage disappeared.

(vi) Wordsworth's comments.

(*a*) The hard and empty setting, "a few sheep, and rocks and stones, and kites." We are prepared for a tale of bare strength.

(*b*) The appeal to "the delight of a few natural hearts."

(*c*) Dignity and simplicity of the description of Michael: "his mind was keen, intense and frugal, apt for all affairs." We respect and admire him, and so are all the more moved when he is overcome.

(*d*) Quiet repetition of "His bodily frame had been from youth to age of an unusual strength." The vigour which had once made his life happy now prolongs it in sadness.

(*e*) Restrained description of his suffering.

(*f*) The final reminder: an oak tree and a heap of stones.

Question 22

Give an account of Parson Maybold and *either* Geoffrey Day *or* Elizabeth Endorfield, showing their importance in the scheme of *Under the Greenwood Tree.*

POINTS TO CONSIDER

(1) Straight character sketches, followed by consideration of why Hardy put them into the book.

(2) Consider plot, picture of country life and people, and the theme of new ways versus old.

SUGGESTIONS FOR AN ANSWER

(1) Characters.

(*a*) Maybold.

(i) As seen by the villagers: intrusive, tactless, fond of change, enemy of the choir, too keen on Fancy.

(ii) As seen by Fancy: refined, educated, handsome, elegant, fascinating.

(iii) The final picture: a good and decent man.

(*b*) Geoffrey Day.

Grim, but honest and unsubtle. Silent and reserved. Resigned to Mrs. Day's odd ways. Anxious for Fancy to marry well; works and makes Fancy work so that she can have money to marry with independence. Concerned over Fancy's fretting and loss of appetite; makes the best of a bad job at last.

(*c*) Elizabeth Endorfield.

Shrewd and penetrating. Lonely dwelling. Not a churchgoer. Red cloak and pointed chin; wore bonnet indoors; i.e. thought to be a witch (name suggests it). But not gaunt and ugly. A deep body. "Makes pretence to common sense, and that's all."

(2) Use.

(*a*) Maybold.

(i) Plot. Turns out choir as part of his reforms. Rival to Dick; arouses his jealousy when Fancy first moves into her house. Almost wins Fancy by offer of refinement and position.

(ii) Picture of country life. Contrast to Mr. Grinham; disliked by villagers for changes.

(iii) New v. old. Illustrates movement for reform in Church in nineteenth century. Represents new ways in general: successful about church music, but defeated when Fancy prefers Dick's old-fashioned country life to the new ways offered by Maybold.

(*b*) Geoffrey.

(i) Plot. Opposition to Dick. Prefers Shiner. Beaten by Fancy and Mrs. Endorfield.

(ii) Country life. Description of house and job. Relations with Enoch and Mrs. Day. Bee-keeping.

(iii) New v. old. Favours new. Fancy's education and his ambitions for her. Yields to old. Wedding celebrations in old style.

(*c*) Elizabeth Endorfield.

(i) Plot. Enables Fancy to outwit Geoffrey.

(ii) Country life. Survival of belief in witches, and demonstration that witchcraft was mostly common sense.

(iii) New v. old. Country shrewdness defeats Geoffrey's hopes to marry Fancy into the new world of education and city ways.

(C) Reproduction Questions

(i) Straightforward accounts

Question 23

Give an account of the last act of *Twelfth Night*, showing clearly how all complications and misunderstandings are resolved and explained.

POINTS TO CONSIDER

(1) A straightforward test of memory and understanding.

(2) A brief plan is necessary, to make sure that the answer does not get out of proportion, and that nothing essential is missed.

(3) As in all accounts of scenes from plays, dramatic effects must not be

Viola meets Sebastian face to face in the last act of Twelfth Night.

ignored. Feelings and motives are often just as important as actual events.

SUGGESTIONS FOR AN ANSWER

(1) Clown and Fabian with Malvolio's letter.
(2) Duke, Viola, etc. enter, asking for Olivia.
(3) Antonio enters under arrest and complains of Viola's behaviour.
(4) Olivia enters and rebukes Viola for leaving her.
(5) Duke threatens Viola with death.
(6) Olivia sends for a priest and discloses her marriage.
(7) Andrew interrupts, followed by Toby, and complains of Viola.
(8) Sebastian enters and sees Olivia, Antonio and Viola. Confusion of identities cleared up.
(9) Feste re-enters with Malvolio's letter.
(10) Duke offers marriage to Viola.
(11) Malvolio enters and complains of his treatment. Fabian confesses.
(12) Feste ends the play with "the wind and the rain."

There is a lot of material here, and it will not be easy to manage. An answer might perhaps go as follows.

The scene opens with Feste teasing Fabian by not allowing him to see the letter Malvolio has written from prison; but before they have agreed, the Duke enters, attended by Viola (as Cesario) and others, and asks to see

Olivia. Feste, after wittily begging his usual tip, goes to tell her. Meanwhile the men who have arrested Antonio bring him before the Duke, who recognizes him as a brave enemy. Confusions between Viola and Sebastian are now set off again, as one after another takes Viola for her brother.

Antonio reproaches Viola for ingratitude, saying that he had rescued "him" from the sea, and exposed himself to danger of arrest for "his" sake, and yet "he" had denied his acquaintance as soon as he was arrested and needed help. The Duke and Viola cannot understand him, as Viola has been in the Duke's service for three months.

Olivia now enters, so that the question of Antonio's strange behaviour is set aside. She reproaches Viola for not keeping "his" promise to her. Viola is bewildered, and the Duke, finding his suit again rejected, and being jealous of Olivia's regard for "Cesario," says that he will kill "him." Viola gladly accepts a death that will help the Duke, confessing that she loves him

"More than I love these eyes, more than my life,
More by all mores than e'er I shall love wife."

This statement naturally drives Olivia to despair, so that she calls on "Cesario" as her husband to stay. Viola denies the marriage; but the priest, sent for by Olivia, confirms that he has performed "a contract of eternal bond of love" between them. The Duke, disgusted by the "dissembling cub", scornfully dismisses Viola; but her protests are interrupted by the entrance of Sir Andrew, with a broken head and loud wails of complaint against "one Cesario," whom he suddenly sees. Sir Toby follows, drunk and wounded, leaning on Feste; he only increases the confusion, and then staggers off as Sebastian enters.

Sebastian, unaware of the situation, first greets Olivia as his wife, with an apology for having hurt Sir Toby, who had attacked him (believing him to be the cowardly "Cesario"). He then turns to Antonio with friendly words, to Antonio's great astonishment. At last he sees Viola, dressed just as he is. A recognition follows, slow and hesitant, as both fear to believe so happy a meeting. Sure in the end that his sister is alive, Sebastian turns to his wife with an explanation, and the Duke, at last seeing the truth about his feelings, claims "Cesario's" often-promised love, which is gladly given.

A reference by Viola to the captain who helped her, and is now in prison at Malvolio's suit, reminds Olivia of her steward. Feste produces the letter, which is read out by Fabian after Feste has been rebuked for bawling it out. While Malvolio is being fetched, Olivia offers to hold the Duke's marriage with Viola at her house; he gladly accepts, and as the new sisters greet each other, Fabian brings in Malvolio.

He upbraids Olivia vigorously for leading him on and then having him shut up, but she recognizes Maria's writing in the letter Malvolio thrusts upon her, and Fabian admits the whole plot, adding that Sir Toby has married Maria as reward for her share in it. Feste mockingly reminds Malvolio of his contemptuous, "Madam, why laugh you at such a barren rascal?" and says that, "the whirligig of Time brings in his revenges." Malvolio storms out, threatening revenge on the whole pack.

The complications being all settled and the couples departed, Feste ends the play with his rueful song of life in the wind and the rain.

You will see from this essay that to give an account of a whole scene is a long business, which can only be done in outline, with only major dramatic effects noted. All subtlety is bound to be lost, and quotation must be brief and fitted into the story. There is no time for writing out long passages just because they have been learnt by heart.

Question 24

Summarize the *Ode on a Grecian Urn*, showing how Keats came to the conclusion that "Beauty is truth, truth beauty."

POINTS TO CONSIDER

This looks an easy question for anyone who can remember the ode. Actually, it is a very difficult one, involving much more than the mere reproduction its wording suggests. It is really a demand for a critical account of a complicated poem, and should only be attempted if you really enjoy the ode and want to write about it. One of the difficulties is the demand to explain how Keats came to his conclusion; critics are still debating what this conclusion means. The suggestion that follows should be read more as a hint about answering a difficult type of question than as an attempt to settle this debate.

SUGGESTION FOR AN ANSWER

The first stanza shows a contrast between the stillness and purity of the vase, the "still unravished bride of quietness," and the violence of the scene of lovers on its surface. It is a sylvan historian, which can quietly tell us about the energy of the life it records.

In the second stanza, Keats says that unheard melodies, piped to the spirit, are sweeter than those of reality: the lovers may never kiss, but will always be young. This music stands for the finest products of imagination, never to be destroyed by the harshness of dull fact: "the sensual ear" can hear only for a moment, and then its music dies.

The third stanza carries on the same argument: these trees can never shed their leaves; the melodist will always pipe songs for ever new; and love, happier than any earthly feeling, will be for ever warm and still to be enjoyed.

In the fourth stanza, the description of a rustic festival, with exact and delicate detail, makes us feel the closeness of this natural life to the religious solemnities suggested by "mysterious priest" and "pious morn." The town is empty, and its silence can never be explained.

The last stanza leads back from this idea to the stillness of the urn's "fair attitude," its "silent form" that teases us out of thought, but holds a permanent message for men, that the beauty of imagination is a divine and true reality, and that reality is the imagination's understanding of what is felt to be beautiful. The urn is an expression of such an understanding.

(ii) Reproduction with comment.

Question 25

(*a*) Give an account of the visit in *Hamlet* of the players to Elsinore, and (*b*) show what importance this visit has in the play as a whole.

POINTS TO CONSIDER

(*a*) is straightforward. You should notice the word "visit": it includes all their activities, i.e. the play scene as well as their arrival.

(*b*) is an example of the often neglected second part of a reproduction question. You should think of the various uses of the scenes (e.g. effect on plot, revelation of character, excitement, simple entertainment), decide which are relevant, and then illustrate.

SUGGESTIONS FOR AN ANSWER

(*a*) (1) Hamlet's welcome to the players.
(2) The Pyrrhus and Hecuba speeches.
(3) Hamlet's request for *The Murder of Gonzago*.
(4) His instruction to the players on speech and acting.
(5) The play scene (The chief part of this section).

You will not be able to give all these in detail: you should concentrate on 5.

(*b*) (1) An opportunity for Polonius to be laughed at: "comical-historical-pastoral."

(2) Hamlet's behaviour with the players shows the admired prince as he used to be.

(3) The Hecuba speech gives another chance for gibes at Polonius, and is a cue for the "Rogue and peasant slave" speech.

(4) The players give Hamlet the idea of testing the King with the "mousetrap."

(5) Ironically, the King and Queen welcome Hamlet's interest in the players, and encourage it.

(6) The play scene is used by Hamlet to torment Ophelia, to hint to the King that he knows about the murder, and to frighten the King by

repetition of the murder as described by the ghost, whose truthfulness is thus tested. Dramatic end as the King calls for lights.

(7) Hamlet thus gives himself away, and the King at once prepares his next move: Hamlet is to be sent to England.

These points showing the importance of the scenes can be very well included in the account of the scenes themselves: you are not obliged to set out your answer in two parts, provided that you give each part of the question proper attention.

Question 26

(*a*) Give an account of the Banquet scene in *Macbeth*, and (*b*) show its importance in the play.

POINTS TO CONSIDER

(*a*) is quite straightforward, and so will not be outlined here. You have only to remember the main incidents, and to consider how they are treated.

(*b*) is more complex; the scene is rich in meaning.

SUGGESTIONS FOR AN ANSWER TO (*b*)

(1) Plot. The lords realize that Macbeth is implicated in the murders. The separation between Macbeth and Lady Macbeth is shown.

(2) Character. Macbeth's imagination on edge. Lady Macbeth still

During the play, Hamlet (left) watches the King for signs of guilt.

Macbeth is horrified when Banquo keeps his promise to be present.

practical and prosaic: "When all's done, you look but on a stool." Macbeth deludes himself into thinking he can talk the lords into accepting his "infirmity."

(3) Theme of the play. Banquet, an attempt to create order, ends by Macbeth's own act in confusion. "Blood will have blood."

(4) Construction of the play. The turning point: "What is the night? Almost at odds with morning, which is which." Fleance's escape. The lords' departure. Macduff's refusal to attend. Macbeth's acceptance of his role of murderer:

> "I am in blood
> Stepped in so far that, should I wade no more,
> Returning were as tedious as go o'er."

He no longer fears sleep, i.e. his conscience is hardening.

Question 27

Choose *one* of the following essays, and give a lively account of it, pointing out what characteristics of Belloc as a writer it illustrates: *The Honest Man and the Devil*; *On a Winged Horse*; *Ultima Ratio.*

POINTS TO CONSIDER

(1) An account of an essay is given by tracing the line of thought in it.

(2) "Lively": answers to this kind of question often fail because they are dull. Unless you enjoy Belloc's kind of joke, you should avoid a question like this.

SUGGESTIONS FOR AN ANSWER

(1) Devil's request and Honest Man's refusal. Its result.

(2) Dictation of letters. (Comments on phonograph.)

(3) Secretary's concern.

(4) The seven letters. (You cannot give a full account of these. Give the main point of each, and as much as you can of two of them, the funniest you can remember.)

(*a*) Accepts Lady Whernside's invitation because he thinks it good for business to be seen there, though he dislikes her and her house.

(*b*) Refuses suction apparatus for his ships because he can't be bothered to change.

(*c*) Asks doctor to come and see his son to keep the mother quiet.

(*d*) Sends five guineas for a new church because he can't afford to be missing from the published subscription list.

(*e*) Accepts tender for new conservatory because builder has under-estimated in order to get his custom, which he will take elsewhere next time.

(*f*) Refuses his sister a loan because she cannot hurt him if he does so.

(*g*) Subscribes £250 to Party funds, to get a baronetcy.

(5) Secretary told to rewrite the letters.

(6) Devil returns and is defeated.

Belloc's characteristics could be described as follows:

(1) Serious dislike of humbug. The Honest Man pretends to love truth, but in fact will not send truthful letters.

(2) Serious dislike of various characteristics of the English shown in the letters: e.g. social insincerity; feeling that the English are superior to other nations; willingness to muddle through; use of Church as means of social advancement; use of politics to gain honours.

(3) Serious dislike of hardness of heart: treatment of wife and sister.

(4) Comic dislike of gadgets and new devices: phonograph.

(5) Love of jokes and nonsense. Defeat of the Devil, banging the door, etc.

(6) Irony. Apparent approval of the Honest Man's behaviour.

(D) Critical Questions

Question 28

Read the following extract from *The Frank Courtship* by George Crabbe

(1754-1832), and then try to answer the questions which are asked below:

"Grave Jonas Kindred, Sybil Kindred's sire,
Was six feet high, and look'd six inches higher;
Erect, morose, determined, solemn, slow,
Who knew the man could never cease to know;
His faithful spouse, when Jonas was not by,
Had a firm presence and a steady eye;
But with her husband dropp'd her look and tone,
And Jonas ruled unquestion'd and alone.
He read, and oft would quote the sacred words,
How pious husbands of their wives were lords;
Sarah call'd Abraham Lord! and who could be,
So Jonas thought, a greater man than he?
Himself he view'd with undisguised respect,
And never pardon'd freedom or neglect."

(*a*) What impression of Jonas is given by the first two lines?

(*b*) What do you find noticeable in the third line, and what effect is the poet making?

(*c*) Explain the reference to Sarah and Abraham.

(*d*) Comment on the words and word-order of the last line but one.

(*e*) What do "freedom" and "neglect" mean in the last line?

POINTS TO CONSIDER

(1) These questions assume that you can read with very close attention and a sensitive ear. Do not try such a question unless you feel confident that you can see what is being got at.

(2) Look very carefully at each question, and answer it as exactly as you can. Do not wander away into comments that you have not been asked for.

SUGGESTIONS FOR AN ANSWER

(*a*) The first line and a half make Jonas out to be serious, dignified and impressive. The second half of the second line makes him ridiculous, as though he tried to look taller than he was. The ridicule is pointed by absurd and unexpected rhyme.

(*b*) The line is a long string of solemn adjectives; the poet is surveying Jonas all round and finding him pompous.

(*c*) Abraham was the first patriarch in the Old Testament; Sarah was his wife. Jonas likes to claim the same authority for himself as Abraham had.

(*d*) "Himself" stands first in the sentence, an unexpected place, but with Jonas "himself" always comes first. "View'd" suggests that he took a good long look at himself. "Respect" is a word to describe one's idea of other people, not of oneself.

(*e*) "Freedom" means "taking liberties with him"; "neglect" means "ignoring him."

Question 29

Contrast *The Brook* and *Come down, O maid . . .* from any *two* of these aspects: (*a*) subject and feeling, (*b*) language and imagery, (*c*) form or construction.

POINTS TO CONSIDER

(1) You need to know the poems in close detail: quotation and close reference are essential.

(2) The question is limited: stick to the points named and do not go off into vague appreciations.

(3) It is always difficult to separate the parts of a poem in the way this type of question demands, and you need not worry if your two aspects overlap, provided that you do give proper attention to both. Here we shall deal with (*a*) and (*b*), but points from (*c*) will come easily to mind.

SUGGESTIONS FOR AN ANSWER

(*a*) Subject and feeling.

The Brook: permanence of nature compared, lightly and happily, with transience of men's lives:

> "Men may come and men may go
> But I go on for ever."

Come down . . .: an invitation to the happiness of love in the valley, shown as full of life and sweetness, by comparison with the cold splendour or fierceness of the mountains:

> "What pleasure lives in height (the Shepherd sang),
> In height and cold, the splendour of the hills . . .
> For Love is of the valley, come thou down
> And find him."

Life on the mountains is wasted, "So waste not thou, but come."

(*b*) Language and imagery.

The Brook: light babbling rhythm, imitating the flow of water:

> "I chatter over stony ways,
> In little sharps and trebles,
> I bubble into eddying bays,
> I babble on the pebbles."

Note: repetition of *t* and *b* to suggest the sound of a shallow brook, and the repeated sound of *trebles, bubble, babble, pebbles.*

Slower movement as the brook moves nearer to the "brimming river":

"I wind about, and in and out
With here a blossom sailing . . .
I steal by lawns and grassy plots,
I slide by hazel covers;
I move the sweet forget-me-nots
That grow for happy lovers."

Note the longer vowels: *about, sailing, lawns, grassy, slide,* etc., and the verbs *wind, steal, slide, move,* which all suggest a gentler flow than the earlier *sparkle, bicker, hurry* and *slip.*

Come down . . .: blank verse; more solemn than the chattering hurry of *The Brook.* Repetition used to lend weight and dignity:

"Come, for Love is of the valley, come,
For Love is of the valley, come thou down."

Long balanced phrases, and only one full stop in the whole poem.

The valley is described in terms of life and harvest and fulfilment: the happy threshold; hand in hand with plenty in the maize; purple wine being trodden out; smoke rising from the hearth, and children calling; the sweet and gentle music (suggested by Tennyson's choice of words) of

"Sweet is every sound . . .
Myriads of rivulets hurrying
through the lawn,
The moan of doves in immemorial elms,
And murmuring of innumerable
bees."

By contrast, the mountains are associated with coldness and remote splendour: a sunbeam glides by a blasted pine; a star is on the sparkling spire; death walks on the icy horrors of mountains, and glaciers slant down furrow-cloven falls, where wild lean-headed eagles yelp. Waterfalls hang like a broken purpose, wasting; the maid is urged not to waste her life in such remote coldness.

Tennyson, drawn by the Pre-Raphaelite poet and artist, Dante Gabriel Rosetti.

Question 30

Suppose that you have been asked to explain your liking for the following poem by W. B. Yeats. How would you do it?

An Irish Airman Foresees His Death

I know that I shall meet my fate
Somewhere among the clouds above;
Those that I fight I do not hate,
Those that I guard I do not love;
My country is Kiltartan Cross,
My countrymen Kiltartan's poor,
No likely end could bring them loss
Or leave them happier than before.
Nor law, nor duty bade me fight,
Nor public men, nor cheering crowds,
A lonely impulse of delight
Drove to this tumult in the clouds;
I balanced all, brought all to mind,
The years to come seemed waste of breath,
A waste of breath the years behind
In balance with this life, this death.

POINTS TO CONSIDER

(1) This is a disguised way of asking for a critical account of the poem, but note that the question assumes that you like the poem.

(2) The only way to answer such a question is to point out all qualities in the poem that interest you, and to explain any difficulties that might interfere with a reader's understanding.

SUGGESTIONS FOR AN ANSWER

(1) Possible difficulties to clear up:

(*a*) The airman was a real man whom Yeats greatly admired.

(*b*) Irish Nationalists did not necessarily take sides in the First World War.

(*c*) Kiltartan is the name of an Irish village.

(2) Qualities to note:

(*a*) Simplicity and directness of language.

(*b*) Precise balance throughout (like being poised dangerously in the air): fight but do not hate; guard but do not love; bring them loss, or leave them happier; neither law (commands from without) nor duty (commands from within); public men (above him) nor cheering crowds (below him); years to come . . . waste of breath/waste of breath the years behind; in balance; life/death.

(*c*) Careful control and detachment throughout. Feeling not involved on either side. Trim and exact verse form and rhyme scheme. This control of something so strong again suggests an aeroplane.

(*d*) Only once does the phrase overrun the line:

"A lonely impulse of delight
Drove to this tumult in the
clouds."

Strength and energy are emphasized by alliteration (delight/drove) carried over the line-end to come down heavily on the verb. This sudden blaze of excitement (delight—drove—tumult) is at once controlled and ordered by the judgment of the last four lines.

Yeats, Irish poet and playwright.

Question 31

Show the importance of use of the supernatural in *Julius Caesar*.

POINTS TO CONSIDER

(1) This is a critical question, not one of reproduction: i.e. you are not being asked *what* Shakespeare wrote, but how he used this material, and what effect it has in its context.

(2) You should think first what instances of the supernatural there are in the play, and then what use is made of them.

SUGGESTIONS FOR AN ANSWER

(1) Portents described by Casca.

(*a*) Used to make us feel the excitement and importance of the situation: an unusually fierce storm.

"Either there is a civil strife in heaven
Or else the world, too saucy with the gods,
Incenses them to send destruction."

(*b*) Various unnatural happenings, to suggest that the conspiracy and murder are themselves unnatural, contrary to the laws of the universe (a regular use of the supernatural in Shakespeare):

". . . they are portentous things,
Unto the climate that they point upon."

(*c*) Cassius' scorn of Casca's ideas illustrates his nature; he uses portents to suggest that Caesar's power is the unnatural thing that the omens point to:

> "A man . . . prodigious grown,
> And fearful, as these strange eruptions are."

(2) The dream and Calphurnia's account of the prodigies.

(*a*) Used to allow Caesar to show his indifference to danger: "death, a necessary end, will come when it will come."

(*b*) Used to make us feel the importance of Caesar: "The heavens themselves blaze forth the death of princes."

(*c*) Gives Decius an opportunity for the flattery he has already spoken of.

(3) Caesar's ghost at Sardis.

(*a*) Warning to Brutus that his defeat is near: "Thou shalt see me at Philippi."

(*b*) Gives an opportunity to show his Stoicism: "Why, I will see thee at Philippi, then."

(*c*) Makes the audience aware that Julius Caesar is mighty still.

(4) All three incidents remind us of a world outside the political one in which Brutus and Cassius are thinking; murder upsets the universal order, even if it is perhaps politically justified.

Question 32

What use is made of the Chorus in *Henry V*? Illustrate your answer by reference to at least *two* of his speeches.

POINTS TO CONSIDER

Not an invitation to copy out two choruses; you must show what you think Shakespeare used them for. Several short quotations, as always, are much more effective than a few long ones.

SUGGESTIONS FOR AN ANSWER

(*a*) Apology for inadequacy of poet and of stage.
(*b*) Arousing the audience's imagination.
(*c*) Scene-painting.
(*d*) Story-telling.
(*e*) Covering gaps in time.

These points might be worked into an essay as follows.

Chorus has various uses in *Henry V*, the first being to apologize to the audience for the inadequacy of the flat unraised spirits of the poet and his actors, and their impertinence in trying to put the vasty fields of France into the cockpit of the Globe Theatre, or to represent the battle of Agincourt in a place that cannot even hold the helmets that were worn there. This apologetic note is heard again at the end of the speech just before Agincourt, when the audience are asked to excuse the few foils that represent the battle.

These apologies are always linked with a reminder of the greatness of events and of King Henry; his story needs

> "A kingdom for a stage, princes to act,
> And monarchs to behold the swelling scene."

To help in forming this true picture of events, we are encouraged to use our imaginations: "Let us . . . on your imaginary forces work," and "Work, work your thoughts." We are to imagine the scenes:

> "Think, when we talk of horses, that you see them
> Printing their proud hoofs in the receiving earth . . .
> Play with your fancies, and in them behold
> Upon the hempen tackle ship-boys climbing."

Before Agincourt, we are to imagine how darkness and whispering fill the heavens; how the enemy camps are so near that English sentinels can almost hear the French passwords; and night is filled with the sound of horses neighing and armourers busily hammering. Shakespeare's powers of descriptive writing are at their height in these speeches.

The Chorus, who introduces and closes Shakespeare's Henry V.

Much of the King's dignity is suggested to us by the Chorus, describing how the young men of England follow the "mirror of all Christian kings," how he encourages his men before battle, and how modestly he returns to London, which pours out its citizens to hail his victory.

The story is helped by the explanations of the Chorus, who describes the conspiracy of Cambridge, Scroop and Grey, tells us that we are now at Harfleur, now at Agincourt, and now back again in England, and recounts negotiations with the French, the offer of petty and unprofitable dukedoms, and the Emperor's intervention after Agincourt. Gaps in time are thus filled, and the play is prevented from seeming a series of disjointed episodes.

Without the Chorus, the play would lose much of its excitement, dignity and unity, and our imaginations would be far less stimulated.

SPECIMEN EXAMINATION PAPER

(*Answers on page* 425)

Time allowed $2\frac{1}{2}$ hours. Answer **five** questions: **one** on Shakespeare, **one** on another verse writer (including Chaucer), **one** on a Prose work, and **two** others, provided that not more than **two** questions are answered on any one writer.

1. **Chaucer: *Prologue to the Canterbury Tales***
   Show how Chaucer, in his description of the pilgrims, uses contrasts of colour and physical feature.
2. **Chaucer: *The Pardoner's Prologue and Tale***
   Describe the technique of the Pardoner as he himself reveals it in the Prologue to his Tale, bringing out in your account the effrontery of the man. Why, in your opinion, was he so frank?
3. **Shakespeare: *The Merchant of Venice***
   What does Shakespeare reveal of Portia's character in: (*a*) the scene in which she comments to Nerissa upon her suitors; (*b*) the Casket scene, after Bassanio has chosen the leaden casket; (*c*) the Trial scene; (*d*) the Ring episode?
4. **Shakespeare: *Julius Caesar***
   "The tragedy of Brutus is the tragedy of wasted ideals." Discuss, using varied illustration from the play.
5. **Shakespeare: *Macbeth***
   Contrast the motives and behaviour of Banquo and Macduff following the death of Duncan.
6. **Coleridge: *The Ancient Mariner***
   Using close detail from the poem, trace the stages of his redemption.
7. ***Ten Twentieth-century Poets* (edited by Wollman)**
   Making close reference to the poem, show how the poets have presented human problems in (*a*) *The Love Song of J. Alfred Prufrock* (T. S. Eliot), (*b*) *The Horses* (Edwin Muir), and (*c*) *Beyond the Last Lamp* (Hardy).
8. **Milton: *Paradise Lost, Book II***
   Show how Milton presents Satan's encounter with Sin and Death and his subsequent journey through Chaos as an allegorical story.
9. **Conrad: *Heart of Darkness***
   Give with some close detail Marlow's impressions (*a*) of the Middle Station, and (*b*) on his journey up-river to meet Kurtz.
10. **Hardy: *The Trumpet Major***
    Show how Hardy creates atmosphere and background in the novel by introducing historical details from the war with Napoleon.

OUTLINE ANSWERS TO QUESTIONS

CHAPTER 3

1. Chaucer implies admiration or dislike by the detail he gives.
   Parson: C. admires simple sincerity and unworldliness with which he follows teaching of Christ (quote last 2 lines): he shares his meagre income with the poor, visits the sick, teaches his people, and is never absent from his parish or pompous in his attitude; he is no respecter of persons.
   Friar: Contrast with the Parson: greedy for money, he neglects the poor, panders to rich women to gain high fees for absolution, and frequents taverns for drinking and immoral life. He is a hypocrite in self-justification, and sings popular songs on the journey. Scathing detail.
   Prioress: C. admires her beauty (forehead, eyes, nose), her dress (wimple), deportment (coy, smiling), and ornament (rosary). He is amused by her affectation of courtly ways, her delicate table manners, and sentimentality (pet dogs). He implies her lack of religious vocation by not mentioning it.
   Reeve: A thin, ill-tempered man, who has grown rich by servility to his lord and by falsifying the Manor accounts.
   C. also admires the Knight, Squire, Clerk and Host, detests the Summoner, is tolerant of the Monk's laxity, and regards the Pardoner as a clever rogue.

2. **Detailed Description,** Miller: Thick-set build of wrestler; red hair and beard show cunning of fox (embezzlement); wart on nose, gaping nostrils and hairy ears show coarseness; "thumb of gold" implies honesty, as millers go. (The Prioress is another good example of this method—see **1** above.)
   Actions, Doctor: Worldly (ignorance of Bible), miserly, profiteering in Black Death. He and the Chemist assist each other's gains. Medical art based on influence of stars. Skill in diagnosing diseases. (The Parson also illustrates this method; and Chaucer blends both methods in the Knight.)

3. **Country Life** indirectly reflects the Manorial system of open fields in strips. Freehold farmers (Franklin) paid a money rent, and were prosperous; they lived well, and assisted in local government. Villeins (Plowman) worked on strips in the open fields; such humble folk displayed Christian virtue in mutual help. All paid tithes to the Parson. The Reeve, who organized the complicated crop system of the open fields, had scope for dishonesty in rendering accounts. Many village Parsons were humble,

devout and hard-working. The Miller had a lucrative monopoly in grinding corn. Wrestling (Miller) and Archery (Yeoman) were among the village games. Friars and Pardoners travelled about, preying on simple folk.

4. (*a*) Emphasis on widow's poverty: small property (catel) and meagre income (rente). Cottage shared with stock (three pigs, three kine, a sheep and poultry). Restricted, diet: milk and bread (whyt and blak), smoked bacon and occasional egg; no luxuries (wyn). Hardworking (exercise), healthy and contented (hertes suffisaunce), enjoyed life (dancing). Cabbages growing in small fenced yard.
(*b*) Select detail to show dramatic quality of narrative: contrasted lodgings, vivid dreams (friend's appeals for help, vision of "bloody woundes"), drama of climax (dung cart, appeal to town officers, the corpse "gaping upright").
(*c*) Emphasis on rapid action and humour. Widow's alarm; whole village joins in chase with handiest weapons and wind instruments; dogs, cows, ducks, geese join in hullabaloo. Allusion to Peasants' Revolt.

5. **Animal Qualities:** Splendour of Chanticleer, colourful plumage, comb, legs and toes; his instinct in crowing. Pertelote's beauty (83-104). Hens dust-bathing in yard (501) and clucking around Chanticleer (406-20). Detailed description of cock crowing (565-7).
Human Qualities: P.'s gentle disposition (105); singing lovers' songs together (110-15); in husband-wife relationship, she lectures him on cowardice and diagnoses indigestion (142-54); in reply he displays learning (dreams, classical and biblical allusions) and moralizes on women (quote 397-8, showing irony). In encounter with fox, he shows complacent pride which makes him a victim of flattery, but escapes through shrewd wit. Distress of P. likened to lament of Trojan women.

6. As a hypocritical moralist the Pardoner exaggerates vices of the age. He pictures inns as nests of vice, open day and night; players on harps, dancers, tumblers, fruit-sellers, pastrycooks; patronized by young people who dance, gamble, eat and drink. In denouncing Gluttony, P. makes humorous reference to cooks disguising products with sauces to stimulate appetite, and to the dishonesty of vintners in mixing wines. In Gambling, dice are "the bicched bones" leading to breaking of oaths and to murder.
References to biblical and classical stories show the medieval fondness for tales (Herod, Adam, St. Paul, Cato, Stilbon, Attila, etc.). The story of the three "riotours" shows drunkenness and swearing, prevalence of plague, and highways haunted by lawless bands who, though sworn to brotherhood, are treacherous and greedy for gold.

CHAPTER 4

1. ***Edom o' Gordon:*** During Lord's absence, Edom besieges the House of the Rodes in the hope of winning "the fair ladye." Defied by the resolute and loyal defence of the house by the Lady, and wounded by shots that she herself fires, he sets fire to the house. The daughter is thrown from the walls wrapped in sheets, but is killed by Edom's spear, and the mother and small son perish in the flames. The Lord of the House returns to find the house in flames, and pursues and kills Edom in revenge.
   Early Appeal: Legend based on local (Scottish) incident, with strong romantic appeal in passion (Edom), loyalty (the Lady), the tragedy of her fate with the children, and ultimate revenge.
   Appeal Today: Traditional verse-form of ballad with repetitive phrasing and rhythms; dramatic telling of story by dialogue, especially anguish of children in fire; pathos (sadness) of much of the simple detail.

2. **Red Cross Knight** (realistic with allegorical adventures): Questing in service of Truth; courage and hardihood in combat (I 16-26); falls into Error; then, through victory, into Pride (IV); and so, through loss of hardihood into defeat (VII 1-19); wards off Despair (IX 21-54); and through repentance (X) renews strength to slay the Dragon (XI) and wed Truth (XII).
   Una (representing Truth): Beautiful, but humble, pure and innocent (I 4-5). Her beauty tames lion (III), and virtue unassailable by brute force (VI). Delivers Knight from Despair, restores and finally weds him.
   Duessa (fantastic character): Creature of Magician Archimago, able to assume various forms, that of Una to deceive Knight, and, later, Fidessa—hypocrisy (II 21-7). Unmasked by Arthur (VIII 45-50).
   Despair (personification of abstract): Sullen mind, grisly locks, hollow eyes, sunken cheeks (X 35-6). Cunning arguments (death attractive) and tempting offers (halters and daggers) (IX 37-51).
   (References are to cantos and stanzas in Book I.)

3. Herrick's poems show humanist enjoyment of the colour, glitter and movement of life; master of the brief light lyric and musical quality in words.
   A sweet disorder in the dress (G.T. 92): The poet is a man about town and an admirer of women. The poem has a spontaneous quality, but the words are sophisticated.
   To Daffodils (G.T. 110): Humanist feeling of sadness of the passing of time and ultimate death. Thought serious but not deep; links man with nature. Emotive effect of simple words and vowel music; long and short lines delay and hasten rhyme.

Gather ye rosebuds (G.T. 82): Similar theme. Images of rosebuds and the Sun used symbolically; last two stanzas moralize on youth and age. Also, delicate pathos of *Epitaph upon a Virgin*, the appreciation yet rebuke of proud beauty in *To Dianeme*, and the Elizabethan clarity and polish of *To Anthea, who may command him in anything*.

4. Satire: "Frail mortality" is theme of Bacon's prosaic poem *Life* (G.T. 57): Court, country, married and single life, home life and travel are all seen through eyes of disillusionment. Shakespeare's *Blow, blow, thou Winter wind* (G.T. 42) compares cruelty of nature favourably with man's ingratitude, and there are satirical hints of tyrants, slander and censure in his *Fidele* (G.T. 45). Shirley uses symbolic imagery to point the vanity of human greatness in *Death the Leveller* (G.T. 69).
Peasant Life: Realistic in Shakespeare's *Winter* (G.T. 27), romantic in Marlowe's *The Passionate Shepherd to his Love* (G.T. 5). More developed pieces on country life are Herrick's *Corinna's goin' a' Maying* (E.V. II, *p.* 137) and *The Country Life* (E.V. II, *p.* 139) where tetrameter couplets are units of verse and thought (see also Milton's *L'Allegro*).

5. *On Adversity:* (*a*) Desirable as prosperity is, a man striving against adversity displays the spirit of a god in human limitations. Adversity, exalted by the New Testament, stimulates fortitude; but the Psalms and Job's patience also enhance it. Adversity brings out the best qualities in a man. In prosperity men become careless and indulgent, but adversity promotes virtues.
(*b*) Opens with a quotation from Seneca. Brief pointed sentences have the force of epigrams. Throughout, qualities of prosperity and adversity are placed in pointed contrast, culminating in final antithesis (quote). Metaphor used to illustrate argument: needlework, and the crushing of odours.

6. (*a*) Many a man, hearing a bell toll, fails to realize its relation to himself. The Church is universal, a single body of which men are the limbs, affected by the gaining of a new limb in baptism or by the loss of a limb in death. A man who recognizes that in any death his own life is affected, has realized a closer union with God. No man can live to himself, so let him realize that, whenever the bell tolls, it tolls for him.
(*b*) Donne uses metaphors or analogies (parallel instances) to point his argument. Thus the unity of mankind is compared with the limbs of the body or the land-mass of Europe. He uses imagery of the sun and the comets in rhetorical questions which have self-evident answers. After a long flowing sentence with build-up of clauses, he makes his point in a brief statement: "All that she does belongs to all"; "It tolls for thee."

CHAPTER 5

1. In the *Wakefield Nativity Play*, comedy of English shepherd life occupies major part of text. The shepherds grumble at cold weather, farming and low wages. A suspicious character, Mak, puts a spell on them as they sleep, and steals a sheep; his wife hides the sheep in a cradle, and Mak tells the shepherds that his wife has given birth; embarrassed, they ask to give a gift to the babe, and discover Mak's deception. As they leave, an Angel appears to announce the birth of Christ. Recalling Old Testament prophecies, and surprised that such humble folk are bidden, they go to the stable and greet the Babe as they would any neighbour's child.
   Emphasize contrasted parallels: the two babes—the sheep and Christ; and the two mothers—Mak's sluttish, scolding wife, and the Virgin Mary. Give some quotations, contrasting the language of the two episodes.

2. An allegory is a story in which incidents are designed to give visible form to an abstract theme, usually moral or political; its object is to enforce a lesson. Characters are frequently personified abstractions, such as Death or Fellowship (friends) in *Everyman.*
   The theme of *Everyman* enforces the supremacy and eternal significance of moral and spiritual truth, as distinct from the temporal nature of the material things of life. Summoned to die, Everyman seeks the support before God's Judgment throne of his earthly friends, wealth (Goods) and physical powers (Strength, Five Wits), only to find that all desert him except Good Deeds, who lies wounded but is revived by Discretion, Knowledge and Confession.

3. "Settle thy studies, Faustus, and begin . . .": Faustus dismisses limited subjects to envisage Magic, which promises unlimited riches and power. Good and Evil Angels represent his divided mind. In "How am I glutted with conceit of this," he indulges in visions of riches and military power. (Quote from rich imagery.) In brief passages, "Now Faustus must thou needs be damned . . ." and "My heart's so hardened, I cannot repent . . ." he betrays his misgivings; but recklessness prevails. "Was this the face that launch'd a thousand ships . . .": the vision of Helen (Beauty), a passage of rich lyrical imagery, is the summit of F.'s abandonment.
   Final soliloquy: A clock strikes the quarters of his last hour; F. appeals to the redeeming blood of Christ, and prays for dissolution; he is appalled by eternal torment, the price of having a soul, and prays to be changed to a brutish beast. The clock strikes; he sees the wrath of God's face and tormenting adders as devils seize him.

4. ***Volpone:*** Jonson's manipulation of intricate plot, and his strong construction, make grotesque characters and situations credible. Volpone, a miserly sensualist, is as fond of his intricate deceptions as of the wealth they bring. Three dupes, greedy to inherit V.'s wealth, succumb to Mosca's cunning deceptions: Corbaccio disinherits his son (I i); Corvino yields his wife, Celia (II iii). In Act III, Mosca over-reaches himself in a counter-plot with Bonario, who rescues Celia from V.'s lust. Here virtue effects a contrast and relieves the tension. In a grotesque trial scene (IV ii), V.'s dupes vie with one another in testimony for Volpone, one betraying his son and another his wife. Untaught by experience, Mosca plays his supreme trick (V); V.'s pretended death, with Mosca as inheritor; he then double-crosses V., who can only gain vengeance by unmasking himself and sharing M.'s punishment. Thus virtue prevails. (Three or four incidents should be selected and developed with detail.)

5. (*a*) The Duchess is gay and playful, independent, full-blooded, witty, innocent and credulous (Bosola's wiles).
Act I, Sc. i: Her brothers distrust her high spirits; she disregards their warning, and woos Antonio. (Quote "This is flesh and blood . . . tomb.")
Act III, Sc. ii (comedy swinging to tragedy): The Duchess is playful with Antonio in the happiness of her love; then, handed a dagger by her brother, she realizes the danger, and plans Antonio's safety; she is duped by Bosola.
(*b*) Act III, Sc. v: Pathos of her parting from husband and children.
Act IV, Sc. i and ii: Persecution: dead hand, effigies of husband and children, serenade of madmen, finally strangled. In suffering she never loses reason and control (contrast with Cariola), and is transfigured by suffering into a lofty solemn figure; executioners cannot break her spirit.

6. ***The Shoemaker's Holiday:*** Intimate picture of Livery Company. Shoemakers are independent, and proud of their skill, wealth and tradition. In workshop scenes, master and men are merry and hearty, always quarrelling but sound at heart. Simon Eyre, the master, is jovial; even his profane abuse is cordial; magnificent health; fond of eating and drinking. Hodge, the foreman, is steady and self-possessed. Firk, a journeyman, is drunken and mischievous.
The play celebrates Simon Eyre's rise to mayoralty; he builds Leadenhall Market and founds an annual feast for apprentices. The King honours the feast, and the independent craftsmen treat him as an equal.
When romance blossoms, both Lacy's noble father and the mayor show pride of class which hinders the match, but love triumphs, as also in Jane's humble affair with Ralph.
There is nothing derisory or satirical in Dekker's picture of London life.

CHAPTER 6

Context Questions

A. (i) Brutus is speaking, in the early hours of the morning, in his orchard.
(ii) Evils begin to develop in times of security and peace; we should therefore be cautious and vigilant at such times.
(iii) The exercise of great power becomes an evil thing when the ruler uses his power without scruple or conscience.
(iv) *The general:* Opposed to *personal*; it means the general welfare of the community. *Would be*: He wishes or intends to be crowned.
(v) The passage shows Brutus' idealism, his zeal for political freedom and for the people's welfare. The argument is an academic one and shows his unpractical mind. Caesar is not yet dangerous.

B. (i) Viola (Cesario) has been forced into a duel with Sir Andrew Aguecheek. Antonio intervenes and is arrested by the Watch. He claims his purse, mistaking Viola for Sebastian, and is angrily indignant when Viola denies all knowledge of him or of it.
(ii) Antonio, saving Sebastian from the sea, has developed a deep affection for him. Sebastian has now, like a false god, proved unworthy of Antonio's trust.
(iii) Viola deduces that Sebastian is still alive.
(iv) Sir Toby Belch, Sir Andrew Aguecheek and Fabian are present. They deduce that Cesario is a coward who dare not stand by his friend in trouble. Therefore they urge Sir Andrew to attack him again, with the result that he attacks Sebastian and gets a thrashing. Olivia intervenes.
(v) Your conduct shows that fine features often conceal an evil nature. It is an evil mind, and not ugly features, that debase a man.

C. (i) Your over-anxiety for my safety is an earnest prayer for this unfortunate man's punishment. If we cannot overlook small offences committed in the anger of the moment, how shall we be able to show mercy for serious crimes that have been long premeditated?
(ii) A man who, under the influence of drink, railed on Henry as he entered Southampton. The king intended to set him free.
(iii) Henry is speaking to Cambridge, Scroop and Grey. He knows that they have plotted to kill him.
(iv) He gives them documents purporting to be their appointments as High Commissioners during the King's absence; the documents are in fact accusations of high treason, and the three men beg for mercy.
(v) He is merciful, but ruthless when offences endanger the state.

The Merchant of Venice

1. Act I, Sc. iii: Bassanio and Antonio approach Shylock for a loan of 3,000 ducats for three months. S. reveals in soliloquy (39-50) his hatred of A., a Christian who lends money free of interest and so lowers usury rates. S. defends interest, citing Jacob's shrewdness (68-78), and upbraids A. for persecuting him on the Rialto (quote parts of 104-26), but offers to lend money free of interest if Antonio will sign a "merry bond" to forfeit a pound of flesh if he defaults. B. has misgivings, but A. is confident that his ships will return. Sympathy goes to Shylock for his treatment by Christians, but he is obviously contemplating murder.

Act IV, Sc. i: The essential points of Portia's method in the trial are a plea for mercy, an offer of repayment, and, both these failing, use of S.'s insistence on the letter of the bond to forbid bloodshed and to insist on an exact pound. Citing of laws and penalties follows. Little sympathy is felt for Shylock (who is attempting legal murder) until penalties are imposed that he become a Christian and leave his wealth to his daughter.

2. Morocco (II i and vii) combats a sense of inferiority by proud and pompous language. A "golden mind" will not stoop to Lead. He tries to weigh deserving (Silver) impartially, and is swayed by his birth, fortune and breeding, but is convinced by the seemingly obvious invitation of the Gold casket. He judges by outward appearance.

Arragon (II ix), proud of rank, conceited and self-centred, barely notices Lead, and dismisses Gold through contempt for the uncultured masses. In arguing that rewards should go only to the deserving (Silver), he fails to realize his own lack of merit.

Bassanio (III ii) rejects Gold, since he knows that outward appearance is deceptive. He illustrates from law, religion, cowardice and beauty. He rejects Silver as the currency of petty bargaining, and chooses Lead because its plainness appeals to his humility. He genuinely loves Portia.

Twelfth Night

1. Orsino: Sentimental indulgence in feeling of love for its own sake (I i); he can woo by proxy (I iii), and is changeable (as Feste sees in II iv); but a deeper feeling subconsciously grows towards Viola through the play (I iii; II iv), and he finds true love at last.

Olivia is uncontrolled in her feelings, and dramatic in declaring them (I v; III iv). Determined to mourn her brother, she falls in love at first sight, with a woman. She loses her dignity before lovers (V. and S.), but maintains it before her household.

Viola, a deep constant lover, can control and conceal her feeling ("Patience on a monument"). She too mourns a brother, but neither this nor thwarted love impairs her resolute facing of life, nor daunts her high spirits. **Sebastian,** a lover of the conventional type, is bewildered (IV i), but accepts fortune gratefully (IV iii), and probably will not be disappointed.

2. (Outline, with careful attention to sequence, climaxes and significant points.) *Significance:* (*a*) Revellers representing the "cakes and ale" of life are confronted with repression in the form of self-righteous Malvolio. In the spirit of Twelfth Night, repression is routed, and the plot hatched (letter in garden) that is to inflame M.'s fantastic passion for O. and bring him to the dark room.
(*b*) Malvolio, already fancying O.'s fondness for him, is convinced by the letter. Conceit makes him credulous and blind to the figure of ridicule he cuts before O. Sir Toby, put in charge by a bewildered O., consigns him to a dark room, a cruel joke which wins him sympathy.
(*c*) Sir Toby's practical joke, and Antonio's intervention, bring Sebastian into the main plot of the play. Sir Andrew, renewing the duel, mistakes Sebastian for V., Olivia intervenes, marries S., and thus resolves the situation of mistaken identities.

King Richard II

1. **Richard's visit to dying Gaunt** (II i): G. denounces the extravagant court, R.'s dependence on favourites, and his shameful methods of raising money. R. insults G.'s age and experience, and threatens him for treason. On hearing of G.'s death, R. confiscates the Lancaster estates to finance Irish wars, an act of political folly, striking at the nobles' right of succession and inviting Bolingbroke's return. Thus R.'s frivolous life, arrogant demeanour and political ineptitude alienate sympathy.
Richard's death in prison (V v): R. is resigned, in a philosophic and imaginative mood comparing his prison to the world and realizing his fatal errors. A wellwisher plays music outside, and a loyal groom visits him. When murderers appear, he shows courage, killing two before Exton strikes him down. Suffering has purged his character of vanities; he dies the victim of mean men.

2. **Aumerle,** the characterless and irresponsible son of York, becomes involved in rebellion against Bolingbroke. York denounces his son: he has with difficulty accepted B. as King, but sees the danger of B.'s rebellion becoming a precedent, and so puts his country before natural feeling. A. is saved by his mother's pleading (V ii and iii).
Carlisle upholds the Divine Right of Kings in a speech opposing Richard's deposition (IV i 114). He prophesies the Wars of the Roses.
Northumberland is Bolingbroke's right-hand man in rebellion. Richard, on

his way to the Tower, denounces N.'s complicity, and prophesies that distrust between B. and N. will produce further rebellion by N. (V i).

The Gardener (III iv) is used by Shakespeare to comment on the political situation. He likens R.'s misrule to a disordered garden. The Queen overhears, and is pitied by the Gardener.

King Henry V

1. **The heroic quality of war:** opening Prologue, Prol. II (spirit of Henry's followers), Prol. III (picture of fleet), Henry's speech before Harfleur (III i) and H.'s speech on honour (IV i 18).
   The realism of war: H.'s speech to Gov. of Harfleur (III iii), Prol. IV ("lank-lean cheeks and war-worn coats"), and the misgivings of Court, Bates and Williams thinking of wives, children and debts (but they intend to fight bravely, IV i 78). Burgundy's speech (V ii 36) shows the devastation of the kingdom; also H.'s order to kill the prisoners (IV vii 54), and perhaps H.'s practical joke on Williams.
   Mock-heroic: Bardolph, Nym and Pistol, hangers-on bent on plunder. B. is mocking Henry at the opening of III ii. B. hanged for stealing (III vi) and P.'s motives are described by Gower (III vi 68) and by himself (end of V i). P.'s capture of a prisoner is mock-heroic (IV iv). Fluellen has a heroic spirit, but is always practical.

2. Act III, Sc. vii: The French nobility long for morning; the Dauphin boasts of his horse, the Constable of his armour, amid a general display of wit. They scorn the English, who are brave but thick-headed, and do not realize their danger.
   Act IV, Sc. ii: Preparing for battle, and confident of victory, they suggest sending their superfluous courage, food and provender to the English, so that they will make a fight of it; they show contempt for the peasantry. Grandpré enters and gives a graphic picture of the dejected English.
   These two scenes precede and follow Henry's tour of the English camp, and dramatically contrast the spirit of the armies: the French boasting, confident, dicing for prisoners, despising common soldiers; the English dejected but resolute and united ("band of brothers," IV iii 60). Direct contrast of Henry with the Dauphin. Prol. IV epitomizes the contrast.

Julius Caesar

1. **Cassius,** "lean and hungry" (I ii 193), is motivated by self-interest (I ii 92); he is a practical, unscrupulous politician (attitude to Antony, II i 155, and to Lucius Pella, IV iii), with shrewd insight into character (Brutus, I ii 306; Casca, I ii 295; Antony, II i 156), but impetuous (III i 19; kills himself upon mistaken notion, V iii 36).

Brutus has an academic unpractical mind; he kills C. on a theory, and has an idealistic zeal for freedom (II i 10; speech to people, III ii). He does not understand his fellow-men (fails to see Cassius' self-interest, and makes wrong estimate of Antony, II i 165, III i 143), and through idealism makes political blunders (allowing Antony to speak, and failing to understand mob); his disposition is gentle (treatment of Portia and Lucius), and he shows courage (Caesar's ghost, IV iii).
Although, in Sardis, Cassius remains less scrupulous than Brutus, his contact with Brutus' nobility has elevated his mind. His love for Brutus, and grief at their quarrel, make him agree to Brutus' mistaken battle tactics (IV iii). With Brutus he gains our sympathy in death.

2. Act I, Sc. ii: Cassius approaches Brutus to gain a respected leader. Shouts at the Lupercal, and Casca's story, emphasize Caesar's ambition.
Act I, Sc. iii: Cassius, by using portents of the storm, wins the superstitious Casca. He plans to throw anonymous letters into Brutus' window.
Act II, Sc. i: Brutus, after revealing the conflict between his love for Caesar and for Rome, meets the conspirators in his orchard and agrees to lead them. He refuses to have an oath, or to kill Antony. The murder is fixed for the morrow. B. wins Ligarius to the conspiracy.
Caesar is at first daunted by Calphurnia's dreams and by omens of the Augurers; but Decius, by flattering interpretation, persuades him to go to the Senate (II ii). On the way he disregards warnings by the Soothsayer and Artemidorus (whose petition names the conspirators). Conspirators, supporting Cimber's petition, gather round C. and murder him (III i).

Macbeth

1. Act IV, Sc. i: M. goes to see the witches after the appearance of Banquo's ghost to get a promise of security. (Describe this scene in outline, with detail of the Apparitions and quotation of promises.) A vision of Banquo's children as kings contradicts the promise of security. Though professing to believe the prophecies, M.'s subsequent behaviour shows his insecurity.
Baulked by Macduff's flight to England (IV i 141), M. orders Macduff's wife and children to be slain—a crime of senseless vengeance (IV ii).
He prepares to stand siege in Dunsinane (where he was promised security). Opening and closing speeches of V iii show his confidence in the prophecies. On hearing the news that Birnam Wood is moving, he curses the witches (quote V v 43), and sallies from his castle to fight. Still relying on the prophecy of the second Apparition, he joins battle and kills Young Siward (V vii 5), meets Macduff, fights and taunts him with the prophecy (37-42), to be daunted by Macduff's revelation (44). He again curses the witches (quote 48-51). Under Macduff's taunts, Macbeth dies bravely.

2. (*a*) Act III, Sc. i: M. questions Banquo to get details of his journey—return in the dark with Fleance. M. employs murderers, who are desperate men; he persuades them that B. is their enemy, and flatters them (dogs, "valu'd file"). A place is selected, where the travellers will dismount and walk; Fleance must die too.
Importance: B. threatens M.'s security; M. employs murderers to divert suspicion and to avoid horror (ironical, in view of the ghost).
(*b*) Act IV, Sc. ii: Lady M., deserted by her husband, is alarmed by warnings; her little son defends his father, but son and mother are murdered.
Importance: A momentary glimpse of decent folk, shows the blind fury of M.'s final mood in the play—an irrational crime.
(*c*) Act II, Sc. iv: This brief scene shows the atmosphere and public opinion in Scotland after D.'s murder. Unnatural deeds produce unnatural portents. M. is to be crowned; but Macduff, suspicious, refuses to go to his Coronation, clearly showing future hostility (contrast with Banquo).

The Tempest

1. **Ariel** rides clouds and dives into fire; his activities on the ship give him the form of lightning. Being a spirit of air, he has an instinctive love of freedom which occasionally makes him rebel against control; but his nature is benevolent (unable to perform evil commands of Sycorax), and he shows human feeling, e.g. gratitude for deliverance from the tree-prison. P.'s benevolent magic controls him for useful service.
Caliban (I ii 319) is a creature of earth (demon father, witch mother), and therefore evil. He early responded to P.'s kindness, but a brutish nature led to confinement and menial service, which he does grudgingly, cursing P. but cowed by his magic. He regards P. as an enemy who robbed him of the isle. (Redeeming features appear later.)

2. **Miranda** is ingenuous and natural, with sound instincts. She is a lady of high birth brought up in a simple environment, with delicate feelings (pity for ship's company, I ii 1-13); she is dutiful and affectionate to her father (175), until love makes her wily (III i 20-1). In love, she is very sure of her feelings, expressing them frankly (III i), having no knowledge of the conventional world. Ferdinand finds her sincerity refreshing after the flattery of Court. She feels wonder at the "brave new world" (V i 183).
Alonso has an ingrained sense of honour; he once committed a crime, but has been pursued by guilt ever since, and looks on every disaster as a punishment (II i 107; III iii 95). He fears the supernatural (won't eat feast laid by spirits, III iii 42). He is repentant, unlike Sebastian and Antonio (contrast differing attitudes to Ariel's speech, 94), so he can be forgiven and reconciled to Prospero.

CHAPTER 7

1. Lines 64-84: The theme of *Lycidas* is the tragedy of accidental death in youth (45-9), which threatens Milton's long-term project ultimately to write a great epic poem. In the meantime his poems are mere experiments to develop his poetic art. He is tempted to write slighter poetry (love lyrics, 67-9) which would win immediate success. He argues that his lofty aim may be a weakness in a gifted mind, since chance death (blind Fury) may deprive him of ultimate achievement. He is reassured by a conviction that achievement does not lie in mere worldly success, but is assessed by God in the light of eternal values.
   Lines 108-31: M.'s denunciation of Laudian clergy is also personal, reflecting his Puritan zeal. He rebukes priests for worldliness (scramble for best livings, tithes, etc.), for lack of learning (shepherds' art), and for empty sermons (flashy songs). The people, untaught by the clergy, fall victims of false Jesuit doctrine (the "grim wolf") of the Roman Church.

2. Milton, King and minor characters are seen as shepherds composing songs and accompanying them on oaten flutes in an Arcadian landscape, after the manner of Theocritus and Virgil. At Cambridge M. and K. submit exercises in poetry to their tutor (23-36). The pastoral convention enables M. to give a colourful Nature background to the poem; Nature mourns for the poet (37), and flowers come in procession to strew his hearse (132-51). Classical allusions give variety and widen range: Muses (15-22), Nymphs (50), Greek Gods and invented figures (88 *seq*.). M.'s denunciation of the Laudian clergy fits the pastoral mould of shepherd and flock (see *St. John* X 11-14; also Q. 1 above). Thus the poem's theme is not merely personal to Edward King; Milton gives it a universal quality.

3. Simple imagery (snow, shepherds on lawn, star-lit night) conveys the simplicity and weakness of the new-born Babe; in contrast, tremendous imagery conveys the power of the Godhead in Creation (burning axle-tree of Sun, hinges of the world, control of weltering waves).
   Peace, conveyed by hushed winds, calm seas and birds brooding on the sea, contrasts with War, symbolized by the hooked chariot and trumpet marshalling armies. The power of evil, suggested by hideous imagery (speckled vanity, leprous sin, and the scaly horror of the Dragon's tail), contrasts with rainbow orbs of Truth and Justice, the celestial robes of Mercy, and glittering ranks of the Angel Host in bright harness. In the description of the Pagan gods, Apollo's shrieks contrast with the silent weeping of nymphs; contrasts occur at 149-56 and 229-36.

4. Satan, presiding, invites advice on the continuance of war against God. **Moloch,** the fiercest spirit, reckless and fearless, counsels open counter-attack on Heaven, to conquer or die, since death is preferable to torment. **Belial,** a cunning counsellor, diplomatic, timorous and slothful, advises ignoble ease. Counter-attack would excite God's wrath to destroy them, and suffering is preferable to annihilation (145-50: a very human protest); they must appease God's wrath and make their own kingdom in Hell. **Mammon** (Bk. 1, 678) prefers hard liberty to servile surrender; they should exploit Hell for gold, and in time would become inured to fire. **Beelzebub,** an experienced statesman (300-9), recommends compromise: they can build an Empire in Hell, but cannot escape God's wrath; eternal enmity must exist between them. He suggests an easier enterprise, invading Earth to rob God of his new creation by winning Man to Hell.

5. Appearance (I 589-612): Satan is immense and formidable in build (200-10; 221-8), his face furrowed with care; he is proud of his followers, and is capable of remorse. Satan inverts moral values—evil is good and to be desired; but in the duel with God, M. gives S. heroic dimensions. He alone dares to venture on voyage to Earth (II 26; 430 *seq.*), and is undaunted in the encounter with Sin and Death (II 629 *seq.*). The legions are re-animated by his call (I 331-8); he has the power to inspire followers with stirring eloquence (I 330; 663-6). His indomitable spirit gives him tragic greatness (I 94-124, 157-8, 262-3, 660-2; II 14).

6. In *A.* the poet tramps the countryside, observing peasant life; when visiting cities, he watches tournaments and pageants. In *P.* the poet's haunt is his study, in a lonely tower at midnight, studying philosophy and the stars, or meditating in a secluded fire-lit room. In *A.* the poet watches villagers dancing on a village green to the music of a rebeck; in *P.* he listens to organ music in the dim religious light of a Gothic cathedral. Sun-rise, the lark, and hunting in *A.* are countered in *P.* with the Moon, a nightingale and the curfew's solemn sound, and in daytime the student in *P.* seeks twilight groves. In the evening the poet of *A.* visits peasants' cottages to listen to their folk-tales. In both poems the poet visits a theatre, to see in *A.* Comedy and in *P.* Tragedy. Nevertheless, *P.*'s dream for retirement is a peaceful hermitage where he may pursue wisdom.

CHAPTER 8

1. Shaftesbury: Good qualities are diverted to bad ends. He has a powerful intellect, and is energetic (mind overtaxing body). As a judge he is swift, approachable and just. His restless spirit courts danger, so in quiet times he seeks intrigue. He sacrifices principles and friends to personal ambition. He hypocritically poses as a patriot, and has won over the crowd by the arts of a demagogue. Great wits are allied to madness.

Buckingham: One of Shaftesbury's meaner tools, Buckingham is a dilettante, changeable and inconsistent, bigoted, shallow and irresponsible; he feels extremes of love and hate; his wealth is squandered on parasites; he begins movements, but never shows any capacity to lead.

Charles II (character deduced from a speech at the end of Part I): He loves Monmouth, and so is unwilling to proceed against him. His mild rule, to heal the divisions of the Civil War, is mistaken for weakness. Against Shaftesbury's demagogy he raises Divine Right and Royal prerogative.

2. (*a*) Once upon a time, we sylphs were ladies of fashion, in death exchanging our earthly bodies for spirit forms. But our vanities survived death, and the earthly scene still invites our interest and influence. (The mock-heroic satire exalts the trivial vanities of ladies of fashion to be of lasting and even eternal importance.)

(*b*) In the calculated manners of ladies of fashion, we detect age beneath youthful make-up, mannerisms of speech and coy behaviour. Swoons create effect; a dressing-gown is very becoming against a colourful quilt; slight illness is convenient for displaying a new nightgown. (Playful satire upon the insincerities of Court ladies. Pope's divided line is very evident here; "languish'd with pride" and "becoming woe" are paradoxical; sixth line contains anti-climax; the last line is an epigram.)

(*c*) Homage paid to a lady of fashion will not be lasting unless her qualities of mind match her beauty. If the frivolities of social life benefited us in any real sense, we should be justified in despising domestic virtues and in refusing to acquire any useful knowledge. (Satire bites deeper here: the most valuable qualities are those of mind and character, but Court ladies often fail to recognize intrinsic virtues.)

3. Crusoe's clumsy attempts to make baskets and clay pots show primitive man's helplessness, and demonstrate the skill and perseverance that has given us common amenities which we take for granted. At first he makes sun-dried pots; then the chance discovery of fire-baked clay makes cooking possible; shallow pots inverted over the hearth make an oven. Crusoe also laboriously hollows a wooden mortar, and makes clothes.

Man Friday is an apt scholar in learning to speak; he learns to use a gun, and to cook goat's flesh (to divert him from cannibalism). In religious instruction, Friday's innocent questions and good nature put Crusoe's knowledge and religious practice to shame, showing Defoe's moral aim.

4. Details of **Vanity Fair** are based on ancient English fairs and town life of Bunyan's day: attractive goods on stalls (worldly possessions and pleasures); jugglers, cheats and rogues; and some murders and thefts. Passions, easily roused, lead to violence; punishments and corruption of justice. These details serve B's purpose, to expose worldly sin. (Answers could be based on the Slough of Despond, Delectable Mountains, etc.)

5. A typical pattern of construction is seen in the essay on *The Evils of the Party Spirit* (Sp. 125). It opens with an anecdote of Sir Roger's in which he tells of the high feelings roused by conflicting religious views and of the dilemma in which this placed him when asking the way to St. Anne's Lane. Addison proceeds to plead against divisions within a country, which can be more bitter than national divisions. He quotes Plutarch to enforce his point, and argues that party spirit affects not only morals, but reason and judgment as well, and will accept any incredible scandal. He gives historical instances of civil strife, and concludes with a plea for the union of all honest minds in a co-operative effort to purge criminal and evil elements that thrive by party divisions.

6. Ruling an isolated and self-sufficing country, the King of Brobdingnag was guided by common sense and reason, justice and lenity. Theorizing (e.g. Political Science) and glosses on laws were departure from simplicity, usually determined by private motive. He was shocked by Gulliver's account of English life: place-seeking politicians, servile churchmen, and the delays and expense of the Law. Horrified by G.'s advocacy of War (recipe for gunpowder), he insisted that the art of government should be productive, aiming to improve mankind's lot (Chapters VI and VII).
The Houyhnhnms also lived by Nature and Reason. They led simple lives and were ignorant of lying. There was no controversy because Reason is free from passion or interest (*opinion* was an unknown word). Their chief virtue was benevolence; they felt equal love for their own and other children, and had an unemotional attitude to marriage. Children were trained in temperance, industry, exercise and cleanliness. They had no books (knowledge was traditional); they lived on a vegetarian diet, had no diseases, and died only of old age (Chapter VIII).

CHAPTER 9

1. Cowper gives simple, realistic description of homely things, with sensibility: in *The Task*, vignettes of postman, waggoner and gipsies (Crazy Kate). He expresses affection for hedges, trees, greenhouse and carpenter's shop, and for wild and tame animals (*Epitaph on Hare*). Cowper describes children's games (*Task* VI 304) and domestic scenes (*Task* III 34). His letters show simple country incidents, and the conversation of a country-house; his works contain little passion (*Oxford Book of Prose*, 296-301). **Crabbe's** realistic verse portrays country life under the shadow of the Industrial Revolution, with sad and ugly stories about crime (*Peter Grimes*), fallen virtue (*Clelia*) and cynical satire (Vicar and Doctor in *The Village* I 282). He describes a decaying countryside. (I 63 and *Ancient Mansion*).

2. **Blank Verse** (Thomson, *Seasons*): Each line is a metrical unit (modulations on the iambic pentameter). To achieve concerted music of a sustained passage, variety and power of single lines blend with overflow from line to line, giving a varying sense-pause. (See Chorus of Birds and Fly-fishing in *Spring*, and Storm in *Winter*, especially Robin Redbreast.)
   Pindaric Ode (Gray, *The Bard*): Complex pattern of formal music for elevated theme. Three similar divisions correspond to divisions of theme; each consists of three stanzas, 1 and 2 of three quatrains and a couplet, 3 of twenty lines and more complex. Rhythm depends on varying line-length and rhyming pattern, and a longer concluding Alexandrine.
   Rhymeless Lyric (Collins, *Ode to Evening*): Two long pentameter lines followed by two shorter (really one longer) give a leisurely pace; frequency of *s*, *m*, *l*, *v* and *w* produce muted music suiting the prevailing greyness of the poem (occasional contrast, e.g. *shriek*).

3. Blake's simple poems revive Elizabethan lyrical quality; words and images spring direct from deep feeling. Perception of man's link with Nature and poems on childhood anticipate Wordsworth (*Echoing Green*). Theme of B.'s imaginative vision: beauty, love and freedom (eternal values) are obstructed by man-made laws and inhibitions (*Garden of Love; Ah, Sunflower; London*); love casts out fear and makes freedom possible. *Songs of Innocence and Experience* contrast joy and sadness of these opposites (two poems *Holy Thursday* and two poems *Chimney Sweeper*). Much of B.'s imagery is symbolic (*Sick Rose*; Preface to *Milton*). His later prophetic books are in free verse (*Milton*, Book II, second half), and blank verse is used in the song from *Edward III* ("O Sons of Trojan Brutus . . .") which shows B.'s patriotism.

4. **Fielding:** *Joseph A.*: high life at Lady Booby's town house and at her country-seat; low life in the countryside on J.'s journey home; highway robbery, inns (Mrs. Towouse), gross farmer-parson Trulliber, hunt horse-play. *Tom J.*: upper-class, wealthy and benevolent Allworthy, irascible and full-blooded Squire Western, moods and apprehensions of Sophia W.,

hypocritical Blifil, and (seamier side) Lady Bellaston; low life at inns. **Smollett:** novels more violent than Fielding's; Hogarthian candour. *Roderick R.*: scenes on shipboard, horrors of a hospital ship. *Peregrine P.*: dress, drink, card-games, etiquette of low life and prison interiors.

5. **Goldsmith:** Poet, *Deserted Village*, decay of the countryside through enclosures. Playwright, *She Stoops to Conquer*, social comedy. Novelist, *Vicar of Wakefield*, modern Job bearing affliction with fortitude. Essayist, *Citizen of the World*, satirical comment on English life through the letters of a Chinaman visiting London.
Johnson: More academic, with a wider range. Poet, *Vanity of Human Wishes*, imitation of the satires of Juvenal. Playwright, *Irene*, a tragedy. Novelist, *Rasselas*, dissertations on the pursuit of happiness. Essayist, *Rambler*, character-sketches, allegories and criticism. Critic, *Preface to Shakespeare* and *Lives of the Poets*. Scholar, *Dictionary*.

6. ***School for Scandal:*** Lady Sneerwell's salon is the background to the play. The main characters are the brothers Charles (a good-hearted spendthrift) and Joseph (a hypocrite), in their relations with Lady Teazle and Maria. C. loves M., but is suspected of an affair with Lady T. J. would marry M. for her money, and is having an affair with Lady T. Sir Oliver, interested in the brothers, and Sir Peter, interested in his wife and ward, resolve complications. Thus the auction and screen scenes are counterparts.
The Rivals: The central situation is Capt. A.'s pose as Beverley to win Lydia. Each is flanked by a watch-dog (Sir A. and Mrs. M.). Captain A. becomes his own rival. Other rivals (Acres and Sir Lucius) provide variety and the mechanics of comedy. Doubling of the love theme in the affair of F. and J. The servants ape their betters.

CHAPTER 10

1. **Wordsworth:** *The Prelude*, growth of a poet's mind. Books I and II show his developing feeling for Nature in childhood; careless early years (Skating: I 425-63); Guilt producing sense of personality in Nature (Boat, I 357-400; Snares, I 306-25. See the poem *Nutting*); later refinement of feeling (IV 311-38); mystical sense of Mind in Nature (XIV 1-67, and see also *Tintern Abbey*). Many poems reflect personal experiences: *Immortality Ode*, fading of natural joy of child in adult mind; *Resolution and Independence*, fears of future allayed by meeting with a leech-gatherer; *Duty*, reason as a check on feeling and impulse. Sonnets reflect zeal for political liberty and distrust of Industrial Revolution.

2. ***Euganean Hills:*** Island of hills in Lombard plain whence Shelley views Venice and Padua: S.'s joy in beauty, his hopes for man, and his solitude of spirit in Italy ruled by foreign tyrant. Rapidity of rhyming couplets; single-word and sustained metaphors; rich fancy in imagery of Venice.
   West Wind: Same disharmony between Shelley's mind and the world of experience. Poetry of sound and movement, some colour. Stanzas 1 and 2, Titanic fury of wind, personal as in a myth; 3, Quieter passage; 4 and 5, Shelley craves to become identified with the Wind, and to renew mankind as wind renews the earth (Seeds in 1st stanza). Images, similes and metaphors in breathless succession—leaves in 1, become clouds in 2; ghosts, angels, plague-stricken multitudes and frenzied women. "Congregated might" of words.

3. Success of an historical novel depends on skilfully weaving a personal story into a sequence of historical events.
   Old Mortality takes place during the war between the troops of Charles II, led by Claverhouse, and the Scottish Covenanters. Henry Morton, a moderate Presbyterian, joins the Covenanters, but loves Edith, the daughter of Royalist Lady Bellenden. The Presbyterians are finally defeated at Bothwell Brig, owing to the follies of their religious fanaticism. Morton is exiled, but ultimately wins Edith.
   Quentin D. is a Scottish archer in the bodyguard of Louis XI of France. His adventures as escort of Isabelle de Croye, a political hostage whom he loves, are interwoven with the intrigues of Louis XI against Charles of Burgundy. By disobeying orders he saves the King and wins Isabelle.

4. Clarity; imaginative depth (*Eve of S.A.* II); atmosphere (*La Belle Dame*, also "dismal cirque of druid stones," *Hyperion* II 94); lavish detail and rich colour (*Eve of S.A.* XXIV-XXVI); use of adjectives to give condensed effect (XIII). Contrasts in *Eve of S.A.*: Ascetic chill of opening and warmth of revelry (IV and V) and love (XXIII onwards); youth and age (Angela); delicacy and grossness (Porter, Hildebrand); hushed chamber and storm outside. *Grecian Urn*: Pictures of arrested motion. *Autumn:* (1) Scented abundance, mellow colours; (2) Figures symbolize man's labours; (3) Symphony of sound creates picture. Exotic description of the palace in *Lamia*, and Hyperion's palace (I 176, flames as tapestries).

5. The wise and good usually represented by the husband of the heroine (Darcy, Mr. Knightley, Edmund Bertram, Tilney), who tends to be priggish and Olympian. Fanny Price, Jane Bennet and Anne Elliott almost escape criticism. J.A. insists that feeling (sensibility) must be controlled by reason: her heroines commonly offend against this, Elizabeth B. by her

prejudice against Darcy (though D.'s pride is also a foible), Emma by her disastrous match-making and irresponsible flirtation with Churchill, and Catherine Morland by translating the romance of novels of terror into real life. Other targets are snobbery (Caroline Bingley), blind egoism (Mr. Bennet), and class-conscious pride (Lady Catherine).

6. Fools are entertaining because J.A. spices their conversation with ironical humour. Mrs. Bennet's obsession is to get her daughters married; her stupidity shows in all her remarks, especially her reactions to Charlotte Lucas' engagement and to Lydia's elopement. Mr. Collins is stupid, pompous, servile, hypocritical and worldly: his proposal to Elizabeth, his letter after Lydia's elopement, and his behaviour towards Lady C. at Rosings. In *Emma*, Mr. Woodhouse and Miss Bates are bores whose talk is tedious but made amusing by skilful selection of irrelevancies. Mr. W. will recommend only an egg boiled by his own cook.

CHAPTER 11

1. (*a*) English scenery incidental to story (*Enoch Arden*), mood (*Mariana*), thought and feeling (*In Memoriam* XI, XC, C, CXIV). River, wolds, and autumn woods in *Lady of Shalott*. Condensed detail is a result of close observation (*Now sleeps the crimson petal*). Wider landscape effects in *Morte d'Arthur* and background to *Idylls of the King*. Stately homes (*Lord Burleigh*). *The Brook*.
(*b*) Revolution in Europe prompted Tennyson to exalt British freedom, political stability and evolutionary progress ("Freedom slowly broadening down"); see *You ask me why*, *Of old sat Freedom*, *Love thou thy land*.
(*c*) Heroic quality of *The Revenge*, *Charge of the Light Brigade*, *Defence of Lucknow*, *Death of the Duke of Wellington*.

2. The Grammarian rejects easy worldly satisfactions for studies he can complete only in eternity. *Childe Roland*, coming to the Dark Tower, blows the horn, thus accepting a challenge in spite of daunting influences on his journey thither. The lover in *The Last Ride Together*, while accepting the discriminating choice of his mistress to part, begs a last experience of approximate perfection, which he believes is the utmost attainable in this life. Browning condemns indecision or lack of choice: lovers in *The Statue and the Bust* fail to seize the critical moment; in *Youth and Art*, youth, cherishing ambition (which proves worthless), fails to realize the moment; while *Porphyria's Lover* strangles his wavering lady to prevent her going back on a decision.

3. A classical scholar, influenced by Homer and Sophocles, Arnold cultivates simplicity and severity of the Grand Style; less direct and impassioned than the Romantics, he gives structure and proportion to poems, and disciplines feeling and thought by passing them objectively through the mind of, say, a scholar-gipsy; nostalgia for the leisured culture of Greece, as against the "sick hurry and divided aims" of his own time. *Sohrab and Rustum*: Epic structure in imitation of Homer, similes (see Milton); hubris (sin of pride) in Rustum, with stages of "recognition" similar to those of *Oedipus*. A. derived his knowledge of the East from reading, but catches landscape (beds of sand and matted rushy isles of Oxus) and atmosphere (simile of pedlars crossing the Himalayas) with colour and contrasts of the East (barbaric Tartar host and uniform might of Persia).

4. Dickens was a great original, carried along by his own fancy. He was always genuine; his high charitable temper (Pickwick is a modern Don Quixote, eccentric but warm-hearted) and large indignant spirit lived to make war (*Oliver T., Nicholas N.*). Humour: his gaiety and goodness as well as his pathos can run into sentiment (*Christmas Books*). Rapidity of stories: his characters are always speaking, gesturing, moving; fond of violent motion (mobs in *Two Cities* and *Barnaby R.*). Settings create the atmosphere of a town (usually London), a river (the Thames) or the marshes (in *Gt. Ex.*); detail of furniture and interiors, prisons, etc. Characters: D. presents the lower and lower-middle class without condescension. Crowded canvas: a character is instantly realized by some idiosyncrasy of appearance or by a characteristic remark often repeated. Gallery of eccentrics: melodramatic blighted women (Miss Havisham, Rosa Dartle); criminals and malicious characters (Fagin, Sikes, Uriah Heep); morbid conditions (Barnaby, Spike); "Humours" (Mrs. Gamp, Micawber, Sam Weller); hypocrites (Pecksniff, Pumblechook)—D. saw the oddity of life. Rarely any half-tones or mixed characters (perhaps Magwitch). Feeling for child life, partly derived from D.'s own memories (Copperfield, Pip, Oliver, Esther Summerson). D.'s characters often show caricatured truth, but many normally dull characters are imaginatively presented. When the plot is weak, characters or drama carry the tale.

5. In *Mill on the Floss*, G.E.'s didactic habit is not intrusive; she is content to tell a story in simple, sometimes lyrical, style (Snow, in Book II, Chapter 2). Childhood relations of brother and sister may reflect G.E.'s own. The novel contains powerful scenes (Mr. T.'s unforgiving passion on his deathbed), humour (the Dodson sisters), pathos and tragedy. G.E.'s characters convey her ideas better than does her own abstract moralizing. In *Silas Marner*, retribution depends on coincidence, and Silas' life is too patterned; but the humours of Rainbow Inn atone. In these books and *Adam Bede*, G.E. instinctively understands characters from her early life; more sophisticated characters are products of later life and learning. Ethical problems predominate, chiefly of marriage choice (*Middlemarch* and *Deronda*), reflecting G.E.'s agnostic and rationalist outlook. *Romola* contains faithful historical settings, but Victorian ethical problems.

6. Capt. Brown brings an air of reality from the outside world, but disappears early. Miss Matty's frustrated love for Mr. Holbrook is genuinely poignant; and she has courage when ruined by failure of the bank. Her friends' kindly contrivances to help her, and Martha's fidelity, spring from something deeper than Cranford veneer. The story of Peter is a sterner element.

CHAPTER 12

1. Plays in which theses dominate, or attack on respectability is emphasized, will date; wit designed to make unpalatable ideas acceptable may misfire. But Shaw is a consummate artist, with a feeling for the theatre, and insight into character and interplay of character in dialogue. *St. Joan* is his classic work: its issue, individual genius *v.* authority, is a universal one; S. is more objective than in his other plays; Joan is a convincing and inspiring figure, a brave, simple, unsophisticated genius. *Candida* is almost purely a play of character. *Doctor's D.* will live through the creation of Dubedat (thesis is in Preface only), *Caesar and Cleopatra* by its freshness of approach, and *Arms and the Man* for its anti-romantic view of war and for its comedy. Shaw's conception of Woman as the depository of the Life Force should survive (*Man and Superman*).

2. ***The Silver Box:*** John Barthwick, son of wealthy middle-class parents, is assisted home after a convivial evening by Jones, lower-class and unemployed. John has "won" a lady's purse, and Jones steals a silver box before leaving. At Jones' trial John is forced to give evidence, but lawyers manage to gloss over the lady's purse, giving an impression of one law for the rich and another for the poor. Mrs. Jones is honest but victimized.
Strife: In an industrial dispute in S. Wales, the Directors fear for their dividends. The men and their womenfolk are starving, but two leaders, Anthony and Roberts, are determined to fight to a finish. The death of Roberts' wife shocks both sides into compromise. The two rejected leaders realize that they have more in common with each other than with their followers. G.'s impartiality is superficial; suffering sways our sympathy to the lower class in both plays.

3. Eliot's characters often fail to communicate because they are living on different planes of experience. In *Murder in the Cathedral*, Henry is on the political level following expediency (politics "but arrest disorder"); Becket is applying eternal values on a spiritual level ("the still point of the turning world"). B.'s martyrdom has a reconciling effect between temporal and eternal, seen in the consolation of the Women of Canterbury at the close of the play. In *The Cocktail Party* the theme of martyrdom is secularized. Victims of a loveless marriage, E. and L. try to realize wishful thinking in unsuccessful affairs with Celia and Peter. C., not egocentric like E., looks for fulfilment outside herself, and finds it in missionary service and martyrdom. E. and L., facing the truth, renew their marriage.

4. **De La Mare** is a poet of intuition, dreams, wistful wonder (*The Scribe*) and unseen presences (*The Listeners*). Delicate imagery and lyrical quality (*Silver*). Poetry for children (*Nod*). Relish of beauty (*Farewell*).
Poets of Great War: Some killed; precocious genius stimulated by suffering. Few poems on glory or heroism; rather moral revolt against conditions and human degradation (Rosenberg, *Break of Day in the Trenches*). No hatred; patriotism recalls the beauty of home and of English life (Rupert Brooke, *The Soldier* and *The Dead;* Sassoon, *Concert Party*). Owen is outstanding; the stark reality of staccato phrasing, assonance (*Dulce et Decorum est*) and symbolism (*Strange Meeting*) have provided models for later poets. His masterpiece *Anthem for Doomed Youth* merges horror into beauty.

5. Polish by birth, Conrad was a master of English style. Background of sea and ships (Far East). Psychological insight into character (influence of Henry James). A narrator within the story (Marlow—Conrad himself) makes events and judgments convincing. *Lord Jim*: a young Englishman loses his honour through a panic decision to desert ship, but retrieves it by sacrificing his life in an eastern native state; meditative study of Jim's mind when taking a decision. *Youth*: A voyage to the East is a symbol of life; struggle against failure is more inspiring than success. *Heart of Darkness*: Among commercial and moralizing exploiters of the Congo, Marlow discovers Kurtz, honest and sensitive, reverting to subconscious primitive. M.'s descriptions of forest scenery give clues to the working of his mind.

6. Portrait of an Age: disintegrating Victorian attitudes of possessive upper middle class before the Great War. Death of Aunt Anne symbolic. Property gives stability, but conflicts with love, art, youth, imagination. Soames Forsyte loses proprietary rights in wife; Irene shows emancipation of married woman. No villain. Galsworthy shows psychological insight into character, impartiality, and compassion.

OUTLINE ANSWERS TO SPECIMEN EXAMINATION PAPER

1. C. sensitively observant of colourful variety in medieval dress: sets drab background of Knight's soiled fustian (modesty) and Clerk's threadbare cloak (humility) against Lincoln green of Yeoman, motley stripes of Merchant and Lawyer (prosperity), and flower-embroidered tunic of Squire (youthful love). Bright colours in small but significant detail: green "gauds" and gold brooch of Prioress (vanity), pipe-clay white of Gildsmen's equipment (wealth), and "hosen" of Wife of Bath (ostentation). **Physical features:** Dignified beauty of forehead and nose of Prioress (with soft red mouth suggesting dalliance), bold red face of Wife of Bath, unhealthy pimples of Summoner, coarseness of Miller's gaping nostrils and red hair (sow or fox), bucolic complexion of Franklin.

2. Displays his licences (Papal Bulls, probably forged); invariable theme, *Radix malorum est cupiditas*; flavours speech with Latin; displays bogus relics—mitten and shoulder-bone. Brazenly avows indifference to spiritual welfare of his patrons, and intention to avoid hard work and live sumptuously; blackmails his opponents by insinuations against their characters.

Pardoner drinking; vanity may account for frankness; effrontery in later soliciting of contributions; and sins he denounces are his own. Common knowledge that Pardoners were rogues, but belief in relics nevertheless.

3. (*a*) High spirits and nimble wit in satirical review of European nationalities; dutiful towards father and shows faith in his wisdom. (*b*) Great lady suddenly becomes modest schoolgirl, afraid of excess of happiness and submitting to her husband (quote III ii 149-75). On arrival of news from Venice, P. shows decision, generosity and loyalty. (*c*) At trial, she shows intellectual powers (allied to wit). Pleads for mercy, offers repayment, then plays on weakness of S.'s argument ("I will have my bond") to undo him. Vindictiveness determined by Elizabethan anti-semitism, but, after all, S. was contemplating murder. (*d*) Playfulness again emerges, and love of a practical joke.

4. Brutus' aim to restore democracy in Rome. Soliloquy in orchard (II i 10-34) reveals that he will kill C., not for what he is, but for what he may become. Fails to see that conspirators need him to make murder honest. Idealism prompts him to refuse oath, and to spare Antony, but he fails to realize that murder is essentially evil. A.'s speech (allowed by

B.'s generosity) sways people, who become determining factor in conspirators' defeat. Their fickleness shows they are unfit for democracy ("Let him (Brutus) be Caesar!"); conditions in Rome demand dictatorship. Thus C.'s spirit lives on. B. realizes this cardinal mistake when Cassius resorts to sordid motives in Sardis similar to those of Antony (C.'s successor) in IV i. Ghost of Caesar clinches impression of coming defeat, and B. dies acknowledging it.

5. **Banquo** had heard witches salute M. as "king hereafter" (I iii), and, though he had warned M. of danger of trusting them, the prophecy to himself had poisoned his mind too. In II i he is struggling with his own temptations (116-9). When D. is murdered, B. determines to bide his time, outwardly supporting M.'s kingship (III i 1-10). He thus sells himself to evil, and this dissembling costs him his life.
Macduff is the disinterested patriot. His shrewdness tells him of M.'s guilt, and he refuses to dissemble or compromise with murder. Does not attend Coronation, and refuses invitation to Banquet (III vi and III iv 128). Promptness in supporting Malcolm and seeking help from England costs him wife and children, but he himself lives to avenge Duncan.

6. A.M.'s sin was hard-hearted lack of sympathy and imagination. His punishment is loneliness (crew die), which makes him realize beauty of companionship ("the many men so beautiful") and he gains humility ("A thousand, thousand slimy things lived on; and so did I"). Realizes natural beauty: moon and stars and transfiguring effect of moonlight on water and slimy things; blesses them, and weight of guilt drops off. Wins boon of sleep (quote) and rain quenches thirst. Crew arise as "spirits blest" to navigate ship, and their "sweet sounds" remind him of music of countryside (jargoning of birds, quiet tune of hidden brooks). Reaches his "own countree," and gains relief by confession to Hermit; has learnt "love and reverence to all things that God made and loveth," but periodically agony returns, and he can only gain relief by retelling story.

7. ***Prufrock*** is a failure: mean streets beset by prowling fog symbolize his life. Two selves ("You and I"), the one living in social circle of superficial culture (Michelangelo) and formal convention (coffee-spoons, morning-coat), the other wishing to put the "overwhelming question," which will penetrate behind the veneer of time and existence. Lacks confidence to put question, fearing failure to communicate and misunderstanding ("That is not what I meant at all"). He has seen himself in prophetic vein (John the Baptist and Lazarus), and has heard mermaids singing; but always he retreats and drowns in his superficial existence.

The Horses: Poet sees nuclear war as culmination of age of machines, divorce of Man from Nature. A few isolated survivors begin life again; tractors rusting in fields. To them come the horses to renew the old alliance of man and beast, and life resumes its primitive simplicity.

Beyond the Last Lamp: Lovers frustrated by circumstances (Fate). The scene in twilight with rain ("drip, drip, drip"), and the last lamp of the town before it meets the uncharted darkness of the Common is symbolic of the lovers' plight. Ending *-ly* gives faltering rhythm to verse.

8. Sin is the child of Satan, and by illicit union their child is Death; the "conscious terrors" that beset mankind are the offspring of Sin and Death. The Abyss of Chaos is matter before Creation has harmonized the four elements. The Anarch Chaos represents the confusion of "no rule"; Night is consort of Chaos (the first act of Creation gave Light); the realm of Chaos is dominated by rumour, chance and tumult. Chaos is a natural ally of Satan and Sin, destroying harmony in the human community.

9. (*a*) Inefficiency and waste. Manager conventional in morality and outlook, actuated by profit motive: hence intrigue to reach Inner Station, and jealousy towards Kurtz, who has "jumped the queue" through influence. Hypocritical anxiety for Kurtz. M. and engineer alone doing good job. (*b*) Primitive exuberance of forest growth diminishes human significance (beetle on portico of temple); natives dancing on bank awake primitive instincts (anticipating Kurtz, and giving M. power to sympathize with him); fantastic scene countered by navigation problems (snags); relief on finding book in hut, which restores real values; fog and native wailing suggest mystery surrounding Kurtz.

10. Hardy had spoken with old men who remembered threat of French invasion. Dragoons encamped on Downs bring military atmosphere into Overcombe Mill; comic guardians of alarm bonfire (Corporal Stannidge's iron plate); humorous drilling of local militia; false alarm, women in flight, men joining militia. At Royal Review on Downs, Hardy observes that behind seeming uniformity of dragoons beats an individual heart with its personal drama. Thus Anne Garland and John and Bob Loveday enact their hopes, rivalries and fears before a collective background that is indifferent to them and makes constant demands on them: Bob sails to Trafalgar, and John goes to die in Spain. Captain Hardy appears and Nelson is remotely "felt." Anne's sight of the *Victory* from Portland Bill brings Trafalgar dramatically into the picture—the most moving incident in the novel.

INDEX

The works of major authors are given under their own titles. Figures in heavy type indicate a developed treatment of the topic. Figures in brackets indicate a suggested answer in the section on Answering the Question.

INDEX

ACKNOWLEDGEMENTS

The publishers wish to thank the following for the use of photographs and illustrations on the pages indicated:

Birmingham Museum and Art Gallery, 383, 396. The Birmingham Post and Mail Ltd., 116(L). The Bodleian Library, Oxford, 199(R). The British Broadcasting Corporation, 21, 245, 360. British Lion Films Ltd., 120, 225(TR), 227(BR), 300. The Trustees of the British Museum, 11, 30, 35, 42(TR), 45, 46, 49, 116(R). The British Tourist Authority, 52, 58, 137, 190, 218, 239, 249, 271(R). Michael Brown, 133. J. Allan Cash, 155(L), 229, 247. Central Press Photos Ltd., 228(TR). J. W. Debenham, 373(TL). Walt Disney Productions Ltd. (for a still from Walt Disney's *Robin Hood*), 55. The French Embassy, 227(TL). Gala Film Distributors Ltd., 41(TR). Lisel Haas, 317. Nicholas Horne, 69. Karsh of Ottawa, 303(L). Angus McBean, 15(T), 15(B), 43(TR), 43(BL), 83, 85, 87, 92, 97, 100, 129, 145, 193, 206, 209, 225(BL), 226(TL), 226(BR), 234, 295, 305, 310, 313, 364, 369, 374(BR), 375(TR), 376(BL), 377, 387, 392, 400. The Raymond Mander and Joe Mitchenson Theatre Collection, 65, 125(B), 126(T, 2), 127(2), 321. Metro-Goldwyn-Mayer Pictures Ltd., 18, 44(BL), 109. 242, 283, 359, 374(TL). Milton's Cottage Trust, Chalfont St. Giles, 141, 148. The National Portrait Gallery, 58, 61, 65, 73(2), 133, 155, 199(L), 203(2), 215, 223, 230, 234, 240, 251, 271(L), 276(2), 296(L), 330 Michael Peto, 228(BR). Paul Popper Ltd., 227(BL), 228(TL), 376(TL). Radio Times Hulton Picture Library, 27, 41(TL), 41(BR), 42(TL), 42(BR), 43(TL), 43(BR), 44(TL), 44(BR), 69, 113, 159, 167(2), 196, 212, 216, 225(TL), 225(BR), 226(TR), 226(BL), 227(TR), 287(2), 373(TR), 373(BL), 374(TR), 374(BL), 375(TL), 375(BR), 376(BR), 384, 398. Paul Popper (8). The Rank Organisation, 17, 44(TR), 105, 293(R), 296(R), 327, 353, 354, 363, 379, 391. Houston Rogers, 23, 151, 228(BL). The Scottish Tourist Board, 79. P. W. & L. Thompson, Coventry, 128(T). Desmond Tripp, Bristol, 126(B). United Artists Corporation Ltd., 41(BL), 161, 186, 303(R). Valentine and Sons Ltd., 128(B). John Vickers, 82, 306. Victoria and Albert Museum, Crown copyright, 293(L). Warner-Pathé Distributors Ltd., 373(BR), 375(BL), 376(TR). Woodfall Film Productions Ltd., 315. York Festival Society, 77, 125(T).

The publishers also wish to thank the following publishers and authors for the use of copyright quotations:

The Bodley Head Ltd.: James Joyce, *Ulysses*, p. 22. Chatto & Windus Ltd., and James Strachey: Lytton Strachey, *Characters and Commentaries*, p. 331. Clarendon Press: Robert Bridges, *Testament of Beauty*, p. 318. Wm. Collins Sons & Co. Ltd.: Edmund Blunden, *The Barn* (from *Poems of Many Years*), p. 322. Curtis Brown Ltd.: John Galsworthy, *Strife*, p. 306, *The Skin Game*, p. 307. J. M. Dent & Sons Ltd.: Joseph Conrad, *The Rover*, p. 14. Faber & Faber Ltd. and Helen Thomas: Edward Thomas, *Words*, p. 22. Faber & Faber Ltd.: T. S. Eliot, *Murder in the Cathedral*, pp .309-10, *The Family Reunion*, p. 311; Louis MacNeice *Flight of the Heart* (from *Collected Poems*), p. 323; Siegfried Sassoon, *At the Cenotaph* (from *Collected Poems*), p. 322; Stephen Spender, *The Express* (from *Collected Poems*), p. 319. Samuel French Ltd.: Dodie Smith, *Dear Octopus*, p. 316. Hamish Hamilton Ltd.: Terence Rattigan, *The Winslow Boy*, p. 316. Wm. Heinemann Ltd.: John Galsworthy, *The White Monkey*, p. 325; Graham Greene, *The Potting Shed*, p. 318; W. Somerset Maugham, *The Moon and Sixpence*, p. 325, *A Writer's Notebook*, p. 325. Hodder & Stoughton Ltd.: J. M. Barrie, *The Twelve-Pound Look*, p. 315; Rudyard Kipling, *The Secret of the Machines*, p. 318, *The Land*, p. 328. The Hogarth Press Ltd.: C. Day-Lewis, *A Time to Dance*, p. 320. Macmillan & Co. Ltd.: W. B. Yeats, *The Countess Cathleen*, p. 308. Macmillan & Co. Ltd. and the Trustees of the Hardy Estate: Thomas Hardy, *In Time of the Breaking of Nations* (from *The Collected Poems of Thomas Hardy*), p. 324. Macmillan & Co. Ltd. and Mrs. W. B. Yeats: W. B. Yeats, *An Irish Airman Foresees his Death* (from *Collected Poems of W. B. Yeats*), p. 397. Jack Marriott, *The Kiss*, p. 323. Methuen & Co. Ltd. and Miss D. E. Collins: G. K. Chesterton, *The Old Song*, p. 252; A. Noyes, *The Old Grey Squirrel*, p. 319; Hilaire Belloc, *The North Sea*, p. 330, *On His Books*, p. 330. John Murray Ltd.: John Betjeman, *In Westminster Abbey*, p. 322. Oxford University Press: Christopher Fry, *A Sleep of Prisoners*, p. 314, *The Dark is Light Enough*, pp. 312-3, *The Lady's Not For Burning*, p. 312 and p. 332. Putnams Ltd.: John Pudney, *For Johnny* (from *Collected Poems*), pp. 323-4. Sidgwick & Jackson Ltd.: Rupert Brooke, *Sonnet III, The Dead* (from *The Collected Poems of Rupert Brooke*), p. 320. The Society of Authors and the Royal Society for the Protection of Birds: W. H. Hudson, *A Shepherd's Life*, p. 329. The Society of Authors and the Public Trustee: George Bernard Shaw, *St. Joan*, p. 251 and p. 304.